USB Complete

Everything You Need
to Develop Custom USB Peripherals

Second Edition

Jan Axelson

Lakeview Research LLC
Madison, WI

Lakeview Research LLC   Phone: 608-241-5824
5310 Chinook Ln.   Fax: 608-241-5848
Madison, WI 53704   Email: info@Lvr.com
USA   Web: www.Lvr.com

14 13 12 11 10 9 8 7 6 5 4

ISBN 0-9650819-5-8   Printed and bound in the United States of America

Contents

Contents

Contents

Contents

Contents

Contents

Introduction

The Universal Serial Bus (USB) is a fast and flexible interface for connecting devices to computers. Every new PC has at least a couple of USB ports. The interface is versatile enough to use with standard peripherals like keyboards and disk drives as well as more specialized devices, including one-of-a-kind designs. USB is designed from the ground up to be easy for end users, with no user configuring required in hardware or software.

In short, USB is very different from the legacy interfaces it's replacing. A USB device may use any of four transfer types and three speeds. On attaching to a PC, a device must respond to a series of requests that enable the PC to learn about the device and establish communications with it. In the PC, every device must have a low-level driver to manage communications between applications and the system's USB drivers.

Developing a USB device and the software that communicates with it requires knowing something about how USB works and how the PC's operating system implements the interface. In addition, the right choice of controller chip, device class, and tools and techniques can go a long way in avoiding snags and simplifying what needs to be done. This book is a guide for developers of USB devices. Its purpose is to introduce you to USB and to help get your project up and running and troublefree as quickly and easily as possible.

Who should read this book?

This book is for you if you want to know how to design a USB peripheral, or if you want to know how to communicate with USB peripherals from the applications you write. These are some of questions the book answers:

- *What is USB and how do peripherals use it to communicate with PCs?* There's a lot to the USB interface. Learning about it can be daunting at first. This book's focus is on the practical knowledge you'll need to complete your project.

- *How can I decide if my project should use a USB interface?* Maybe your design isn't suited for USB. I'll show you how to decide whether it is. If the answer is yes, I'll help you decide which of USB's speeds and transfer types to use.

- *How do I choose a USB controller chip for my peripheral design?* Every USB peripheral must contain an intelligent controller. There are dozens of controller chips designed for use in USB peripherals. In this book, I compare popular chip families and offer tips on how to decide, based on both your project's needs and your own background and preferences.

- *How do applications communicate with USB peripherals?* To communicate with a USB peripheral, a PC needs two things: a device driver that knows how to communicate with the PC's USB drivers and an application that knows how to talk to the device driver. Some peripherals can use drivers that are built into Windows. Others may require a custom driver. This book will show you when you can use Windows' built-in drivers and how to communicate with devices from Visual Basic and Visual C++ applications. You'll also find out what's involved in writing a device driver and what tools can help to speed up the process.

- *How do USB peripherals communicate?* USB peripherals typically use a combination of hardware and embedded code to communicate with PCs. In this book, I show how to write the code that enables Windows to identify a device and load the appropriate device driver, as well as the code required for exchanging data with applications.

- *How do I decide whether my peripheral can use bus power, or whether it needs its own supply?* A big advantage to USB is that many peripherals can be powered entirely from the bus. Find out whether your device can use this capability and how to manage power use, especially for devices that use battery power.

- *How can I be sure that my device will operate as smoothly as possible for its end users?* On the peripheral side, smooth operation requires understanding the specification's requirements and how the device can meet them. In the PC, proper operation requires a correctly structured information (INF) file that enables Windows to identify the device and software that knows how to communicate with the device as efficiently as possible. This book has information and examples to help with each of these.

What's new in the Second Edition?

In the months after the publication of the first edition of *USB Complete*, much happened in the world of USB, including the release of version 2.0 of the USB specification. USB 2.0 supports a bus rate of 480 Megabits per second, forty times faster than USB 1.1. This and other developments in hardware and software prompted this second edition of the book.

Rather than just tacking on a chapter about USB 2.0, I've revised the book from start to finish to reflect the changes in 2.0. By popular request, another addition is Visual C++ code to accompany the Visual Basic examples for application communications with USB devices. I've also expanded the material about Windows drivers and applications to include Windows 2000, and have added information on new controller chips and development tools. Other additions and updates are sprinkled throughout, many prompted by reader suggestions.

Is this book really complete?

Although the title is *USB Complete*, please don't expect this book to contain every possible fact about USB. That would take a library. The *Complete* in the title means that this book will guide you from knowing nothing about USB to developing all of the code required to get a USB peripheral up and communicating with a PC.

There are many other worthy topics related to USB, but limitations of time and space prevent me from including them all.

My focus is on communicating with Windows PCs. Although the basic principles are the same, I don't include details about how to communicate with peripherals on a Macintosh or a PC running Linux or other non-Windows operating systems.

I cover the basics of the device driver's responsibilities and what's involved in writing a driver, but the details of driver writing can easily fill a book (and in fact there are excellent—and lengthy—books on this topic). This book will help you decide when you need to write a custom driver and when and how to use a class driver included with Windows.

To understand the material in the book, it's helpful to have basic knowledge in a few areas. I assume you have some experience with digital logic, application programming for PCs and writing embedded code for peripherals. You don't have to know anything at all about USB.

Additional Resources, Updates, and Corrections

For more about using USB, I invite you to visit my USB Central page at Lakeview Research's website, *www.Lvr.com*. This is where you'll find complete code examples, updates, links to vendors, information and tools from other sources, as well as links to anything else I find that's relevant to developing USB products. If you have a suggestion, code, or other information that you'd like me to post or link to, let me know at *jan@lvr.com*.

In spite of my very best efforts, I know from experience that errors will slip through in this book. As they come to light, I'll document them and make a list available at Lakeview Research's website. If you find an error in the book, please let me know and I'll add it.

Thanks!

USB is way too complicated to write about without help. I have many people to thank.

I owe an enormous thank you to my technical reviewers, who generously read my rough and rocky drafts and provided feedback that has improved the book enormously. (With that said, every error in this book is mine and mine alone.)

I thank Paul E. Berg of PEB Consulting; Brian Buchanan, Mark Hastings, Lane Hauck, Bijan Kamran, Kosta Koeman, Tim Williams, and Dave Wright of Cypress Semiconductor; Joshua Buergel of BSQUARE Inc.; Gary Crowell of Micron Technology; Fred Dart of Future Technology Devices International (FTDI); Dave Dowler; Mike Fahrion and the engineers at B&B Electronics; John M. Goodman, author of *Hard Disk Secrets, Peter Norton's Inside the PC, Memory Management for All of Us,* and other books; John Hyde, USB enthusiast and author of *USB Design by Example;* David James of 1Zero1 Technologies; Christer Johansson of High Tech Horizon; Jon Lueker of Intel Corporation; Bob Nathan of NCR Corporation; Robert Severson of USBMicro; and Craig R. Smith of Ford Motor Company, R&VT department.

Others I want to thank for their help in my researching and writing this book are Walter Banks of Byte Craft; Jason Bock; Michael DeVault of DeVaSys Embedded Systems; Pete Fowler, Joseph McCarthy, and Don Parkman of Cypress Semiconductor; Brad Markisohn of INDesign LLC; Daniel McClure of Tyco Electronics; Tawnee McMullen of Belkin Components; Rich Moran of RPM Systems Corporation; Dave Navarro of PowerBasic; and Amar Rajan of American Concepts Consulting.

I hope you find the book useful. Comments invited!

Jan Axelson, June 2001
jan@lvr.com

1

A Fresh Start

Computer hardware doesn't often get a chance to start fresh. Anything new usually has to remain compatible with whatever came before it. This is true of both computers and the peripherals that connect to them. Even the most revolutionary new peripheral has to use an interface supported by the computers it connects to.

But what if you had the chance to design a peripheral interface from scratch? What qualities and features would you include? It's likely that your wish list would include these:

- **Easy to use**, so there's no need to fiddle with configuration and setup details.

- **Fast**, so the interface doesn't become a bottleneck of slow communications.

- **Reliable**, so that errors are rare, with automatic correction of errors that do occur.

- **Flexible**, so many kinds of peripherals can use the interface.

- **Inexpensive**, so users (and the manufacturers who will build the interface into their products) don't balk at the price.

- **Power-conserving**, to save battery power on portable computers.

- **Supported by the operating system**, so developers don't have to struggle with writing low-level drivers for the peripherals that use the interface.

The good news is that you don't have to create this ideal interface, because the developers of the Universal Serial Bus (USB) have done it for you. USB was designed from the ground up to be a simple and efficient way to communicate with many types of peripherals, without the limitations and frustrations of existing interfaces.

Every new PC has a couple of USB ports that you can connect to a keyboard, mouse, scanners, external disk drives, printers, and standard and custom hardware of all kinds. Inexpensive hubs enable you to add more ports and peripherals as needed.

But one result of USB's ambitious goals has been challenges for the developers who design and program USB peripherals. A result of USB's versatility and ease of use is an interface that's more complicated than the interfaces it replaces. Plus, any new interface will have difficulties just because it's new. When USB first became available on PCs, Windows didn't yet include device drivers for all popular peripheral types. Protocol analyzers and other development tools couldn't begin to be designed until there was a specification to follow, so the selection of these was limited at first. Problems like these are now disappearing, and the advantages are increasing with the availability of more controller chips, new development tools, and improved operating-system support. This book will show you ways to get a USB peripheral up and running as simply and quickly as possible by making the best possible use of tools available now.

This chapter introduces USB, including its advantages and drawbacks, a look at what's involved in designing and programming a device with a USB interface, and a bit of the history behind the interface.

What USB Can Do

USB is a likely solution any time you want to use a computer to communicate with devices outside the computer. The interface is suitable for one-of-kind and small-scale designs as well as mass-produced, standard peripheral types.

To be successful, an interface has to please two audiences: the users who want to use the peripherals and the developers who design the hardware and write the code that communicates with the device. USB has features to please both.

Benefits for Users

From the user's perspective, the benefits to USB are ease of use, fast and reliable data transfers, flexibility, low cost, and power conservation. Table 1-1 compares USB with other popular interfaces.

Ease of Use

Ease of use was a major design goal for USB, and the result is an interface that's a pleasure to use for many reasons:

One interface for many devices. USB is versatile enough to be usable with many kinds of peripherals. Instead of having a different connector type and supporting hardware for each peripheral, one interface serves many.

Automatic configuration. When a user connects a USB peripheral to a powered system, Windows automatically detects the peripheral and loads the appropriate software driver. The first time the peripheral connects, Windows may prompt the user to insert a disk with driver software, but other than that, installation is automatic. There's no need to locate and run a setup program or restart the system before using the peripheral.

No user settings. USB peripherals don't have user-selectable settings such as port addresses and interrupt-request (IRQ) lines. Available IRQ lines are in short supply on PCs, and not having to allocate one for a new peripheral is often reason enough to use USB.

Table 1-1: Comparison of popular computer interfaces. Where a standard doesn't specify a maximum, the table shows the typical maximum.

Interface	Format	Number of Devices (maximum)	Length (maximum, feet)	Speed (maximum, bits/sec.)	Typical Use
USB	asynchronous serial	127	16 (or up to 96 ft. with 5 hubs)	1.5M, 12M, 480M	Mouse, keyboard, disk drive, modem, audio
RS-232 (EIA/TIA-232)	asynchronous serial	2	50-100	20k (115k with some hardware)	Modem, mouse, instrumentation
RS-485 (TIA/EIA-485)	asynchronous serial	32 unit loads (up to 256 devices with some hardware)	4000	10M	Data acquisition and control systems
IrDA	asynchronous serial infrared	2	6	115k	Printers, hand-held computers
Microwire	synchronous serial	8	10	2M	Microcontroller communications
SPI	synchronous serial	8	10	2.1M	Microcontroller communications
I^{2}C	synchronous serial	40	18	3.4M	Microcontroller communications
IEEE-1394 (FireWire)	serial	64	15	400M (increasing to 3.2G with IEEE-1394b	Video, mass storage
IEEE-488 (GPIB)	parallel	15	60	8M	Instrumentation
Ethernet	serial	1024	1600	10M/100M/ 1G	Networked PC
MIDI	serial current loop	2 (more with flow-through mode)	50	31.5k	Music, show control
Parallel Printer Port	parallel	2 (8 with daisy-chain support)	10–30	8M	Printers, scanners, disk drives

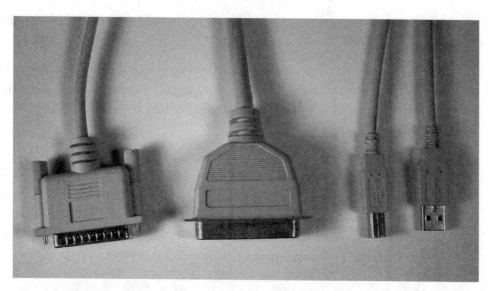

Figure 1-1: The two USB connectors (right) are much more compact than typical RS-232 serial (left) and Centronics parallel (center) connectors.

Frees hardware resources for other devices. Using USB for as many peripherals as possible frees up IRQ lines for the peripherals that do require them. The PC dedicates a series of port addresses and one interrupt-request (IRQ) line to the USB interface, but beyond this, individual peripherals don't require additional resources. In contrast, each non-USB peripheral requires dedicated port addresses, often an IRQ line, and sometimes an expansion slot (for a parallel-port card, for example).

Easy to connect. With USB, there's no need to open the computer's enclosure to add an expansion card for each peripheral. A typical PC has at least two USB ports. You can expand the number of ports by connecting a USB hub to an existing port. Each hub has additional ports for attaching more peripherals or hubs.

Simple cables. The USB's cable connectors are keyed so you can't plug them in wrong. Cables can be as long as 5 meters. With hubs, a device can be as far as 30 meters from its host PC. Figure 1-1 shows that the USB connectors are small and compact in contrast to typical RS-232 and parallel connectors. To ensure reliable operation, the specification includes detailed requirements that all cables and connectors must meet.

Hot pluggable. You can connect and disconnect a peripheral whenever you want, whether or not the system and peripheral are powered, without damaging the PC or peripheral. The operating system detects when a device is attached and readies it for use.

No power supply required (sometimes). The USB interface includes power-supply and ground lines that provide +5V from the computer's or hub's supply. A peripheral that requires up to 500 milliamperes can draw all of its power from the bus instead of having its own supply. In contrast, most other peripherals have to choose between including a power supply in the device or using a bulky and inconvenient external supply.

Speed

USB supports three bus speeds: high speed at 480 Megabits per second, full speed at 12 Megabits per second, and low speed at 1.5 Megabits per second. Every USB-capable PC supports low and full speeds. High speed was added in version 2.0 of the specification, and requires USB 2.0-capable hardware on the motherboard or an expansion card.

These speeds are signaling speeds, or the bit rates supported by the bus. The rates of data transfer that individual devices can expect are lower. In addition to data, the bus must carry status, control, and error-checking signals. Plus, multiple peripherals may be sharing the bus. The theoretical maximum rate for a single transfer is over 53 Megabytes per second at high speed, about 1.2 Megabytes per second at full speed, and 800 bytes per second at low speed.

Why three speeds? Low speed was included for two reasons. Low-speed peripherals can often be built more cheaply. And for mice and devices that require flexible cables, low-speed cables can be more flexible because they don't require as much shielding.

Full speed is comparable to or better than the speeds attainable with existing serial and parallel ports and can serve as a replacement for these.

After the release of USB 1.0, it became clear that a faster interface would be useful. Investigation showed that a speed increase of forty times was feasible while keeping the interface backwards-compatible with low- and full-speed devices. High speed became an option with the release of version 2.0 of the USB specification.

Reliability

The reliability of USB results from both the hardware design and the data-transfer protocols. The hardware specifications for USB drivers, receivers, and cables eliminate most noise that could otherwise cause data errors. In addition, the USB protocol enables detecting of data errors and notifying the sender so it can retransmit. The detecting, notifying, and retransmitting are typically done in hardware and don't require any programming or user intervention.

Low Cost

Even though USB is more complex than earlier interfaces, its components and cables are inexpensive. A device with a USB interface is likely to cost the same or less than its equivalent with an older interface. For very low-cost peripherals, the low-speed option has less stringent hardware requirements that may reduce the cost further.

Low Power Consumption

Power-saving circuits and code automatically power down USB peripherals when not in use, yet keep them ready to respond when needed. In addition to the environmental benefits of reduced power consumption, this feature is especially useful on battery-powered computers where every milliampere counts.

Benefits for Developers

The above advantages for users are also important to hardware designers and programmers. The advantages make users eager to use USB peripherals, so there's no need to fear wasting time developing for an unpopular interface. And many of the user advantages also make things easier for developers. For example, USB's defined cable standards and automatic error checking mean that developers don't have to worry about specifying cable characteristics or providing error checking in software.

USB also has advantages that benefit developers specifically. The developers include the hardware designers who select components and design the circuits, the programmers who write the software that communicates with USB peripherals, and the programmers who write the embedded code inside the peripherals.

The benefits to developers result from the flexibility built into the USB protocol, the support in the controller chips and operating system, and the fact that the interface isn't controlled by a single vendor. Although users aren't likely to be aware of these benefits, they'll enjoy the result, which is inexpensive, trouble-free, and feature-rich peripherals.

Flexibility

USB's four transfer types and three speeds make it feasible for many types of peripherals. There are transfer types suited for exchanging large and small blocks of data, with and without time constraints. For data that can't tolerate delays, USB can guarantee a transfer rate or maximum time between transfers. These abilities are especially welcome under Windows, where accessing peripherals in real time is often a challenge. The operating system, device drivers, and application software can still introduce unavoidable delays, but USB makes it as easy as possible to achieve transfers that are close to real time.

Unlike other interfaces, USB doesn't assign specific functions to signals or make other assumptions about how the interface will be used. For example, the status and control lines on the PC's parallel port were defined with the intention of communicating with line printers. There are five input lines with assigned functions such as indicating a busy or paper-out condition. When developers began using the port for scanners and other peripherals that send large amounts of data to the PC, the limitation of having just five inputs was an obstacle. (Eventually the interface was expanded to allow eight bits of input.) USB makes no such assumptions and is suitable for just about any device type.

For communicating with common device types such as printers and modems, there are USB classes with defined device requirements and protocols. This saves developers from having to re-invent these.

Operating System Support

Windows 98 was the first Windows operating system to reliably support USB, and its successors, including Windows 2000 and Windows Me, support USB as well. This book focuses on Windows programming for PCs, but other computers and operating systems also have USB support. On Apple's iMac, the only peripheral connectors are USB. Other Macintoshes also support USB, and support is in progress for Linux, NetBSD, and FreeBSD.

However, a claim of operating-system support can mean many things. The level of support can vary! At the most fundamental level, an operating system that supports USB must do three things:

- Detect when a device is attached to or removed from the system.
- Communicate with newly attached devices to find out how to exchange data with them.
- Provide a mechanism that enables software drivers to communicate with the host computer's USB hardware and the applications that want to access USB peripherals.

At a higher level, operating system support may also mean the inclusion of software device drivers that enable application programmers to access devices by calling functions supported by the operating system. If the operating system doesn't include a device driver appropriate for a specific peripheral, the peripheral vendor has to provide one.

Microsoft has added class drivers with each release of Windows. Device types with included drivers now include human interface devices (keyboards, mice, joysticks), audio devices, modems, still-image cameras and scanners, printers, and mass-storage devices. A filter driver can support device-specific features and abilities. Applications use Applications Program Interface (API) functions or other operating-system components to communicate with the device drivers.

In the future, Windows will likely include support for more device classes. In the meantime, some chip vendors provide drivers that developers can use with their chips, either as-is or with minimal modifications.

USB device drivers use the new Win32 Driver Model (WDM), which defines an architecture for drivers that run under Windows 98, Windows 2000, Windows Me, and future Windows editions. The aim is to enable developers to support all of the operating systems with a single driver. The reality is that some devices still require two, though similar, WDM drivers, one for Windows 98/Windows Me and one for Windows 2000.

Because Windows includes low-level drivers that handle communications with the USB hardware, writing a USB device driver is easier than writing a driver for devices that use other interfaces.

Peripheral Support

On the peripheral side, each USB device's hardware must include a controller chip that handles the details of USB communications. Some controllers are complete microcomputers that include a CPU and memory to store device-specific code that runs inside the peripheral. Others handle only USB-specific tasks, with a data bus that connects to another microcontroller that performs non-USB related functions and communicates with the USB controller as needed.

The peripheral is responsible for responding to requests to send and receive configuration data, and for reading and writing other data when requested. In some chips, some functions are microcoded in hardware and don't need to be programmed.

Many USB controllers are based on popular architectures such as Intel's 8051, with added circuits and machine codes to support USB. If you're already familiar with a chip architecture that has a USB-capable variant, there's no need to learn an entirely new architecture in order to use USB.

Most peripheral manufacturers provide sample code for their chips. Using this code as a starting point for your own developing can give you a quick start.

USB Implementers Forum

Unlike other interfaces, where you're pretty much on your own when it comes to getting a design up and running, USB offers plenty of help via the USB Implementers Forum, Inc. (USB-IF) and its website (*www.usb.org*). The Forum is the non-profit corporation founded by the companies that developed the USB specification. The Forum's mission is to support the advancement and adoption of USB technology.

To that end, the Forum offers information, tools, and testing. The information includes the specification documents, white papers that delve into specific topics in detail, FAQs, and a web board where developers can post and answer questions on any USB-related topic. The tools include software and hardware to help in developing and testing products. Testing includes developing compliance tests to verify proper operation, holding compliance workshops where developers can have their products tested, and granting the rights to use the USB Logo on products that pass the tests.

It's Not Perfect

All of USB's advantages mean that it's a good candidate for use with many peripherals. But one interface can't do it all.

User Challenges

From the user's perspective, the downside to USB includes lack of support in older hardware and operating systems, speed and distance limits that make USB impractical for some uses, and problems with some products due to difficulties experienced by the developers of early USB products.

Lack of Support for Legacy Hardware

Older ("legacy") computers and peripherals don't have USB ports. If you want to connect a non-USB peripheral to a USB port, a solution is a converter that translates between USB and the older interface. Several sources have converters for use with peripherals with RS-232, RS-485, and Centronics-type parallel ports. However, the converter solution is useful only for peripherals that use conventional protocols supported by the converter's device driver. For example, a parallel-port converter is likely to support printers but not other peripheral types.

If you want to use a USB peripheral with a PC that doesn't support USB, the solution is to add USB capabilities to the PC. This requires two things: USB host-controller hardware and an operating system that supports USB. The hardware is available on expansion cards that plug into a PCI slot (or on a replacement motherboard). The version of Windows should be Windows 98 or later. A few peripherals have drivers for use with later releases of Windows 95, but it's best not to count on these being available. If the hardware doesn't meet Windows 98's minimum requirements, it will need upgrades. The upgrades may end up costing more than a new system with USB, so replacing the system may be the best option.

If upgrading the PC to support USB isn't feasible, what about using a converter to translate the peripheral's USB interface to the PC's RS-232, parallel, or other interface? Interface converters are generally designed for use between a USB port on a PC and a peripheral with a legacy interface. A converter for the other direction would be much more complicated because the peripheral would have to contain the host-controller hardware and code that normally resides in the PC. So a converter isn't normally an option when the PC has the legacy interface.

Even on new systems, users may occasionally run applications on older operating systems such as MS-DOS. But the drivers that Windows 98 applications use to communicate with USB devices are specific to Windows. Without a driver, there's no way to access a USB peripheral. Although it's possible to write a USB driver for DOS, the reality is that few peripherals provide one.

However, for the mouse and keyboard, which are standard, essential peripherals, the system's BIOS is likely to include support to ensure that the peripheral is usable any time, including from within DOS, from the BIOS screens that you can view on bootup, and from Windows' Safe mode (used in system troubleshooting). If there is no BIOS or other support, the system will need to have an old-style keyboard interface and a spare keyboard for these uses.

Speed Limits

USB is versatile, but it's not designed to do everything. USB's high speed makes it competitive with the IEEE-1394 (Firewire) interface's 400 Megabits per second, but IEEE-1394b will be faster still, at 3.2 Gigabits per second.

Distance Limits

USB was designed as a desktop bus, with the expectation that peripherals would be relatively close at hand. A cable segment can be as long as 5 meters. Other interfaces, such as RS-232, RS-485, and Ethernet, allow much longer cables. You can increase the length of a USB link to as much as 30 meters by using cables that link five hubs and a device, using 6 cable segments of 5 meters each.

To extend the range beyond this, an option is to use a USB interface on the PC, then convert to RS-485 or another interface for the long-distance cabling and peripheral interface.

Peer to Peer Communications

The assumption that USB is a desktop bus also means that every USB system has a host computer to manage the bus communications. Peripherals can't talk to each other directly. All communications are to or from the host computer. Other interfaces, such as IEEE-1394, allow direct peripheral-to-peripheral communications.

USB provides a partial solution with USB On-The-Go, introduced in 2001 in a supplement to the 2.0 specification. USB On-The-Go defines a host computer with reduced capabilities, suitable for use in embedded devices that need to connect to a single USB peripheral.

Products with Problems

When USB works, it's great. But the reality is that some USB products don't work as well as they should. When something misbehaves, the result can be an inability to communicate with a peripheral or an application or system crash. The source of the problem may be in hardware or software, in the PC or in the peripheral. Problems like these are a result of USB's complexity and newness combined with inadequate testing.

But there are plenty of products that do perform exactly as they should. The problems are diminishing as the operating-system support has improved and developers have become more familiar with USB.

Developer Challenges

From the developer's perspective, the main downside to USB is the increased complexity of the programming. Bugs in the USB hardware in the peripheral or PC can also slow project development and cause problems after a product is released. However, these problems are also diminishing as the operating-system support increases, more chips and development tools are available, and everyone gains more experience.

Protocol Complexity

To program a USB peripheral, you need to know a fair amount about the USB's protocols (the rules for exchanging data on the bus). The controller chips handle much of the communications automatically, but they still must be programmed, and this requires the knowledge to write the programs and the tools to do the programming. Chips vary in how much support they require to perform USB communications. On the PC side, the device driver insulates application programmers from having to know many of the details, but device-driver writers need to be familiar with USB protocols and the driver's responsibilities.

In contrast, some older interfaces can connect to very simple circuits with very basic protocols. For example, the PC's original parallel printer port is just a series of digital inputs and outputs. You can connect to basic input and output circuits such as relays, switches, and analog-to-digital converters, with no computer intelligence required on the peripheral side and no device driver required on the PC (just direct port reads and writes).

Evolving Support in the Operating System

Windows includes class drivers that enable applications to communicate with some devices. This is great if you can design your device to use one of the provided drivers. If not, in many cases you can use or adapt a driver provided by the controller-chip vendor, so you don't have write a driver from scratch. Several vendors offer toolkits that make the job of writing USB drivers easier.

Hardware Bugs

Some early host-controller hardware wasn't bugfree, and some peripheral chips have had problems as well. In most cases, the manufacturers make fixes available with new drivers or coding workarounds. The way to keep on top of these problems is to choose your hardware carefully and visit manufacturers' websites for the latest information and fixes.

Fees

The USB Implementers Forum provides the USB specification, related documents, software for compliance testing, and much more, all for free on its website. Anyone can develop USB software without paying a licensing fee.

However, anyone who sells a device with a USB interface must obtain legal access to use a Vendor ID. The administrative fee for obtaining a Vendor ID from the Forum is $1500. Or if you join the Forum at $2500/year, the Vendor ID is free, along with many other benefits such as compliance workshops. The Vendor ID and a Product ID assigned by the vendor are embedded in each device to identify it to the operating system. The fee is no problem for developers of high-volume products, but it can be an impediment to developers for the hobbyist market who expect to sell only small quantities of inexpensive devices. Some chip manufacturers will assign their Vendor ID and a block of Product IDs to customers for use with the manufacturer's chips.

History

To understand what USB is all about, it helps to know a little history. The main reason that new interfaces don't come around very often is that existing interfaces have the irresistible pull of all of the existing peripherals that users don't want to scrap. Also, using an existing interface saves the time and expense of designing something new. This is why the designers of the original IBM PC chose compatibility with the existing Centronics parallel interface and the RS-232 serial-port interface—to speed up the design process and enable users to connect to printers and modems already on the market. These interfaces proved serviceable for close to two decades. But as computer power and the number of peripherals have increased, the older interfaces have became a bottleneck of slow communications, with limited options for expansion.

The Motivation for Change

A break with tradition is justified when the desire for enhancements overshadows the inconvenience and expense of changing. This is the situation that prompted the development of USB. The result is a versatile interface that can replace existing interfaces to standard and custom peripherals on computers of all types.

In the past, development of a new interface was often the work of a single company. Hewlett Packard developed the HP Interface Bus (HPIB), which came to be known as the GPIB (general-purpose interface bus) for lab equipment, and the Centronics Data Computer Corporation popularized a printer interface that is still referred to as the Centronics interface.

But an interface controlled by a single company isn't ideal. The company may forbid others from using the interface, or charge licensing fees. Even if the interface is freely available, a company may be reluctant to commit its products to an interface controlled by another company who may be a competitor and may change the interface without warning.

For these reasons, more recent interfaces are often the product of a collaboration of manufacturers who share a common interest. In some cases, an organization like the IEEE (Institute of Electrical and Electronics Engineers) or TIA (Telecommunications Industry Association) sponsors committees to develop specifications and publishes the results. In fact, many of the older manufacturers' standards have been taken over by these organizations. The IEEE-1284 standard evolved from the Centronics interface, and the GPIB was the basis for IEEE-488.

In other cases, the developers of a standard form a new organization to release the standard and handle other development issues. This is the approach used for USB. The copyright on the USB 2.0 specification is assigned jointly to seven corporations, all heavily involved with PC hardware or software: Compaq, Hewlett-Packard, Intel, Lucent, Microsoft, NEC, and Philips. All have agreed to make the specification available without charge (which is a refreshing change from the standards published by other organizations). The USB Implementers Forum's website has the latest versions of all USB specifications and other information for both developers and end users.

An early specification with many USB-like features was the ACCESS.bus sponsored by Philips and Digital Equipment Corporation, who made it available as an open standard. ACCESS.bus was in turn derived from the I^2C synchronous serial bus. Although the electrical interface is different, many of the functions and features are a lot like what ended up in USB.

ACCESS.bus was designed for interfacing keyboards, pointing devices, and other devices at speeds of 100 kilobits per second. The bus supports up to 125 devices and 10-meter cables. Devices are hot-pluggable. The cable includes +5V and ground wires. Classes are defined for keyboards, pointing devices (called locators), monitor/display control and text devices. Unlike USB, ACCESS.bus uses open-collector drivers, with one data wire and one clock wire.

ACCESS.bus never caught on with PCs, but is still used in other applications, including smart battery control.

The Specification's Release

Release 1.0 of the USB specification in January 1996 followed several years of development and preliminary releases. The 1.1 release is dated September 1998. USB 1.1 fixed problems identified in release 1.0 and added one new transfer type (Interrupt OUT). In this book, *1.x* refers to USB 1.0 and 1.1. April 2000 saw the release of USB 2.0 with the new high-speed option. An Engineering Change Notice (ECN) in December 2000 provided corrections and defined a new mini-B connector.

Although companies may begin designing products while a specification is still under development, by necessity, the availability of products on the market lags the specification's release.

USB capability first became available on PCs with the release of Windows 95's OEM Service Release 2. There were at least two editions of this release, OSR 2.1 and 2.5. Neither was available directly to retail customers. They were sold only to vendors who installed Windows 95 on the PCs they sold. The USB support in these versions was limited and buggy, and there weren't a lot of USB peripherals available, so use of USB was limited in this era.

Things improved with the release of Windows 98 in June 1998. By this time, many more vendors had USB peripherals available, and USB began to take hold as a popular interface. A service pack for Windows 98 and the release of Windows 98 Second Edition (SE) fixed some bugs and further enhanced the USB support. The original version of Windows 98 is called Windows 98 Gold, to distinguish it from Windows 98 SE.

This book concentrates on PCs running Windows 98 and later Windows editions. Windows NT4 preceded Windows 98 and doesn't have USB support built in, but its successor, Windows 2000, does. Windows 98's successor, Windows Me, also supports USB. Generally, Windows 2000 is more stable and is targeted for business users, while Windows 98 and Windows Me are more flexible and targeted for home users.

Following these editions is Windows XP, which is based on the Windows 2000 kernel but includes editions for both home and business users, with the goal of replacing both Windows 98/Windows Me and Windows 2000.

In this book, the term *PC* includes all of the various computers that share the common ancestor of the original IBM PC. The expression *Windows 98 and later* means Windows 98, Windows 98 SE, Windows 2000, Windows Me, and Windows XP, and is also likely to apply to any Windows editions that follow. A USB-capable PC is assumed to be using Windows 98 or later.

USB 2.0

A big step in USB's evolution was version 2.0, whose main added feature is support for *much* faster transfers. The original hope when researching the new high speed was a 20-times increase in speed, but studies and tests showed that this estimate was low. In the end, a 40-times increase was found to be feasible, for a bus speed of 480 Megabits per second. This makes USB much more attractive for peripherals such as printers, scanners, drives, and even video.

USB 2.0 is backwards compatible with USB 1.1. Version 2.0 peripherals can use the same connectors and cables as 1.x peripherals. To use the new, higher speed, peripherals must connect to 2.0-compliant hosts and hubs. 2.0 hosts and hubs can also communicate with 1.x peripherals. A 2.0-compliant hub with a slower peripheral attached will translate as needed between the peripheral's speed and high speed. This increases the hub's complexity but makes good use of the bus time without requiring different hubs for different speeds.

USB versus IEEE-1394

The other major interface choice for new peripherals is IEEE-1394. Apple Computer's implementation of the interface is called Firewire. USB and IEEE-1394 take complimentary approaches, with IEEE-1394 being faster and more flexible, but more expensive. IEEE-1394 is best suited for video and other links where speed is essential or a host PC isn't available. USB is best suited for typical peripherals such as keyboards, printers, scanners, and disk drives as well as low- to moderate-speed, cost-sensitive applications. For many devices, either interface would work.

With USB, a single host controls communications with many peripherals. The host handles most of the complexity, so the peripherals' electronics can be relatively simple and inexpensive. IEEE-1394 uses a peer-to-peer model, where peripherals can communicate with each other directly. A single communication can also be directed to multiple receivers. The result is a more flexible interface, but the peripherals' electronics are more complex and expensive.

IEEE-1394's 400 Megabits per second is more than 30 times faster than USB 1.x's 12 Megabits per second. As USB is getting faster with version 2.0, IEEE-1394 is getting faster with the proposed IEEE-1394.b. Its 3.2 Gigabits per second is over six times faster than USB 2.0's 480 Megabits per second.

2

Is USB Right for My Project?

Before you can decide if USB is suitable for a project, you need to know a little more about how USB works and what it can do. This chapter presents some fast facts about USB, with the focus on what's relevant when deciding whether or not USB is a good choice for a project. There's also a look at the steps in developing a USB peripheral.

Fast Facts

Some of the first questions you might have relating to whether or not USB is suitable for a project are these:

- What are the minimum requirements that a PC must meet in order to use USB peripherals?
- How do devices connect to the PC?
- In real-world terms, how fast can a peripheral exchange data with a PC?

- How do applications communicate with the peripheral?
- What are the responsibilities of the code inside the peripheral?

This section answers these questions.

Minimum PC Requirements

Before you decide to design a USB peripheral, it makes sense to be sure that the PCs that will use the peripheral can use the interface. To use USB, a PC needs hardware and software support. The hardware consists of a USB host controller and a root hub with one or more USB ports. The software support is an operating system that supports USB.

The Host Controller

An interface won't succeed if PC manufacturers don't support it. Fortunately, both PC and peripheral manufacturers have enthusiastically supported USB. Just about any new PC will have a USB host controller and at least two port connectors. PCs as old as 1997 are likely to have hardware support for USB. Microsoft and Intel's *PC 2001 System Design Guide* requires new PCs to have two user-accessible USB ports. The USB Implementers Forum's website has a *usbready* utility that examines a PC's resources and reports whether or not the PC supports USB.

If a computer doesn't have USB support built into its motherboard, you can add one on an expansion card that plugs into a slot on the PCI bus. For portables, USB controllers on PC cards are available.

Early USB controllers complied with the 1.x specification and supported low and full speeds. 2.0-compliant controllers also support high speed.

The Operating System

The other side of USB support is in the operating system. Your developing will be much easier if you require users to be running Windows 98 or later. Windows 95 had some USB support, but the support was greatly improved and enhanced in Windows 98. Windows 95 and Windows 98 can't use the same device drivers. Windows NT 4 doesn't support USB at all. However, if you're developing a peripheral that needs to run under NT, you can use

BSQUARE's USB Extension to WinDK to write a driver that enables the peripheral to be used under NT. DOS and Windows 3.x have no USB support built in.

The Components

The physical components of the Universal Serial Bus consist of the circuits, connectors, and cables between a host and one or more devices.

The host is a PC or other computer that contains two components: a host controller and a root hub. These work together to enable the operating system to communicate with the devices on the bus. The host controller formats data for transmitting on the bus and translates received data to a format that operating-system components can understand. The host controller also performs other functions related to managing communications on the bus. The root hub has one or more connectors for attaching devices. The root hub, in combination with the host controller, detects the attachment and removal of devices, carries out requests from the host controller, and passes data between devices and the host controller.

The devices are the peripherals and additional hubs that connect to the bus. A hub has one or more ports for connecting devices. Each device must contain circuits and code that knows how to communicate with the host. The specification defines the cables and connectors that connect devices to hubs.

Bus Topology

The topology, or arrangement of connections, on the bus is a tiered star (Figure 2-1). At the center of each star is a hub. Each point on a star is a device that connects to one of the hub's ports. The devices may be additional hubs or other peripherals. The number of points on each star can vary, with a typical hub having two, four, or seven ports. When there are multiple hubs in series, you can think of them as connecting in a tier, or series, one above the next.

The tiered star describes only the physical connections. In programming, all that matters is the logical connection. In communicating with a USB

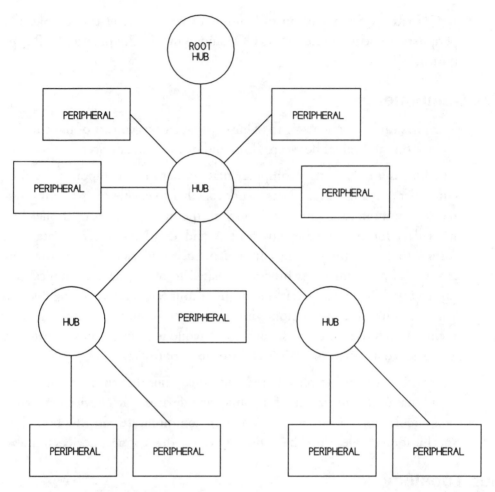

Figure 2-1: USB uses a tiered star topology, where each hub is the center of a star that can connect to peripherals or additional hubs.

device, neither the host or the device knows or cares whether a communication passes through one hub or five. The hubs manage this automatically.

All of the devices on a bus share one data path to the host computer. Only one device can communicate with the host at a time. For more bandwidth, you can add a second data path to the host by installing an expansion card with another host controller and root hub. Expansion cards with multiple host controllers are also available.

Figure 2-2 shows a few of the possible configurations for a PC with two USB connectors. If you have just two USB peripherals, you can plug one into each port on the PC. If you have up to five peripherals, you can plug one peripheral into one of the PC's ports and attach a hub with four downstream connectors to the other. You can then connect the remaining four peripherals to the hub. Some peripherals are compound devices that contain both a peripheral and a hub. You can cascade up to five external hubs in series, up to a total of 127 peripherals and hubs (including the root hub). Of course, it may be impractical to have this many devices sharing a data path.

In some cases, especially with compound devices where the hubs are hidden inside the peripheral, the peripherals may appear to be using a daisy-chain type of connection, where each new peripheral hooks to the last one in a chain. But the USB's topology is more flexible and complicated than a daisy chain. Each peripheral connects to a hub that manages communications with the host, and the peripherals and hubs aren't limited to connecting in a single chain.

Defining Terms

In the universe of USB, several everyday words have specific meanings. Along with *host*, defined earlier as the computer that controls the interface, three other such terms are *function, hub,* and *device*.

The USB specification defines a function as a device that provides a capability to the host. Examples of functions are a mouse, a set of speakers, or a data-acquisition unit.

A hub is a device that contains one or more connectors or internal connections to USB devices along with the hardware to enable communicating with each device. Each connector represents a USB port.

A 1.x hub repeats received USB traffic in both directions, and also contains the intelligence to manage power, send and respond to status and control messages, and prevent full-speed data from transmitting to low-speed devices. A 2.0 hub does all of this and more. A 2.0 hub supports high speed. And instead of just repeating received data, as needed the hub converts

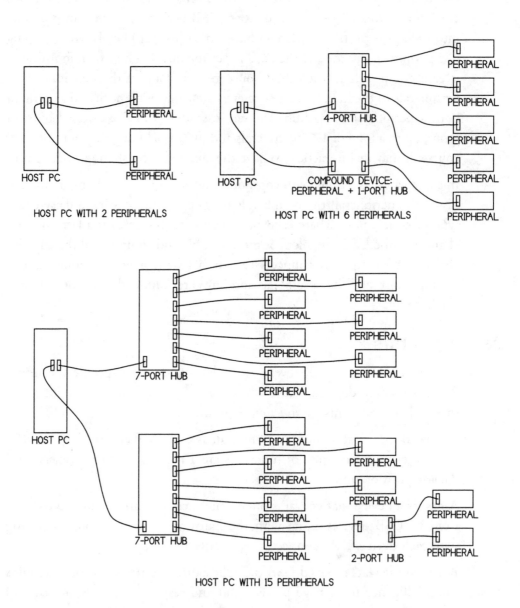

Figure 2-2: There are many possible configurations for connecting USB devices to a host PC. These are a few of the options for a host with two ports.

between low- and full-speed and high-speed data and performs other functions that ensure that bus time is used efficiently.

A device, or peripheral, is something you attach to a USB port on a PC or hub. The official definition of a device is a function or a hub—except for the special case of the compound device, which contains a hub and one or more functions. Generally, the host treats a compound device the same as if the hub and its functions were each a separate physical device. Every device on the bus has a unique address, except again for a compound device, whose hub and functions each have unique addresses.

A composite device is a multi-function device with multiple, independent interfaces. It has one address on the bus but each interface can have a different device driver on the host.

If you're thinking that this terminology is confusing, you're not alone.

What is a Port?

This is also a good time to clarify the meaning of the word *port* in relation to USB. A USB port is different in some ways from the traditional serial and parallel ports on a PC.

In a general sense, a computer port is an addressable location that is available for attaching additional circuits. Usually the circuits terminate at a connector that enables attaching a cable to a peripheral such as a keyboard, display, or printer. In some cases, the peripheral circuits are hard-wired to the port. Software monitors and controls the port circuits by reading and writing to the port's address. Computer memory also consists of addressable locations, but the CPU accesses memory with different machine instructions. On PCs, most memory addresses connect only to the system's data bus, not to other peripheral circuits.

USB ports differ from many other ports because all ports on the bus share a single path to the host. With the RS-232 serial interface, each port is independent from the others. If you have two RS-232 ports, each has its own data path, and each cable carries its own data and no one else's. The two ports can send and receive data at the same time.

USB uses a different approach. Each host controller supports a single bus, or data path. Each connector on the bus represents a USB port, but unlike RS-232, all devices share the available time. So even though there are multiple ports, each with its own connector and cable, there is only one data path. Only one device, or the host, transmits at a time. A single host may support multiple USB host controllers, however, each with its own bus. Other interfaces that share a data path include IEEE-1394 and SCSI.

The Host's Duties

The host PC is in charge of the bus. The host has to know what devices are on the bus and the capabilities of each. The host must also do its best to ensure that all devices on the bus can send and receive data as needed. A bus may have many devices, each with different requirements, and all wanting to transfer data at the same time. The host's job is not trivial!

Fortunately, the host controller's hardware and the USB support in Windows do much of the work of managing the bus. Each device attached to the host must have a device driver, which is a software component that enables applications to communicate with the device. Some peripherals can use device drivers included with Windows, while others require custom drivers. Other system-level software components manage communications between the device driver and the host-controller and root-hub hardware.

Applications don't have to worry about the details of USB communications. All they have to do is send and receive data using standard operating-system functions that are accessible from just about all programming languages.

The tasks below are ones that the host performs. The descriptions are in general terms. Later chapters in this book have more specifics.

Detect Devices

On power-up, the hubs make the host aware of all attached USB devices. In a process called enumeration, the host assigns an address and requests additional information from each device. After power-up, whenever a device is removed or attached, the host learns of the event and enumerates any newly attached device and removes any detached device from the devices available to applications.

Manage Data Flow

The host manages the flow of data on the bus. Multiple peripherals may want to transfer data at the same time. The host controller handles this by dividing the available time into segments called frames and microframes, and by giving each transmission a portion of a frame or microframe.

Transfers that must occur at specific rate are guaranteed to have the amount of time they need in each frame. During enumeration, a device's driver requests the bandwidth it will need for transfers that must have guaranteed timing. If the bandwidth isn't available, the host doesn't allow communications to begin. The driver must then request a smaller portion of the bandwidth, or wait until the requested bandwidth is available. Transfers that have no guaranteed timing use the remaining portion of the frames, and may have to wait.

Error Checking

The host also has error-checking duties. It adds error-checking bits to the data it sends. When a device receives data, it performs calculations on the data and compares the results with the received error-checking bits. If the results don't match, the device doesn't acknowledge receiving the data and the host knows that it should retransmit. (USB also supports one transfer type that doesn't allow re-transmitting, in the interest of maintaining a constant transfer rate.) In a similar way, the host error-checks the data it receives from devices.

The host may receive other indications that a device can't send or receive data. The host can then inform the device's driver of the problem, and the driver can notify the application so it can take appropriate action.

Provide Power

In addition to its two signal wires, a USB cable has +5V and ground wires. Some peripherals can draw all of their power from these lines. The host provides power to all devices on power-up or attachment, and works with the devices to conserve power when possible. Each full-power, bus-powered device can draw up to 500 milliamperes. The ports on a battery-powered host or hub may support only low-power devices, which are limited to 100 milliamperes. Windows doesn't support hosts with low-power ports, however. A device may also have its own power supply, using bus power only during the initial communications with the host.

Exchange Data with Peripherals

All of the above tasks support the host's main job, which is to exchange data with peripherals. In some cases, a device driver requests the host to attempt to send or receive data at a requested rate, while in others the host communicates only when an application or other software component requests it. The device driver reports any problems to the appropriate application.

The Peripheral's Duties

In many ways, the peripheral's duties are a mirror image of the host's. When the host initiates communications, the peripheral must respond. But peripherals also have duties that are unique.

A device can't begin USB communications on its own. Instead, it must wait and respond to a communication from the host. (An exception is the remote wakeup feature, which enables a device to request a communication from the host.)

The USB controller in the device handles many of the communication's responsibilities automatically. The amount of support required in the device's firmware varies with the chip.

The peripheral must perform all of the tasks described below. The descriptions are in general terms. Later chapters in this book have more specifics.

Detect Communications Directed to the Chip

Each device monitors the device address in each communication on the bus. If the address doesn't match the device's stored address, the device ignores the communication. If the address does match, the device stores the data in its receive buffer and generates an interrupt to signal that data has arrived. In almost all chips, this is built into the hardware and thus automatic. The device's program code doesn't have to take action or make decisions until the chip has detected a communication containing its address.

Respond to Standard Requests

On power-up, or when the device attaches to a powered system, the device must respond to the requests made by the host in the enumeration process. The host may also send standard requests any time after enumeration completes.

All USB devices must respond to requests that query the capabilities and status of the device or request the device to take other action. On receiving a request, the device places any data or status information to send in response in its transmit buffer. In some cases, such as setting an address or configuration, the device takes other action in addition to responding with information.

The specification defines eleven requests, and a class or vendor may define additional requests. The device doesn't have to carry out every request, however; it just has to respond to the request in an understandable way. For example, when the host requests a configuration that the device doesn't support, the device responds with an indicator that the request isn't supported.

Error Check

Like the host, the device adds error-checking bits to the data it sends. On receiving data that includes error-checking bits, the device does the error-checking calculations. The device's response or lack of response informs the host whether to re-transmit. These functions are built into the hardware and don't need to be programmed. When appropriate, the device also detects the acknowledgement that the host sends in reply to data it has received.

Manage Power

A device may be bus-powered or it may have its own power supply. For devices that use bus power, when there is no bus activity, the device must enter its low-power Suspend state. During Suspend, the device must continue to monitor the bus and exit the Suspend state when bus activity resumes.

When the host enters a low-power state, such as Windows 98's Standby state, all communications on the bus cease, including the periodic timing markers the host normally sends. When the devices that connect to the bus detect the absence of bus activity for three milliseconds, they must enter the Suspend state and limit the current they draw from the bus. A host may also request to suspend communications with a specific device.

Devices that don't support the remote-wakeup feature can consume no more than 500 microamperes from the bus in the Suspend state. If the remote-wakeup feature is available and enabled by the host, the limit is 2.5 milliamperes. These are average values over a 1 second; the peak current can be greater.

Exchange Data with the Host

All of the above tasks support the main job of the device's USB port, which is to exchange data with the host. After the device is configured, it must respond to requests to send and receive data.

The host may poll the device at regular intervals or only when an application requests to communicate with it. The device's configuration, the host's device driver, and the applications that use the device together determine what type of requests the host makes and how often it makes them.

For most transfers where the host sends data to the device, the device must respond to each transfer attempt by sending a code that indicates whether it accepted the data or was too busy to handle it. For most transfers where the device sends data to the host, the device must respond to each attempt by returning data or a code indicating there was no data to send or the device was busy. Typically, the hardware responds automatically according to settings made previously in firmware. Some transfers don't use acknowledgements and the sender just assumes the receiver has received all transmitted data.

The controller chip's hardware handles the details of formatting the data for the bus. This includes adding error-checking bits to data to transmit, checking for errors in received data, and sending and receiving the individual bits on the bus.

Of course, the device must also do anything else it's responsible for. For example, a mouse must always be ready to detect movement and mouse clicks, a data-acquisition unit has to read the data from its sensors, and a printer must translate received data into images on paper.

What about Speed?

A device controller may support low speed, full speed, or full and high speeds. Virtually all hubs support low- and full-speed devices. The exception is a hub embedded in a compound device that has only low-speed functions. This hub would communicate at full speed with the host, but at low speed with its embedded device(s). A low- or full-speed peripheral can connect to any USB hub. Users can be completely unaware of whether a device is low or full speed, because there are no user settings or configurations to worry about.

High-speed peripherals are likely to be dual-speed devices that are also usable when connected to any hub. A 1.x host or hub doesn't support high speed at all because high speed didn't exist when the 1.x specifications were written. To ensure that high-speed devices don't confuse 1.x hosts and hubs, all high-speed devices must respond to standard enumeration requests at full speed. This enables any host to identify any device.

Other than responding to standard requests, a high-speed device doesn't have to function at full speed. But because 1.x hosts and hubs are likely to remain in use for a while, and because supporting full speed is easy to do, most high-speed devices will also be completely functional at full speed.

The actual rate of data transfer between a peripheral and host is less than the bus speed and isn't always predictable. Some of the transmitted bits are used for identifying, synchronizing, and error-checking rather than data, and the data rate also depends on the type of transfer and how busy the bus is.

For time-sensitive data, USB supports transfer types that have a guaranteed rate or guaranteed maximum latency. Isochronous transfers have a guaranteed rate, where the host can request a specific number of bytes to transfer to or from a peripheral in a defined time period. A full-speed transfer can move up to 1023 bytes in each 1-millisecond frame. A high-speed transfer can move up to 3072 bytes in each 125-microsecond microframe. Isochronous transfers have no error correcting, however. Interrupt transfers have error correcting and guaranteed maximum latency, which means that a precise rate isn't guaranteed, but the time between transfer attempts will be no greater than a specified amount. At low speed, the requested maximum interval may range from 10 to 255 milliseconds. At full speed, the range is 1 to 255 milliseconds. At high speed, the range is 125 microseconds to 4.096 seconds.

Because the bus is shared, there's no guarantee that a particular rate or maximum latency will be available to a device. If the bus is too busy to allow a requested rate or maximum latency, the host will refuse to complete the configuration process that enables the host's software to attempt the transfers. Also, although the host controller can guarantee bandwidth will be available, it's up to the device driver, application software, and device firmware to ensure that there is data to transfer when the host controller is ready for it.

At full speed, the fastest transfers on an otherwise idle bus are bulk transfers, with a theoretical maximum of 1.216 Megabytes/second at full speed and 53.248 Megabytes/second at high speed. The host controller's driver may limit a single bulk transfer to a slower rate, however. The transfers with the most guaranteed bandwidth are high-speed interrupt and isochronous transfers at 24.576 Megabytes/second.

Although the low-speed bus speed is 1.5 Megabits per second, the fastest guaranteed delivery for a single transfer is 8 bytes in 10 milliseconds, or just 800 bytes per second. Low speed has uses, however, because the cables can be cheaper, circuit-board layout is simpler, and the controller chips may be cheaper.

The Development Process

After you've made the decision to use a USB interface with your peripheral, what's next? Designing a USB product involves both getting the peripheral up and running and developing the PC software to communicate with the peripheral.

Elements in the Link

A USB peripheral needs all of the following:

- A controller chip with a USB interface.
- Code in the peripheral to carry out the USB communications.
- Whatever hardware and code the peripheral needs to carry out its other functions (processing data, reading inputs, writing to outputs).
- A host that supports USB.
- Device-driver software on the host to enable applications to communicate with the peripheral.
- If the peripheral isn't a standard type supported by the operating system, the host must have application software to enable users to access the peripheral. For standard peripheral types such as a mouse, keyboard, or disk drive, you don't need custom application software (though you may want to write a test application).

Tools for Developing

To develop a USB peripheral, you need the following tools:

- An assembler or compiler to create the firmware (the code that runs inside the device's controller chip). If you use assembly code, you'll need a cross assembler that runs on a PC and translates your source code into the machine code the controller understands. If you use C or another high-level language, you'll need a compiler that can generate the machine code for your controller.
- A device programmer or development kit that enables you to store the assembled or compiled code in the controller's program memory.

- A programming language and development environment on the host for writing and debugging the host software. The host software may include a device driver or filter driver and/or application code. To write a device driver, you'll need Visual C++, which is capable of compiling the WDM (Win32 Driver Model) drivers required for USB devices.
- A monitor program, protocol analyzer, or other debugging tools to help in developing your firmware.

Steps in Developing a Project

For a project of any size, you'll want to create the project a piece at a time, in modules, and get each piece working before moving on to the next. In writing the firmware, you can begin by writing just enough code to enable Windows to detect and enumerate the device. When that's working, you can move on to exchanging small blocks of data with applications. From there you can add specific code for your application. The steps in project development include initial decisions, enumerating, and exchanging data:

Initial Decisions

Before you begin the developing, you need to gather data and make some decisions:

1. Specify the requirements of your device. For the USB interface, how much data does it need to transfer, and how fast? Do you need error correcting? How much power will the device draw? What else does the device need to do?

2. Use the answer to #1 to specify the requirements of the controller chip.

3. Using your requirements, decide whether the PC will communicate with the peripheral using Windows' built-in drivers, a generic device driver from another source, or a custom driver.

4. Select a controller chip that matches your requirements. If you have a favorite chip family, start by looking for a controller in that family.

Enumerating

Here's what you need to do to get Windows to enumerate your device:

1. Write the code the controller chip needs to be enumerated by its host. The details vary with the chip, but every chip must be able send a series of descriptors to the host. The descriptors are data structures that describe the chip's USB capabilities and how they'll be used. The chip must also have program code or hardware that recognizes and responds to the requests that the host sends when it enumerates the device. Chip vendors generally provide example code that you can use with very few modifications.

2. Create or obtain an INF (information) file so that Windows can identify the device when it enumerates it. The INF file is a text file that you can create with any text editor. The file names the driver that the device will use. At this point, you can use any generic driver supported by the chip's descriptors. Again, chip vendors often provide sample INF files. If your device uses one of the classes supported by Windows, you may be able to use an INF file included with Windows.

3. If necessary, design and build a circuit to connect the chip to the host. In many cases, you'll initially use a development board available from the chip's vendor.

4. Load the code into the device and plug the device into the host's bus. Windows should enumerate the device, adding it to the Control Panel and identifying it correctly.

5. Debug and repeat as needed!

Exchanging Data

These are the steps related to getting the device to perform its intended functions:

1. Add abilities to the device by adding code to the controller chip's firmware and components that connect to the chip.

2. If you're using a custom driver, write the driver code to communicate with the device.

3. If needed, write application code to communicate with the USB device. If you're designing a mouse, keyboard, or other standard device, you can access the device from any application.

When the code is debugged, you're ready to program the code into the chip and test on your final hardware.

But before you begin with any of this, it's useful to know a more about how the host enumerates and transfers data with devices, so you can make the right choices about controller chips and drivers. This is the purpose of the following chapters.

3

Inside USB Transfers

To design and program a USB device, you need to know a certain amount about the inner workings of the interface. This is true even though the hardware and system software handle many of the details automatically.

This and the next three chapters are a tutorial on how USB transfers data. This chapter has essentials that apply to all transfers. The following chapters cover the four transfer types supported by USB, the enumeration process, and the standard requests used in control transfers.

You don't need to know every bit of this information to get a project up and running, but I've found that understanding something about how the transfers work helps in deciding which transfer types to use, in writing the firmware for the controller chip, and in tracking down the inevitable bugs that show up when you try out your circuits and code.

The USB interface is complicated, and much of what you need to know is interwoven with everything else. This makes it hard to know where to start. In general, I begin with the big picture and work down to the details. Unavoidably, some of the things I refer to aren't explained in detail until later. And some things are repeated because they're important and relevant in more than one place.

The information in these chapters is dense. If you don't have a background in USB, you won't absorb it all in one reading. You should, however, get a feel for how USB works, and will know where to look later when you need to check the details.

The ultimate authority on the USB interface is the specification published by its sponsoring members. The specification document, titled not surprisingly, *Universal Serial Bus Specification,* is available on the USB Implementers Forum's website (*www.usb.org*). However, by design, the specification omits information and tips that are unique to any operating system or controller chip. This type of information is essential when you're designing a product for the real world, so I've included it.

Transfer Basics

You can divide USB communications into two categories, depending on whether they're used in configuring and setting up the device or in the applications that carry out the device's purpose. In configuration communications, the host learns about the device and prepares it for exchanging data. Most of these communications take place when the host enumerates the device on power up or attachment. Application communications occur when the host exchanges data for use with applications. These are the communications that perform the functions the device is designed for. For example, for a keyboard, the application communications are the sending of keypress data to the host to tell an application to display a character.

Configuration Communications

During enumeration, the device's firmware responds to a series of standard requests from the host. The device must identify each request, return requested information, and take other actions specified by the requests.

On PCs, Windows performs the enumeration, so there's no user programming involved. However, to complete the enumeration, Windows must have two files available: an INF file that identifies the filename and location of the device's driver, and the device driver itself. If the files are available and the firmware is in order, the enumeration process is invisible to users.

Depending on the device and how it will be used, the device driver may be one that's included with Windows or one provided by the product vendor. The INF file is a text file that you can usually adapt if needed from an example provided by the driver's provider. Chapter 11 has more details about device drivers and INF files.

Application Communications

After the host has exchanged enumeration information with the device and a device driver has been assigned and loaded, the application communications can be fairly straightforward. At the host, applications can use standard Windows API functions to read and write to the device. At the device, transferring data typically requires placing data to send in the USB controller's transmit buffer, reading received data from the receive buffer, and on completing a transfer, ensuring that the device is ready for the next transfer. Most devices also require additional firmware support for handling errors and other events.

Each data transfer on the bus uses one of four transfer types: control, interrupt, bulk, or isochronous. Each has a format and protocol suited for particular uses.

Managing Data on the Bus

USB's two signal lines carry data to and from all of the devices on the bus. The wires form a single transmission path that all of the devices must share. (As explained later in this chapter, a cable segment between a 1.x device and a 2.0 hub on a high-speed bus is an exception, but even here, all data shares the path between the hub and host.) Unlike RS-232, which has a TX line to carry data in one direction and an RX line for the other direction, USB's pair of wires carries a single differential signal, with the directions taking turns.

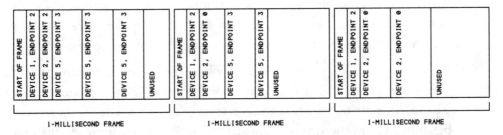

Figure 3-1: At low and full speeds, the host schedules transactions within 1-millisecond frames. Each frame begins with a Start-of-Frame packet, followed by transactions that transfer data to or from device endpoints. The host may schedule transactions anywhere it wants within a frame. The process is similar at high speed, but using 125-microsecond microframes.

The host is in charge of seeing that all transfers occur as quickly as possible. It manages the traffic by dividing time into chunks called frames, or microframes at high speed. The host gives each transfer a portion of each frame or microframe (Figure 3-1). For low- and full-speed data, the frames are one millisecond. For high speed data, the host divides each frame into eight 125-microsecond microframes. Each frame or microframe begins with a Start-of-Frame timing reference.

Each transfer consists of one or more transactions. Control transfers always have multiple transactions because they have multiple stages, each consisting of one or more transactions. Other transfers use multiple transactions when they have more data than will fit in a single transaction. Depending on how the host schedules the transactions and the speed of a device's response, a transfer's transactions may all be in a single frame or microframe, or they may be spread over multiple (micro)frames.

Because all of the transfers share a data path, each transaction must include a device address. Every device has a unique address assigned by the host, and all data travels to or from the host. Each transaction begins when the host sends block of information that includes the address of the receiving device and a specific location, called an endpoint, within the device. Everything a device sends is in response to receiving a request from the host to send data or status information.

Host Speed and Bus Speed

A 1.x host supports low and full speeds. A 2.0 host with user-accessible ports must support low, full, and high speeds.

A 1.x hub doesn't convert between speeds; it just passes received traffic on, changing only the edge rate of the signals to match the destination's speed. In contrast, a 2.0 hub acts as a remote processor. It converts between high speed and low or full speed as needed and performs other functions that help make efficient use of the bus time. The added intelligence of 2.0 hubs is a major reason why the high-speed bus remains compatible with 1.x hardware. It also means that 2.0 hubs are much more complicated internally than 1.x hubs.

The traffic on a bus segment is high speed only if the host controller and all upstream (toward the host) hubs are 2.0-compliant. Figure 3-2 illustrates. A

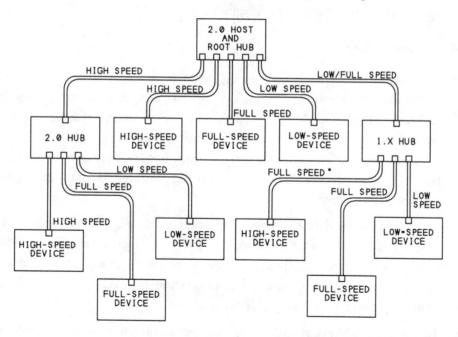

*FULL-SPEED ENUMERATION IS REQUIRED. ADDITIONAL FULL-SPEED FUNCTIONALITY IS OPTIONAL.

Figure 3-2: A USB 2.0 bus uses high speed whenever possible, switching to low and full speeds when necessary.

high-speed bus may also have 1.x hubs, and if so, any bus segments downstream (away from the host) are low or full speed. Traffic to and from low- and full-speed devices travels at high speed between the host and any 2.0 hubs that connect to the host with no 1.x hubs in between. Traffic between a 2.0 hub and a 1.x hub or another low- or full-speed device travels at low or full speed. A bus with only a 1.x host controller supports only low and full speeds, even if the bus has 2.0 hubs and devices.

Elements of a Transfer

Understanding USB transfers requires looking inside them several levels deep. Each transfer is made up of transactions. Each transaction is made up of packets. And each packet contains information. To understand transactions, packets, and their contents, you also need to know about endpoints and pipes. So that's where we'll begin.

Device Endpoints

All transmissions travel to or from a device endpoint. The endpoint is a buffer that stores multiple bytes. Typically it's a block of data memory or a register in the controller chip. The data stored at an endpoint may be received data, or data waiting to transmit. The host also has buffers for received data and for data ready to transmit, but the host doesn't have endpoints. Instead, the host serves as the starting point for communicating with the device endpoints.

The specification defines a device endpoint as "a uniquely addressable portion of a USB device that is the source or sink of information in a communication flow between the host and device." This suggests that an endpoint carries data in one direction only. However, as I'll explain, a control endpoint is a special case that is bidirectional.

The unique address required for each endpoint consists of an endpoint number and direction. The number may range from 0 to 15. The direction is from the host's perspective: IN is toward the host and OUT is away from the host. An endpoint configured to do control transfers must transfer data in both directions, so a control endpoint actually consists of a pair of IN and OUT endpoints that share an endpoint number.

Every device must have Endpoint 0 configured as a control endpoint. There's rarely a need for additional control endpoints. They're allowed, however, and some controller chips support them.

The other transfer types send data in one direction only (though status and control information may flow in the opposite direction). A single endpoint number can support both IN and OUT endpoint addresses. For example, Endpoint 1 on a device might support an IN endpoint address for transfers to the host as well as an OUT endpoint address for transfers from the host.

In addition to Endpoint 0, a full-speed device can have up to 30 additional endpoints (1 through 15, with each supporting both IN and OUT). A low-speed device is limited to two additional endpoints with any combination of directions (for example Endpoint 1 IN and Endpoint 1 OUT, or Endpoint 1 IN and Endpoint 2 IN).

Every transaction on the bus includes an endpoint number and a code that indicates the direction of data flow and whether or not the transaction is initiating a control transfer. The codes are IN, OUT, and Setup:

Transaction Type	Source of Data	Types of Transfers that Use this Transaction Type	Contents
IN	device	all	generic data
OUT	host	all	generic data
Setup	host	control	a request

As with the endpoint directions, the naming convention for IN and OUT transactions is from the perspective of the host. In an IN transaction, data travels from the peripheral to the host. In an OUT transaction, data travels from the host to the peripheral.

In a Setup transaction, data also travels from the host to the peripheral, but a Setup transaction is a special case because it initiates a control transfer. Devices need to identify Setup transactions so they know how to interpret the data they contain. Setup transactions are also the only type that devices must always accept. Any transfer may use IN or OUT transactions, but only control transfers use Setup transactions.

Each transaction contains a device address and an endpoint address. When a device receives an OUT or Setup transaction containing the device's address, the hardware stores the received data in the appropriate location for the endpoint and typically triggers an interrupt. An interrupt-service routine in the device then processes the received data and does whatever else the transaction requires. When a device receives an IN transaction containing its device address, if the device has data ready to send to the host, the hardware sends the data from the specified endpoint onto the bus and typically triggers an interrupt. An interrupt-service routine in the device then does whatever is needed to get ready for the next IN transaction.

Pipes: Connecting Endpoints to the Host

Before a transfer can occur, the host and device must establish a pipe. A USB pipe isn't a physical object; it's just an association between a device's endpoint and the host controller's software.

The host establishes pipes shortly after system power-up or device attachment, on requesting configuration information from the device. If the device is removed from the bus, the host removes the no-longer-needed pipes. The host may also request new pipes or remove unneeded pipes at other times by requesting an alternate configuration or interface for a device. Every device has a Default Control Pipe that uses Endpoint 0.

The configuration information received by the host includes a descriptor for each endpoint that the device wants to use. Each endpoint descriptor is a block of information that tells the host what it needs to know about the endpoint in order to communicate with it. This includes the endpoint address, the type of transfer to use, the maximum size of data packets, and, when appropriate, the desired interval for transfers.

In some cases, the host accepts a requested configuration only after ensuring that the bus has enough idle bandwidth to do the transfers at the requested rate. This is true when the configuration requires pipes that will carry isochronous transfers, which have a guaranteed rate (transactions per second), and interrupt transfers, which have a guaranteed maximum latency (time between transactions).

In these cases, the host examines the available bandwidth before establishing the pipe. If the bandwidth is available, the host accepts the configuration request and ensures that the transfers will have the time they need. If the bandwidth isn't available, the host denies the configuration request and the requesting software must try again, either waiting until the bandwidth is available or selecting a new configuration that requests less bandwidth. For pipes that carry requests without guaranteed timing, the host doesn't check available bandwidth; it just promises to fit the transfers into the available time as best as it can.

Types of Transfers

USB is designed to handle many types of peripherals with varying requirements for transfer rate, response time, and error correcting. The four types of data transfers each handle different needs, and a device can support the transfer types that are best suited for its purpose. Table 3-1 summarizes the features and uses of each transfer type.

Control transfers are the only type that have functions defined by the USB specification. Control transfers enable the host to read information about a device, set a device's address, and select configurations and other settings. Control transfers may also send custom requests that send and receive data for any purpose. All USB devices must support control transfers.

Bulk transfers are intended for situations where the rate of transfer isn't critical, such as sending a file to a printer or receiving data from a scanner. In these applications, quick transfers are nice, but the data can wait if necessary. If the bus is very busy with other transfers that have guaranteed transfer rates, bulk transfers must wait, but if the bus is idle, bulk transfers are very fast. Only full- and high-speed devices can do bulk transfers. Devices aren't required to support bulk transfers, but a specific device class might require it.

Interrupt transfers are for devices that must receive the host's or device's attention periodically. Other than control transfers, interrupt transfers are

Table 3-1: Each of the USB's four transfer types is suited for different application types.

Transfer Type	Control	Bulk	Interrupt	Isochronous
Typical Use	Configuration	Printer, scanner	Mouse, keyboard	Audio
Required?	yes	no	no	no
Allowed on low-speed devices?	yes	no	yes	no
Data bytes/millisecond per transfer, maximum possible per pipe (high speed). Assumes data/transfer = maximum packet size.	15,872 (thirty-one 64-byte transactions/ microframe)	53,248 (thirteen 512-byte transactions/ microframe)	24,576 (three 1024-byte transactions/ microframe)	24,576 (three 1024-byte transactions/ microframe)
Data bytes/millisecond per transfer, maximum possible per pipe (full speed). Assumes data/transfer = maximum packet size.	832 (thirteen 64-byte transactions/ frame)	1216 (nineteen 64-byte transactions/ frame)	64 (one 64-byte transaction/ frame)	1023 (one 1023-byte transaction/ frame)
Data bytes/millisecond per transfer, maximum possible per pipe (low speed). Assumes data/transfer = maximum packet size.	24 (three 8-byte transactions)	not allowed	0.8 (8 bytes per 10 milliseconds)	not allowed
Direction of data flow	IN and OUT	IN or OUT	IN or OUT (1.0 supports IN only)	IN or OUT
Reserved bandwidth for all transfers of the type	10 at low/full speed, 20 at high speed (minimum)	none	90 at low/full speed, 80 at high speed (isochronous & interrupt combined) (maximum)	
Error correction?	yes	yes	yes	no
Message or Stream data?	message	stream	stream	stream
Guaranteed delivery rate?	no	no	no	yes
Guaranteed latency (maximum time between transfers)?	no	no	yes	yes

the only way that low-speed devices can transfer data. Keyboards and mice use interrupt transfers to send keypress and mouse-movement data. Interrupt transfers can use any speed. Devices aren't required to support interrupt transfers, but a specific device class might require it.

Isochronous transfers have guaranteed delivery time but no error correcting. Data that might use isochronous transfers incudes audio files to be played in real time. This is the only transfer type that doesn't support automatic re-transmitting of data received with errors, so occasional errors must be acceptable. Only full- and high-speed devices can do isochronous transfers. Devices aren't required to support isochronous transfers, but a specific device class might require it.

Chapter 4 has more detailed descriptions of each transfer type, with the focus on what you need to know in order to use each. But before we get into that, there are additional things to understand about how the bus transfers data.

Stream and Message Pipes

In addition to classifying a pipe by the type of transfer it carries, the specification defines pipes as either stream or message, according to whether or not information travels in one or both directions. Control transfers are the only transfers that use the bidirectional message pipes; all others use unidirectional stream pipes.

Control Transfers Use Message Pipes

In a message pipe, each transfer begins with a Setup transaction containing a request. To complete the transfer, the host and device may exchange data and status information, or the device may just send status information. There is always at least one transaction that sends information in each direction.

If the device supports the request, it takes the requested action. If the device doesn't support the request, it responds with a code to indicate this.

All Other Transfers Use Stream Pipes

In a stream pipe, the data has no format defined by the USB specification. The receiving device just accepts whatever arrives. The device firmware or host software can then process the data in whatever way is appropriate for the application.

Of course, even with stream data, the sending and receiving devices will need to agree on a format of some type. For example, a host application may define a code that requests a device to send a series of bytes indicating a temperature reading and the time of the reading. Although the host could use control transfers with a vendor-defined Get_Temperature request, it might prefer to use interrupt transfers to guarantee that the host will request a new reading at intervals. In an interrupt transfer, the data is in a stream pipe and doesn't have to conform to the format for control transfers.

Initiating a Transfer

When a device driver in the host wants to communicate with a device, it initiates a transfer. The specification defines a transfer as the process of making and carrying out a communication request. A transfer may be very short, sending as little as a byte of data, or very long, sending the contents of a large file.

Typically, a Windows application opens communications with a device using a handle retrieved using standard API functions. To begin a transfer, an application may use the handle in calling an API function to request the transfer from the device's driver. Applications can request data from a device or provide data to send to the device. A request from an application might be "send the contents of the file *data.txt* on the host" or "get the contents of *Report 0* from the device." When an application requests a transfer, the operating system passes the request to the appropriate device driver, which in turn passes the request to other system-level drivers and on to the host controller. The host controller then initiates the transfer on the bus.

In some cases, the driver is configured to request periodic transfers, and applications read the retrieved data or provide data to send in these transfers. Other transfers, such as those done in enumeration, are initiated by the operating system on detecting the device.

Transactions: the Building Blocks of a Transfer

Figure 3-3 shows the elements of a typical transfer, and Table 3-2 lists the elements that make up each of the four transfer types. A lot of the terminology here begins to sound the same. There are transfers and transactions, stages and phases, data transactions and data packets, Status stages and handshake phases. Data stages have handshake packets and Status stages have data packets. It takes a while to absorb it all. I created Table 3-2 to use as a memory-jogging reference when I found myself getting confused about the terminology. With that reminder to take it slowly, we can move on to the details.

Each transfer consists of one or more transactions, and each transaction in turn consists of one, two, or three packets.

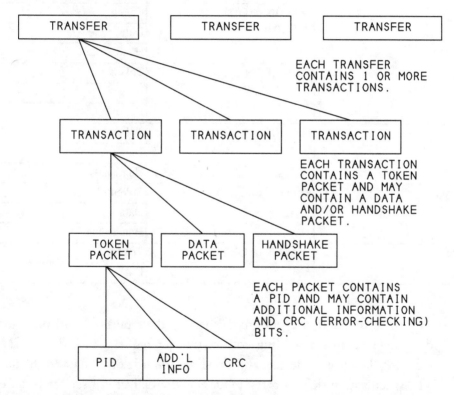

Figure 3-3: A USB transfer consists of transactions. The transactions in turn contain packets, and the packets contain a packet identifier (PID), PID-check bits, and sometimes additional information.

Table 3-2: Each of the four transfer types consists of one or more stages, with each stage made up of two or three phases. (This table doesn't show the additional transactions required for the split transactions and PING protocol used in some transfers.)

Transfer Type	Stages (0 or more transactions)	Phases (packets). Each downstream, low-speed packet is also preceded by a PRE packet.
Control	Setup	Token
		Data
		Handshake
	Data (IN or OUT) (optional)	Token
		Data
		Handshake
	Status (IN or OUT)	Token
		Data
		Handshake
Bulk	Data (IN or OUT)	Token
		Data
		Handshake
Interrupt	Data (IN or OUT)	Token
		Data
		Handshake
Isochronous	Data (IN or OUT)	Token
		Data

The three transaction types are defined by their purpose and direction of data flow: Setup for sending control-transfer requests to a device, IN for receiving data from a device, and OUT for sending other data to the device. The specification defines a transaction as the delivery of service to an endpoint. *Service* in this case can mean either the host's sending a chunk of information to the device, or the host's requesting and receiving a chunk of information from the device.

Each transaction includes identifying, error-checking, status, and control information, as well as any data to be exchanged. A complete transfer may take place over multiple frames, but a transaction is a single communication that must complete uninterrupted. No other communication on the bus can break into the middle of a transaction.

Devices must be able to respond quickly with requested data or status information in a transaction. Program code in the device may prepare an endpoint to respond to a transaction request, but hardware handles responding to the request when it arrives.

A transfer with a small amount of data may require just one transaction. If the amount of data is large, a transfer may use multiple transactions, with a portion of the data in each.

Transaction Phases

Each transaction has up to three phases, or parts that occur in sequence: token, data, and handshake. Each phase consists of one or two transmitted packets. Each packet is a block of information with a defined format. All packets begin with a Packet ID (PID) that contains identifying information, as Table 3-3 shows. Depending on the transaction, the PID may be followed by an endpoint address, data, status information, or a frame number, along with error-checking bits.

In the token phase of a transaction, the host sends a communications request in a token packet. The PID indicates the transaction type, such as Setup, IN, OUT, or Start-of-Frame.

In the data phase, the host or device may transfer any kind of information in a data packet. The PID indicates the data-toggle value used to indicate the data's position when there are multiple data packets.

In the handshake phase, the host or device sends status, or handshaking, information in a handshake packet. The PID holds the status code (ACK, NAK, STALL, NYET). The specification sometimes uses the terms *status phase* and *status packet* to refer to the handshake phase and packet.

The token phase has one additional use. A token packet may carry a Start-of-Frame (SOF) marker, which is a timing reference that the host sends at 1-millisecond intervals at full speed and 125-microsecond intervals

Table 3-3: The PID (packet identifier) provides information about a transaction. (Sheet 1 of 2)

Packet Type	PID Name	Value	Transfer types used in	Source	Bus Speed	Description
Token (identifies transaction type)	OUT	0001	all	host	all	Endpoint address for OUT (host-to-device) transaction.
	IN	1001	all	host	all	Endpoint address for IN (device-to-host) transaction.
	SOF	0101	Start-of-Frame	host	all	Start-of-Frame marker and frame number.
	SETUP	1101	control	host	all	Endpoint address for Setup transaction.
Data (carries data or status code)	DATA0	0011	all	host, device	all	Data toggle, data sequencing
	DATA1	1011	all	host, device	all	Data toggle, data sequencing
	DATA2	0111	isoch.	host, device	high	Data sequencing
	MDATA	1111	isoch., interrupt	host, device	high	Data sequencing
Handshake (carries status code)	ACK	0010	all	host, device	all	Receiver accepts error-free data packet.
	NAK	1010	control, bulk, interrupt	device	all	Receiver can't accept data or sender can't send data or has no data to transmit.
	STALL	1110	control, bulk, interrupt	device	all	A control request isn't supported or the endpoint is halted.
	NYET	0110	control Write, bulk OUT, split transactions	device	high	Device accepts error-free data packet but isn't yet ready for another or hub doesn't yet have complete-split data.

Table 3-3: The PID (packet identifier) provides information about a transaction. (Sheet 2 of 2)

Packet Type	PID Name	Value	Transfer types used in	Source	Bus Speed	Description
Special	PRE	1100	control, interrupt	host	full	Preamble issued by host to indicate that the next packet is low speed.
	ERR	1100	all	device hub	high	Returned by a hub to report a low- or full-speed error in a split transaction.
	SPLIT	1000	all	host	high	Precedes a token packet to indicate a split transaction.
	PING	0100	control Write, bulk OUT	host	high	Busy check for bulk OUT and control Write data transactions after NYET.
	reserved	0000	-	-	-	For future use.

at high speed. This packet also contains a frame number that increments and rolls over on reaching the maximum. The number indicates the frame count, so the eight microframes within a frame all use the same number. An endpoint may synchronize to the Start-of-Frame packet, or use the frame count as a timing reference. The Start-of-Frame marker also keeps devices from entering the low-power Suspend state when there is no other USB traffic.

Low-speed devices don't see the SOF packet. Instead, the device's hub uses a simpler End-of-Packet (EOP) signal called the low-speed keep-alive signal, sent once per frame. As the SOF does for full-speed devices, the low-speed keep-alive keeps low-speed devices from entering the Suspend state.

Of the four special PIDs, one is used only with low-speed devices, one is used only with high-speed devices, and two are used when a low- or full-speed device's 2.0 hub communicates at high speed with the host.

The special low-speed PID is PRE, which contains a preamble code that tells hubs that the next packet is low speed and the hub should enable communications with any attached low-speed devices. On a low- and full-speed bus, the PRE PID precedes all token, data, and handshake packets directed to low-speed devices. High-speed buses encode the PRE in the SPLIT packet, so they don't send it separately. Low-speed packets sent by a device don't require a PRE PID.

The PID used only with high-speed devices is PING. The host sends a PING to find out if a high-speed device endpoint is busy before sending the next data packet in a bulk or control transfer with multiple data packets. The device responds with a status code.

The SPLIT PID identifies a token packet as part of a split transaction. To make better use of bus time, 2.0 hosts and hubs send low- and full-speed traffic at high speed. When the host begins a transaction destined for a low- or full-speed device, the 2.0 hub nearest to the device is responsible for completing the transaction with the device, storing any returned data or status information, and reporting it back in one or more later transactions. This way, the entire bus doesn't have to wait for a transaction to complete at a lower speed. These special transactions between the hub and host are called split transactions.

The ERR PID is used only in split transactions. A 2.0 hub uses this PID to report an error to the host in a low- or full-speed transaction. The ERR and PRE PIDs have the same value, but won't be confused because a hub never sends a PRE to the host or an ERR to a device.

Packet Sequences

Every transaction has a token packet. The host is always the source of the this packet, which sets up the transaction by identifying the packet type, the receiving device and endpoint, and the direction of any data that the transaction will transfer. If it's a low-speed transaction on a full-speed bus, a PRE packet precedes the token packet. If it's a split transaction, a SPLIT packet precedes the token packet.

Depending on the transfer type and whether or not a device has information to send, a data packet may follow the token packet. The direction specified in the token packet determines whether the host or device sends the data packet.

In all transfer types except isochronous, the device that receives a data packet returns a handshake packet containing a code that indicates the success or failure of the transaction. The absence of an expected handshake packet indicates a more drastic failure.

Timing Constraints and Guarantees

The allowed delays between the token, data, and handshake packets of a transaction are very short, intended to allow only for cable delays and switching times, plus a brief time to allow the hardware to prepare a response, such as a status code, in response to a received packet.

The maximum packet sizes for the transfer type and endpoint limit the amount of data a transaction can contain. A transfer with multiple transactions may take place over multiple frames, which don't have to be contiguous. For example, in a full-speed bulk transfer of 512 bytes, the maximum number of bytes in a single transaction is 64, so transferring all of the data would require at least 8 transactions.

Although devices must complete each transaction quickly, the bus can accommodate transfers with devices that need extra time to respond. The amount of time allowed varies with the transfer type, but can be as long as five seconds. If a request will take a long time to carry out, the request should be defined so that the request and response use separate transfers. This way, after receiving a request for data, the device can prepare its response for later retrieval by the host. The host uses this technique when it requests a hub to reset a port. The host requests the hub to reset a port, and the hub responds that it has received the request and has begun the reset signaling. Later, the host sends a second request to find out if the reset is complete.

Split Transactions

A 2.0 hub communicates with a 2.0 host at high speed unless a 1.x hub lies between them. When a low- or full-speed device is attached to a 2.0 hub, the hub converts between speeds as needed. But speed conversion isn't the only thing the hub does to manage multiple speeds. High speed is 40 times faster than full speed and 320 times faster than low speed. It doesn't make

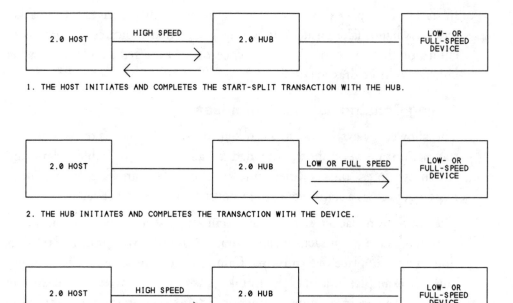

1. THE HOST INITIATES AND COMPLETES THE START-SPLIT TRANSACTION WITH THE HUB.

2. THE HUB INITIATES AND COMPLETES THE TRANSACTION WITH THE DEVICE.

3. THE HOST INITIATES AND COMPLETES THE COMPLETE-SPLIT TRANSACTION WITH THE HUB.

Figure 3-4: In a transfer that uses split transactions, the host communicates at high speed with a 2.0 hub, and the hub communicates at low or full speed with the device. Isochronous transactions may use multiple start-split or complete-split transactions.

sense for the entire bus to wait while a hub exchanges low- or full-speed data with a device.

The solution is split transactions (Figure 3-4). A 2.0 host uses split transactions when it communicates with a low- or full-speed device on a high-speed bus. What would be a single transaction at low or full speed usually requires two types of split transactions, one or more start-split transactions to send information to the device and one or more complete-split transactions to receive information from the device. The exception is isochronous OUT transactions, which don't use complete-split transactions because there is nothing to return.

Even though there are more transactions, split transactions make better use of the bus time because they minimize the amount of bus time spent waiting for a low- or full-speed device to respond. Table 3-4 compares the structure and contents of transactions with low- and full-speed devices at different bus speeds.

I'll start by explaining how split transactions work in bulk and control transfers, which don't have the timing constraints of interrupt and isochronous transfers. In the start-split transaction, the 2.0 host sends the start-split token packet (SSPLIT), followed by the usual low- or full-speed token packet, and any data packet destined for the device. The device's 2.0 hub returns ACK or NAK. The host is then free to use the bus for other transactions. The device knows nothing of the transaction yet.

On returning ACK in a start-split transaction, the hub has two responsibilities. It must complete the transaction with the device. And it must continue to handle any other bus traffic it receives from the host or other attached devices.

To complete the transaction, the hub converts the packet or packets received from the host to the appropriate speed, sends them to the device, and stores the device's response, if any. Depending on the transaction, the device may return data, a handshake, or nothing. To the device, the transaction has proceeded at the expected low or full speed and is now complete. The device has no knowledge that it's a split transaction. The host hasn't yet received the device's response.

While the hub is completing the transaction with the device, the host may initiate other bus traffic that the device's hub must handle as well. The two functions are handled by separate hardware modules within the hub.

For all but isochronous OUT transactions, when the host thinks the hub has had enough time to complete the transaction with the device, it begins a complete-split transaction with the hub.

In the complete-split transaction, the host sends a complete-split token packet (CSPLIT), followed by the usual low- or full-speed token packet to request the data or status information the hub has received from the device. The hub returns the requested data or a status code. This completes the transaction. The host doesn't return ACK. If the hub doesn't have the packet ready to send, it returns a NYET status code, and the host retries later. The

Table 3-4: When a low- or full-speed device has a transaction on a high-speed bus, the host uses start-split (SSPLIT) and complete-split (CSPLIT) transactions with the device's 2.0 hub. The hub is responsible for completing the transaction at low or full speed and reporting back to the host.

Bus Speed	Transaction Type	Transaction Phase		
		Token	Data	Handshake
Low/Full-speed communications with the device	Setup, OUT	PRE if low speed, LS/FS token	PRE if low speed, data	status (except for isochronous)
	IN	PRE if low speed, LS/FS token	data or status	PRE if low speed, status (except for isochronous)
High-speed communications between the 2.0 hub and host in transactions with a low- or full-speed device	Setup, OUT (isochronous OUT has no CSPLIT transaction)	SSPLIT, LS/FS token	data	status (bulk and control only)
		CSPLIT, LS/FS token	-	status
	IN	SSPLIT, LS/FS token	-	status (bulk and control only)
		CSPLIT, LS/FS token)	data or status	-

device has no knowledge of the complete-split transaction because it completed the transaction with its hub earlier.

In split transactions in interrupt and isochronous transfers, the process is similar, but with more strictly defined timing. The goal is to transfer data to the host as soon as possible after the device has data available to send, and to transfer data to the device just before the device is ready for new data. To achieve this, isochronous transactions with large packets use multiple start or complete splits, transferring a portion of the data in each.

Unlike with bulk and control transfers, the start-split transactions in interrupt and isochronous transfers have no handshake phase, just the start-split token followed by an IN, OUT, or Setup token and data if it's an OUT or Setup transaction.

In an interrupt transaction, the hub schedules the start split in the microframe just before the earliest time that the hub is expected to begin the transaction with the device. For example, assume that the microframes in a frame are numbered in sequence, Y0 through Y7. If the start split is in Y0, the transaction with the device may occur as early as Y1. The device may have data or a handshake response to return to the host as early as Y2. The results of previous transactions and bit stuffing can affect when the transaction with the device actually occurs, so the host schedules complete-split transactions in Y2, Y3, and Y4. If the hub doesn't yet have the information to return in the complete split, it returns a NYET status code and the host retries.

Full-speed isochronous transactions can transfer up to 1023 bytes. To ensure that the data transfers just in time, or as soon as the device has data to send or is ready to receive data, transactions with large packets use multiple start splits or complete splits, with up to 188 bytes of data in each. This is the maximum amount of full-speed data that can transfer in a microframe. A single transaction's data can require up to eight start-split or complete-split transactions.

In an isochronous IN transaction, the host schedules complete-split transactions in every microframe where it's expected that the device will have at least a portion of the data to return. Requesting the data in smaller chunks ensures that the host receives the data as quickly as possible. The host doesn't have to wait for all of the data to transfer from the device at full speed before beginning to retrieve it.

In an isochronous OUT transaction, the host sends the data in one or more start-split transactions. The host schedules the transactions so the hub's buffer will never be empty, but will contain as few bytes as possible. Each SPLIT packet contains bits to indicate its data's position in the low- or full-speed data packet (beginning, middle, end, or all). There is no complete-split transaction.

Ensuring that Transfers Are Successful

To help ensure that every transfer succeeds, USB uses handshaking and error-checking.

Handshaking

Like other interfaces, USB uses status and control, or handshaking, information to help to manage the flow of data. In hardware handshaking, dedicated lines carry the handshaking information. An example is the RTS and CTS lines in the RS-232 interface. In software handshaking, the same lines that carry the data also carry handshaking codes. An example is the XON and XOFF codes transmitted on the data lines in RS-232 links.

USB uses software handshaking. A code indicates the success or failure of all transactions except in isochronous transfers. In addition, in control transfers, the Status stage enables a device to report the success or failure of the entire transfer.

Most handshaking signals transmit in the handshake packet, though some use the data packet. The defined status codes are ACK, NAK, STALL, NYET, and ERR. A sixth status indicator is the absence of an expected handshake code, indicating a more serious bus error. In all cases, the receiver of the handshake, or lack of one, uses the information to help it decide what to do next. Table 3-5 shows the status indicators and where they transmit in each transaction type.

ACK

ACK (acknowledge) indicates that a host or device has received data without error. Devices must return ACK in the handshake packets of Setup transactions. Devices may also return ACK in the handshake packets of OUT transactions. The host returns ACK in the handshake packets of IN transactions.

NAK

NAK (negative acknowledge) means the device is busy or has no data to return. If the host sends data at a time when the device is too busy to accept it, the device sends a NAK in the handshake packet. If the host requests data from the device when the device has nothing to send, the device sends a NAK in the data packet. In either case, NAK indicates a temporary condition, and the host retries later.

Table 3-5: The location, source, and contents of the handshake signal depend on the type of transaction.

Transaction type or PING query	Data packet source	Data packet contents	Handshake packet source	Handshake packet contents
Setup	host	data	device	ACK
OUT	host	data	device	ACK, NAK, STALL, NYET (high speed only), ERR (from hub in complete split)
IN	device	data, NAK, STALL, ERR (from hub in complete split)	host	ACK
PING (high speed only)	none	none	device	ACK, NAK, STALL

Hosts never send NAK. Isochronous endpoints don't support NAK because they have no handshake packet for returning the NAK. If a device or the host misses isochronous data, it's gone.

STALL

The STALL handshake can have any of three meanings: unsupported control request, control request failed, or endpoint failed.

When a device receives a control-transfer request that the endpoint doesn't support, the device returns a STALL to the host. The device also sends a STALL if it supports the request but for some reason can't take the requested action. For example, if the host sends a Set_Configuration request that requests the device to set its configuration to 2, and the device supports only configuration 1, the device returns a STALL. To clear this type of STALL, the host just needs to send another Setup packet to begin a new control transfer. The specification calls this type of stall a protocol stall.

Another use of STALL is to respond to transfer requests when the endpoint's Halt feature is set, indicating that the endpoint is unable to send or receive data at all. The specification calls this type of stall a functional stall.

Bulk and interrupt endpoints must support the functional stall. Although control endpoints may also support this use of STALL, it's not recommended. A control endpoint in a functional stall must continue to respond normally to other requests related to controlling and monitoring the STALL condition. And if the endpoint is capable of doing this, it's clearly capable of sending and receiving data and shouldn't be stalled! Isochronous endpoints don't support STALL because they have no handshake packet for returning the STALL.

On receiving a functional STALL, the host drops all pending requests to the device and doesn't resume communications until it has sent a successful request to clear the Halt feature on the device. Hosts never send STALL.

NYET

Only high-speed devices use NYET, which stands for *not yet*. High-speed bulk and control transfers have an improved protocol that enables the host to find out before sending data if a device is ready to receive it. At full and low speeds, when the host wants to send data in a control, bulk, or interrupt transfer, it sends the token and data packets and receives a reply from the device in the handshake packet of the transaction. If the device isn't ready for the data, it returns a NAK and the host tries again later. This can waste a lot of bus time if the data packets are large and the device is often not ready.

High-speed bulk and control transactions with multiple data packets have a better way to do it. After receiving a data packet, a device endpoint can return a NYET handshake, which says that the data was accepted but the endpoint isn't yet ready to receive another data packet. When the host thinks the device might be ready, it sends a PING token packet, and the endpoint returns an ACK to indicate it's OK to send the next data packet or NAK or STALL if it's not OK. Sending a PING is more efficient than sending the entire data packet only to find out the device wasn't ready and having to resend later.

Even after responding to a PING or OUT with ACK, the endpoint is allowed to return NAK on receiving the data packet that follows, though this should be rare. The host then tries again with another PING.

A 2.0 hub may also use NYET in complete-split transactions, as described earlier. Hosts and low- and full-speed devices never send NYET.

ERR

The ERR handshake is used only by high-speed hubs in complete-split transactions. ERR indicates the device didn't return an expected handshake in the transaction the hub is completing with the host.

No Response

The final type of status indication occurs when the host or a device expects to receive a handshake, but receives nothing. This usually indicates that the receiver's error-checking calculation detected an error and informs the sender that it should try again or if multiple tries have failed, take other action.

Reporting the Status of Control Transfers

In addition to reporting the status of transactions, the same ACK, NAK, and STALL codes report the success or failure of complete control transfers. An additional status code is a zero-length data packet, which reports successful completion of a control transfer with a host-to-device Data stage. Table 3-6 shows the locations of the different status indicators for control transfers.

For control Write transfers, where the device receives data in the Data stage, the transfer's status is returned in the data packet of the Status stage. A zero-length data packet means the transfer was successful. Or the device may return a NAK or STALL. The host then returns an ACK in the handshake packet of the Status stage to indicate that it received the response.

For control Read transfers, where the host receives data in the Data stage, the device returns the status of the transfer in the handshake packet of the Status stage. The host normally waits to receive all of the packets in the Data

Table 3-6: Depending on the direction of the Data stage, the status information for a control transfer may be in the data or handshake packet of the Status stage.

Transfer Type and Direction	Status Stage Direction	Status stage's data packet	Status stage's handshake packet
Control Write (Host sends data to device)	IN	Device sends status: 0-length data packet (success), NAK (busy), or STALL (failed)	Host returns ACK
Control Read (Device sends data to host)	OUT	Host sends 0-length data packet	Device sends status: ACK (success), NAK (busy), or STALL (failed)

stage, then sends a zero-length data packet in the Status stage. The device responds with ACK, NAK, or STALL. However, if the host begins the Status stage before all of the data packets have been sent, the device must abandon the Data stage and return a status code.

Error Checking

The specification for USB hardware, including the drivers, receivers, and cables, spells out design and performance requirements that ensure that errors due to line noise will be rare. Still, especially because the interface uses external cabling, there is a chance that a noise glitch or an unexpectedly disconnected cable could corrupt a transmission. For this reason, USB packets include error-checking bits that enable a receiver to identify virtually any received data that doesn't match what was sent. In addition, for transfers that require multiple transactions, a data-toggle value keeps the transmitter and receiver synchronized to ensure that no transactions are missed entirely.

Error-checking Bits

All token, data, and Start-of-Frame packets include bits for use in error-checking. The bit values are calculated using a mathematical algorithm, or procedure, called the cyclic redundancy check (CRC). The specification has details on how the CRC is calculated. It's not something you'll ever have to do in code, however, because the hardware handles it.

The CRC is applied to the data to be checked. The transmitting device performs the calculation and sends the result along with the data. The receiving device performs the identical calculation on the received data. If the results match, the data has arrived without error and the receiving device returns an ACK. If the results don't match, the receiving device sends no handshake. This tells the sender to retry.

Typically, the host tries a total of three times, though the specification gives the host some flexibility in determining the number of retries. If there's still no handshake, the host gives up and informs the driver of the problem.

The PID field in token packets uses a simpler form of error checking. The lower four bits in the field are the PID, and the upper four bits are its complement. The receiver can check the integrity of the PID by complementing the upper four bits and ensuring that they match the PID. If not, the packet is corrupted and is ignored.

The Data Toggle Bit

In transfers that require multiple transactions, the data-toggle bit can ensure that no transactions are missed by keeping the transmitting and receiving devices synchronized. The data-toggle bit is included in the PID field of the token packets for IN and OUT transactions. DATA0 is a code of 0011, and DATA1 is 1011, so bit 3 indicates the data-toggle state. In controller chips, a register bit often indicates the data-toggle state. Another name for this bit is DATA0/1, sometimes also called DATA1/0 (!).

Both the sender and receiver keep track of the data toggle. On configuring the device, the bits on both are set to DATA0.

When the receiver detects an incoming data transaction, it compares the received data-toggle bit to the state of its own data toggle. If the bits match, the receiver toggles its bit and returns an ACK handshake packet to the sender. The ACK causes the sender to toggle its bit.

The next received packet in the transfer should contain a data-toggle of DATA1, and again the receiver toggles its bit and returns an ACK. The data toggle continues to alternate until the transfer completes.

If the receiver is busy, it returns a NAK. If it detects corrupted data, it returns no response. If the sender doesn't receive an ACK, it doesn't toggle its bit and instead tries again with the same data and data toggle.

If a receiver returns an ACK but for some reason the sender doesn't see it, the sender will think that the receiver didn't get the data and will try again, with the same data and data-toggle bit. In this case, the receiver of the repeated data doesn't toggle its bit and ignores the data, but does return an ACK. This re-synchronizes the data toggles. The same thing happens if the sender mistakenly sends the same data toggle twice in a row.

A Windows host handles the data toggles without requiring any user programming. Some peripheral controller chips also handle the data-toggles completely automatically, while others require some firmware control.

In some cases, if the device is interested only in receiving the newest data and doesn't care about the sequence, it won't bother to compare the data toggles. Instead, it can just return ACKs without comparing or toggling the bit.

In full-speed isochronous transfers, the host always uses a data toggle of DATA0. Full-speed isochronous transfers can't use the data toggle because they have no handshake packet for returning an ACK or NAK and no time to resend missed data.

Some high-speed isochronous transfers use DATA0, DATA1, and additional PIDs of DATA2 and MDATA. High-speed isochronous IN transfers that have two or three transactions per microframe use DATA0, DATA1, and DATA2 encoding to indicate the transaction's position in the microframe:

Number of IN Transactions in the Microframe	Data PID		
	First Transaction	Second Transaction	Third Transaction
1	DATA0	-	-
2	DATA1	DATA0	-
3	DATA2	DATA1	DATA0

High-speed isochronous OUT transfers that have two or three transactions per microframe use DATA0, DATA1, and MDATA encoding to indicate whether more data will follow in the microframe:

Number of OUT Transactions in the Microframe	Data PID:		
	First Transaction	Second Transaction	Third Transaction
1	DATA0	-	-
2	MDATA	DATA1	-
3	MDATA	MDATA	DATA2

4

A Transfer Type for Every Purpose

Now that you know a little more about how transfers work, it's time to look in more detail at the four transfer types: control, bulk, interrupt, and isochronous.

Control Transfers

Control transfers have two uses. They carry the requests that are defined by the USB specification and used by the host to learn about and configure devices. And they can also carry requests defined by a class or vendor for any other purpose.

Availability

Every device must support control transfers over the default pipe at Endpoint 0. A device may also have additional pipes configured for control transfers, but in reality there's no need for more than one. Even if a device needs to send a lot of control requests, the host may allocate bandwidth according to the number and size of requests, rather than by the number of control pipes, so additional control endpoints would offer no advantage.

Structure

As Chapter 3 explained, control transfers use a defined structure with two or three stages: Setup, Data (optional), and Status. A stage consists of one or more transactions.

Every control transfer must have Setup and Status stages. The Data stage is optional, though a particular request may require it. Because every control transfer requires transferring information in both directions, the control transfer's message pipe uses both the IN and OUT addresses of the endpoint.

In a control Write transfer, the data in the Data stage travels from the host to the device. In a control Read transfer, data in the Data stage travels from the device to the host. Figure 4-1 and Figure 4-2 show the stages of control Read and Write low- and full-speed transfers on a low/full-speed bus. There are differences, described later in this chapter, for some high-speed transfers and for low- and full-speed transfers with 2.0 hubs.

In the Setup stage, the host begins a Setup transaction by sending information about the request. The token packet contains a PID that identifies the transfer as a control transfer. The data packet contains information about the request, including the request number, whether or not the transfer has a Data stage, and if so, in which direction the data will travel.

The USB specification defines 11 standard requests. Successful enumeration requires specific responses to some requests, such as the one that sets the device's address. For other requests, a device can return a code that indicates that the request isn't supported. A specific class may require a device to support class-specific requests, and any device may support vendor-specific or device-specific requests.

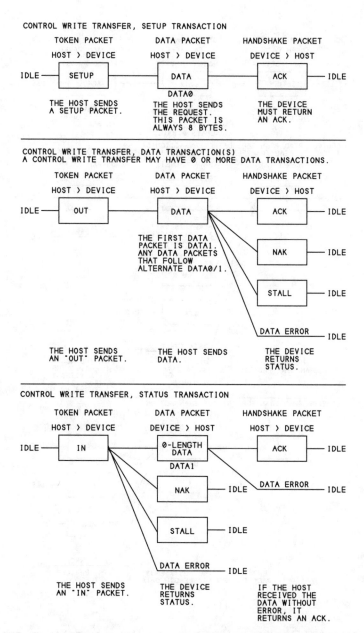

Figure 4-1: A control Write transfer contains a Setup transaction, zero or more Data transactions, and a Status transaction. Not shown are the PING protocol used in high-speed transfers with multiple data packets and the split transactions used with low- and full-speed devices on a high-speed bus.

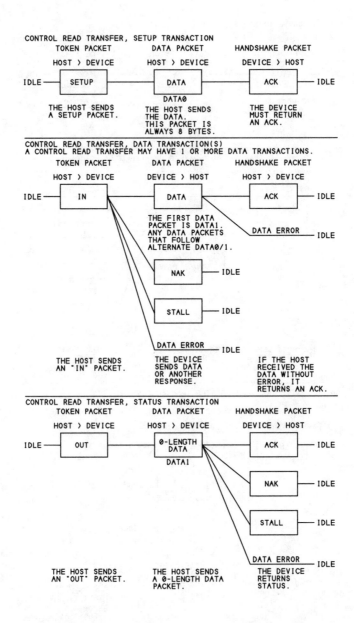

Figure 4-2: A control Read transfer contains a Setup transaction, one or more data transactions, and a status transaction. Not shown are the split transactions used with low- and full-speed devices on a high-speed bus.

When a Data stage is present, it consists of one or more IN or OUT transactions, also called Data transactions. Depending on the request, the host or peripheral may be the source of these transactions, but all data packets in this (or any) stage must be in the same direction.

As described in Chapter 3, if a high-speed control Write transfer has more than one data packet in the Data stage, and if the device returns NYET after receiving a data packet, the host uses the PING protocol before sending the next packet.

The Status stage consists of one IN or OUT transaction, also called the status transaction. In the Status stage, the device reports the success or failure of the previous stages. The source of the Status stage's data packet is the receiver of the data in the previous Data transaction. When there is no Data stage, the device sends the Status stage's data packet. The data or handshake packet sent by the device in the Status stage contains a code that indicates the success or failure of the transfer's Setup and Data stages.

If a host is doing a control transfer with a low- or full-speed device on a high-speed bus, the host uses the split transactions described in Chapter 3 for all of the transfer's transactions. To the device, the transaction is no different. The device's hub carries out the transaction with the device and reports back to the host when requested.

Data Size

The maximum size of the data packet in the Data stage varies with the device's speed. For low-speed devices, the maximum is 8 bytes. For full speed, the maximum may be 8, 16, 32, or 64 bytes. For high speed, the maximum must be 64 bytes. These bytes include only the information transferred in the data packet, excluding the PID and CRC bits.

All data packets except the last must be the maximum packet size. The host reads the maximum packet size from the descriptors retrieved during enumeration. For the Default Control Pipe, the size is in the device descriptor. For other control endpoints, the size is in the endpoint descriptor. If a transfer has more data than will fit in one data transaction, the host sends or requests the data in multiple transactions.

In some control Read transfers, the amount of data returned by the device can vary. If the amount is less than the requested number of bytes and an even multiple of the maximum packet size, the device should indicate that there is no more data to send by returning a 0-byte data packet in response to the next IN token packet.

Speed

The host must make its best effort to ensure that all control transfers get through as quickly as possible. The host controller reserves a portion of the bus bandwidth for control transfers: 10 percent for low and full speed and 20 percent for high speed. If the control transfers don't need this much time, bulk transfers may use what remains. If the bus has unused bandwidth, control transfers may use more than the reserved amount.

The host attempts to parcel out the available time as fairly as possible to all requests. Within a transfer, one frame or microframe may carry multiple transactions, or the transactions may be in different (micro)frames.

There are two opinions on whether control transfers are appropriate for transferring data other than configuration data. Some say that control transfers should be reserved for servicing the standard USB requests as much as possible. This helps to ensure that the transfers complete quickly by keeping the bandwidth reserved for them as open as possible. But the specification doesn't forbid other uses for control transfers, and others believe that devices should be free to use control transfers for any purpose. Low-speed devices have no other choice except periodic interrupt transfers, which can waste bandwidth if data transfers are infrequent.

Table 4-1 compares the amount of data that each transfer type can move at each of the three speeds. Control transfers aren't the most efficient way to transfer data. In addition to the data being transferred, each transfer with one data packet has an overhead of 63 bytes (low speed), 45 bytes (full speed), or 173 bytes (high speed). Each Data stage requires token and handshake packets, so stages with larger data packets are more efficient.

A single low-speed control transfer with 8 data bytes uses 29% of a frame's bandwidth, though the transfer's individual transactions may be spread

Table 4-1: The maximum possible rate of data transfer varies greatly with the transfer type and bus speed.

Transfer Type	Maximum data-transfer rate per endpoint (kilobytes/second with data payload/transfer = maximum packet size for the speed)		
	Low Speed	Full Speed	High Speed
Control	24	832	15,872
Interrupt	0.8	64	24,576
Bulk	not allowed	1216	53,248
Isochronous		1023	24,576

among multiple frames. In a control transfer with multiple data packets in the data stage, the data may transfer in the same or different (micro)frames.

If the bus is very busy, all control transfers may have to share the reserved portion of the bandwidth. At low speed, the reserved bandwidth requires three frames to complete one 8-byte transfer. At full speed, the reserved bandwidth can carry one 64-byte transfer per frame (though again, any one transfer may be spread over multiple frames). And at high speed, the reserved bandwidth can carry six 64-byte transfers per microframe, or 512 per frame.

Devices don't have to respond immediately to control-transfer requests. The specification has timing limits that apply to most requests. However, a device class may require faster response to standard and class-specific requests. Where stricter timing isn't specified, in a transfer where the host requests data from the device, the device may delay as long as 500 milliseconds before it has the data ready for the host. To find out if data is available, the host sends a token packet requesting the data. If the data is ready, the device sends it immediately in that transaction's data packet. If not, the device returns a NAK to advise the host to retry later. The host keeps trying at intervals, for up to 500 milliseconds.

In a transfer where the host sends data to the device, the device can delay as long as 5 seconds before accepting all of the data and completing the Status stage. The 5 seconds doesn't include any delays the host adds between packets. In a transfer with no Data stage, the device must complete the request and the Status stage within 50 milliseconds.

Detecting and Handling Errors

If a device doesn't return an expected handshake packet during a control transfer, the host tries twice more. If the host receives no response after a total of three tries, it notifies the software that requested the transfer and stops communicating with the endpoint until the problem is corrected. The two retries include only those sent in response to no handshake at all. A NAK isn't an error.

Control transfers use data-toggle bits to ensure that no data is lost. In the data stage of a Control Read transfer, on receiving a data packet from the device, the host normally returns an ACK, then sends an OUT token packet to begin the Status stage. If the device for any reason doesn't see the ACK returned after the transfer's final data packet, it must interpret a received OUT token packet as evidence that the handshake was returned and the Status stage can begin.

Devices must accept all Setup packets. If a new Setup packet arrives before a previous transfer completes, the device must abandon the previous transfer and start the new one.

Bulk Transfers

Bulk transfers are useful for transferring data when time isn't critical. A bulk transfer can send large amounts of data without clogging the bus, because the transfers defer to the other transfer types and wait until time is available. Uses for bulk transfers include sending data from the host to a printer, sending data from a scanner to the host, and reading and writing to a disk. On an otherwise idle bus, bulk transfers are the fastest transfer type.

Availability

Only full- and high-speed devices can do bulk transfers. Devices aren't required to support bulk transfers, though a specific device class may require it.

Structure

A bulk transfer consists of one or more IN or OUT transactions (Figure 4-3). A bulk transfer is one-way. A transfer's transactions must all be IN transactions, or all OUT transactions. Transferring data in both directions requires a separate pipe and transfer for each direction.

A bulk transfer ends in one of two ways: when the requested amount of data has transferred, or when a data packet contains less than the maximum data, including a zero-length packet.

To conserve bus time, the host uses the PING protocol in some high-speed control transfers. If a high-speed bulk OUT transfer has more than one data packet and if the device returns NYET after receiving one of these packets, the host uses PING to find out when it's OK to begin the next data transaction. In a bulk transfer on a high-speed bus with a low- or full-speed device, the host uses split transactions for all of the transfer's transactions.

Data Size

A full-speed bulk transfer can have a maximum packet size of 8, 16, 32, or 64 bytes. For high speed, the maximum must be 512 bytes. During enumeration, the host reads the maximum packet size for each bulk pipe from the device's descriptors. The amount of data in a transfer may be less than, equal to, or greater than the maximum size. If the amount of data won't fit in a single packet, the host completes the transfer using multiple transactions.

Speed

The host controller guarantees that bulk transfers will complete eventually, but doesn't reserve any bandwidth for the transfers. Control transfers are guaranteed to have 10 percent of the bandwidth at low and full speeds, and 20 percent at high speed. Interrupt and isochronous transfers may use the rest. So if a bus is very busy, a bulk transfer may take very long.

However, when the bus is otherwise idle, bulk transfers can use the most bandwidth of any type, and they have a low overhead, so they're the fastest of all. When an endpoint's maximum packet size is less than the maximum,

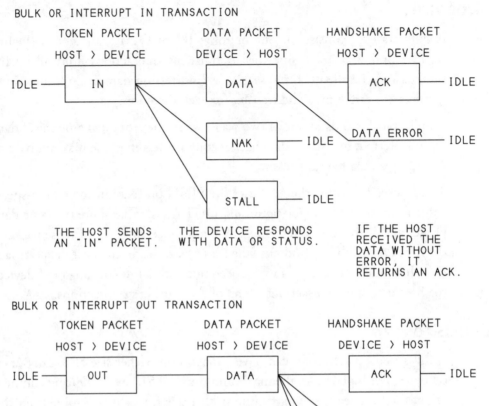

BULK OR INTERRUPT IN TRANSACTION

Figure 4-3: Bulk and interrupt transfers use IN and OUT transactions. Their structure is identical, but the host schedules them differently. Not shown are the PING protocol used in high-speed bulk OUT transfers with multiple data packets or the split transactions used with low- and full-speed devices on a high-speed bus.

USB Complete

some hosts schedule no more than one packet per frame, even if more bandwidth is available.

At full speed on an otherwise idle bus, up to nineteen 64-byte bulk transfers can transfer up to 1216 data bytes per frame, for a data rate of 1.216 Megabytes per second. This leaves 18% of the bus bandwidth free for other uses. The protocol overhead for a bulk transfer with one data packet is 13 bytes at full speed and 55 bytes at high speed.

At high speed on an otherwise idle bus, up to thirteen 512-byte bulk transfers can transfer up to 6656 data bytes per microframe, for an impressive data rate of 53.248 Megabytes per second, using all but 2% of the bus bandwidth. The protocol overhead for a bulk transfer with one data packet is 55 bytes.

Detecting and Handling Errors

Bulk transfers use error detecting. If a device doesn't return an expected handshake packet, the host tries up to twice more. The host will also retry without limit on receiving NAK handshakes. Bulk transfers use data-toggle bits to ensure that no data is lost.

Interrupt Transfers

Interrupt transfers are useful when data has to transfer within a specific amount of time. Typical applications include keyboards, mice and other pointing devices, joysticks, and hub status reports. Users don't want a noticeable delay between pressing a key or moving a mouse and seeing the result on screen. And a hub needs to report the attachment or removal of devices promptly. Low-speed devices, which support only control and interrupt transfers, are likely to use interrupt transfers for generic data. Interrupt transfers are also popular because Windows includes drivers that enable applications to do interrupt transfers with devices that conform to the HID specification.

At low and full speeds, the bandwidth available for an interrupt endpoint is limited, but high speed loosens the limits and enables an interrupt endpoint to transfer almost 400 times as much data as full speed.

The name *interrupt transfer* suggests that a device can cause a hardware interrupt that results in a fast response from the PC. But the truth is that interrupt transfers, like all other USB transfers, occur only when the host polls a device. The transfers are interrupt-like, however, because they guarantee that the host will request or send data with minimal delay.

Availability

All three speeds support interrupt transfers. Devices aren't required to support interrupt transfers, but a device class may require it. For example, a HID-class device must support interrupt IN transfers for sending data to the host.

Structure

An interrupt transfer consists of one or more IN transactions or one or more OUT transactions. The structure of an interrupt transfer is identical to that of a bulk transfer (Figure 4-3). The only difference is in the scheduling. An interrupt transfer is one-way; the transactions must be all IN transactions, or all OUT transactions. Transferring data in both directions requires a separate transfer and pipe for each direction.

An interrupt transfer ends in one of two ways: when the requested amount of data has transferred, or when the data packet contains less than the maximum data, including a zero-length packet.

In an interrupt transfer on a high-speed bus with a low- or full-speed device, the host uses the split transactions described in Chapter 3 for all of the transfer's transactions. Unlike high-speed bulk OUT transfers, high-speed interrupt OUT transfers don't use the PING protocol when a transfer has multiple transactions.

Data Size

For low-speed devices, the maximum packet size can be any value from 1 to 8 bytes. For full speed, the maximum can range from 1 to 64 bytes. For high speed, the range is 1 to 1024 bytes. If the amount of data in a transfer won't fit in a single transaction, the host uses multiple transactions to complete the transfer.

Speed

An interrupt transfer guarantees a maximum latency, or time between transaction attempts. In other words, there is no guaranteed transfer rate, just the guarantee that there will be no more than the request maximum latency between transaction attempts.

High-speed interrupt transfers can be very fast. A high-speed transfer can request up to three 1024-byte packets in each 125-microsecond microframe, which works out to 24.576 Megabytes per second. An endpoint that requires more than 1024 bytes per microframe is a high-bandwidth endpoint. A full-speed transfer can request up to 64 bytes in each 1-millisecond frame, or 64 kilobytes per second. And a low-speed transfer can request up to 8 bytes every 10 milliseconds, or 800 bytes per second.

The endpoint descriptor stored in the device specifies the maximum latency. For low-speed devices, the maximum latency can be any value between 10 and 255 milliseconds. For full speed, it can be anywhere between 1 and 255 milliseconds. For high speed, the range is from 125 microseconds to 4 seconds, in increments of 125 microseconds (the width of a microframe). In addition, a high-speed interrupt endpoint with a maximum latency of 125 microseconds can request 1, 2, or 3 transactions per interval. The host controller ensures that transaction attempts occur within the specified time.

The host may begin each transaction at any time up to the specified maximum, compared to when the previous transaction began. So, for example, with a 10-millisecond maximum at full speed, 5 transfers could take as long as 50 milliseconds or as little as 5 milliseconds. However, OHCI host controllers use values that correspond to powers of 2, with a maximum of 32 milliseconds. So for a full-speed device that requests a maximum anywhere from 8 to 15 milliseconds, the OHCI host begins a transaction every 8 milliseconds. A maximum latency anywhere from 32 to 255 will cause a transaction attempt every 32 milliseconds. However, a device should assume only that the host will comply with the specification. The device shouldn't rely on behavior that is specific to a type of host controller.

Because the host is free to transfer data more quickly than the requested rate, interrupt transfers don't guarantee a precise rate of delivery. The only exceptions are when the maximum latency equals the fastest possible rate. For example, with a 1.x host, a full-speed interrupt pipe configured for 1 transaction per millisecond will use this exact rate.

An otherwise idle bus can carry up to six low-speed, 8-byte transactions per frame. At full speed, the limit is nineteen 64-byte transactions. Since the minimum time between transfers is one frame or more, each transaction in the frame would have to be for a different endpoint address. In reality, a host may not be able to schedule as many as nineteen full-speed interrupt transactions in a single frame, so the practical maximum number of interrupt transactions is likely to be less.

At high speed, the limit is two transfers per microframe, each consisting of three 1024-byte transactions.

The protocol overhead per transfer with one data packet is 19 bytes at low speed, 13 bytes at full speed, and 55 bytes at high speed. High-speed interrupt and isochronous transfers combined can use no more than 80 percent of a microframe. Full-speed isochronous transfers and low- and full-speed interrupt transfers combined can use no more than 90 percent of a frame. The section *More about Time-critical Transfers* later in this chapter has more about the capabilities and limits of interrupt transfers.

Detecting and Handling Errors

If a device doesn't return an expected handshake packet, host controllers in PCs will retry up to twice more. The host will also retry without limit on receiving NAKs. Interrupt transfers can use data-toggle values to ensure that all data is received without errors. As explained earlier, if the receiver cares only about the most recent data, it may ignore the data toggle.

Isochronous Transfers

Isochronous transfers are streaming, real-time transfers that are useful when data must arrive at a constant rate, or by a specific time, and occasional errors can be tolerated. At full speed, isochronous transfers can transfer more data per frame than interrupt transfers. But there is no provision for retransmitting data received with errors.

Examples of uses for isochronous transfers include encoded voice and music to be played in real time. But data that will eventually be used at a constant rate doesn't necessarily require an isochronous transfer. For example, a host may use a bulk transfer to send a music file to a device. After the device has received the entire file, it can play it at the appropriate rate.

Nor does the data in an isochronous transfer have to be used at a constant rate. An isochronous transfer is a way to ensure that a large block of data gets through quickly on a busy bus, even if the data doesn't need to transfer in real time. Unlike with bulk transfers, once an isochronous transfer begins, the host guarantees that the time will be available to send the data at a constant rate, so the completion time is predictable.

Availability

Only full- and high-speed devices can do isochronous transfers. Devices aren't required to support isochronous transfers but a device class may require it.

Structure

Isochronous means that the data has a fixed transfer rate, with a defined number of bytes transferring in every frame or microframe. None of the other transfer types guarantee to send a specific number of bytes in each frame (with the exception of interrupt transfers with the shortest possible maximum latency).

A full-speed isochronous transfer consists of one IN or OUT transaction per frame in one or more frames at equal intervals. High-speed isochronous transfers are more flexible. They can request as many as three transactions per microframe or as little as one transaction every 32,768 microframes. Figure 4-4 shows the packets in full-speed isochronous IN and OUT transactions. An isochronous transfer is one-way; the transactions in a transfer must all be IN transactions, or all OUT transactions. Transferring data in both directions requires a separate transfer and pipe for each direction.

Before configuring a pipe for isochronous transfers, the host controller compares the requested buffer size with the available remaining, unreserved bandwidth on the bus to determine whether the requested bandwidth is available. A full-speed transfer with the maximum 1023 bytes per frame uses 69 percent of the USB's bandwidth. If two full-speed devices want to establish pipes for transferring 1023 bytes per frame, the host will refuse to configure the second pipe because the data won't fit in the remaining bandwidth. If the device supports an alternate interface with smaller data packets or fewer packets per microframe, the device driver can request this.

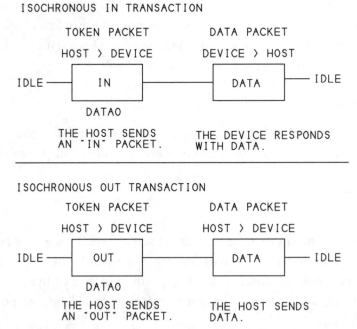

Figure 4-4: Isochronous transfers don't have handshake packets, so occasional errors must be acceptable. Not shown are the split transactions used with full-speed devices on a high-speed bus or the data sequencing in high-speed transfers with multiple data packets per microframe.

Or the driver can try again later in the hope that the bandwidth will be available. When the device is configured, the transfers are guaranteed to have the time they need.

Although isochronous transfers may send a fixed number of bytes per frame, the data doesn't transfer at a constant number of bits per second. Each transaction has overhead and must share the bus with other devices. So the data is actually a burst at 12 or 480 Megabits per second that may occur any time within the frame or microframe. If the receiving end wants to use the data at a constant rate, such as sending it to a speaker, the receiver must convert the received bits to signals that span the frame time.

Isochronous transfers may also synchronize to another data source or recipient, or to USB's Start-of-Frame signals. For example, a microphone's input may synchronize to the output of speakers. The specification describes several methods of synchronizing to internal and external clocks. The descriptor for a 2.0 isochronous endpoint can specify a synchronization type and a usage value that indicates whether the endpoint is contains data or feedback information used to maintain synchronization.

If a host is doing an isochronous transfer on a high-speed bus with a full-speed device, the host uses the split transactions described in Chapter 3 for all of the transfer's transactions. Isochronous OUT transactions use start-split transactions, but not complete-splits, because there is no status information to report back to the host. Isochronous transfers don't use the PING protocol.

Data Size

For full-speed endpoints, the maximum packet size can range from 0 to 1023 data bytes. High-speed endpoints can have a maximum packet size up to 1024 bytes. If the amount of data won't fit in a single packet, the host completes the transfer in multiple transactions.

The amount of data in each frame doesn't have to be the same. For example, data at 44,100 samples per second could use a sequence of 9 frames containing 44 samples each, followed by 1 frame containing 45 samples.

Speed

A full-speed isochronous transaction can transfer up to 1023 bytes per frame, or up to 1.023 Megabytes per second. This leaves 31% of the bus bandwidth free for other uses. The protocol overhead is 9 bytes per transfer for a transfer with one data packet, or less than 1% for a single 1023-byte transaction. The minimum requested bandwidth for a full-speed transfer is one byte per frame, or 1 kilobyte per second.

A high-speed isochronous transaction can transfer up to 1024 bytes. An isochronous endpoint that requires more than 1024 bytes per microframe can request 2 or 3 transactions per microframe, for a maximum rate of 24.576 Megabytes per second. An endpoint that requires multiple transactions per microframe is a high-bandwidth endpoint. The protocol overhead is 38 bytes per transfer for a transfer with one data packet.

Because high-speed isochronous transfers don't have to do a transaction in every frame or microframe, they can also request less bandwidth than full-speed transfers. The minimum requested bandwidth is one byte every 32,678 microframes, which works out to one byte every 4.096 seconds. However, any endpoint can transfer less data than the maximum reserved bandwidth by skipping available transactions or transferring less than the maximum data per transfer.

High-speed interrupt and isochronous transfers can use no more than 80 percent of a microframe. Full-speed isochronous transfers and low- and full-speed interrupt transfers combined can use no more than 90 percent of of a frame. An otherwise idle high-speed bus can carry two isochronous transfers at the maximum rate.

The section *More about Time-critical Transfers* later in this chapter has more about the capabilities of isochronous transfers.

Detecting and Handling Errors

The price to pay for guaranteed on-time delivery of large blocks of data is no error correcting. Isochronous transfers are intended for uses where occasional, small errors are acceptable. For example, listeners may tolerate or not notice a short dropout in voice or music. And in reality, under normal circumstances, a USB transfer should experience no more than a very occasional error due to line noise. Because isochronous transfers must keep to a schedule, the receiver can't request a retransmit of data if it's busy or detects an error. If the receiver suspects errors, it can ask the sender to resend the entire transfer, but this isn't very efficient.

More about Time-critical Transfers

Just because an endpoint is capable of a rate of data transfer doesn't mean that a particular device and host will be able to achieve it. Several things can limit an application's ability to send or receive data at the maximum rate that an endpoint and host controller are capable of. The limiting factors include bus bandwidth, the device's capabilities, the capabilities of the device driver and application software, and the latencies due to how Windows manages multi-tasking.

Bus Bandwidth

When a device requests more interrupt or isochronous bandwidth than is available, the host will refuse to configure the device. Low- and full-speed interrupt transfers use little bandwidth, so the host isn't likely to deny a configuration due to the requirements of these. High-speed interrupt transfers are a different story. A high-speed endpoint can request up to three 1024-byte data packets in each microframe, using as much as 40 percent of the bus bandwidth. To help ensure that devices will enumerate without problems, the initial, default data payload of an interrupt endpoint must be 64 bytes or less. The device driver is then free to try to increase the endpoint's reserved bandwidth by requesting alternate interface settings or configurations.

Isochronous endpoints can also cause bandwidth problems. A frequent problem with isochronous endpoints on 1.x devices was devices requesting more bandwidth than was available. The host would properly refuse to configure the device and the user was left with a device that didn't work without knowing why.

To help ensure that devices will enumerate without problems, the default interface setting of a 2.0-compliant device must use no isochronous bandwidth. In other words, the default interface can transfer no isochronous data at all. An obvious way to ensure this is to include no isochronous endpoints in the default interface. After enumeration, the device driver is free to attempt to request isochronous bandwidth by requesting an alternate interface or configuration with an isochronous endpoint. Note that even full-speed endpoints must meet this requirement to be 2.0-compliant. Microsoft and Intel's *PC 2001 System Design Guide* also requires the default interface setting to use zero isochronous bandwidth.

Device Capabilities

If the host has promised that the requested USB bandwidth will be available, there's still no guarantee that the device will be ready to send or receive data when needed.

To use interrupt and isochronous transfers effectively, both the sender and receiver have to be capable of sending and receiving at the desired rate. If the device is sending data, it must write the data to send into the transmit buffer in time to enable the hardware to place it on the bus when the host requests it. If the device is receiving data, it must read the previous data from its buffer before the new data arrives, or either the old data will be overwritten or the device will refuse the new data.

One way to help ensure that the device is always ready for a transfer is to use double buffering, as described in Chapter 7. This gives the firmware extra time to load the next data to transfer or to retrieve the just-received data.

Host Software Capabilities

Another thing that can affect whether or not all available transfers take place is the capabilities of the device driver and application software on the host.

A device driver requests a transfer by submitting an I/O request packet (IRP) to a lower-level driver. For interrupt and isochronous transfers, if there is no outstanding IRP for an endpoint when its scheduled time comes up, the transaction is skipped. To ensure that no transfer opportunities are missed, drivers typically submit a new IRP immediately on completing the previous one.

For some devices, including keyboards and mice, the driver begins to request interrupt transfers as soon as the driver is loaded into memory. For other devices, the host's driver may begin requesting transfers only after an application requests to send or receive data.

The application software that uses the data also has to be able to keep up with the transfers. For example, the driver for HID-class devices places report data received in interrupt transfers in a buffer, and applications use ReadFile to retrieve reports from the buffer. If the buffer is full when a new report arrives, the driver discards the oldest report and replaces it with the newest one. If the application can't keep up, some reports are lost. In some cases, applications can increase the size of the buffer the driver uses to store received data. This can help if the application is sometimes busy, but at other times is free to retrieve the data.

As a general rule, Visual-Basic applications are slower than applications compiled with Visual C++ or Delphi.

One way to help ensure that an application sends or receives data with minimal delays is to place the code that communicates with the device driver in its own program thread. The thread should have few responsibilities other than managing these communications. In Visual Basic, an ActiveX Exe server can run in its own thread and communicate with an application.

Doing fewer, larger transfers rather than multiple, small transfers can also help. When there are multiple transactions per transfer, the lower-level drivers take care of the scheduling. An application can typically send or request a few large chunks of data more quickly than it can send or request many smaller chunks.

Windows Latencies

Another factor in the performance of time-critical USB transfers is the latencies, or delays, due to how Windows handles multi-tasking. Windows was never designed as a real-time operating system that could guarantee a rate of data transfer with a peripheral.

Multi-tasking means that multiple program threads can run at the same time. The operating system grants a portion of the available time to each thread. Different threads can have different priorities, but under Windows 98, Windows 2000, and Windows Me, no thread can be guaranteed CPU time at a defined, precise rate, such as once per millisecond.

Latencies under Windows are often well under 1 millisecond, but in some cases a thread can keep other code from executing for over 100 milliseconds. Windows 98's performance tends to be worse than that of Windows 2000 or Windows Me in this respect.

A USB device and its software have no control over what other tasks the host CPU is performing, so dealing with these latencies can be one of the biggest challenges when timing is critical.

In general, it's best to let the device handle any real-time processing required and make the timing of the host communications as non-critical as possible. For example, imagine a device that reads a sensor once per millisecond. The device could attempt to send each reading to the host in a separate interrupt transfer, but this would require the driver and application to be able to read a transfer every millisecond. If the device instead collects a series of readings and transfers them using less frequent, but larger transfers, the timing in the host software is less critical. Data compression can also help by reducing the amount of data that transfers.

5

Enumeration: How the Host Learns about Devices

Before applications can communicate with a device, the host needs to learn about the device and assign a device driver. Enumeration is the initial exchange of information that accomplishes this. The process includes assigning an address to the device, reading data structures from the device, assigning and loading a device driver, and selecting a configuration from the options presented in the retrieved data. The device is then configured and ready to transfer data using any of the endpoints in its configuration.

This chapter describes the enumeration process, including the structure of the descriptors that the host reads from the device during enumeration. You don't need to know every detail about enumeration in order to design a USB peripheral, but understanding a certain amount is essential in creating the descriptors that will reside in the device and writing the firmware that responds to enumeration requests.

The Process

One of the duties of a hub is to detect the attachment and removal of devices. Each hub has an interrupt IN pipe for reporting these events to the host. On system boot-up, the host polls its root hub to learn if any devices are attached, including additional hubs and devices attached to the first tier of devices. After boot-up, the host continues to poll periodically to learn of any newly attached or removed devices.

On learning of a new device, the host sends a series of requests to the device's hub, causing the hub to establish a communications path between the host and the device. The host then attempts to enumerate the device by sending control transfers containing standard USB requests to Endpoint 0. All USB devices must support control transfers, the standard requests, and Endpoint 0. For a successful enumeration, the device must respond to each request by returning the requested information and taking other requested actions.

From the user's perspective, enumeration should be invisible and automatic, except for possibly a window that announces the detection of a new device and whether or not the attempt to configure it succeeded. Sometimes on first use, the user needs to provide a disk containing the INF file and device driver.

When enumeration is complete, Windows adds the new device to the Device Manager display in the Control Panel. Figure 5-1 shows an example. To view the Device Manager, in Windows 98, click the Start menu > Settings > Control Panel >System > Device Manager. In Windows 2000, it's the same except that after clicking System, you click Hardware, then Device Manager. When a user disconnects a peripheral, Windows automatically removes the device from the display.

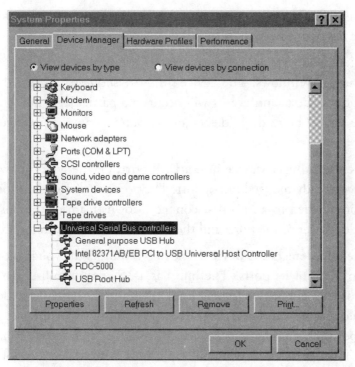

Figure 5-1: The Device Manager in Windows' Control Panel lists all detected USB devices. Some devices are listed under Universal Serial Bus controllers, and others are listed by type, such as keyboard or modem.

In a typical peripheral, the device's program code contains the information the host will request, and a combination of hardware and firmware decodes and responds to requests for the information. Some application-specific chips (ASICs) manage the enumeration entirely in hardware and require no firmware support. On the host side, under Windows there's no need to write code for enumerating, because Windows handles it automatically. Windows will look for a special text file called an INF file that identifies the driver to use for the device.

Enumeration Steps

During the enumeration process, a device moves through four of the six device states defined by the specification: Powered, Default, Address, and

Configured. (The other states are Attached and Suspend.) In each state, the device has defined capabilities and behavior.

The steps below are a typical sequence of events that occurs during enumeration under Windows. The device firmware shouldn't assume that the enumeration requests and events will occur in a particular order, however. The device should be ready to detect and respond to any control request at any time.

1. The user plugs a device into a USB port. Or the system powers up with a device already plugged into a port. The port may be on the root hub at the host or attached to a hub that connects downstream of the host. The hub provides power to the port, and the device is in the Powered state.

2. The hub detects the device. The hub monitors the voltages on the signal lines of each of its ports. The hub has a 15-kilohm pull-down resistor on each of the port's two signal lines (D+ and D-), while a device has a 1.5-kilohm pull-up resistor on either D+ for a full-speed device or D- for a low-speed device. High-speed devices attach at full speed. When a device plugs into a port, the device's pull-up brings that line high, enabling the hub to detect that a device is attached. Chapter 18 has more on how hubs detect devices.

On detecting a device, the hub continues to provide power but doesn't yet transmit USB traffic to the device, because the device isn't ready to receive it.

3. The host learns of the new device. Each hub uses its interrupt pipe to report events at the hub. The report indicates only whether the hub or a port (and if so, which port) has experienced an event. When the host learns of an event, it sends the hub a Get_Port_Status request to find out more. Get_Port_Status and the other requests described here are standard hub-class requests that all hubs understand. The information returned tells the host when a device is newly attached.

4. The hub detects whether a device is low or full speed. Just before the hub resets the device, the hub determines whether the device is low or full speed by examining the voltages on the two signal lines. The hub detects the speed of a device by determining which line has the higher voltage when idle. The hub sends the information to the host in response to the next

Get_Port_Status request. USB 1.x allowed the hub the option to detect device speed just after reset. USB 2.0 requires speed detection to occur before reset so it knows whether to check for a high-speed-capable device during reset, as described below.

5. The hub resets the device. When a host learns of a new device, the host controller sends the hub a Set_Port_Feature request that asks the hub to reset the port. The hub places the device's USB data lines in the Reset condition for at least 10 milliseconds. Reset is a special condition where both D+ and D- are a logic low. (Normally, the lines have opposite logic states.) The hub sends the reset only to the new device. Other hubs and devices on the bus don't see it.

6. The host learns if a full-speed device supports high speed. Detecting whether a device supports high speed uses two special signal states. In the Chirp J state, the D+ line only is driven and in the Chirp K state, the D- line only is driven.

During the reset, a device that supports high speed sends a Chirp K. A high-speed hub detects the chirp and responds with a series of alternating Chirp Ks and Js. When the device detects the pattern KJKJKJ, it removes its full-speed pull up and performs all further communications at high speed. If the hub doesn't respond to the device's Chirp K, the device knows it must continue to communicate at full speed. All high-speed devices must be capable of responding to enumeration requests at full speed.

7. The hub establishes a signal path between the device and the bus. The host verifies that the device has exited the reset state by sending a Get_Port_Status request. A bit in the data returned indicates whether the device is still in the reset state. If necessary, the host repeats the request until the device has exited the reset state.

When the hub removes the reset, the device is in the Default state. The device's USB registers are in their reset states and the device is ready to respond to control transfers over the default pipe at Endpoint 0. The device can now communicate with the host, using the default address of 00h. The device can draw up to 100 milliamperes from the bus.

8. The host sends a Get_Descriptor request to learn the maximum packet size of the default pipe. The host sends the request to device address 0, Endpoint 0. Because the host enumerates only one device at a time, only one device will respond to communications addressed to device address 0, even if several devices attach at once.

The eighth byte of the device descriptor contains the maximum packet size supported by Endpoint 0. A Windows host requests 64 bytes, but after receiving just one packet (whether or not it has 64 bytes), it begins the status stage of the transfer. On completion of the status stage, a Windows host requests the hub to reset the device (step 5). The specification doesn't require a reset here, because devices should be able to handle the host's abandoning a control transfer at any time by responding to the next Setup packet. But resetting is a precaution that ensures that the device will be in a known state when the reset ends.

9. The host assigns an address. The host controller assigns a unique address to the device by sending a Set_Address request. The device reads the request, returns an acknowledge, and stores the new address. The device is now in the Address state. All communications from this point on use the new address. The address is valid until the device is detached or reset or the system powers down. On the next enumeration, the device may be assigned a different address.

10. The host learns about the device's abilities. The host sends a Get_Descriptor request to the new address to read the device descriptor, this time reading the whole thing. The descriptor is a data structure containing the maximum packet size for Endpoint 0, the number of configurations the device supports, and other basic information about the device. The host uses this information in the communications that follow.

The host continues to learn about the device by requesting the one or more configuration descriptors specified in the device descriptor. A device normally responds to a request for a configuration descriptor by sending the descriptor followed by all of that descriptor's subordinate descriptors. But a Windows host begins by requesting just the configuration descriptor's nine bytes. Included in these bytes is the total length of the configuration descriptor and its subordinate descriptors.

Windows then requests the configuration descriptor again, this time using the retrieved total length, up to FFh bytes. This causes the device to send the configuration descriptor followed by the interface descriptor(s) for each configuration, followed by endpoint descriptor(s) for each interface. If the descriptors total more than FFh bytes, Windows obtains the full set of descriptors on a third request. Each descriptor begins with its length and type, to enable the host to parse (pick out the individual elements in) the data that follows. The Descriptors section in this chapter has more on what each descriptor contains.

11. The host assigns and loads a device driver (except for composite devices). After the host learns as much as it can about the device from its descriptors, it looks for the best match in a device driver to manage communications with the device. In selecting a driver, Windows tries to match the information stored in the system's INF files with the Vendor and Product IDs and (optional) Release Number retrieved from the device. If there is no match, Windows looks for a match with any class, subclass, and protocol values retrieved from the device. After the operating system assigns and loads the driver, the driver often requests the device to resend descriptors or send other class-specific descriptors.

An exception to this sequence is composite devices, which have multiple interfaces, with each interface requiring a driver. The host can assign these drivers only after the interfaces are enabled, which requires the device to be configured (as described in the next step).

12. The host's device driver selects a configuration. After learning about the device from the descriptors, the device driver requests a configuration by sending a Set_Configuration request with the desired configuration number. Many devices support only one configuration. If a device supports multiple configurations, the driver can decide which to use based on whatever information it has about how the device will be used, or it may ask the user what to do, or it may just select the first configuration. The device reads the request and sets its configuration to match. The device is now in the Configured state and the device's interface(s) are enabled.

The host now assigns drivers for the interfaces in composite devices. As with other devices, the host uses the information retrieved from the device to find a matching driver.

The device is now ready for use.

The other two device states, Attached and Suspended, may exist at any time.

Attached state. If the hub isn't providing power (VBUS) to the port, the device is in the Attached state. This may occur if the hub has detected an over-current condition, or if the host requests the hub to remove power from the port. With no power on VBUS, the host and device can't communicate, so from their perspective, the situation is the same as when the device isn't attached at all.

Suspend State. The Suspend state means the device has seen no activity, including Start-of-Frame markers, on the bus for at least 3 milliseconds. In the Suspend state, the device must consume minimal bus power. Both configured and unconfigured devices must support this state. Chapter 19 has more details.

Enumerating a Hub

Hubs are also USB devices, and the host enumerates a newly attached hub in exactly the same way as it enumerates a device. If the hub has devices attached, the host also enumerates each of these after the hub informs the host of their presence.

Device Removal

When a user removes a device from the bus, the hub disables the device's port. The host learns that the removal occurred after polling the hub, learning that an event has occurred, and sending a Get_Port_Status request to find out what the event was. Windows then removes the device from the Device Manager's display and the device's address becomes available to another newly attached device.

Descriptor Types and Contents

Descriptors are data structures, or formatted blocks of information, that enable the host to learn about a device. Each descriptor contains information about either the device as a whole or an element in the device.

All USB peripherals must respond to requests for the standard USB descriptors. This means that the peripheral must do two things: store the information in the descriptors, and respond to requests for the descriptors in the expected format.

Types

As described above, during enumeration the host uses control transfers to request descriptors from the device. As enumeration progresses, the requested descriptors concern increasingly small elements of the device: first the entire device, then each configuration, each configuration's interface(s), and finally each interface's endpoint(s). Table 5-1 lists the descriptor types.

The higher-level descriptors inform the host of any additional, lower-level descriptors. Each device has one and only one device descriptor that contains information about the device as a whole and specifies the number of configurations the device supports. Each device also has one or more configuration descriptors that contain information about the device's use of power and the number of interfaces supported by the configuration. Each interface descriptor has zero or more endpoint descriptors that contain the information needed to communicate with an endpoint. An interface with no endpoint descriptors can still use the control endpoint for communications.

On receiving a request for a configuration descriptor, the device should return the configuration descriptor and all of the configuration's interface, endpoint, and other subordinate descriptors, up to the requested number of bytes. There is no request to retrieve, for example, only an endpoint descriptor. Devices that support both full and high speeds support two additional descriptor types: device_qualifier and other_speed_configuration. These and their subordinate descriptors contain information about the device's behavior when using the speed not currently selected.

Table 5-1: The specification defines standard descriptor types. A device class may require additional descriptor types.

Descriptor Type	Required?
device	Yes
device_qualifier	Yes, for devices that support both full and high speeds. Not allowed for other devices.
configuration	Yes
other_speed_configuration	Yes, for devices that support both full and high speeds. Not allowed for other devices.
interface	Yes
endpoint	No, if the device uses only Endpoint 0.
string	No. Optional descriptive text.
interface_power	No. Supports interface-level power management.

A string descriptor can store text such as the vendor's or device's name. The other descriptors can store indexes that point to these string descriptors, and the host can read the string descriptors using Get_Descriptor requests.

The 2.0 specification added an interface_power descriptor that enables power management at the interface level in addition to the device level. The document describing this descriptor's structure and use is *USB Feature Specification: Interface Power Management.*

In addition to the standard descriptors, a device may contain class- or vendor-specific descriptors. These offer a structured way for a device to provide more detailed information about itself. For example, an interface descriptor may specify that the interface belongs to the HID class and supports a HID class descriptor.

Each descriptor contains a value that identifies the descriptor type. Table 5-2 lists values defined by the USB and HID specifications. Bit 7 is always zero. Bits 6 and 5 identify the descriptor type: 00h=standard, 01h=class, 02h=vendor, 03h=reserved. Bits 4 through 0 identify the descriptor.

Each descriptor consists of a series of fields. Most of the field names use prefixes to indicate something about the format or contents of the data in that

Table 5-2: Each descriptor has a value that defines the information the descriptor contains.

Type	Value (hexadecimal)	Descriptor
Standard	01	device
	02	configuration
	03	string
	04	interface
	05	endpoint
	06	device_qualifier
	07	other_speed_configuration
	08	interface_power
Class	21	HID
	29	hub
Specific to the HID class	22	report
	23	physical

field: b = byte (8 bits), w = word (16 bits), bm = bit map, bcd = binary-coded decimal, i = index, id = identifier.

Device Descriptor

The device descriptor has basic information about the device. It's the first descriptor the host reads on device attachment and includes the information the host needs so it can retrieve additional information from the device.

The descriptor has 14 fields. Table 5-3 lists the fields in the order they occur in the descriptor. The descriptor includes information about the descriptor itself, the device, its configurations, and its classes. The following descriptions group the information by function.

The Descriptor

bLength. The length in bytes of the descriptor.

bDescriptorType. The constant DEVICE (01h).

Table 5-3: The device descriptor has 14 fields in 18 bytes.

Offset (decimal)	Field	Size (bytes)	Description
0	bLength	1	Descriptor size in bytes
1	bDescriptorType	1	The constant DEVICE (01h)
2	bcdUSB	2	USB specification release number (BCD)
4	bDeviceClass	1	Class code
5	bDeviceSubclass	1	Subclass code
6	bDeviceProtocol	1	Protocol Code
7	bMaxPacketSize(0)	1	Maximum packet size for Endpoint 0
8	idVendor	2	Vendor ID
10	idProduct	2	Product ID
12	bcdDevice	2	Device release number (BCD)
14	iManufacturer	1	Index of string descriptor for the manufacturer
15	iProduct	1	Index of string descriptor for the product
16	iSerialNumber	1	Index of string descriptor containing the serial number
17	bNumConfigurations	1	Number of possible configurations

The Device

bcdUSB. The USB specification number that the device and its descriptors comply with. In BCD (binary-coded decimal) format. If you think of the version as a decimal number, the upper byte represents the integer, the next four bits are tenths, and the final four bits are hundredths. So version 1.0 is 0100h; version 1.1 is 0110h, and version 2.0 is 0200h.

idVendor. Members of the USB Implementers Forum and others who pay an administrative fee receive the rights to use a unique Vendor ID. The device descriptor for every commercial product must have a Vendor ID. The host may have an INF file that contains this value, and if so, Windows uses the value to help decide what driver to load for the device.

idProduct. The manufacturer assigns a Product ID to identify the device. Both the device descriptor and the device's INF file on the host may contain this value, and if so, Windows uses the value to help decide what driver to load for the device. Each Product ID is specific to a Vendor ID, so multiple vendors can use the same Product ID without conflict.

bcdDevice. The device's release number in BCD format. Assigned by the manufacturer. Optional. This value can also be used in deciding which driver to load.

iManufacturer. An index that points to a string describing the manufacturer. Optional. Zero if unused.

iProduct. An index that points to a string describing the product. Optional. Zero if unused.

iSerialNumber. An index that points to a string containing the device's serial number. Optional. Zero if unused. Serial numbers are useful if users may have more than one identical device on the bus and the host needs to keep track of which is which, even after rebooting. They also enable the host to determine whether a peripheral is the same one used previously or a new installation of a peripheral with the same Vendor and Product ID. If a device has a serial number and a user plugs the device into a different port on a PC, Windows won't need to reload the device driver.

The Configuration

bNumConfigurations. The number of configurations the device supports.

bMaxPacketSize0. The maximum packet size for Endpoint 0. The host uses this information in the requests that follow. Low-speed devices must use 8. Full-speed devices may use 8, 16, 32, or 64. High-speed devices must use 64.

Classes

bDeviceClass. For devices that belong to a class, this field may name the class. Values from 1 to FEh are reserved for the USB's defined classes. Examples of classes are hubs, printers, and communications devices. The value FFh means that the class is specific to the vendor and defined by the vendor. Some devices (such as HIDs) specify a class in the interface descriptor, and for these devices, the bDeviceClass field in the device descriptor is 0. Not all devices belong to a class.

bDeviceSubclass. For devices that belong to a class, this field may specify a subclass within the class. If DeviceClass is 0, the Subclass must be 0. If DeviceClass is between 1 and FEh, the Subclass must be a code defined in a USB class specification. A value of FFh means that the subclass is specific to the vendor. A subclass may add support for additional features and abilities shared by a group of functions within a class.

bDeviceProtocol. This field may specify a protocol defined by the selected class or subclass. For example, a 2.0 hub uses this field to indicate whether the hub is currently supporting high speed and if so, if the hub supports one or multiple transaction translators. If DeviceClass is between 1 and FEh, the protocol must be a code defined by a USB class specification.

Device_Qualifier Descriptor

Devices that support both full and high speeds must have a device_qualifier descriptor. If the device switches speeds, some fields in the device descriptor may change. The device_qualifier descriptor holds the values to use for these fields at the speed not currently in use. The contents of fields in the device and device_qualifier descriptors swap, depending on which speed is selected.

The descriptor has 9 fields. Table 5-4 lists the fields in the order they occur in the descriptor. The descriptor includes information about the descriptor itself, the device, its configurations, and its classes. The fields are the same as the ones in a device descriptor. The only difference is that they describe the device at the speed that isn't currently active.

The Vendor and Product IDs, device release number, and manufacturer, product, and serial-number strings don't change when the speed changes, so the device_qualifier descriptor doesn't include these.

The host can use a Get_Descriptor request to retrieve the device_qualifier descriptor. The following descriptions group the information by function.

The Descriptor

bLength. The length in bytes of the descriptor.

bDescriptorType. The constant DEVICE_QUALIFIER (06h).

Table 5-4: The device_qualifier descriptor has 9 fields in 10 bytes.

Offset (decimal)	Field	Size (bytes)	Description
0	bLength	1	Descriptor size in bytes
1	bDescriptorType	1	The constant DEVICE_QUALIFIER (06h)
2	bcdUSB	2	USB specification release number (BCD)
4	bDeviceClass	1	Class code
5	bDeviceSubclass	1	Subclass code
6	bDeviceProtocol	1	Protocol Code
7	bMaxPacketSize(0)	1	Maximum packet size for Endpoint 0
8	bNumConfigurations	1	Number of possible configurations
9	Reserved	1	For future use

The Device

bcdUSB. The USB specification number that the device and its descriptors comply with. Must be at least 0200h.

The Configuration

bNumConfigurations. The number of configurations the device supports.

bMaxPacketSize0. The maximum packet size for Endpoint 0.

Classes

bDeviceClass. For devices that belong to a class, this field may name the class.

bDeviceSubclass. For devices that belong to a class, this field may specify a subclass within the class.

bDeviceProtocol. This field may specify a protocol defined by the selected class or subclass. For example, a 2.0 hub must support both a low- and full-speed protocol and a high-speed protocol. The device descriptor contains the code for the currently active protocol, and the device_qualifier descriptor contains the code for the not-active protocol.

Reserved. For future use.

Configuration Descriptor

After retrieving the device descriptor, the host can retrieve the device's configuration, interface, and endpoint descriptors.

Each device has at least one configuration descriptor that describes the device's features and abilities. Often a single configuration is enough, but a device with multiple uses or modes can support multiple configurations. Only one configuration is active at a time. Each configuration requires a descriptor. The configuration descriptor contains information about the device's use of power and the number of interfaces supported. Each configuration descriptor has subordinate descriptors, including one or more interface descriptors and optional endpoint descriptors.

The host selects a configuration with the Set_Configuration request, and reads the current configuration number with a Get_Configuration request.

The descriptor has eight fields. Table 5-5 lists the fields in the order they occur in the descriptor. The fields contain information about the descriptor itself, the configuration, and the device's use of power in that configuration. For many configurations, some fields don't apply. The following descriptions group the information by function.

The Descriptor

bLength. The length (in bytes) of the descriptor.

bDescriptorType. The constant CONFIGURATION (02h).

wTotalLength. The number of data bytes that the device returns, including the bytes for all of the configuration's interfaces and endpoints.

The Configuration

bConfigurationValue. Identifies the configuration for Get_Configuration and Set_Configuration requests. A Set_Configuration request with a value of zero causes the device to enter the Not Configured state.

iConfiguration. Index to a string that describes the configuration. Optional.

Table 5-5: The configuration descriptor has 8 fields.

Offset (decimal)	Field	Size (bytes)	Description
0	bLength	1	Descriptor size in bytes
1	bDescriptorType	1	The constant Configuration (02h)
2	wTotalLength	2	Size of all data returned for this configuration in bytes
4	bNumInterfaces	1	Number of interfaces the configuration supports
5	bConfigurationValue	1	Identifier for Set_Configuration and Get_Configuration requests
6	iConfiguration	1	Index of string descriptor for the configuration
7	bmAttributes	1	Self power/bus power and remote wakeup settings
8	MaxPower	1	Bus power required, expressed as (maximum milliamperes/2)

bNumInterfaces. The number of interfaces the configuration supports. The minimum is 1.

Power Use

bmAttributes. Bit 6=1 if the device is self-powered. Bit 5=1 if the device supports the remote wakeup feature. This enables a suspended USB device to tell its host that it wants to communicate. A USB device must enter the Suspend state if there has been no bus activity for 3 milliseconds. If an event at a suspended device requires action from the host, a device that supports remote wakeup and with this feature enabled can request the host to resume communications.

The other bits are unused. Bits 0 through 4 must be 0. Bit 7 must be 1. (In USB 1.0, bit 7 was set to 1 to indicate that the configuration was bus powered. In USB 1.1 and higher, setting bit 6 to 0 is enough to indicate that the configuration is bus powered.)

MaxPower. Specifies how much bus current a device requires. MaxPower in milliamperes equals one half the number of milliamperes required. If the device requires 200 milliamperes, MaxPower=100. The maximum allowed current is 500 milliamperes. Storing half the number of milliamperes enables one byte to store values up to the maximum. If the host determines that the requested current isn't available, it will refuse to configure the device.

Other_Speed_Configuration Descriptor

The other descriptor unique to devices that support both full and high speeds is the other_speed_configuration descriptor. The structure of the descriptor is identical to that of the configuration descriptor. The only difference is that it describes the configuration when the device is operating at the speed not currently active. The other_speed_configuration descriptor has subordinate descriptors the same as the configuration descriptor does.

The descriptor has eight fields. Table 5-6 lists the fields in the order they occur in the descriptor.

Interface Descriptor

The term *interface* may of course describe USB as a whole, but in terms of a device and its descriptors, interface means a set of endpoints used by a device feature or function. A configuration's interface descriptor contains information about the endpoints the interface supports.

Each configuration must support one interface, and for many devices, one is enough. But a configuration can have multiple interfaces that are active at the same time, as well as multiple, mutually exclusive interfaces. Each interface has its own interface descriptor and a subordinate endpoint descriptor for each endpoint supported by the interface.

A device with a configuration that has multiple interfaces that are active at the same time is a composite device. The host loads a driver for each interface.

When there are multiple ways to use a device, instead of using multiple configurations, a configuration may support alternate, mutually exclusive interfaces. Changing interfaces is simpler than changing configurations, which affects the entire device. The host requests an alternate interface with a Set_Interface request, and reads the current interface number with a

Table 5-6: The other_speed_configuration descriptor has the same 8 fields as the configuration descriptor.

Offset (decimal)	Field	Size (bytes)	Description
0	bLength	1	Descriptor size in bytes
1	bDescriptorType	1	The constant OTHER_SPEED_CONFIGURATION (07h)
2	wTotalLength	2	Size of all data returned for this configuration in bytes
4	bNumInterfaces	1	Number of interfaces the configuration supports
5	bConfigurationValue	1	Identifier for Set_Configuration and Get_Configuration requests
6	iConfiguration	1	Index of string descriptor for the configuration
7	bmAttributes	1	Self power/bus power and remote wakeup settings
8	MaxPower	1	Bus power required, expressed as (maximum milliamperes/2)

Get_Interface request. Each interface has its own interface descriptor and subordinate descriptors.

An interface descriptor has nine fields. Table 5-7 lists the fields in the order they occur in the descriptor. Many devices don't need all of the fields, such as those that enable alternate settings and protocols. The following descriptions group the information by function.

The Descriptor

bLength. The number of bytes in the descriptor.

bDescriptorType. The constant INTERFACE (04h).

The Interface

iInterface. Index to a string that describes the interface.

bInterfaceNumber. Identifies the interface. In a composite device, a configuration has multiple interfaces that are active at the same time. Each interface must have a descriptor with a unique value in this field. The default is 0.

Table 5-7: The interface descriptor has 9 fields.

Offset (decimal)	Field	Size (bytes)	Description
0	bLength	1	Descriptor size in bytes
1	bDescriptorType	1	The constant Interface (04h)
2	bInterfaceNumber	1	Number identifying this interface
3	bAlternateSetting	1	Value used to select an alternate setting
4	bNumEndpoints	1	Number of endpoints supported, except Endpoint 0
5	bInterfaceClass	1	Class code
6	bInterfaceSubclass	1	Subclass code
7	bInterfaceProtocol	1	Protocol code
8	iInterface	1	Index of string descriptor for the interface

bAlternateSetting. When a configuration supports multiple, mutually exclusive interfaces, each interface must have a descriptor with the same value in bInterfaceNumber but a unique value in bAlternateSetting. The Get_Interface request retrieves the currently active setting. The Set_Interface request selects the setting to use. The default is 0.

bNumEndpoints. The number of endpoints the interface supports in addition to Endpoint 0. For a device that supports only Endpoint 0, NumEndpoints is 0.

bInterfaceClass. Similar to DeviceClass in the device descriptor, but for devices with a class specified by the interface. Values from 01h to FEh are reserved for USB-defined classes. HID is class 03h. FFh indicates a vendor-defined class. Zero is reserved.

bInterfaceSubClass. Similar to bDeviceSubClass in the device descriptor, but for devices with a class defined by the interface. For interfaces that belong to a class, this field may specify a subclass within the class. If bInterfaceClass is 0, bInterfaceSubclass must be 0. If bInterfaceClass is between 1 and FEh, InterfaceSubclass must be a code defined by a USB specification. A value of FFh means that the subclass is specific to the vendor.

bInterfaceProtocol. Similar to bDeviceProtocol in the device descriptor, but for devices whose class is defined by the interface. May specify a protocol defined by the selected bInterfaceClass or bInterfaceSubClass. If bInterfaceClass is between 1 and FEh, bInterfaceProtocol must be a code defined by a USB specification.

Endpoint Descriptor

Each endpoint specified in an interface descriptor has an endpoint descriptor. Endpoint 0 never has a descriptor because every device must support Endpoint 0, the device descriptor contains the maximum packet size, and the specification defines everything else about the endpoint. Table 5-8 lists the endpoint descriptor's six fields in the order they occur in the descriptor. The following descriptions group the information by function.

The Descriptor

bLength. The number of bytes in the descriptor.

bDescriptorType. The constant ENDPOINT (05h).

The Endpoint

bEndpointAddress. Includes the endpoint number and direction. Bits 0 through 3 are the endpoint number. Low-speed devices can have a maximum of 3 endpoints (usually numbered 0 through 2), while full- and high-speed devices can have 16 (0 through 15). Bit 7 is the direction: Out=0, In=1, Bidirectional (for control transfers)=ignored. Bits 4, 5, and 6 are unused and must be zero.

bmAttributes. Bits 1 and 0 specify the type of transfer the endpoint supports. 00=Control, 01=Isochronous, 10=Bulk, 11=Interrupt. For Endpoint 0, Control is assumed.

In USB 1.1, bits 2 through 7 were reserved. USB 2.0 uses bits 2 through 5 for full- and high-speed isochronous endpoints. Bits 3 and 2 indicate a synchronization type: 00=no synchronization, 01=asynchronous, 10=adaptive, 11=synchronous. Bits 5 and 4 indicate a usage type: 00=data endpoint, 01=feedback endpoint, 10=implicit feedback data endpoint, 11=reserved. For non-isochronous endpoints, bits 2 through 5 must be 0. For all endpoints, bits 6 and 7 must be 0.

Table 5-8: The endpoint descriptor has 6 fields.

Offset (decimal)	Field	Size (bytes)	Description
0	bLength	1	Descriptor size in bytes
1	bDescriptorType	1	The constant Endpoint (05h)
2	bEndpointAddress	1	Endpoint number and direction
3	bmAttributes	1	Transfer type supported
4	wMaxPacketSize	2	Maximum packet size supported
6	bInterval	1	Maximum latency/polling interval/NAK rate

wMaxPacketSize. The maximum number of data bytes the endpoint can transfer in a transaction. The allowed values vary with the device speed and type of transfer.

Bits 10 through 0 are the maximum packet size, from 0 to 1024 (0 to 1023 in USB 1.x). In USB 2.0, bits 12 and 11 indicate how many additional transactions per microframe a high-speed endpoint supports: 00=no additional transactions (1 transaction per microframe), 01=1 additional (2 transactions per microframe), 10=2 additional (3 transactions per microframe), 11=reserved. In USB 1.x, these bits were reserved and set to zero. Bits 13 through 15 are reserved and must be zero.

bInterval. The maximum latency for polling interrupt endpoints, or the interval for polling isochronous endpoints, or the maximum NAK rate for high-speed bulk OUT or control endpoints. The allowed range and how the value is used varies with the device speed, the transfer type, and whether or not the device supports USB 2.0.

For low-speed interrupt endpoints, the maximum latency equals bInterval in milliseconds. The value may range from 10 to 255.

For all full-speed interrupt endpoints and for full-speed isochronous endpoints on 1.x devices, the interval also equals bInterval in milliseconds. For interrupt endpoints, the value may range from 1 to 255. For isochronous endpoints in 1.x devices, the value must be 1. For isochronous endpoints in full-speed 2.0 devices, values from 1 to 16 are allowed, and the interval is calculated as $2^{bInterval-1}$. This allows a range from 1 millisecond to 32.768 seconds.

For full-speed bulk and control transfers, the value is ignored.

For high-speed endpoints, the value is in units of 125 microseconds, which is the width of a microframe. The value for interrupt and isochronous endpoints may range from 1 to 16, and the interval is calculated as $2^{bInterval-1}$. This allows a range from 125 microseconds to 4.096 seconds.

For high-speed bulk OUT and control endpoints, the value indicates the endpoint's maximum NAK rate. This value is relevant when the device has received data and returned ACK, and the host has more data to send in the transfer. By returning ACK, the device is saying that it expects to be able to accept the next transaction's data. (Otherwise the device would return NYET.) If the next data packet arrives and for some reason the device can't accept it, the endpoint returns NAK. The bInterval value says that the endpoint will return NAK no more than once in each period specified by bInterval. The value can range from 0 to 255 microframes. A value of zero means the endpoint will never NAK. The host isn't required to use the maximum-NAK-rate information.

String Descriptor

A string descriptor contains descriptive text. The specification defines string descriptors for the manufacturer, product, serial number, configuration, and interface. A device may support additional string descriptors as well. String descriptors are optional. Table 5-9 shows the descriptor's fields and their purposes.

The Descriptor

bLength. The number of bytes in the descriptor.

bDescriptorType. The constant STRING (03h).

Table 5-9: A string descriptor has 3 or more fields.

Offset (decimal)	Field	Size (bytes)	Description
0	bLength	1	Descriptor size in bytes
1	bDescriptorType	1	The constant String (03h)
2	bSTRING or wLANGID	varies	For string descriptor 0, an array of 1 or more Language Identifier codes. For other string descriptors, a Unicode string.

The String

Each string has an index. String 0 has the special function of providing language IDs, while the other strings may contain any text.

wLANGID[0...n]. Used in string descriptor 0 only. String descriptor 0 contains one or more 16-bit language ID codes that indicate the languages that the strings are available in. The code for English is 0009h, and the subcode for U.S. English is 0004h. These seem to be the only codes that are valid in U.S. versions of Windows 98. This value must be valid for any of the other strings to be valid. Devices that return no string descriptors must not return an array of language IDs. The USB Implementers Forum's website has a list of defined USB language IDs.

bString. For Strings 1 and up, the String field contains a Unicode string. Unicode uses 16 bits to represent each character. With a few exceptions, ANSI character codes 00h through 7Fh correspond to Unicodes 0000h through 007Fh. For example, a product string for a product called "Gizmo" would contain five 16-bit Unicodes representing the characters in the product name: 0047 0069 007A 006D 006F. The strings are not null-terminated.

Descriptors in 2.0-compliant Devices

If you're upgrading a 1.x-complaint device to 2.0, what changes are required in the descriptors? In a dual-speed device, can you detect a device's current speed by reading its descriptors? This section answers these questions.

Making 1.x Descriptors 2.0-compliant

Table 5-10 lists the descriptor fields whose contents may require changes to enable a 1.x device to comply with the 2.0 specification. For all except some devices that have isochronous endpoints, the one and only required change is this: in the device descriptor, the bcdUSB field must be 0200h.

A device's default interface settings must request no isochronous bandwidth, as Chapter 4 explained. And because these interfaces are of no use for transferring isochronous data, a device that wants to do isochronous transfers must support at least one alternate interface setting, which will require at least one endpoint descriptor. Some 1.x devices meet this requirement already.

The 2.0 spec also adds two new descriptors and functions for bits in existing fields, but the new descriptors are used only in dual-speed devices and the existing descriptors are backwards compatible with 1.x.

Full-speed isochronous endpoints have a few new, optional abilities. The endpoint descriptor can specify synchronization and usage types (bmAttributes field), and the interval can be greater than 1 millisecond (bInterval field). In 1.x descriptors, these bits default to 0 (no synchronization) and 1 (one millisecond).

Detecting the Current Speed of a Dual-Speed Device

A high-speed device must respond to enumeration requests at full speed, and may also be completely functional at full speed. As Chapter 2 explained, a high-speed capable device must use full speed if it has a 1.x host or if there is a 1.x hub between the host and device. Applications and device drivers normally have no need to know which speed a dual-speed device is using because all of the speed-related details are handled at a lower level. And Windows in fact provides no straightforward way to learn a device's speed. But if the host wants to know, there are a few techniques that can provide this information for many devices.

If a device has a bulk endpoint, you can learn the current speed by examining the endpoint descriptor in the active configuration. The MaxPacketSize

Table 5-10: The descriptors in a 1.x-compliant device require very few changes to comply with 2.0.

Descriptor	Field	Change
Device	bcdUSB	Set to 0200h.
Endpoint	bmAttributes	Isochronous only: bits 3..2 are a synchronization type, bits 5..4 are a usage type.
	bInterval	Isochronous only: the interval is $2^{bInterval-1}$ milliseconds instead of milliseconds.
	wMaxPacketSize	Isochronous only: must be 0 in the default configuration.

field must be 512 in a high-speed device, and it can't be 512 in a full-speed device. If there is no bulk endpoint, the MaxPacketSize of an interrupt or isochronous endpoint provides speed information if the endpoint uses a maximum packet size available only at high speed. For an interrupt endpoint, a MaxPacketSize greater than 64 indicates high speed, but a high-speed interrupt endpoint can have a MaxPacketSize of 64 or less. For isochronous endpoints, a MaxPacketSize of 1024 indicates high speed, but a high-speed isochronous endpoint can have a MaxPacketSize of 1023 or less.

If you're writing the device firmware, you can provide speed information in the optional configuration strings indexed by the configuration and other_speed_configuration descriptors. For example, the string indexed by the configuration descriptor might contain the text "high speed," and the string indexed by the other_speed_configuration descriptor might contain the text "full speed." Applications can then read the configuration string to learn the current speed.

The USBView application in the Windows DDK shows how applications can read endpoint and string descriptors.

6

Control Transfers: Structured Requests for Critical Data

Of the four transfer types, control transfers have the most complex structure. They're also the only transfer type with functions defined by the specification. This chapter takes a more detailed look at control transfers. The focus is on what you need to know to implement standard and custom requests in device firmware, along with some background about the structure of the requests.

Elements of a Control Transfer

As Chapter 3 explained, control transfers enable the host and a device to exchange information about the device's configuration. They also offer a way that any device can use to transfer any type of information. Each control transfer has a defined format consisting of a Setup stage, an optional Data stage, and a Status stage. Each stage consists of one or more transactions that contain a token phase, a data phase, and a handshake phase. Each phase transfers a token, data, or handshake packet. Chapter 4 has diagrams that show the packets that transfer in each stage.

As described in Chapter 3, low-speed transfers also use PRE packets, high-speed transfers use the PING protocol, and some low- and full-speed transfers use split transactions. Each packet also contains error-checking bits. Application programmers, device-driver writers, and firmware developers don't have to worry about PREs, PINGs error-checking, or split transactions because the hardware and low-level drivers handle them.

The Setup Stage

The Setup stage consists of a Setup transaction, which has two purposes: to identify the transfer as a control transfer and to transmit the request and other information that the device will need to complete the request.

Devices must accept and acknowledge every Setup transaction. If a device is in the middle of another control transfer, it must abandon that transfer and respond to the new Setup transaction. Here are more details about each of the packets in the Setup stage's transaction:

Token Packet

Purpose: identifies the receiver and identifies the transaction as a Setup transaction.

Sent by: the host.

PID: SETUP

Additional Contents: the device and endpoint addresses.

Data Packet

Purpose: transmits the request and related information.

Sent by: the host.

PID: DATA0

Additional Contents: eight bytes in five fields: bmRequestType, bRequest, wValue, wIndex, and wLength.

bmRequestType is a byte that specifies the direction of data flow, the type of request, and the recipient.

Bit 7 is a Direction bit that names the direction of data flow for data in the Data stage. Host to device (OUT) or no Data stage is 0; device to host (IN) is 1. Just remember that *0* looks like *O* for OUT and *1* looks like *I* for IN.

Bits 6 and 5 are Request Type bits that specify whether the request is one of the USB's eleven standard requests (00), a request defined for a specific USB class (01), or a request defined by a vendor for use with a particular product or products (10).

Bits 4 through 0 are Recipient bits that define whether the request is directed to the device (00000) or to a specific interface (0001), endpoint (00010), or other element (00011) in the device.

bRequest is a byte that specifies the request. When the Request Type bits in bmRequestType are 00, bRequest contains the number of one of the USB's standard requests. When the Request Type bits are 01, bRequest names a request defined for the device's class. When the Request Type bits are 10, bRequest names a request defined by the device's vendor.

wValue is two bytes that the host may use to pass information to the device. Each request may define the meaning of these bytes in its own way. For example, in a Set_Address request, wValue contains the device address.

wIndex is two bytes that the host may use to pass information to the device. A typical use is to pass an index or offset such as an interface or endpoint number, but each request may define the meaning of these bytes in any way. When passing an endpoint index, bits 0-3 indicate the endpoint number, and bit 7 is 0 for a Control or OUT endpoint or 1 for an IN endpoint. When passing an interface index, bits 0-7 are the interface number. All unused bits are 0.

wLength is two bytes containing the number of data bytes in the Data stage that follows. For a host-to-device transfer, wLength is the exact number of bytes the host will transfer. For a device-to-host transfer, wLength is a maximum, and the device may return this number of bytes or fewer. If the wLength field is 0, there is no Data stage.

Handshake Packet

Purpose: transmits the device's acknowledgement.

Sent by: the device.

PID: ACK.

Additional Contents: none. The handshake packet consists of the PID alone.

Comments: If the device detected an error in the received Setup or Data packet, it returns no handshake. The device's hardware typically handles the error checking and sending of the ACK, with no programming required.

The Data Stage

When a control transfer contains a Data stage, the stage consists of one or more IN or OUT transactions. The endpoint's descriptor specifies the number of data bytes that each transaction can carry. (For Endpoint 0, the device descriptor specifies this.)

When the Data stage uses IN transactions, the device sends data to the host. An example is Get_Descriptor, where the device sends a requested descriptor to the host. When the Data stage uses OUT transactions, the host sends data to the device. An example is Set_Report, where the host sends a report to a HID-class device. If the wLength field in the Setup transaction is 0, there is no Data stage at all. For example, in the Set_Configuration request, the host passes a configuration value to the peripheral in the wValue field of the Setup stage's data packet, so there's no need for the Data stage.

If all of the data can't fit in one packet, the stage uses multiple transactions. The number of transactions required to send all of the data for the transfer equals the value in the Setup transaction's wLength field divided by wMax-PacketSize value in the endpoint's descriptor, rounded up. For example, in a Get_Descriptor request, if wLength is 18 and wMaxPacketSize is 8, the transfer requires 3 Data transactions. The transactions in the Data stage must all be in the same direction.

The host uses split transactions in the Data stage when the device is low or full speed and the device's hub connects to a high-speed bus. The host uses the PING protocol when the device is high speed, the Data stage uses OUT transactions, and there is more than one data transaction.

Each IN or OUT transaction in the Data stage contains token, data, and handshake packets. Here are more details about each of the packets in the Data stage's transaction(s):

Token Packet

Purpose: identifies the receiver and identifies the transaction as an IN or OUT transaction.

Sent by: the host.

PID: if the request requires the device to send data to the host, the PID is IN. If the request requires the host to send data to the device, the PID is OUT.

Additional Contents: the device and endpoint addresses.

Data Packet

Purpose: transfers all or a portion of the data specified in the wLength field of the Setup transaction's data packet.

Sent by: if the token packet's PID is IN, the device sends the data packet; if the token packet's PID is OUT, the host sends the data packet.

PID: The first packet is DATA1. Any additional packets in the Data stage alternate DATA0/DATA1.

Additional Contents: the data.

Handshake Packet

Purpose: the data packet's receiver returns status information.

Sent by: the receiver of the Data stage's data packet. If the token packet's PID is IN, the host sends the handshake packet. If the token packet's PID is OUT, the device sends the handshake packet.

PID: Any device may return ACK (valid data was received), NAK (the endpoint is busy), or STALL (the request isn't supported or the endpoint is halted). A high-speed device that is receiving multiple data packets may return NYET (the current transaction's data was accepted but the endpoint isn't yet ready for another data packet). The host can return only ACK.

Additional Contents: None. The handshake packet consists of the PID alone.

Comments: If the receiver detected an error in the token or data packet, it returns no handshake packet.

The Status Stage

The Status stage is where the device reports the success or failure of the entire transfer. Its purpose is similar to that of a transaction's handshake packet, and in fact the information sometimes travels in the handshake packet of the Status stage. But the Status stage reports the success or failure of the entire transfer, rather than of a single transaction.

In some cases (such as after receiving the first packet of a device descriptor during enumeration), the host may begin the Status stage before the Data stage has completed, and the device must detect this, abandon the Data stage, and complete the Status stage.

Here are more details about each of the packets in the Status stage's transaction:

Token Packet

Purpose: identifies the receiver and indicates the direction of the Status stage's data packet.

Sent by: the host.

PID: the opposite of the direction of the previous transaction's data packet. If the Data stage's PID was OUT or if there was no Data stage, the Status stage's PID is IN. If the Data stage's PID was IN, the Status stage's PID is OUT.

Additional Contents: the device and endpoint addresses.

Data Packet

Purpose: enables the receiver of the Data stage's data to indicate the status of the transfer.

Sent by: if the Status stage's token packet's PID is IN, the device sends the data packet; if the Status stage's token packet's PID is OUT, the host sends the data packet.

PID type: DATA1

Additional Contents: The host sends a zero-length data packet consisting only of the PID and error-checking bits, with no data bits. A device may send a zero-length data packet (success), NAK (busy), or STALL (endpoint halted).

Comments: For most requests, the zero-length data packet indicates that the request has been carried out. An exception is Set_Address, which isn't carried out until the Status stage has completed.

Handshake Packet

Purpose: the sender of the Data stage's data indicates the status of the transfer.

Sent by: the receiver of the Status stage's data packet. If the Status stage's token packet's PID is IN, the host sends the handshake packet; if the token packet's PID is OUT, the device sends the data packet.

PID type: the device's response may be ACK (success), NAK (busy), or STALL (the request isn't supported or the endpoint is halted). The host's response to the received data packet must be ACK.

Additional Contents: none. The handshake packet consists of the PID alone.

Comments: The Status stage's handshake packet is the final transmission in the transfer. If the receiver detected an error in the token or data packet, it returns no handshake packet.

For any request that's expected to take many milliseconds to carry out, the protocol should define an alternate way to determine when the request has completed. This ensures that the host doesn't waste a lot of time looking for an acknowledgement that will take a long time to appear. An example is the Set_Port_Feature(PORT_RESET) request sent to a hub. The reset signal lasts at least 10 milliseconds. Rather than forcing the host to wait this long for the device to complete the reset, the hub acknowledges receiving the request when it first places the port in the reset state. When the reset is complete, the hub sets a bit that the host can retrieve at its leisure, using a Get_Port_Status request.

Handling Errors

Not every control-transfer request is carried out by the device. The device's firmware may not support a request. Or the device may be unable to respond because its firmware has crashed, or the endpoint is in the Halt condition, or the device is no longer attached to the bus. The host may also decide for any reason to end a transfer early, before all of the data has been sent.

An example of an unsupported request is one that uses a request code that the device's firmware doesn't know how to respond to. Or the device may support the request but other information in the Setup stage doesn't match what the device expects or supports. When this occurs, a Request Error condition exists and the device notifies the host by sending a STALL code in a handshake packet. Devices must respond to the Setup transaction with an ACK, so the STALL must transmit in the handshake packet of the next Data stage or the Status stage.

If the host fails to get an expected response, or if it detects an error in received data or a Halt condition at the endpoint, it abandons the transfer. The host then tries to re-establish communications by sending the token packet for a new Setup transaction. If a device receives a token packet for a

Setup transaction before it has completed a previous control transfer, it must abandon the previous transfer and begin the new one. If the transfer is using the Default Control Pipe and a new token packet doesn't cause the device to recover, the host takes more drastic action, requesting the device's hub to reset the device's port.

The host may also end a transfer early by initiating the Status stage before completing all of the Data stage's transactions. In this case, the device must abandon the rest of the data and respond to the Status stage as if all of the data had transferred.

The Requests

Table 6-1 summarizes the USB's 11 standard requests, followed by a description of each request. All devices must respond to these requests (though the response may be just a STALL). The values range from 00 to 0Ch, with some values unused.

Most of the requests are in pairs, with each Set request having a corresponding Get or Clear request. The exceptions are Set_Address, Synch_Frame, and Get_Status.

Table 6-1: The USB specification defines eleven standard requests for Control transfers.

Request #	Request	Data source (Data stage)	Recipient	Value	Index	Data Length (bytes) (in Data stage)	Data (in Data stage)
00h	Get_Status	device	device, interface, endpoint	0	device, interface, endpoint	2	status
01h	Clear_Feature	none	device, interface, endpoint	feature	device, interface, endpoint	0	none
03h	Set_Feature	none	device, interface, endpoint	feature	device, interface, endpoint	0	none
05h	Set_Address	none	device	device address	0	0	none
06h	Get_ Descriptor	device	device	descriptor type & index	device or language ID	descriptor length	descriptor
07h	Set_ Descriptor	host	device	descriptor type & index	device or language ID	descriptor length	descriptor
08h	Get_ Configuration	device	device	0	device	1	configura- tion
09h	Set_ Configuration	none	device	configura- tion	device	0	none
0Ah	Get_Interface	device	interface	0	interface	1	alternate setting
0Bh	Set_Interface	none	interface	interface	interface	0	none
0Ch	Synch_Frame	device	endpoint	0	endpoint	2	frame number

Set_Address

Purpose: The host specifies an address to use in future communications with the device.

Request Number: 05h

Source of Data: none

Data Length: 0

Contents of Value field: new device address. Allowed values are 1 through 127. Each device on the bus, including the root hub, has a unique address.

Contents of Index field: 0

Contents of data packet in the Data stage: none

Supported States: Default, Address.

Behavior on error: not specified.

Comments: When a hub enables a port after power-up or attachment, the port uses the default address of 0 until it completes a Set_Address request from the host.

This request is unlike most other requests because the device doesn't carry out the request until it has completed the Status stage of the request by sending a 0-length data packet. The host sends the Status stage's token packet to the default address, so the device must detect and respond to this packet before changing its address.

After completion of this request, all communications use the new address.

A device using the default address of 0 is in the Default state. After completing Set_ Address request to set an address other than 0, the device enters the Address state.

A device must send the handshake packet within 50 milliseconds after receiving the request, and it must complete the request within 2 milliseconds after completing the Status stage.

Get_Descriptor

Purpose: The host requests a specific descriptor.

Request Number: 06h

Source of Data: device

Data Length: the number of bytes to return. If the descriptor is longer than Data Length, the device returns bytes up to Data Length. If the descriptor is shorter than Data Length, the device returns the descriptor. If the descriptor is shorter than Data Length and an even multiple of the endpoint's maximum packet size, the device follows the descriptor with a 0-length data packet. The host detects the end of the data when it has received the requested amount of data or a packet containing less than the maximum packet size (including 0 bytes).

Contents of Value field: High byte: descriptor type. Low byte: descriptor value.

Contents of Index field: for String descriptors, Language ID. Otherwise 0.

Contents of data packet in the Data stage: the requested descriptor.

Supported states: Default, Address, Configured.

Behavior on error: If a device receives a request that it doesn't support, it should return a STALL.

Comments: There are seven types of descriptors. All devices may have device, configuration, interface, endpoint, and string descriptors. Two other descriptors, device_qualifier and other_speed_configuration, are only for devices that support both full and high speeds. Chapter 5 described the purpose and contents of the descriptor types. Every USB device must have a device descriptor and at least one configuration and one interface descriptor.

A request for a configuration descriptor causes the device to return the configuration descriptor, plus all interface descriptors for that configuration and all endpoint descriptors for the interfaces.

Set_Descriptor

Purpose: The host adds a descriptor or updates an existing descriptor.

Request Number: 0Bh

Source of Data: host

Data Length: The number of bytes the host will transfer to the device.

Contents of Value field: high byte: descriptor type. (See Get_Descriptor) Low byte: descriptor index.

Contents of Index field: For string descriptors, Language ID. Otherwise 0.

Contents of data packet in the Data stage: descriptor length.

Supported states: Address and Configured.

Behavior on error: If a device receives a request that it doesn't support, it should return a STALL.

Comments: This request makes it possible for the host to add descriptors other than those stored in the device's firmware, or to change an existing descriptor. Many devices don't support this request because it allows errant software to place incorrect information in a descriptor.

Set_Configuration

Purpose: Instructs the device to use the selected configuration.

Request Number: 09h

Source of Data: none

Data Length: 0

Contents of Value field: The lower byte specifies a configuration. If the value matches a configuration supported by the device, the device selects the requested configuration. A value of 0 indicates not configured. If the value is 0, the device enters the Address state and requires a new Set_Configuration request to be configured.

Contents of Index field: 0

Contents of data packet in the Data stage: none

Supported states: Address, Configured.

Behavior on error: If Value isn't equal to 0 or a configuration supported by the device, the device returns a STALL.

Comments: After completing a Set_Configuration request specifying a supported configuration, the device enters the Configured state. Many of the standard requests require the device to be in the Configured state.

Get_Configuration

Purpose: The host requests the value of the current device configuration.

Request Number: 08h

Source of Data: device

Data Length: 1

Contents of Value field: 0

Contents of Index field: 0

Contents of data packet in the Data stage: Configuration value

Supported states: Address (returns 0), Configured

Behavior on error: not specified.

Comments: If the device isn't configured, it returns 0.

Set Interface

Purpose: For devices with configurations that support multiple, mutually exclusive settings for an interface, the host requests the device to use a specific setting.

Request Number: 0Bh

Source of Data: host

Data Length: 0

Contents of Value field: alternate setting to select

Contents of Index field: interface number

Contents of data packet in the Data stage: none

Supported states: Configured

Behavior on error: If the device supports only a default interface, it may return a STALL. If the requested interface or setting doesn't exist, the device returns a STALL.

Comments: See Get_Interface

Get_Interface

Purpose: For devices with configurations that support multiple, mutually exclusive settings for an interface, the host requests the current setting.

Request Number: 0Ah

Source of Data: device

Data Length: 1

Contents of Value field: 0

Contents of Index field: interface number

Contents of data packet in the Data stage: the current setting

Supported states: Configured

Behavior on error: If the interface doesn't exist, the device returns a STALL.

Comments: The interface number in the Index field of this request refers to the bInterface field in an interface descriptor. This value distinguishes an interface from other interfaces that may exist at the same time. The setting in the Data field in this request refers to the bAlternateInterface field in the interface descriptor. This value identifies which of two or more mutually exclusive settings an interface is currently using. For each setting supported by an interface, there is an interface descriptor and optional endpoint descriptors. Many devices support only one interface setting.

Set_Feature

Purpose: The host requests to enable a feature on a device, interface, or endpoint.

Request Number: 03h

Source of Data: none

Data Length: 0

Contents of Value field: the feature to enable

Contents of Index field: For a device, 0. For an interface, the interface number. For an endpoint, the endpoint number.

Contents of data packet in the Data stage: none

Supported states: Default: undefined. Address: OK for address 0, Endpoint 0. Otherwise the device returns a STALL. Configured: OK.

Behavior on error: If the endpoint or interface specified doesn't exist, the device responds with a STALL.

Comments: The USB specification defines two features.

DEVICE_REMOTE_WAKEUP, with a value of 1, applies to devices. When the host sets the DEVICE_REMOTE_WAKEUP feature, a suspended device can signal the host to resume communications.

ENDPOINT_HALT, with a value of 0, applies to endpoints. Bulk and interrupt endpoints must support the Halt condition. Two types of events may cause a Halt condition: a communications problem such as the device's not receiving a handshake packet or receiving more data than expected, or the device's receiving a Set_Feature request to halt the endpoint. A Clear_Feature request to halt the endpoint removes a Halt condition caused by a Set_Feature request.

The Get_Status request tells the host what features, if any, are enabled.

Clear_Feature

Purpose: The host requests to disable a feature on a device, interface, or endpoint.

Request Number: 01h.

Source of Data: none

Data Length: 0

Contents of Value field: the feature to disable

Contents of Index field: For a device feature, 0. For an interface feature, the interface number. For an endpoint feature, the endpoint number.

Contents of data packet in the Data stage: none

Supported states: Default: undefined. Address: OK for address 0, Endpoint 0. Otherwise the device returns a STALL. Configured: OK.

Behavior on error: If the feature, device, or endpoint specified doesn't exist, or if the feature can't be cleared, the device responds with a STALL. Behavior is undefined when Data Length is greater than 0.

Comments: The USB specification defines only two features. DEVICE_REMOTE_WAKEUP, with a value of 1, applies to devices. ENDPOINT_HALT, with a value of 0, applies to endpoints. See Set_Feature for more details.

Get_Status

Purpose: The host requests the status of the features of a device, interface, or endpoint.

Request Number: 00h

Source of Data: device

Data Length: 2

Contents of Value field: 0

Contents of Index field: For a device, 0. For an interface, the interface number. For an endpoint, the endpoint number.

Contents of data packet in the Data stage: the device, interface, or endpoint status

Supported states: Default: undefined. Address: OK for address 0, endpoint 0. Otherwise the device returns a STALL. Configured: OK.

Behavior on error: The device returns a STALL if the interface or endpoint doesn't exist.

Comments: For device requests, only two bits are defined. Bit 0 is the Self-Powered field: 0=bus-powered, 1=self-powered. The host can't change this value. Bit 1 is the Remote Wakeup field. The default on reset is 0 (disabled). All other bits are reserved. For interface requests, all bits are reserved. For endpoint requests, only bit 0 is defined. Bit 0=1 indicates a Halt condition. See Set_Feature for more details on Remote Wakeup and Halt.

Synch_Frame

Purpose: The device sets and reports an endpoint's synchronization frame.

Request Number: 0Ch

Source of Data: host

Data Length: 2

Contents of Value field: 0

Contents of Index field: endpoint number

Contents of data packet in the Data stage: frame number

Supported states: Default: undefined. Address: The device returns a STALL. Configured: OK.

Behavior on error: If the endpoint doesn't support the request, it should return a STALL.

Comments: In isochronous transfers, a device endpoint may request data packets that vary in size, following a sequence. For example, an endpoint may send a repeating sequence of 8, 8, 8, 64 bytes. The Synch_Frame request enables the host and endpoint to agree on which frame will begin the sequence.

When an endpoint receives a Synch_Frame request, it returns the number of the frame that will precede the beginning of a new sequence

This request is rarely used because there is rarely a need for the information it provides.

Class-Specific Requests

A class may define requests for devices in its class. A class-specific request may be required or optional. Some requests are unrelated to the standard requests, while others build on the standard requests by defining class-specific fields in a request.

An example of a request that's unrelated to the standard requests is the Get Max LUN request supported by some mass-storage devices. The host uses this request to find out the number of logical units the interface supports.

An example of a request that builds on an existing request is the Get_Port_Status request that hubs must support. This request is structured like the standard Get_Status request. But Get_Port_Status has different values in two fields. In bmRequestType, bits 6 and 5 are 01 to indicate that the request is defined by a standard USB class, and bits 4 through 0 are 00011 to indicate that the request applies to a unit other than the device or an interface or endpoint. (It applies to a port on the hub.) The index field holds the port number.

Vendor-Specific Requests

A vendor may define custom requests for control transfers with specific devices. In order to use a custom request in a control transfer, you need all of the following:

• Vendor-defined fields as needed in the Setup and optional Data stages. Bits 6 and 5 in the Setup stage's data packet are set to 10 to indicate a vendor-defined request.

• Code in the device that detects the request number and knows how to respond. If you have code for the standard requests, you can use it as a model for custom requests.

• A custom device driver in the host that initiates the request. Windows has no built-in driver that enables applications to send custom control requests, so the only option is a custom driver with this ability.

7

Chip Choices

When it's time to select a USB controller for a project, the good news is that there are plenty of chips to choose from. The downside is that there are so many that deciding which chip to use in a project can be overwhelming at first.

As with any project involving embedded controllers, the decision depends on what functions the chip has to perform, cost, availability, and ease of development. Ease of development depends on the availability and quality of development tools, device-driver software for the host, and sample code, plus your experience with the device's architecture and instruction set or language compiler.

This chapter is a guide to selecting a USB controller. It includes a tutorial about what you need to consider and descriptions of a sampling of chips with a range of abilities. The chips covered include inexpensive ones with simple architectures and basic USB support as well as more full-featured, high-end chips.

Elements of a USB Controller

The complexity of the USB protocol means that USB peripherals must have intelligence. The peripheral controller has to know how to detect and respond to events at a USB port, and it has to provide a way for the device to store data to be sent and retrieve and use data that's been received.

Controller chips vary in how much firmware support they require for USB communications. Some require little more than accessing a series of registers to store and retrieve USB data. Others require the device's program code to do more, including managing the sending of descriptors to the host, setting data-toggle values, and ensuring that the appropriate handshake packets are sent.

Some controllers have a general-purpose CPU on-chip, while others take a more minimalist approach and interface to an external CPU that handles the non-USB tasks while communicating with the USB controller as needed. All USB controllers have one or more USB ports as well as buffers, registers, and other I/O. A controller chip with a general-purpose CPU also has program and data memory on-chip or an interface to these in external memory.

For high-volume applications that require fast performance, another option is to design and manufacture an application-specific integrated circuit (ASIC). VAutomation is one source for USB controllers and other components that are available as synthesizable VHDL (very high speed integrated circuit hardware description language) or Verilog Source code.

Not all controllers support all four transfer types, and different controllers support different bus speeds. Most chips support fewer than the maximum number of endpoints (1 control endpoint and 30 other endpoints).

The USB Port

A USB peripheral controller must of course have a USB port and supporting circuits for communicating with the host. A USB transceiver provides the hardware interface to the bus. The circuits that communicate with the transceiver form a unit with the generic name of serial interface engine (SIE).

The SIE typically handles the sending and receiving of data in transactions. It doesn't interpret or use the data, but just sends the data that has been made available to it and stores any data received. A typical SIE does all of the following:

- Detect incoming packets.
- Send packets.
- Detect and generate Start-of-Packet, End-of-Packet, Reset, and Resume signaling.
- Encode and decode data in the format required on the bus (NRZI with bit stuffing).
- Check and generate CRC values.
- Decode and generate Packet IDs.
- Convert between USB's serial data and parallel data in registers or memory.

Implementing these functions requires about 2500 gates.

Buffers for USB Data

A USB controller must also have buffers for storing data that was recently received and data that's ready to be sent on the bus. Some chips, such as Netchip's NET2888, use registers, while others, such as Cypress' EZ-USB, reserve a portion of data memory for the buffers.

Registers that hold transmitted or received data are often structured as FIFOs (first in, first out buffers). Each read of a receive FIFO returns the byte that has been in the FIFO the longest. Each write to a transmit FIFO stores a byte that will transmit after all of the bytes already in the FIFO have transmitted. An internal pointer to the next location to be read or written to increments automatically as the firmware reads or writes to the FIFO.

In some chips, like Cypress' enCoRe series, the USB buffers are in ordinary data memory and the firmware explicitly selects each location to read and write to. There is no pointer that increments automatically when the firmware reads or writes to the buffers. The bytes in the USB transmit buffer go out in order from the lowest address to the highest, and the bytes in a USB receive buffer are stored in the order they arrive, from lowest address to highest. These buffers technically aren't FIFOs, but are sometimes called that anyway.

To enable faster transfers, some chips have double buffers that can store two full sets of data in each direction. While one block is transmitting, the firmware can write the next block of data into the other buffer so it will be ready to go as soon as the first block finishes transmitting. In the receive direction, the extra buffer enables a new transaction's data to arrive before the firmware has finished processing data from the previous transaction. The hardware automatically switches, or ping-pongs, between the two buffers.

CPU

A USB controller's central-processing unit (CPU) controls the chip's actions by executing instructions in the firmware stored in the chip. Each CPU supports an instruction set that includes machine-language instructions for moving data, performing math and logic operations, and program branching. The instruction set also enables the CPU to communicate with the SIE. The CPU may be based on a general-purpose microcontroller such as the 8051, or it may be a design developed specifically for use in USB applications.

Chips that don't have a general-purpose CPU may support a command set for USB-related communications, or they may just use a series of registers for storing USB data and configuration information. These chips provide a way to add USB capabilities to any microcontroller with an external data bus.

Program Memory

The program memory holds the code that the CPU executes. The program code assists in USB communications and carries out whatever other tasks the chip is responsible for. This memory may be in the CPU chip or a separate chip.

The program storage may use any of a number of memory types: ROM, EPROM, EEPROM, Flash EPROM, or RAM. All except RAM (unless it's battery-backed) are nonvolatile; they retain the data stored in them after powering down. The amount of program memory may range from a couple of kilobytes on up. Chips that can access memory off-chip may support a Megabyte or more of program memory.

Another name for the code stored in program memory is firmware, which indicates that the memory is non-volatile and not as easily changed as program code that can be loaded into RAM, edited, and re-saved on disk. In this book, I use the term firmware to refer to a controller's program code, with the understanding that the code may be stored in a variety of memory types, some more volatile than others.

ROM (read-only memory) must be mask-programmed at the factory and can't be erased. It's practical only for product runs in the thousands.

EPROM (erasable programmable ROM) is user-programmable. Many chips have inexpensive programming hardware and software available. To erase an EPROM, you insert the chip into an EPROM eraser, which exposes the circuits beneath the chip's quartz window to ultraviolet light. Erasing typically takes 10 to 30 minutes. The chip is then ready to be reprogrammed. Data sheets rarely specify the number of erase/reprogram cycles that the chip can withstand, but it's typically at least 100.

OTP (one-time programmable) PROMs are a cheaper, non-erasable alternative to erasable EPROMs. Internally, they're identical to EPROMs, and you program them exactly like EPROMs. The difference is that the chips lack the quartz window for erasing. The erasable varieties are useful for product development. Then to save cost, you can switch to OTP PROMs for the final product run. Many CPUs have both EPROM and OTP PROM variants.

Flash EPROM is a more recent electrically-erasable memory technology that doesn't need a quartz window and often doesn't need the special programming voltage required by other EPROMs. Current Flash EPROM technology enables around 100,000 erase/reprogram cycles.

EEPROM (electrically erasable PROM) also doesn't need a window, nor does it need the special programming voltage required by other EPROMs. EEPROMs tend to have longer access times than Flash EPROMs.

EEPROMs are available both with the parallel interface used by EPROMs and Flash EPROMs, and with a variety of synchronous serial interfaces, including Microwire, I^2C, and SPI. Serial EEPROMs are useful for storing small amounts of data that changes only occasionally, such as configuration data, including Vendor and Product IDs. Current EEPROM technology enables around 10 million erase/reprogram cycles.

RAM (random-access memory) can be erased and rewritten endlessly, but the stored data disappears when the chip powers down. It's possible to use RAM for program storage by loading the code from a PC on each power-up or by using battery backup. Cypress Semiconductor's EZ-USB uses RAM for program storage, along with special hardware and driver code that loads code into the chip on power up or attachment. Any CPU with external program memory could use battery-backed RAM for program storage. Host-loadable RAM has no practical limit on the number of erase/rewrite cycles. For battery-backed RAM, the limit is the battery life. Access times for RAM are fast.

Data Memory

Data memory provides temporary storage during program execution. The contents of data memory may include data received from the USB port, data to be sent to the USB port, values to be used in calculations, or anything else the chip needs to remember or keep track of. Data memory is usually RAM. Typical amounts of internal data memory are 128 to 1024 bytes.

Registers

Registers are another option for temporary storage. Registers are memory locations the CPU accesses using different instructions than it uses to access other data memory. Most registers have defined functions. Most CPUs can access registers more quickly than other data memory.

USB controller chips typically have status and control registers that hold information about what endpoints are enabled, the number of bytes received, the number of bytes ready to transmit, Suspend-state status, error-checking information, and other information about how the chip will be used and the current status of transmitted or received data. For example, setting a bit in a configuration register may enable an endpoint. The number of registers and the specifics of their contents vary with the chip family.

Other I/O

Just about every controller will also have an interface to the world outside of itself, other than the USB port. This often includes a series of general-purpose input and output (I/O) pins that can connect to other circuits. A chip may also have built-in support for other serial interfaces, such as an asynchronous interface for RS-232, or synchronous interfaces such as I^2C, Microwire, and SPI.

Some chips have special-purpose interfaces. For example, Philips' USA1321 contains a digital-to-analog converter (DAC) for use in USB speakers and other audio devices. The chip converts received USB data to analog signals at sampling frequencies of up to 55 kilohertz. FTDI's FT8U232AM is a USB UART that makes it as easy as possible to upgrade RS-232 designs to USB.

Other Features

A chip may also have any number of other features such as hardware timers or counters. Just about any feature that you might find in a general-purpose microcontroller is likely to be available in a USB controller.

Simplifying the Development Process

Besides the abilities and features of the chip itself, ease of development can make a huge difference in how long it takes to get a project up and running. The simplest and quickest USB project is one that uses a controller chip with all of the following:

- A chip architecture and programming language that you're familiar with.
- Detailed, well-organized hardware documentation.

- Well-documented, bug-free sample firmware code for an application similar to yours.
- A development system that enables easy downloading and debugging of firmware.
- Device-driver availability, either using drivers included with Windows or a well-documented driver provided by the chip vendor or another source and usable as-is or with minimal modifications.

These are not trivial considerations. The right choice will save you many hours and much aggravation.

Architecture Choices

In selecting a controller chip, you can use a chip designed from the ground up as a standalone USB controller, a chip that's compatible with an existing chip family, or a chip that requires an interface to a generic microcontroller. Which to use depends on your own background and experience as well as the project specifics. Manufacturers frequently release new chips and improved versions of existing chips, so it's always a good idea to check the manufacturers' websites for the latest offerings.

Chips Designed for USB from the Ground Up

Some controllers are designed specifically for USB applications. Instead of adding USB capability to an existing architecture, these designs are optimized for USB from the start. Two sources for this type of chip are Cypress Semiconductor and ScanLogic. Table 7-1 compares the features of a selection of their chips.

Cypress' M8 family has a variety of inexpensive chips that share an instruction set optimized for USB. The enCoRe series has low-speed chips, each with a USB port and 8 to 16 lines of general-purpose I/O. Other M8-series chips have more I/O and support full-speed transfers.

ScanLogic's SL11R contains a BIOS ROM that supports USB's four transfer types. The ROM also has boot-up code that enables executing user firmware either from external parallel memory or by loading code from serial EEPROM to RAM. The chip has 32 general-purpose I/O lines.

Table 7-1: Cypress and ScanLogic have microcontrollers that are designed for USB from the ground up.

Feature	CY7C637XX (enCoRe)	CY7C64113	SL11R
Manufacturer	Cypress	Cypress	ScanLogic
Speed	Low	Full	Full
Number of Endpoints	3	5	4
RAM (bytes)	96	256	3K
Program Memory Type	OTP PROM	OTP PROM	BIOS ROM + serial EEPROM or external parallel memory
Program Memory Size (bytes)	6K-8K	8K	2K internal or 26K external
General Purpose I/O Pins	10-16	32	32
Other I/O capability	SPI, USB or PS/2 option	I^2C, hardware-assisted parallel interface, DAC	parallel data bus, UART, serial EEPROM
Power Supply Voltage	4.0-5.5	4.0-5.25	3.3 ±10%
Number of Pins	18, 24	48	100

Chips Based on Popular Families

Some USB controllers are compatible with existing chip families. These have two advantages. One is that many developers are already familiar with the architecture and instruction set, and familiarity gives a big head start to any project. Certainly if you're designing a USB-capable version of an existing product that uses an 8051 variant, sticking with the 8051 makes sense. But even if you're not already familiar with the architecture, selecting a popular family means that programming and debugging tools are available, and sample code and other advice is likely to be available from other users on the Internet.

If your microcontroller of choice is the 8051, you're in luck. Cypress, Infineon, and Standard Microsystems have 8051-compatible, USB-capable chips. (But not Intel. Although Intel originated the 8051 family and was the first to release 8051-compatible USB controllers with the 8x930 and 8x931,

Table 7-2: Many manufacturers produce USB controllers that are compatible with existing microcontroller families.

Company	Compatibility	Example Chip
AMD	Intel 80C186	AM186
Atmel	Atmel AVR	AT76C711
Cypress	Intel 8051, Dallas Semi DS80C320	AN2121 (EZ-USB series)
Infineon	Intel 8051	C541U
Microchip Technology	Microchip PIC	16C7x5
Mitsubishi	Mitsubishi 740	7640, 7532/36
Motorola	Motorola 68HC05	68HC05JB3/4
	Motorola 68HC08	68HC08JB8
	Motorola Power PC	MPC850 (host or device)
Standard Microsystems (SMSC)	Intel 8051	USB97C100
STMicroelectronics	STMicroelectronics ST7	ST7261

Intel discontinued these in 2000.) Cypress' FX2 series in its 8051-compatible EZ-USB family supports high speed.

Chips compatible with other families are available as well, including Atmel's AVR, Microchip's PIC, and Motorola's 68HC05/8. Table 7-2 lists these and others.

Chips that Interface to an External Microcontroller

Some USB controllers handle only the USB communications and must be controlled by an external microcontroller. These enable you to add a USB port to just about any microcontroller circuit. The downside is that you need two chips, while other USB controllers have both the CPU and the USB controller on a single chip. Also, you may or may not be able to find example circuits and code for the CPU you want to use. Table 7-3 compares a selection of these chips.

The chips have external, local data buses that typically use a synchronous serial or parallel interface to connect to the CPU. An interrupt pin can signal the CPU when the controller has received USB data or needs new data

Table 7-3: A Selection of USB Controllers that Interface to a Generic Microcontroller.

Chip	USS820C	USBN9603	NET2888	PDIUSBD11	PDIUSBD12
Manufacturer	Lucent	National Semiconductor	NetChip	Philips	Philips
Bus Speed	Full	Full	Full	Full	Full
Number of Endpoint addresses	1 control + 14 others	1 control + 6 others	1 control + 5 others	1 control + 6 others	1 control + 4 others
Double Buffered?	yes	no	no	no	yes
Microprocessor Interface	Non-multiplexed parallel	Multiplexed or non-multiplexed parallel, Microwire	Non-multiplexed parallel	I^2C	Multiplexed or non-multiplexed parallel
Power Supply Voltage	3.3	3.3 or 5	3.3	3.3	3.3
Number of Pins	44/48	28	48	16	28
Comments	Programmable FIFO size	Programmable clock output	Occupies 32 bytes of address space	Programmable clock output	Programmable-clock output, status-LED outputs

to send. With some chips, the local-bus interface is slower than USB's maximum transfer rate, so the chip is suitable only for intermittent data.

Netchip's NET2888 uses a parallel data bus with 8 data lines and 5 address lines. It can read and write data at 10 Megabytes per second, or faster in DMA mode. National Semiconductor's USBN9603 has more options. It has a data bus that can transfer multiplexed parallel data, non-multiplexed parallel data, or Microwire synchronous serial data. Microwire requires just four lines and can interface to just about any microcontroller with four spare I/O pins.

Philips Semiconductors offers both the PDIUSBD11 with an I²C interface and the PCIUSBD12 with a parallel interface. Lucent's USS820C has a parallel interface and supports the maximum number of endpoint addresses.

Chip Documentation

The ultimate authority on a chip's abilities is its data sheet, and for chips with CPUs, the documentation for the instruction set. The data sheet documents the hardware, including the functions of the registers and voltages and timing for all pins.

The documentation for the chip's instruction set defines the assembly-code syntax for each of the instructions that the CPU understands. If you're programming in assembly code, these are the instructions you use in writing the firmware. If you're using a higher-level language such as C, you may not need to use the assembly-code instructions at all, though compilers typically allow in-line assembly code.

To supplement the basic documentation, many vendors provide a user manual with more detailed information about how to use the chip.

Sample Firmware

The best way to get a head start on writing firmware is to begin with sample code that's similar to what you want to achieve. Having an example to refer to is much, much easier than trying to put something together from scratch. Chip and tool vendors vary widely in the amount and quality of sample code provided, so it's worth looking into what's available before you commit to a chip.

In some cases you can find code samples from other sources, especially via the Internet, from other users who are willing to share what they've done.

Driver Choices

The other side of programming a USB device is the driver and application software at the host. Here again, samples are useful.

If your device fits into one of the classes supported by Windows, you don't have to worry about writing or finding a device driver. For example, applications can access a HID-class device using standard API functions that communicate with Windows' HID drivers. A chip vendor may offer a sample application, as National Semiconductor does in its sample HID application for the '9603.

Some vendors provide a generic driver that you can use to exchange data with the device. Cypress' EZ-USB is an example. The chip has a unique architecture that enables the PC to load the chip's firmware on attachment. To use this feature, the chip requires a special driver. Cypress' generic driver can load firmware into the chip and can also exchange data using each of the four transfer types.

Chapter 10 has more about device drivers.

Debugging Tools

Ease of debugging also makes a big difference in how easy it is to get a project up and running. Products that can help include development boards and software offered by the chip vendors and other sources.

A protocol analyzer is also very useful during debugging. Protocol analyzers aren't specific to a particular chip. Chapter 17 has more about these and related tools.

Development Boards from Chip Vendors

Chip manufacturers offer development boards and basic debugging software to make it easier for developers to use their chips. A development board enables you to load a program from a PC to the chip's program memory, or to circuits that emulate the chip's hardware.

The debugging software provided with the board is typically a monitor program that enables you to control program execution and watch the results. Standard features include the ability to step through a program line by line, set breakpoints, and view the contents of the chip's registers and memory. You can run the monitor program and a test application at the same time.

Figure 7-1: The I2C/IO board from DeVaSys contains an EZ-USB and a variety of options for I/O.

You can look inside the emulated chip and see exactly what happens when your application communicates with it.

If you have a general-purpose development system for your favorite microcontroller, you can use it for USB developing as well. For example, development tools for Microchip's 16C5x series are also usable with the USB-capable 167Cx5 chips.

Boards from Other Sources

In general, the evaluation kits offered by the manufacturers are well worth the cost. But if you're on a strict budget, there are inexpensive printed-circuit boards that can serve as an alternative. You can also use these boards as the base for one-of-a-kind or small-scale projects, saving you the trouble of designing and making a board to hold the controller chip.

The EZ-USB is a natural choice for this type of board because its firmware is downloadable from the host so you don't have to worry about programming hardware. The I2C/IO board from DeVaSys Embedded Systems (Figure 7-1) contains an AN2131 EZ-USB chip, a connector with 20 bits of I/O, an I²C interface for synchronous serial communications, and an asynchronous serial interface. The on-board 24LC128 is an I²C EEPROM that can store 16 kilobytes of data, including Vendor and Product IDs and firmware. The board can load its firmware from EEPROM or from the host on attachment or power-up.

DeVaSys provides the board's schematic and a free custom device driver that enables applications to open communications and read and write to ports, including the I²C port. If you prefer, you can load your own firmware into the device and use your own driver or a driver provided by Windows. An early version of the I2CIO won an award in *Circuit Cellar* magazine's annual design contest.

Another option for developing is to interface a basic controller like the PDIUSBD11 to a PC's parallel port for debugging code that will eventually reside in a microcontroller. DeVaSys also has a board that takes this approach.

The parallel port has 8 lines that are bidirectional on all but the oldest PCs, plus four outputs and five inputs. PC applications can access the port's bits using port reads and writes. PC software can communicate with the PDIUSBD11's I²C interface by using parallel-port lines as clock and data lines for sending and receiving data.

With this approach, you can write PC applications that perform the functions of the firmware that will eventually control the chip, including sending descriptors during enumeration and whatever other functions the device is responsible for. This approach is most useful if the device firmware will be written in C, because the PC software can also use C and will be somewhat portable. Every controller has chip-specific operations, however, and will require some modifying for the final product.

With all of the available controller chips and the many options for accessing them from PCs, it's likely that many more inexpensive boards will become available in time.

Project Needs

Along with looking for a chip that will be easy to work with, you can further narrow the choice of controllers by specifying your project's needs and looking for chips that meet the needs. These are some of the areas to consider:

How fast does the data need to transfer? A device's rate of data transfer depends on several things: whether the device supports low, full, or high speed, the transfer type being used, and how busy the bus is. As a peripheral designer, you don't control how busy users' buses will be, but you can design your product to work in the worst case expected.

If a product requires no more than low-speed interrupt and control transfers, a low-speed chip may save money not only in chip cost, but also in the circuit-board design and cables. HID-class devices can use low-speed chips. But remember that low-speed devices can transfer only eight data bytes per transaction, and the specification limits the transfer rate of an endpoint to much less than the bus rate of 1.5 Megabits/second. Even if low speed is feasible, don't rule out full speed automatically. You may find a full-speed chip that can do the job at the same or even a lower price.

Devices that support high speed should also support full speed, at least until 2.0 hosts become common.

How many and what type of endpoints do you need? Each endpoint address is configured to support a transfer type and direction. A device that does only control transfers needs just the default endpoint. Interrupt, bulk, or isochronous transfers require additional endpoint addresses. Not all chips support all transfer types.

Do you want the device to be software upgradable? For program memory, many USB devices use windowed EPROM, OTP PROM, or other memory that isn't easily erased and re-written. To change the program, you need to insert a new chip or remove, erase, re-program, and replace the chip. Cypress' EZ-USB has an easier way, with the ability to load firmware from the host into RAM on each power up or attachment. Another option is to store the program code in a microcontroller with electrically reprogrammable memory. ScanLogic's SL11N has the ability to store code received from the host in serial EEPROM. The contents of the EEPROM then load into RAM on power up. The *Device Class Specification for Device Firmware Upgrade,* available from the USB Implementers Forum's website, describes a mechanism for loading firmware from a host to a device.

Do you need a flexible cable? One reason why mice are almost certain to be low-speed devices is that the less stringent requirements for a low-speed cable mean that the cable can be thinner and more flexible. However, 2.0-compliant low-speed cables have the same requirements as full and high speed except that the braided outer shield and twisted pair are recommended, but not required.

Do you need a long cable? Low-speed cables are limited to three meters, while full-speed cables can be five meters.

What other hardware features and abilities do you need? These include everything from general-purpose or specialized I/O, the size of program and data memory, on-chip timers, and so on. As with any embedded computer project, the requirements depend on the application.

A Look at Some Chips

The following descriptions of popular USB controller chips will give an idea of what's available. They include only a sampling, and new chips are being released all the time, so any new project warrants checking the latest offerings.

Cypress enCoRe

The chips in Cypress Semiconductor's enCoRe series (yes, that annoying capitalization is how Cypress has trademarked it) are inexpensive and simple in design. They're intended for applications that transfer small blocks of information at low speed. Examples of uses include standard peripherals such as mice and joysticks, as well as specialized devices such as data-acquisition units and controllers.

CPU Architecture

Unlike most other USB chips, the enCoRe series isn't based on an existing chip family. Using these chips means having to learn a new instruction set. However, the instruction set is small and the instructions are similar to those used by other microcontrollers, Learning the syntax is fairly painless if you have experience with assembly-code programming. A C compiler is also available.

The chips support 37 instructions that cover the basics of moving data, performing mathematical operations, and program branching. Because the instruction set is short, learning it isn't difficult. However, it also means that you won't find fancy instructions that do a lot of the work for you. For example, there are no instructions for multiplying or dividing; all calculations must be done by adding, subtracting, and bit-shifting. (The C compiler has math and other functions.)

The chips in the series share a common architecture, but they vary in the amount of program memory, number of I/O pins, and packaging. The '63743 has 256 bytes of RAM, 8 kilobytes of OTP EPROM for program memory, 16 I/O pins, and is available in both surface-mount and through-hole packaging. The through-hole packages are useful for prototyping on hand-assembled boards because they don't require soldering a tiny surface-mount chip.

The chips contain internal oscillators that eliminate the need to add external crystals or resonators. The USB port can be configured for PS/2 (synchronous serial) communications, which enables a pointing device to support both interfaces.

USB Controller

The simplicity of the enCoRe's design is a benefit but also a limitation. Although the chips comply fully with the USB specification, they don't support the full range of USB capabilities. They're limited to low-speed transfers, which means that they can't use bulk or isochronous transfers. The '63743 has three endpoints, the required Endpoint 0 for control transfers, plus endpoints 1 and 2 for interrupt transfers. The chip can support one interrupt IN endpoint and one interrupt OUT endpoint, or two in the same direction. Some other low-speed chips, especially earlier releases, don't support interrupt OUT endpoints, which were added in USB 1.1. Each endpoint has an 8-byte buffer in RAM.

For project development, Cypress offers a development kit that includes a printed-circuit board with an emulated chip and a monitor program for loading and testing code.

The only memory available for the chips is OTP PROM. This isn't too much of a drawback because the development kit works well for testing. You can test the chips in the product itself when the programming is nearly complete. To program the PROMs, you'll need a device programmer. Cypress offers an inexpensive programmer from Hi-Lo.

The USB communications require a fair amount of firmware support, but Cypress provides example code for common applications.

If you like the chips but need more I/O or full speed, Cypress' CY7C64013 and CY7C64113 are alternatives.

Cypress EZ-USB

Cypress' EZ-USB family is notable for two reasons: it's 8051-compatible, and the chips support a different and flexible approach to storing firmware. Rather than storing the firmware on-chip, an EZ-USB can store its firmware on the host, which loads it into the chip on each power-up or attachment.

Having the firmware stored on the host has pluses and minuses. The obvious advantage—and it's a big one—is easy updates to firmware. To update the firmware, you store the new version on the host and the driver sends it to the device on the next power up or attachment. There's no need to replace the chip or use a special programmer.

The downsides are increased driver complexity, the need to have the firmware available on the host, and longer enumeration time. Cypress helps with the driver by providing the complete source and executable code for a driver that handles the downloading of firmware. You can use the supplied driver as-is, or use the source code as the base for a custom driver.

The EZ-USB also supports storing its firmware in an external serial EEPROM or in parallel EPROM or other non-volatile memory.

The EZ-USB family originated with Anchor Chips, which Cypress acquired in 1999. You may see the name *Anchor* in older documentation.

CPU Architecture

The EZ-USB's architecture is similar to Dallas Semiconductor's DS80C320, which is an 8051 whose core has been redesigned for enhanced performance. The chip uses four clock cycles per instruction cycle, compared to the 8051's twelve. Each instruction takes between one and five instruction cycles. The CPU is clocked at 24 Megahertz. On average, an EZ-USB is 2.5 times as fast as an 8051 with the same clock speed.

The instruction set is compatible with the 8051's. All of the 8-kilobytes of combined code and data memory is RAM; there is no non-volatile memory on-chip. However, the chips do support non-volatile storage in the I^2C serial interface that can read and write to serial EEPROM, or in external parallel memory.

The EZ-USB family includes three series: the basic EZ-USB (AN21XX) and the FX (CY7C646XX) and FX2 (CY7C68013) series. Within each series are chips that vary in features such as the number of I/O pins or availability of an external data bus. Table 7-4 summarizes the features of each series. The FX series adds faster I/O and a general programmable interface that supports configurable, automated handshaking. The FX2 series also supports high speed.

Keil has a C compiler for the EZ-USB, or you can use assembly code. The compiler has a limited but free evaluation version. If you have the full version of the compiler, you can base your code on Cypress' Frameworks firmware, which handles much of the work of USB communications.

USB Controller

Most EZ-USBs support the maximum number of endpoints: one control endpoint, plus 30 additional endpoint addresses and all four transfer types. For simpler designs, chips with fewer capabilities are available. The

Table 7-4: Cypress Semiconductor's EZ-USB family is compatible with the 8051 microcontroller.

Feature	AN21xx (EZ-USB)	CY7C646xx (EZ-USB-FX)	CY7C68013 (EZ-USB-FX2)
Speed	Full	Full	Full/High
Number of endpoints	13, 16, 31	31	11
Compatibility	80C320, 8051	80C320, 8051	80C320, 8051
RAM (bytes)	256 + 4-8K combined data and program memory	256 + 4-8K combined data and program memory	256 + 8K combined data and program memory
Program memory type	RAM, serial EEPROM, external parallel	RAM, serial EEPROM, external parallel	RAM, serial EEPROM, external parallel
Internal program memory (bytes)	4-8K combined data and program memory	4-8K combined data and program memory	8K combined data and program memory
External memory bus (bytes)	64K	64K	one or two 64K
General-purpose I/O pins	16-24	16-40	16-40
Other I/O	2 UARTs, I^2C	2 UARTs, I^2C	2 UARTs, I^2C
Power Supply Voltage	3-3.6	3-3.6	3-3.6
Number of Pins	44, 48, 80	52, 80, 128	56, 100, 128

EZ-USB's many options for storing firmware make its architecture more complicated compared to other chips. The options are useful because they make the chip very flexible, so I'll describe them in some detail.

When an EZ-USB wants to use firmware stored in the host, it enumerates twice. When an EZ-USB attaches to the bus, the host attempts to enumerate it, as it would for any device. But how can it enumerate a device with no stored firmware? The answer is that the chip contains an EZ-USB core that knows how to respond to enumeration requests. This core controls communications when the device first attaches to the bus. The EZ-USB core is independent from the 8051 core that normally takes control when the chip has completed the enumeration process. The EZ-USB core communicates with the host while holding the normal 8051 circuits in the reset state.

The EZ-USB core also responds to vendor-specific requests that enable the chip to receive, store, and run firmware received from the host. For basic testing, the core circuits can also enable the device to transfer data using all four transfer types, without any firmware programming.

The ReNum register bit determines whether the EZ-USB or 8051 core responds to requests at Endpoint 0. On power-up, ReNum is zero and the EZ-USB core controls Endpoint 0. When ReNum is set to one, the 8051 core controls Endpoint 0.

The source of an EZ-USB's firmware depends on two things: the contents of the initial bytes in an external EEPROM and the state of the chip's EA input. On power-up and before enumeration, the EZ-USB core attempts to read bytes from a serial EEPROM on the chip's I²C interface. The result, along with the state of the chip's EA input, tell the core what to do next: use the default mode, load firmware from the host, load firmware from EEPROM, or boot from code memory on the external parallel data bus.

Default Mode. The default mode is the most basic mode of operation. It doesn't use the serial EEPROM or other external memory. The EZ-USB core uses this mode if EA is a logic low and the core detects no EEPROM, or if the first byte read from EEPROM is not B0h or B2h.

When the host enumerates the device, the EZ-USB core responds to requests. During this time, the 8051 core is held in the reset state. This reset state is controlled by a register bit in the chip. The host can write directly to this bit to place the chip in and out of reset. This reset affects the 8051 circuits and is unrelated to USB's Reset signaling.

The descriptors retrieved by the host identify the device as a Default USB Device. The host matches the retrieved Vendor and Product IDs with values in a Cypress-provided INF file that instructs the host to load Cypress' General Purpose Driver to communicate with the chip. The ReNum bit remains at zero.

This default mode is intended for use in debugging. You can use it to get the USB interface up and transferring data. In addition to supporting transfers over Endpoint 0, the Default USB Device can also use the other three transfer types on other endpoints. All of this is possible without having to write any firmware or device drivers.

Identify the Device from EEPROM Bytes. The core can also read identifying bytes from the EEPROM on power-up, and then provide this information to the host during enumeration. If the first value read from the EEPROM is B0h, the core reads EEPROM bytes containing the chip's Vendor and Product IDs and Version Number. When the host enumerates the device the first time, it uses these bytes to find a matching INF file that identifies a driver for the device. The driver contains the firmware to download before re-enumerating. Cypress provides instructions for building a driver with this ability.

The driver uses the vendor-specific Firmware Load request to download the firmware to the device. The firmware contains a new set of descriptors and the code the device needs to carry out its purpose. For example, a HID-class device will have report descriptors and code for transferring HID report data.

On completing the download, the driver causes the chip to exit the reset state and run the firmware. The firmware electrically simulates removal from, then reattachment to the bus by writing to a register that controls the chip's DISCON# pin. The pin either pulls up or floats (provides no connection to) one end of a resistor whose opposite end connects to D+. The pin indicates device attachment when pulled up and simulated device removal when floating. The firmware also sets ReNum to 1 to cause the 8051 core, instead of the EZ-USB core, to respond to Endpoint 0 requests.

When the host detects the simulated re-attachment, it enumerates the device again, this time retrieving the newly stored descriptors and using the information in them to select a device driver to load. Cypress has trademarked the term ReNumeration to describe this process.

Load Firmware from EEPROM. A third mode of operation provides a way for the chip to store its own firmware. If the first byte read from the EEPROM is B2H, the core loads the EEPROM's entire contents into RAM on power-up. The EEPROM must contain the Vendor ID, Product ID, and Version Number bytes as well as all descriptors required for enumeration and whatever other code and data the device requires to carry out its purpose. When the chip exits the reset state, it has everything it needs for USB communications. The core sets the ReNum bit to 1 on completing the loading of the code. When the host enumerates the device, it reads the stored descriptors and loads the appropriate driver. There is no re-enumeration.

Run Code from External Parallel Memory. If no EEPROM is detected, or if the first byte isn't B0h or B6h, and if EA is a logic high, the chip boots from code memory on the external parallel data bus. This memory can be EPROM, EEPROM, FLASH EPROM, or battery-backed RAM. The memory contains the descriptors and other firmware. ReNum is set to 1. The host enumerates the device and loads a driver, and there is no re-enumeration.

Microchip PIC 16C7x5

Microchip's PIC microcontrollers have many devotees because of their low cost, wide availability, many variants, speed, low power consumption, and simple instruction set. The 16C745 and 16C765 are PICs with low-speed USB ports.

Architecture

The chips are enhanced members of Microchip's 16C5x series. Code written for the 16C5x is portable to the 16C7x5. The chips support 35 instructions.

In addition to the USB interface, there are 19 I/O pins, plus the '65 has an 8-bit parallel slave port for connecting to a microcontroller with an external data bus. Up to 8 of the I/O pins can function as analog-to-digital converter inputs. A USART supports asynchronous and synchronous serial communications. The chips have three timers.

A crystal or ceramic resonator can clock the chip. Program memory is EPROM or OTP PROM. The chips are available in through-hole and surface-mount packages.

USB Controller

The chips support Endpoint 0 plus Endpoints 1 and 2 in any combination of IN and OUT. To manage communications, there are 7 status and control registers, plus each endpoint has a control register and a 4-byte buffer descriptor. The microcontroller and the bus share access to the buffer descriptors, which contain information such as the data-toggle state and the number of bytes received or to be transferred. The chip supports firmware simulation of attaching to and removal from the bus.

Like the enCoRes, these chips require a fair amount of firmware support. Microchip provides assembly and C code for enumeration and other standard USB tasks. For HIDs, there is example mouse code that you can adapt for other HID applications.

NetChip NET2888

NetChip's NET2888 doesn't contain a general-purpose CPU or memory. It has only a USB controller and an interface to a generic data bus, which you can connect to any CPU that has a complimentary bus.

Architecture

The NET2888 has no program or data memory other than its USB buffers. The local bus has five address bits (A0 - A4) and eight data bits (D0-D7) to enable reading and writing bytes to 32 addresses.

Transferring data over the local bus uses a ChipSelect line to select the chip and separate IOR and IOW signals to control reads and writes. Most microcontrollers that support external data buses can use this interface with little or no added logic.

The chip also supports direct memory access (DMA) transfers, for the fastest possible transfer of blocks of data. The CPU that the NET2888 connects to must also support DMA. In a DMA transfer, the chip takes control of the local bus. Once the DMA transfer is requested, the transfer of a block of data to or from memory occurs without requiring the external CPU to initiate individual read and write operations.

The chip reserves a block of memory to hold the data that will transfer. A DMA address counter holds the address of the block, and a DMA byte counter holds the number of bytes left to transfer. In a host-to-device transfer, on receiving USB data, the device copies the data into the reserved memory. In a device-to-host transfer, the device copies data into the transmit buffer whenever space is available.

The chip responds to the standard control requests without requiring any firmware support other than storing the appropriate information (such as Vendor and Product IDs) in registers.

USB Controller

The NET2888 supports five endpoints and all four transfer types:

Endpoint Number	Transfer Type(s) Supported
0	control
1	bulk OUT
2	interrupt IN
3	bulk or isochronous OUT
4	bulk or isochronous IN

The 32 bytes that the CPU can access using the address and data buses correspond to registers in the chip. For Endpoints 1 and 2, the peripheral's CPU can send and receive USB data using two 8-byte mailbox registers. Each mailbox's data uses a single address on the local bus, with a second address containing an index that indicates the byte in the mailbox to be read or written to. For Endpoints 3 and 4, the peripheral's CPU can send and receive USB data using two 64-byte buffers. Each buffer uses a single address, with a count register that indicates the number of data bytes in the buffer.

The NET2888 automatically stores data received from the host. To detect data received from the host at Endpoint 1, the peripheral's CPU can poll the chip's receive-mailbox-valid bit or respond to an interrupt that occurs when the bit is set.

To send data from Endpoint 2 to the host, the peripheral's CPU writes the data to the transmit mailbox and sets the chip's transmit-mailbox-valid bit. The NET2888 then handles the details of sending the USB data.

Other registers hold various status and handshaking values and configuration information.

The peripheral's CPU is responsible for writing some configuration information to the NET2888's registers. But because the endpoints are configured in hardware, there's less to do than for other chips.

National Semiconductor USBN9603

National Semiconductor's USBN9603 is another chip that requires an interface to a microcontroller. It can interface to any microcontroller with a parallel data bus, a Microwire interface, or even just four spare I/O pins controlled entirely in firmware

Architecture

The '9603 has a serial interface engine for handling USB transmissions, a set of USB endpoint buffers, and a series of status and control registers. A CPU can access the endpoint buffers and status and control registers at addresses 00h through 3Fh via an external, local bus.

The chip offers three options for accessing the local data bus: non-multiplexed parallel, multiplexed parallel, and Microwire synchronous serial.

Multiplexed parallel transfers read or write a byte of data in one bus cycle. The address is latched with ALE, and the data with RD or WR. Most microcontrollers with external data buses can use these signals with little or no additional logic.

For non-multiplexed parallel transfers, the '9603 transfers both data and addresses on D0-D7, but in separate bus cycles. One bus cycle sends the address to the '9603, and another transfers data to or from the chip. To save on bus accesses, the chip supports a burst mode where the CPU writes a starting address to the controller chip, and then transmits or receives multiple bytes that go to consecutive addresses. The external CPU must also support this mode. The parallel interface also supports DMA transfers.

Not all microcontrollers have an external parallel data bus, and for those that don't, the '9603 offers a solution in its Microwire interface. Microwire is a synchronous serial interface that uses four lines: the two data lines SIN (serial in) and SOUT (serial out), CS (chip select), and SYNC (the clock line). Command/address and data bytes shift in and out, bit by bit, using transitions on the SYNC line as a timing reference. The external CPU controls SYNC. There is no minimum SYNC frequency, and the signal doesn't have to have a constant frequency; the CPU can toggle line as needed. The interface just has to be fast enough to keep up with the USB traffic. If the USB port transfers only small, occasional blocks of data, you can program a Microwire interface in firmware without having to worry about critical timing. Some microcontrollers, such as National Semiconductor's COP888, have Microwire interfaces built in.

USB Controller

The '9603 supports seven endpoint addresses: Endpoint 0 for control transfers, three IN endpoints, and three OUT endpoints. Endpoint 0's buffer is 8 bytes; the others are 64 bytes. An endpoint may also send or receive packets larger than the buffer size, if the firmware reads data from the buffer as it arrives to prevent the buffer from overflowing, or writes data to the buffer as it transmits to prevent the buffer from emptying before all of the data has transmitted.

Philips Semiconductors PDIUSBD11/12

Philips Semiconductors offers additional choices for minimal USB controllers in its PDIUSBD11 and PDIUSBD12.

Architecture

The chips are similar except for their external data buses. The '12 has a parallel data bus, while the '11 has an I²C bus. Like Microwire, I²C is a synchronous serial bus. It requires just two signal wires: serial clock (SCL) and a bidirectional serial-data line (SDA). In a typical transfer, the CPU sends a command that specifies the function of the data to follow, followed by transmitted or received data. The bus can transfer data at up to 1 Megabit per second, and some of the bits are commands. So although the USB interface is full speed, the local bus limits the amount of USB data that the chip can send and receive in a period of time. There is no minimum speed for SCK. Some microcontrollers have built-in I²C interfaces.

Like National Semiconductor's USBN9603, Philips' PDIUSBD12 supports multiplexed, non-multiplexed, and DMA parallel transfers. The interface can transfer data at up to 2 Megabytes per second.

Instead of using status and control registers, the chips respond to commands for performing functions such as selecting an endpoint or reading or writing to a buffer.

USB Controller

Both chips are full speed. The '12 supports a control endpoint and four additional endpoint addresses. One endpoint's buffer holds up to 128 bytes, with double buffering for a total of 256 bytes. The '11 supports a control endpoint and six additional endpoint addresses with 8-byte buffers.

On both chips, the USB connection is under firmware control. The chip appears detached from the host until the peripheral's CPU sends a command to simulate attachment to the bus. This ensures that the chip has time to initialize on power-up before being enumerated by the host. A status output on the '12 can connect to an LED that lights when a USB connection has been established and blinks on data transfers.

Intel StrongARM

An example of a high-end controller with USB capability is Intel's StrongARM series. The StrongARM is a 32-bit CPU designed for use in portable, wireless, multimedia devices. USB communications isn't the primary purpose of the StrongARM, but it has a full-speed peripheral interface with three endpoints that support control, bulk OUT, and bulk IN transfers.

Chapter 7

8

Inside a USB Controller: the Cypress enCoRe

Now that you know something about the USB protocols and the controller chips available for USB peripherals, it's time to take a closer look at a controller chip and how to use it. The chip I've chosen for the examples in the book is the CY7C63743 in Cypress Semiconductor's enCoRe series.

This chapter explains how I chose the chip to use for my examples, then describes the chip and its abilities in detail. Because describing the hardware often involves showing code that accessing the hardware, I've also included information about the chip's assembler and C compiler. The focus as always is on what you'll need to know to put the chip to use. No matter which chip your project uses, this chapter will give you an idea of how USB controllers carry out their responsibilities.

Selecting a Chip

If you're going to design a USB peripheral, you eventually need to decide which controller chip the peripheral will contain. The same principle holds true for the examples in this book. In order to show application examples, I need to choose a chip to base the examples on. So the first order of business is selecting the chip.

Requirements

A major purpose of this book is to show how to design and program a USB peripheral. I wanted to use a chip that would be suitable for simple monitoring and control projects. The focus is on getting a basic design up and running quickly, rather than on supporting a complex design and every capability of USB. With this in mind, I decided to look for these features in a chip:

- Easy to learn. A simple design is good.

- Contains a microcontroller, rather than requiring an interface to an external microcontroller. This keeps the design simpler and avoids the issue of which microcontroller to interface to.

- Supports interrupt transfers. One of the easiest ways to communicate with a USB device is using Windows' HID drivers. The drivers use interrupt and control transfers for transferring data in both directions.

- Inexpensive.

- Available.

- Has an easy-to-use development system. The development system should enable transferring of code from a PC to the controller, viewing the code and chip registers, and debugging using functions such as single-stepping and breakpoints.

- Reprogrammable. A chip whose program memory is easily reprogrammed makes development simpler and cheaper.

- Available sample code. This provides a quick start in developing firmware and application software.

The Choice

There are many excellent products available, and the truth is that no chip meets every requirement perfectly. Every controller I've seen supports interrupt transfers, so that part is easy. Cypress' products rose to the top of the list because Cypress has done a very good job of supporting developers with example code and documentation. Cypress' EZ-USB is a powerful chip and requires no PROM programming, but its complexity means that it's likely to be programmed in C, requiring an expensive C compiler.

In the end, I decided on Cypress' enCoRe series. The chips aren't reprogrammable, except by swapping the PROM, but the development system enables testing code before storing it in PROM. The development system costs a little more than I'd like, but the chips themselves are inexpensive. The chips are low speed, which limits their performance, but makes printed-circuit-board design less critical. The USB communications require a fair amount of firmware support, but you can begin with example code that includes the essentials and change only the portions that are specific to your application. The instruction set is simple enough that you can use the free assembler.

The specific chip I'll use is the CY7C63743. It can do USB communications and generic I/O. There are no external buses; the chip stands alone as a complete controller for managing USB communications and other processing.

If you're using a different chip, following my examples will give you a head start on figuring out what you'll need to do. Even if you need a full-speed interface or a custom driver, the examples will introduce many topics that are relevant to all USB devices.

The Assembler

Before getting into the details about the chip, it's helpful to know a little about how to program it. The enCoRe's CPU supports 37 instructions. Everything that the firmware does must use these instructions. Cypress provides a free assembler for converting the assembly code you write into object files for programming into the chip's EPROM. If you prefer to program in C, Cypress also offers a C compiler.

If you have experience with microcontroller assembly-language programming, programming for the enCoRe will be familiar. If you're used to programming in Basic, C, or another high-level language, the limited operations available in assembly code may come as a shock. There are no for or while loops, no fancy variable types, and no object-oriented anything. But for a chip like the enCoRe, which is intended for fairly uncomplicated control and monitoring tasks, using assembly code is feasible. For short programs, the code is manageable and executes quickly. And there are no compilers to buy.

This book isn't a tutorial on assembly-language programming, but I'll present some basic information for beginners, as well as specific details about the enCoRe for those who have programming experience and want to see how the Cypress chip compares.

Assembly Programming Basics

An assembly-language program contains a series of instructions, each corresponding to a machine code that the chip supports. For example, the instruction iord, which reads an I/O location, corresponds to the code 29h. Instead of having to remember 29h, you can write iord, and the assembler will translate for you. The iord instruction also requires an operand that specifies the location to read. For example, iord 01h reads the port at address 01h.

An assembly-language program may also contain directives and comments. A directive is an instruction for the assembler, rather than for the CPU. Directives enable you to assign locations in program memory, define variables, and in general instruct the assembler to perform operations besides specifying what machine-code instructions to execute. A semicolon (;) or double slash (//) introduces a comment, which the assembler ignores.

The assembler provided by Cypress, *cyasm.exe*, is a command-line program that you can run in a DOS window. Cypress provides a User's Guide that documents the instructions, directives, and how to use the assembler.

The assembler supports two similar instruction sets, for the A- and B-series CPUs. The enCore chips are B-series. Cypress' older chips, such as the '63001, are A-series and support all but a few of the same instructions.

Assembler Codes

The User's Guide has complete documentation for the assembly codes and directives, and I won't repeat the details here. Table 8-1 is a summary of the codes, and Table 8-2 is a summary of the directives. The chip's machine codes translate to 37 instructions, with some supporting multiple sources or destinations.

The instructions do basic arithmetic and logic functions, program branching and control, and copying of data to and from registers, ports, and RAM. Two flag bits, the carry flag and zero flag, provide additional information, such as whether an add instruction resulted in an overflow or whether the result of an instruction is zero.

The chip supports three addressing modes that determine how an instruction uses its operand. Not all instructions support all three addressing modes.

In immediate addressing, the instruction uses the operand's value directly. This instruction uses immediate addressing to add 60h to the value in the accumulator.

```
Add A, 60h
```

In direct addressing, the instruction treats the operand as an address and uses the value stored at that address. This instruction uses direct addressing to add the value stored at address 60h in RAM to the contents of the accumulator:

```
Add A, [60h]
```

In indexed addressing, the instruction uses the data stored at an address obtained by adding a value to the contents of the X register. Indexed addressing is useful for copying blocks of data. The X register holds the starting address of data to be copied. The code adds an index value to the contents of the X register to obtain the address of a byte to copy. By incre-

Table 8-1: The Cyasm assembler supports 37 assembly-language instructions for the enCoRe. (Sheet 1 of 2)

Instruction Type	Instruction	Description
Arithmetic and logic functions	ADD	Add without carry
	ADC	Add with carry
	AND	Bitwise AND
	ASL	Arithmetic shift left
	ASR	Arithmetic shift right
	CMP	Non-destructive compare
	CPL	Complement accumulator
	DEC	Decrement
	INC	Increment
	OR	Bitwise OR
	RLC	Rotate left through carry
	RRC	Rotate right through carry
	SUB	subtract without borrow
	SBB	Subtract with borrow
	XOR	Bitwise XOR
Program branching and control	CALL	Call function
	HALT	Halt execution
	RETI	Return from interrupt
	JACC	Jump accumulator
	JC	Jump if carry
	JMP	Jump
	JNC	Jump if no carry
	JNZ	Jump if not zero
	JZ	Jump if zero
	RET	Return
	XPAGE	Memory page

Table 8-1: The Cyasm assembler supports 37 assembly-language instructions for the enCoRe. (Sheet 2 of 2)

Instruction Type	Instruction	Description
Moving data	INDEX	Table read
	IORD	Read I/O
	IOWR	Write I/O
	IOWX	Indexed I/O write
	MOV	Move
	POP	POP data stack into accumulator
	PUSH	PUSH accumulator into data stack
	SWAP	Swap
Other	DI	Disable interrupts
	EI	Enable interrupts
	NOP	No operation

menting the index value after each copy, the code can step through a block of data.

Using the Assembler

The assembler uses a command-line interface that you can run from a DOS window. This command:

```
cyasm test.asm
```

assembles the file *test.asm*.

The assembler creates three files:

test.rom is the assembled code in a format for use with the Development Kit. You can use this file to load the code from a PC to the development board's RAM.

Here is a portion of a *.rom* file as it appears when loaded into a text editor:

```
80 99 80 10 80 15 81 24
80 8C 80 99 80 85 80 10
2D 1A 20 1E 20 2D 2A 21
1A 37 16 00 A0 20 27 37
```

Table 8-2: The Cyasm assembler supports 13 directives.

Directive	Description
CPU	Product specification
DB	Define byte
DS	Define ASCII string
DSU	Define UNICODE string
DW	Define word (2 bytes)
DWL	Define word with little endian ordering
EQU	Equate label to variable value
FILLROM	Define value for unused program memory
INCLUDE	Include source file
MACRO	Macro definition
ORG	Origin
XPAGEON	XPAGE enable
XPAGEOFF	XPAGE disable

The file contains lines consisting of eight ASCII hex bytes with a space between each and a carriage return/line feed at the end.

In ASCII hex format, each byte is represented by two ASCII codes, with each code representing a hexadecimal character. For example, the byte 80h is represented by the ASCII codes 38h for *8*, and 30h for *0*. Using ASCII hex format enables you to easily view the byte values (*80* in the example) in a text editor. When the code is stored in the development board's RAM, the RAM contains the binary bytes represented by the ASCII Hex bytes. For example, 80h translates to 10000000 in binary.

test.hex is the assembled code in Intel Hex format. Many EPROM programmers, including the Hi-Lo programmer available from Cypress, support this format. The Development Kit can use this format as well, instead of the *.rom* format. Intel Hex format uses ASCII hex characters and adds checksums for error-checking and addressing information to enable the file to specify where each line of bytes should be stored.

Here is the same data in one line of a **.hex* file (the line wraps on the page):

```
:20000000809980108015812480BC8099808580102D1A201E202D
2A211A371600A0202737A1
```

test.lst is the listing file generated by the assembler. It shows each line of the assembly code and comments, along with the program code generated from it and the address where each byte will be stored. The listing file is useful when you're using the monitor program. For example, if you want to stop program execution at a breakpoint, you can use the listing file to find the address that corresponds to the line of code where you want to break.

Here is an excerpt from a **.lst* file, showing an interrupt-service routine for Endpoint 1:

```
03BC                    endpoint1:
03BC 2D     [05]        push     A
03BD
03BD                    ; change data toggle
03BD 19 80 [04]         mov             A, 80h
03BF 37 21 [07]         xor             [ep1_data_toggle], A
03C1
03C1 19 00 [04]         mov             A,NO_EVENT_PENDING
03C3 31 2D [05]         mov             [event_machine], A
03C5
03C5                    ; set response
03C5 1A 29 [06]         mov             A, [ep1_stall]
03C7 16 FF [04]         cmp             A, FFh
03C9 B3 CF [05]         jnz             endpoint1_done
03CB 19 03 [04]         mov             A, STALL_IN_OUT
03CD 2A 14 [05]         iowr            ep1_mode
03CF
03CF                    endpoint1_done:
03CF 2B     [04]        pop             A
03D0 73     [08]        reti
```

The leftmost column is the address in program memory. The address doesn't change when a line contains only a comment or label. The next two columns are the bytes stored at each address. For example, at location 03CD, 2Ah is the code for `iowr`, and 14h identifies the register to write to. The next column is the number of clock cycles the instruction uses (5). The rightmost columns contain the assembly code and comments.

Programming in C

Another option for developing code for these Cypress chips is the C compiler and development environment. These tools were developed by Byte-Craft, a provider of C compilers for many embedded-controller families.

Advantages to C

Compared to assembly-language programming, C has several advantages:

- Standardization. If you're an experienced C programmer, you know the syntax and can get a quick start. You may be able to use C code written for another chip with minimal changes.

- More structures. Instead of being confined to simple jumps, your code can use structures like `if...else` and `case` statements and `for` and `do...while` loops.

- More operators. The compiler supports many more math and relational operators than the assembler. You can add, subtract, multiply, divide, and do a variety of comparisons.

- Libraries and examples. The included libraries will save you much time in performing common functions. There are libraries for a firmware UART, I²C and Microwire interfaces, delay timing, LCD and keypad interfacing, and more math functions. The examples include complete code for a keyboard and mouse/trackball.

- Optimization. The compiler optimizes the code for compactness and speed.

The downside is that you have to buy the compiler, while the assembler is free. But it's likely that the time saved with even a single project will justify the expense.

Using the Compiler

You can run the compiler from DOS or use the included Windows-based BCLIDE development environment (Figure 8-1). BCLIDE enables you to

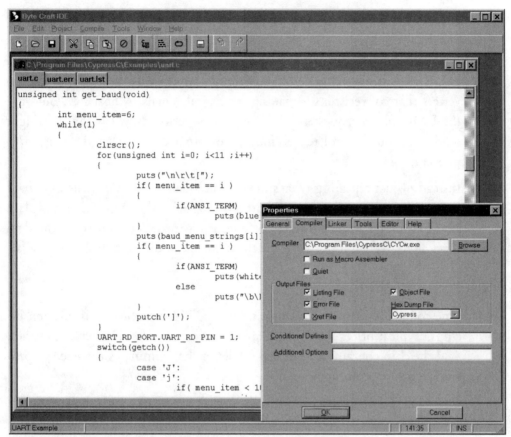

Figure 8-1: Byte Craft's C compiler includes a development environment that enables you to set project options and edit and compile code.

create a project, add files, define file paths, and set compiler and editor options. You can edit source-code files and compile and link the file or files to create executable code. The compiler can create a file in Intel hex or *.rom* format.

Chip Architecture

Chapter 7 introduced the enCoRe series. The chips are inexpensive and simple in design. They're intended for use in applications that transfer small blocks of information at moderate speeds. Uses include standard peripherals such as mice and other pointing devices, as well as specialized devices such as data-acquisition units and controllers.

For example, a data acquisition unit might send periodic sensor readings to a PC. The controller chip's I/O pins could connect to analog-to-digital converters that convert sensor readings to digital signals. A host PC could use the USB link to request the latest readings periodically. Or the PC might send signals to control relays, motors, or other devices that the chip's I/O pins control.

Instead of just repeating what's in the chip's data sheet, I'll focus on what's important to know before you start working with the chip. I'll also explain anything that I found difficult or confusing to understand from the data sheet alone. When it's time to use the chip, check the data sheet for details.

Features and Limits

One compelling reason for choosing the '63743 for a project is inexpensive chips. Typical prices for the chip are a few dollars each in small quantities. And the chip contains an internal oscillator that eliminates the need to provide an external timing reference.

The chip is available in both through-hole (DIP) and surface-mount (SOIC) packages. If you have experience with assembly-language programming (or are willing to learn), the assembly-code instructions aren't too hard to master. The chip has 8 Kilobytes of program memory. With optimization, the code required to support USB communications can fit in 1 Kilobyte, leaving 7 Kilobytes for other functions.

The essential tool for developing is the Developer's Kit, which includes a development board, assembler, and debugging application. You'll probably also want the CY3649 Hi-Lo PROM Programmer with the adapter base and matrix card for the enCoRes, all available from Cypress.

The '63743 isn't suitable for every project. The chip is low speed, which means that you can't use bulk or isochronous transfers and the fastest maximum latency for interrupt transfers is 8 bytes per 10 milliseconds. Unlike some early controllers, the '63743 does support Interrupt OUT transfers. If

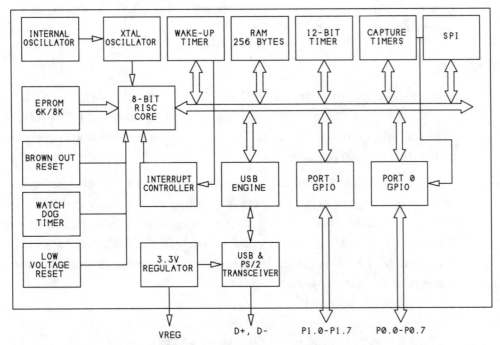

Figure 8-2: The chips in Cypress' enCoRe series have the essentials for USB communications and general port I/O.

you can get by with less memory or I/O, the series has chips with 6K of program memory and twelve I/O pins.

Inside the Chip

Figure 8-2 shows the chip's architecture. The CPU is an 8-bit RISC (reduced instruction set computer). It can access program memory, RAM, general-purpose I/O ports, and of course, a USB port. The USB port is actually an auto-switching port that supports both USB and the PS/2 interface for mice and other pointing devices. This feature is handy for designing devices that can plug into either port type. A variety of interrupt and reset sources can interrupt the CPU.

The frequency of the internal 6-Megahertz oscillator is accurate to within 1.5%, as required for low-speed USB. If an application requires a more precise clock source, the chip can instead use an external oscillator.

Figure 8-3 shows the pinouts of the '63743 and the '63723, which has four fewer I/O pins.

Memory

The on-chip memory of the '63743 consists of 8 kilobytes (0000h to 1FFFh) of OTP PROM for program storage and 256 bytes of RAM (00h to FFh) for temporary data storage. There are also 34 byte-wide I/O registers, each with a defined purpose.

The organization of the program memory is similar to that of other micro-controllers. Program execution begins at 00h. Addresses 00h and 01h contain a jump to the address where the main program code begins. Addresses 02h through 17h are interrupt vectors that hold the addresses to jump to when one of the chip's eleven interrupts occurs. Here is an example inter-rupt-vector table in firmware:

```
ORG 00h
jmp   reset       ; device reset
jmp   bus_reset   ; USB reset interrupt
jmp   error       ; 128-microsecond interrupt
jmp   1ms_timer   ; 1.024-millisecond interrupt
jmp   endpoint0   ; Endpoint 0 interrupt
```

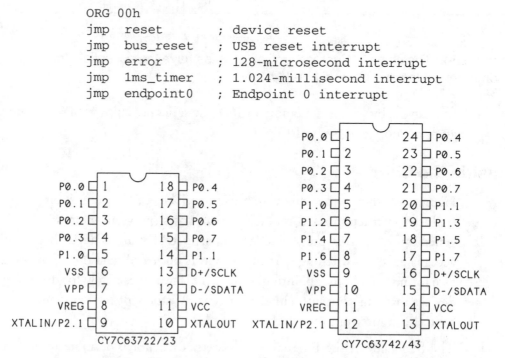

Figure 8-3: The enCoRe series includes chips with 12 and 16 I/O pins.

```
jmp   endpoint1   ; Endpoint 1 interrupt
jmp   endpoint2   ; Endpoint 2 interrupt
jmp   spi         ; SPI interrupt
jmp   capture_a   ; Capture timer A interrupt
jmp   capture_b   ; Capture timer B interrupt
jmp   gpio        ; GPIO interrupt
jmp   wakeup      ; Wake-up interrupt
```

Each interrupt vector jumps to the location specified by a label. Unused interrupts should never occur, but the firmware should include jumps even for these interrupts. A typical interrupt-service routine (ISR) for an unused interrupt would just return the firmware to the calling location with registers unchanged.

The interrupt vectors are stored in order of priority, with the highest priority at 0002h. Program memory from 0018h to 1FDFh is available for storing the rest of the code.

The 256 bytes of RAM must hold two data stacks and 8 bytes each of buffer data for Endpoints 0, 1, and 2 (if all are used), as well as any other temporary data (Figure 8-4). The endpoint buffers use addresses E8h through FFh.

The stacks are last in, first out (LIFO) structures for short-term storage of addresses and register contents. The RAM has two pointers for accessing the two stacks. The Program Stack Pointer (PSP) begins at 00h on reset and grows up, while the Data Stack Pointer (DSP) may be set by firmware to E8h or lower and grows down. The firmware needs to be sure that the stacks don't grow so large that they bump into each other in the middle. To reserve general-purpose RAM for other uses, such as storage for variables, set the DSP to an address lower than E8h. This frees the locations from that address through E7h for other uses without having to worry that one of the stacks will overwrite them.

The Program Stack Pointer

The Program Stack Pointer (PSP) holds the address the code will jump to on returning from a call to a subroutine or interrupt-service routine. For interrupts, the PSP also stores the states of the zero and carry flags. The firmware

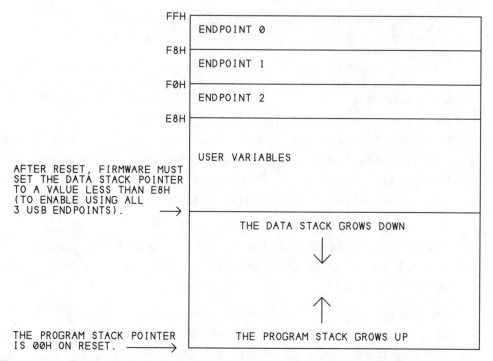

Figure 8-4: The enCoRe's RAM contains the USB endpoint buffers, the program and data stacks, and whatever variables the firmware requires.

doesn't have to do anything to manage the PSP. It's all done automatically by the hardware and the CALL, RET, and RETI instructions.

On reset, the PSP points to 00h. The PSP can handle multiple, nested subroutines and interrupts. Each routine returns to the instruction after the last instruction that executed before the call.

For example, if the PSP is pointing to 00h when an instruction in program memory calls a subroutine, the CALL instruction will cause the PSP to save the address of the following instruction in addresses 00h and 01h. The CALL also increments the PSP by two bytes (to 02h in the example) so it's ready to store another location if needed. The RET instruction that returns from the routine places the value pointed to by the PSP in the program counter and decrements the PSP by two. Program execution then continues where it left off before the routine was called.

The same thing happens in interrupt-service routines, except that the values of the zero and carry flags are also saved and restored.

The Data Stack Pointer

The Data Stack Pointer (DSP) holds data stored by PUSH instructions. For example, PUSH A stores the contents of the accumulator on the data stack. The DSP decrements one byte before storing a byte. A POP instruction removes the most recently stored byte and increments the DSP.

The default value of DSP on reset is *not* where it should remain. Unless the chip isn't using USB at all, the firmware *must* set the DSP to a new value before doing any PUSH instructions. On reset, the DSP is 00h. From here, the first PUSH instruction would cause the DSP to decrement to the top of RAM (FFh), which is byte 7 in Endpoint 0's buffer. For this reason, before pushing any bytes, the firmware should set the DSP pointer to E8h or lower:

```
; Store the DSP's new beginning address
; in the accumulator.
mov A, 70h
; Swap the contents of the accumulator with the DSP.
swap A, dsp
```

Use a lower value if you want to reserve more bytes for firmware use, or a higher value the firmware needs fewer bytes.

USB Communications

The firmware monitors and controls the serial interface engine (SIE) by accessing registers. There are nine registers whose functions relate directly to USB communications: an address register, three endpoint mode registers, three endpoint counter registers, a status and control register, and an interrupt-enable register.

Device Address

The **USB Device Address Register** holds the 7-bit address assigned by the host during enumeration. The firmware must detect the Set_Address request, send a handshake in response to the request, and store the received address in this register. Bit 7 must be set to 1 to enable the serial interface engine to respond to USB traffic.

Modes

The **USB Endpoint 0 Mode Register** contains information about the last received data packet at Endpoint 0. Both the SIE and firmware can change the register's contents.

Three PID bits indicate the type of the transaction's token packet: Setup, IN, or OUT. During the data phase of a Setup transaction, the SIE sets the Setup bit to 1. To prevent incoming data from being overwritten, the chip doesn't allow firmware to write to any USB buffer while the Setup bit is 1. Firmware can't change this bit until all of the transaction's data bytes have been received.

The ACK bit is set when a transaction completes with ACK.

Four Mode bits determine how the SIE will respond to Setup, IN, and OUT transactions. Depending on the type of transaction, the firmware can request the SIE to return ACK, NAK, Stall, a 0-byte data packet, or nothing at all. In some cases, the SIE changes the mode after a transaction's ACK. For example, when the mode is Ack OUT, after returning an ACK in response to receiving OUT data, the SIE sets the mode to Nak OUT. This gives the firmware time to retrieve the data that was ACKed. After retrieving the data, the firmware can change the mode bits back to Ack OUT to enable accepting new data at the endpoint.

For me, understanding the use of these mode bits was the most confusing part in using these chips. Cypress provides four pages of documentation about how the chip responds in every circumstance. I found it useful to group the modes according to what type of endpoint would use them, and in what situations. Table 8-3 shows the modes used by Endpoint 0. Each of these modes accepts Setup transactions, as control endpoints must.

The complements to Endpoint 0's mode register are the **USB Endpoint 1 Mode Register** and **USB Endpoint 2 Mode Register**. These have the same

Table 8-3: Modes used by Endpoint 0 in the USB Endpoint 0 Mode Register. Endpoint 0 must accept Setup transactions.

Mode	Encod-ing	Response to Transaction			Mode after ACK	Typical Use
		Setup	IN	OUT		
Nak In/Out	0001	accept	NAK	NAK	same	No transfer is in progress; waiting for a Setup transaction.
Status Out Only	0010	accept	Stall	check	same	Control Read transfer, status stage. Return ACK on receiving a 0-byte data packet with the correct data toggle.
Stall In/Out	0011	accept	Stall	Stall	same	No transfer is in progress; waiting for a Setup transaction.
Ignore In/Out	0100	accept	ignore	ignore	same	No transfer is in progress; waiting for a Setup transaction.
Status In Only	0110	accept	0-byte data	Stall	same	Control Write transfer, status stage. For an IN transaction, return a 0-byte data packet.
Nak Out - Status In	1010	accept	0-byte data	NAK	same	Control Write transfer, status stage. For an IN transaction, return a 0-byte data packet.
Ack Out - Nak In	1011	accept	NAK	ACK	Nak In/Out	Control Write transaction, data stage.
Nak In - Status Out	1110	accept	NAK	check	same	Control Read transfer, data or status stage. For an IN transaction, return NAK. For an OUT transaction, return ACK on receiving a 0-byte data packet with the correct data toggle.
Ack In - Status Out	1111	accept	data	check	Nak In - Status Out	Control Read transfer, data or status stage. For an IN transaction, return data. For an OUT transaction, return ACK on receiving a 0-byte data packet with the correct data toggle.

mode and ACK bits as Endpoint 0's mode register. They don't have the PID bits because these endpoints support either IN or OUT transactions only. These registers also each have a Stall bit.

Endpoints 1 and 2 use different mode settings than Endpoint 0 because they never respond to Setup packets, while Endpoint 0 must do so. Table 8-4 shows the modes used by Endpoints 1 and 2. The table also shows how firmware can use the Stall bit to cause the SIE to return Stall in Ack In and Ack Out modes.

Endpoint Status and Control

Each of the three endpoints also has a **USB Endpoint Counter Register** that contains information about the data packet that is next to transmit, is being transmitted, or has just transmitted. Each contains a four-bit count, a data-toggle bit, and a data-valid bit.

The four Byte Count bits hold the number of data bytes in a transaction. For IN transactions, the value indicates how many bytes will be sent from the endpoint's buffer in the next transaction, not including the CRC bytes. Valid values are 0 through 8. For Setup and OUT transactions, the value indicates how many data bytes were received in the last transaction, plus the two CRC bytes. Valid values are 2 through 10. Setup and OUT counts are locked until the firmware reads the register.

For Setup and OUT transactions, the Data Valid bit is 1 if the received CRC value was correct.

The Data 0/1 Toggle bit indicates the data packet's data toggle state. For IN transactions, firmware sets the value. For Setup and OUT transactions, the SIE sets the bit to match the received data-toggle state.

USB Status and Control

The **USB Status and Control register** has two bits used in USB communications, four bits that USB or PS/2 communications may use, and one bit for PS/2 communications only.

The SIE sets the USB Bus Activity bit to 1 on detecting any USB activity or in other words, a non-idle bus. The firmware can use this bit along with the 1-millisecond interrupt-service routine to decide whether the chip should

Table 8-4: Modes used by Endpoints 1 and 2 in their USB Endpoint Mode Registers. Endpoints 1 and 2 don't accept Setup transactions.

Mode	Encoding	Response to Transaction			Mode after ACK	Typical Use
		Setup	IN	OUT		
Disable	0000	ignore	ignore	ignore	-	The endpoint is disabled.
Nak Out	1000	ignore	ignore	NAK	-	An OUT endpoint isn't ready to receive data.
Ack Out (Stall=0)	1001	ignore	ignore	ACK	Nak Out	An OUT endpoint is ready to receive data.
Ack Out (Stall=1)		ignore	ignore	stall	-	An OUT endpoint is halted.
Nak In	1100	ignore	NAK	ignore	-	An IN endpoint has no data to send.
Ack In (Stall=0)	1101	ignore	data	ignore	Nak In	An IN endpoint has data to send.
Ack In (Stall=1)		ignore	stall	ignore	-	An IN endpoint is halted.

enter the Suspend state. If the bit remains 0 for more than three milliseconds, the chip must enter the Suspend state.

The VREG Enable bit can enable 3.3V at the chip's VREG output. This output is intended for pulling up the USB's pull-up resistor to D- on the bus. Because VREG is under firmware control, code can remove and restore the output voltage to simulate device removal and attachment. VREG's output impedance is about 200 ohms, so the resistor's value should be 1.3K to meet the 1.5K specification.

The USB Reset - PS/2 Activity Interrupt Mode bit selects whether to interrupt on a USB reset or on PS/2 activity.

Three Control bits enable firmware to set the USB or PS/2 lines to specific states, including USB's J, K, and SE0 states. If the host has previously enabled a device's Remote-Wakeup ability with a Set_Feature request, the firmware can use the Force-K state to send a Resume signal to tell the host that the device wants to communicate. Chapter 19 has more on resume signaling.

The PS/2 Pullup Enable bit can enable internal pull-up resistors on the SCLK and SDATA lines used in PS/2 communications.

The **Port 2 Data Register** holds the states of four read-only bit values at an auxiliary input port (Port 2). Two bits are the states of D+ and D- when using USB, or the states of SCLK and SDATA when using PS/2. The other two bits can sometimes serve as general-purpose inputs. If the pull-up on USB's D- uses an external voltage source or if the device doesn't support USB, the VREG output can be disabled and the pin can serve as a general-purpose input whose state is read at P2.0. When the internal clock is enabled, there is no timing reference at XTALIN, and this pin can serve as a general-purpose input whose state is read at Bit P2.1.

The final USB-related register is the **USB Endpoint Interrupt Enable Register**, which enables interrupts for Endpoints 0, 1, and 2. I cover this register in more detail below, under Interrupt Processing.

Other I/O

In addition to the USB port, the enCoRe has built-in support for three other I/O interfaces. Firmware can use the general-purpose ports for any purpose. Some of the general-purpose bits can function as an SPI synchronous serial interface. And the USB interface is switchable between USB and a PS/2 interface.

General-purpose I/O

For interfacing to circuits besides the USB port, the chip has 16 versatile I/O pins on two 8-bit ports. Each can function as an input or output. Inputs can have pull-ups or not, and CMOS or TTL thresholds. Outputs can be CMOS with selectable driver strength or open drain. Each input can trigger an interrupt. A data register and two mode registers for each port control the configuration of each pin.

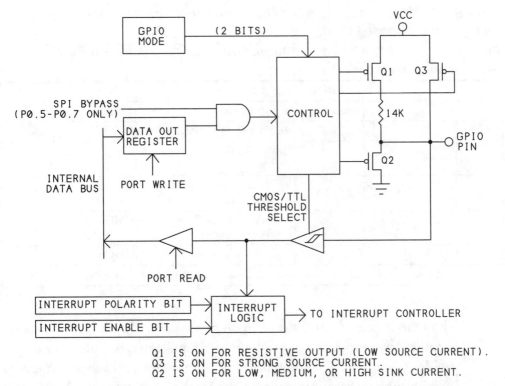

Q1 IS ON FOR RESISTIVE OUTPUT (LOW SOURCE CURRENT).
Q3 IS ON FOR STRONG SOURCE CURRENT.
Q2 IS ON FOR LOW, MEDIUM, OR HIGH SINK CURRENT.

Figure 8-5: Two GPIO register bits for each pin determine whether the pin is an input or output and the amount of source and sink current an output is capable of.

The Circuits Inside

Figure 8-5 shows the circuits inside each port pin. Table 8-5 shows the effects of combinations of settings.

To configure a bit as an input, the firmware writes 0 to the matching bits in the Mode 0 and Mode 1 registers. For TTL input thresholds, write 1 to the Data bit; for CMOS, write 0. A TTL low input must be 0.8V or less, and a TTL high input must be 2.0V or greater. CMOS input thresholds are centered at around half the power-supply voltage. For low-to-high transitions, the thresholds are 40% and 60% of the supply voltage. For high-to-low transitions, the thresholds are slightly lower. This adds hysteresis to keep inputs from oscillating on noisy or slowly changing inputs.

Table 8-5: Two Mode bits and a Data bit determine the configuration and state of each general-purpose I/O bit.

Register			Output State	Output Drive Strength	Input Threshold
Data	Mode 1	Mode 0			
0	0	0	undefined	high impedance	CMOS
1	0	0	undefined	high impedance	TTL
0	0	1	0	medium (8 mA) sink current	CMOS
1	0	1	1	strong (2mA) source current	CMOS
0	1	0	0	low (2 mA) sink current (open drain on)	CMOS
1	1	0	1	resistive (14K pull-up, low source current)	CMOS
0	1	1	0	high (50 mA) sink current	CMOS
1	1	1	1	strong (2 mA) source current	CMOS

The other modes control the strength of the source and sink currents for outputs. Any output pin can sink up to 50 milliamperes, but only one pin can do so at a time. The combined sink current for all pins shouldn't exceed 70 milliamperes. For source current, the combined maximum is 30 milliamperes. Use current-limiting resistors to limit the output current.

Interrupts

A transition on a GPIO pin can cause an interrupt. Additional register bits configure the pin's interrupt capability. Writing 1 to a pin's bit in the **GPIO Interrupt Enable Register** enables a transition on the pin to trigger a GPIO interrupt. The GPIO bit in the **Global Interrupt Enable Register** must be set to 1 as well. A pin's bit in the **GPIO Interrupt Polarity Register** determines whether a rising (1) or falling (0) edge triggers the interrupt.

All of the GPIO pins share an interrupt, so the firmware may need to determine which pin caused the interrupt. It can do so by reading the port. The interrupt latency, or time it takes for the CPU to enter the interrupt-service routine, is under 3 microseconds, so an interrupt signal should be greater than 3 microseconds wide if the interrupt-service routine needs to detect which pin caused the interrupt.

SPI Port

The enCoRe includes hardware support for an SPI (Serial Peripheral Interface) port. SPI is a synchronous serial interface suitable for short-range communications, often on the same circuit board, though cables of ten feet or so shouldn't be a problem in most environments. Compared to USB, SPI doesn't require nearly as much support in hardware or code, so it's used by many simple and inexpensive chips.

Chips with SPI interfaces include serial EEPROMs and analog-to-digital converters. The enCoRe's Development System includes a couple of SPI peripherals that can connect to the chip. Motorola introduced SPI, so the 68HC11 and other Motorola microcontrollers have SPI interfaces. A peripheral that needs more processing power than the enCoRe could use an enCoRe to manage USB communications and use the SPI interface to pass information between the enCoRe and another microcontroller.

An SPI bus has one master and one or more slaves. As with USB's host, the master initiates all SPI traffic. The enCoRe's SPI can function as a master or slave. The number of wires varies with the application. In addition to a common ground, an SPI interface has MISO (master in, slave out), MOSI (master out, slave in), and SCK (serial clock) lines. When there is more than one slave connected, each must also have an *SS (slave select) line. If there is just one slave, *SS can often be tied low at the slave to select it permanently.

On a master, MOSI, SCK, and any *SS pins are outputs and MISO is an input. On a slave, MISO is an output and MOSI, SCK, and *SS are inputs.

On the enCoRe, the SPI interface uses GPIO pins. Four pins have assigned functions: MOSI is P0.5, MISO is P0.6, and SCK is P0.7. On a slave, *SS is P0.4. On a master, the *SS outputs can be any spare GPIO pins.

The hardware handles the clocking and sending and receiving of the SPI data bits. A communication consists of the master writing one or more bytes to a slave, followed by an optional reply. For example, to write a byte to serial EEPROM, the master sends a write instruction, followed by an address and data. The slave sends nothing. To read a byte from EEPROM, the master sends a read instruction followed by an address, and the slave sends the data in reply.

Writing to the **SPI Data Register** fills a transmit buffer, which causes the data to load into a shift register for transmitting. Received SPI data is loaded into a receive buffer, where the firmware can retrieve it by reading the SPI Data Register.

The enCoRe's interface is flexible enough to communicate with just about any SPI chip. An **SPI Control Register** enables the firmware to select master or slave mode, a clock frequency from 62.5 Kbits/sec. to 2 Mbits/sec., and a clock polarity and phase. The clock polarity and phase select the clock's idle state (0 or 1) and whether data is written and read on rising or falling clock edges. Some SPI chips support only master or slave or a single clock phase and polarity.

Two additional bits in the SPI Control Register indicate when the transmit buffer is full and when an 8-bit transfer is complete. Completing a transfer also triggers an SPI interrupt so the firmware can get ready for another transfer.

The PS/2 Interface

Although this book is about USB, I shouldn't entirely neglect the enCoRe's PS/2 option. The term PS/2 can refer to the mouse, keyboard, or parallel-port interface IBM included years ago in its model PS/2 computer. In this case, we're talking about the mouse interface, which became a favored alternative to the serial (RS-232) and bus interfaces that were the options until USB came along.

A PS/2 mouse uses a synchronous serial interface that has a single data line and a clock line. The interface also has +5V and ground lines. The device provides the clock for communications in both directions. The device sends mouse data synchronized to the clock pulses. The data format uses 11 bits: a Start bit of 0, eight data bits sent least significant bit first, an odd parity bit, and a Stop bit of 1. The host reads the data on the clock's falling edge. As with a USB mouse, the data contains information about button presses and the amount and direction of mouse movement.

A long low on the data line tells the device that the host wants to send a command and generates a PS/2 interrupt in the device.

Having an interface that supports both USB and PS/2 makes it easy to design a pointing device that can use either. The device will need firmware to support both. For PS/2, the firmware is responsible for writing each clock pulse and data bit by setting Control bits in the USB Status and Control Register. Of course, a design can also use only USB, only PS/2, or even neither.

Other Chip Capabilities

The enCoRe has many other capabilities worthy of mention. Timer functions enable performing periodic tasks and measuring intervals. Many event types can trigger interrupts. And several registers enable monitoring and controlling the CPU and managing power.

Timer Functions

The chips have hardware support for a variety of timing functions, including generating interrupts for periodic tasks and measuring intervals.

Performing Periodic Tasks

For tasks to be done periodically, there are three options: the 1-millisecond, 128-microsecond, and Wake-up timer interrupts. The Wake-up interrupt provides less precise, but longer, timing intervals than the other two timers. If the chip is in the Suspend state, this interrupt will wake it. But firmware can also use this interrupt to perform periodic tasks when the chip isn't suspended.

The timing interval of the Wake-up interrupt is the chip's tWAKE period multiplied by the value indicated by three Wake-up Timer Adjust bits in the **Clock Configuration Register**. The available values are the eight powers of 2 from 1 through 128. The tWAKE value varies with the supply voltage and temperature, and can range from 1 to 5 milliseconds. So for example, if tWAKE is 128, the interval may be anywhere from 128 to 640 milliseconds.

To select an interval more precisely, the firmware can enable the Wake-up timer, use the chip's free-running timer to measure the interval, and select the Wake-up Timer Adjust value that most closely matches the desired interval.

With any of these timers, to time a longer interval, the firmware can maintain a counter in the interrupt-service routine. The routine increments the counter on each interrupt until the desired number of intervals has elapsed.

Measuring Intervals

The enCoRe has a free-running timer that provides a way to measure intervals and timer capture registers that enable measuring the time between events at I/O pins.

The 12-bit free-running timer increments once per microsecond, The timer rolls over on a count of FFFh, enabling firmware to measure periods up to 4.096 milliseconds (or longer by cascading counts). The count is stored in two registers. The firmware can read just one register at a time, yet it will want to know the states of all 12 bits at the same time. To make this possible, reading the **Timer LSB (least significant byte) Register** also loads the timer's upper four bits into a temporary register. Reading the **Timer MSB (most significant byte) Register** reads the temporary register. So sequential reads of these two registers gives the count at the time of the first read.

The chip can also measure intervals between events at the GPIO pins Port 0.0 (Capture A) and Port 0.1 (Capture B). Six registers configure the timers and hold the results, which can correspond to the times of rising and falling edges at each pin.

The **Capture Timers Configuration Register** has three functions. Four bits enable interrupts on the rising and falling edges of Capture A and B. One bit selects whether to save the time of the first edge or the most recent edge. Three bits select a prescale value that determines which 8 of the free-running timer's 12 bits are saved on an interrupt. Using lower bits gives better precision but shorter range, while higher bits give longer range but less precision.

The **Capture Timers Status Register** indicates whether a rising or falling edge has occurred on Capture A or B. The four **Capture Timer Data Registers** hold the timer counts for rising and falling edges at the two port pins. The difference between the counts stored at two events equals the time in microseconds between them.

Interrupt Processing

The firmware uses two registers to control which interrupts are enabled, plus two additional registers to enable individual GPIO interrupts. The **USB Endpoint Interrupt Enable Register** has three bits that enable interrupts for Endpoints 0, 1, and 2. The **Global Interrupt Enable Register** enables the other interrupt sources: Wake up, General-purpose I/O, Capture Timer A, Capture Timer B, SPI, 1.024-millisecond timer, 128-microsecond timer, and USB Reset or PS/2 Activity. Writing 1 to an interrupt's bit enables the interrupt, while writing 0 masks, or disables, the interrupt.

Interrupt Service Routines

When an interrupt occurs, the chip's hardware disables all interrupts, clears the Global Interrupt Enable bit and jumps to the interrupt's assigned interrupt-vector location in program memory. This location typically contains a jump to an interrupt-service routine. The interrupt-service routine is responsible for carrying out whatever needs to be done in response to the interrupt's event and for ensuring that all registers are in the expected states on exiting the routine.

On entering an interrupt-service routine, the hardware automatically stores the Program Counter's value and the states of the Carry and Zero flags. On exiting the routine, these values are automatically restored. So the interrupt-service routine can do what it wants with these values, and other code won't be affected. The firmware is responsible for saving and restoring any other values that need to be preserved. A typical example saves and restores the contents of the accumulator (A) and index register (X). Here is an example interrupt-service routine that uses push and pop to preserve the contents of these registers while also allowing the interrupt-service routine to use the registers:

```
DoNothing_ISR:
;Save the contents of the accumulator
push A
;Push the contents of the index register
push X
;Add code to service the interrupt here
;Pop values that were preserved
;in the reverse order they were saved (last first)
pop X
pop A
reti
```

GPIO Interrupts

For the general-purpose I/O (GPIO) interrupts, a **Port Interrupt Enable Register** for each port allows the firmware to enable or disable the interrupt for each I/O pin. A transition on a port pin will result in an interrupt only if several things are true:

- The GPIO bit in the Global Interrupt Enable register is set to 1.
- The pin's bit in its port's Port Interrupt Enable register is 1.
- The polarity of the transition on the port pin matches the polarity set in the pin's bit in the corresponding Port Interrupt Polarity Register.
- If any previous GPIO interrupt has occurred, that pin's state must have returned to the inactive, or non-trigger state, or the pin's bit in the Port Interrupt Enable register must have been set to 0 (and may optionally then be set back to 1). For a low-to-high interrupt trigger, the non-trigger state is low; for a high-to-low trigger, the non-trigger state is high.

USB Endpoint Interrupts

The USB endpoint interrupts trigger on sending or receiving the last packet in a transaction. In a Setup transaction, an interrupt occurs when the device returns ACK or receives a flawed data packet. In an IN transaction, an interrupt occurs on receiving the host's ACK or if the device returns a NAK or Stall. In an OUT transaction, an interrupt occurs when the device returns ACK, NAK, or Stall or receives a flawed data packet.

Timer Interrupts

The timer interrupts occur at intervals of 1.024 milliseconds and 128 microseconds. The firmware can use these interrupts for any purpose. One use for the 1-millisecond interrupt is to measure the amount of time with no USB activity to determine whether or not to enter the Suspend state.

Deciding whether to enter the Suspend state requires firmware support. The code must maintain a count of the number of milliseconds that the bus has been idle and cause the chip to enter the Suspend state when the count equals or exceeds 3. The count can be stored in any spare location in RAM.

To find out if the bus has been idle, the firmware reads the bus-activity bit in the USB Status and Control register. If the bit is 0, there has been no bus activity and the firmware should increment the suspend counter. If the bit is 1, there has been activity, and the firmware should clear the suspend counter and the bus activity bit by writing 0 to each:

```
1ms_timer:
; Sample 1-millisecond timer routine
; that checks bus activity and enters the Suspend
; state if there has been no bus activity for over
; 3 milliseconds.

push A

1ms_suspend_timer:
; To check for bus activity,
; read the bus-activity bit
; in the USB Status register.
iord usb_status
and  A, BUS_ACTIVITY
;If it's not 0, there has been bus activity.
jnz  bus_activity

;If it's 0, there has been no bus activity
;since the last 1-millisecond interrupt.
;Increment the suspend counter to keep track of
;the amount of time with no bus activity.
inc  [suspend_count]
mov  A, [suspend_count]
;Has it been over 3 milliseconds?
```

```
cmp   A, 04h
;If yes, enter the Suspend state.
jz    usb_suspend
;If no, we're finished checking for bus activity.
jmp   ms_timer_done

usb_suspend:
; Before entering the Suspend state,
; enable the Reset interrupt.
mov   A, (USB_RESET_INT)
iowr global_int

; Set the Suspend bit in the control register
; and re-enable interrupts.
iord control
or    A, SUSPEND
ei
iowr control

;On exiting Suspend, program execution begins here.
nop

; Look for bus activity.
; If there has been none, return to the Suspend state.
iord usb_status
and   A, BUS_ACTIVITY
jz    usb_suspend

; Exit the Suspend state.
; Enable the 1-milliscond and Reset interrupts.
mov   A, (1MS_INT | USB_RESET_INT)
iowr global_int

bus_activity:
; Bus activity was detected.

; Reset the Suspend counter to 0.
mov   A, 00h;
mov   [suspend_count], A

; Clear the bus-activity bit.
iord usb_status
and   A, ~BUS_ACTIVITY
```

```
iowr usb_status

ms_timer_done:
;Exit the 1-millisecond timer ISR.
pop A
reti
```

The Wake-up interrupt occurs at intervals set by firmware. If the chip is in the Suspend state, the Wake-up interrupt will wake it. The Wake-up interrupt is enabled whenever the Wake-up Interrupt Enable bit in the Global Interrupt Enable Register is 1, even if hardware or firmware has disabled interrupts.

Interrupt Status

The **Processor Status and Control Register** has two bits that relate to interrupts.

The Interrupt Enable Sense bit shows whether interrupts are enabled (1) or disabled (0). Firmware can control its state with the instructions DI (disable interrupts), EI (enable interrupts), and RETI (return from interrupt-service routine and re-enable interrupts. The hardware disables interrupts on entering an interrupt-service routine and re-enables them on exiting.

When interrupts are disabled, the IRQ Pending bit in the Processor Status and Control register indicates when an interrupt has occurred but has been ignored because interrupts are disabled. The bit remains set until the interrupt(s) are enabled and serviced.

CPU Status, Control, and Clocking

The **Processor Status and Control Register** contains seven bits that relate to the chip's overall operation. Two bits can stop the CPU, two bits relate to resets, and three bits relate to interrupts. In addition the **Clock Configuration Register** has bits that relate to resets and CPU clocking.

Halting the CPU

To stop the CPU, the HALT instruction sets the Run bit in the Processor Status and Control Register to 0. The CPU stops executing instructions until a reset occurs. The CPU resumes at address 0.

Writing 1 to the Suspend bit in the Processor Status and Control Register puts the chip in the Suspend state. The chip stops executing instructions until there is USB activity or a pending, enabled interrupt occurs. The CPU resumes at the instruction following the instruction that set the Suspend bit.

Resets

The CPU supports three types of reset: Low Voltage, Brown Out, and Watch Dog. Each is triggered by a different event. A fourth type of reset is the bus reset that a USB host may request to restart USB communications.

On a Low-Voltage or Brown-Out reset, the chip is placed in a known state: the PSP and DSP are set to 0, the USB address is set to 0, interrupts are disabled, and registers return to their default states. The GPIO, USB, and VREG pins are high impedance. USB communications are disabled. A chip using an external clock switches to the internal clock. After a short delay, program execution begins at 0. After reset, the firmware is responsible for writing the desired default values to registers and variables. After enabling USB communications, the chip has to wait to be enumerated by the host before it can do other USB communications.

A useful feature is the ability to shut the chip down automatically if the supply voltage is low and start it up again when voltage is restored. The Low-Voltage and Brown-Out resets perform this function.

A Low-Voltage Reset occurs when the supply voltage is below the low-voltage-reset voltage of 3.5 to 4.0V. This reset also acts as a power-on reset that occurs when power is first applied to the chip. The internal oscillator runs, but the chip is held in reset until the supply voltage reaches the reset threshold and 24 to 60 milliseconds has elapsed. The delay gives the supply voltage time to stabilize.

After power up, a Low-Voltage Reset occurs any time the supply voltage falls below the threshold, unless firmware has set the Low Voltage Reset Disable bit in the Clock Configuration Register, or unless the device is in the Suspend state.

When the Low-Voltage Reset isn't enabled, the Brown-Out Reset takes over. This reset does nothing until the supply voltage is below about 2.5V. The Brown-Out Reset is also active when the chip is in the Suspend state. This enables a suspended chip to have a lower supply voltage and still preserve the states of registers and memory. If the voltage falls below 2.5V and a Brown-Out reset occurs, the chip remains in reset until the supply reaches the low-voltage reset threshold.

The Watch-Dog Reset prevents the firmware from hanging by requiring the firmware to reset a watch-dog timer periodically. If the timer isn't reset, something has gone wrong and the firmware restarts. To prevent a Watch-Dog Reset, firmware must write any value to the **Watch Dog Restart Register** at least once every 10 milliseconds. If it fails to do so, the watch-dog timer overflows and triggers a reset. This reset behaves like the Low-Voltage and Brown-Out resets, except that the chip will continue to use an enabled external clock and the reset delay is just 2 to 4 milliseconds.

The interrupt-service routine for the 1-millisecond timer might seem a natural place to write to the Watch Dog Restart Register, but it's possible for firmware to stall or get stuck in a loop while still being able to service this interrupt. So it's best to reset the watch dog in the firmware's main task loop and also in any other routines that may take longer than 10 milliseconds.

Firmware can't disable the Watch Dog interrupt. The Processor Status and Control Register has a bit that indicates if a Watch Dog reset has occurred, and a bit that indicates if a Low Voltage or Brown-out reset has occurred.

A USB Bus reset occurs when the host sends a reset by bringing both USB signal lines low for at least 10 milliseconds. This doesn't reset the CPU. It just calls the USB Bus Reset interrupt-service routine. The bus-reset routine must cause the chip to stop USB communications and wait to be enumerated. And if this is necessary, the firmware is likely to want to start fresh from 00h as it does on the other resets. Here is example bus-reset code that does this:

```
bus_reset:
```

```
;Disable USB communications, then reset the firmware.
; Return Stall to IN and OUT token packets.
mov  a, STALL_IN_OUT
iowr ep0_mode

; Enable USB address 0.
mov  a, ADDRESS_ENABLE
iowr usb_address
; Disable Endpoints 1 and 2.
mov  a, DISABLE
iowr ep1_mode
iowr ep2_mode

; Set the program stack pointer to 0.
mov  A, 00h
mov  psp, a
; Execute reset code.
jmp  reset
```

Selecting and Controlling the Clock

A very convenient feature of the enCoRe is its on-chip oscillator. There's no need to connect an external crystal or resonator unless the device needs a more precise frequency for other functions. An external clock can be a crystal oscillator or ceramic resonator, plus any required capacitors at the XTALIN and XTALOUT pins.

The Clock Configuration Register has four bits that relate to clocking the CPU. The chip always uses the internal clock on power up and on returning from a Low-Voltage or Brown-Out reset. Firmware can then set the External Oscillator Enable bit to 1 to switch the CPU to an external clock. If this bit is 0, the XTALIN pin is a general-purpose input (P2.1).

When using the internal clock, the Internal Clock Output Disable bit determines whether XTALOUT is a logic high or a 6-Megahertz clock.

When using an external clock, the External Clock Resume Delay bit selects one of two delay times when switching to the external clock or waking from the Suspend state with the external clock enabled. As a rule, ceramic resonators can use the 128-microsecond delay, while crystals will need the 4 millisecond delay.

When firmware has set the Precision USB Clocking Enable bit to 1, the clock frequency meets USB's 1.5% tolerance requirements.

Power Management

The chip requires a power supply of 4.0 to 5.5V DC.

To save power and to comply with the USB specification, the chip can enter a Suspend state that powers down everything except what's needed to detect USB activity and whatever external interrupts are enabled. The on-chip oscillator stops, so there is no clock to cause program instructions to execute. The chip just waits for an event that will end the Suspend state.

The events that will end the Suspend state are non-idle activity at the USB receiver, the triggering of an enabled interrupt at an I/O pin, an SPI slave interrupt, or a Wake-Up interrupt.

The chip enters the Suspend state by writing 1 to the Suspend bit in the Processor Status and Control Register. Program execution stops. When an event brings the chip out of the Suspend state, program execution begins at the instruction following the `iowr` instruction that suspended the chip.

The firmware can put the chip into the Suspend state at any time, but it must do so if there has been no USB activity (including low-speed keep-alive signals) for three milliseconds. And as Chapter 19 explains, a device suspended for this reason must consume very little bus power, as little as 500 microamperes in some cases.

There are some things the firmware can do to ensure the lowest possible power consumption. The firmware should set unused bits on ports 0 and 1 to pull-up mode. On 18-lead packages, this includes P1.2 though P1.7, which are not brought out to external pins. The GPIO interrupt bits in the Port 0 and 1 Interrupt Enable Registers should all be 0, even if the GPIO bit in the Global Interrupt Enable Register is 0.

9

Writing Firmware: the Cypress enCoRe

Whatever controller chip you select for a project, it won't be much use until you write the code that enables it to communicate with the host and the other circuits in your peripheral. In this chapter, I again use the Cypress enCoRe series an example, this time to show what's involved in writing and debugging USB firmware, including a review of development tools. Even if you're using a different chip, this chapter will give you an idea of what the process involves.

Hardware and Firmware Responsibilities

In a USB transfer, the CY7C63743's serial interface engine handles many of the tasks, but the firmware still has plenty to do. Here is a look at the responsibilities of each.

What the Hardware Does

These are the tasks the hardware does on its own:

- Detects new incoming packets.
- Translates received information from the encoded format used on the USB's data lines.
- Determines whether a transaction is directed to the chip's USB address and if not, ignores the transaction.
- For transactions with Endpoint 0, determines the transaction type (Setup, IN, or OUT) and sets a bit in the endpoint's USB Mode register to indicate which type it is.

For received data, the hardware also does the following:

- Stores valid received data in the endpoint's buffer or toggles a register bit to indicate an error in received data.
- Sets the count in the Endpoint Counter Register to match the number of received bytes.
- Stores the data-toggle state of valid received data.
- Calculates CRC values, compares them to the received CRC values, and takes action on detecting an error.
- Sends the appropriate handshake to the host.
- Triggers an interrupt so the firmware can prepare for the next transaction.

For data to be transmitted, the hardware also does the following:

- Translates data to be transmitted from the bytes in the USB buffer to the format used on the USB's data lines.
- Sends the number of bytes specified in the Endpoint Counter Register onto the USB lines in response to the host's IN token packet.
- Calculates and sends CRC bits with the data.
- Sends a data-toggle code with the data.
- On receiving a handshake from the host, triggers an interrupt.

What the Firmware Does

The firmware's job in USB communications is to supplement the hardware's capabilities and ensure that the device exchanges data as needed in both directions. The following code is adapted from Cypress' example firmware.

Endpoint 0 Interrupts

An interrupt at Endpoint 0 indicates activity that the firmware should check into. On receiving an Endpoint 0 interrupt, the firmware pushes the accumulator and index registers. The firmware checks the ACK bit in the Endpoint 0 Mode Register and exits if the transaction didn't complete with an ACK. Otherwise, the firmware checks the same register to find out whether a Setup, IN, or OUT token packet was received, then jumps to a routine to handle it:

```
endpoint0:
push X
push A

; Read the ep0_mode register to enable writing to
; the endpoint's buffer.
iord ep0_mode
; If EP0_ACK isn't set, the transaction didn't
; complete with an Ack, so exit the routine.
and  A, EP0_ACK
jz   ep0_done

; Bit 5, 6, or 7 in ep0_mode is set to indicate
; whether the transaction type is Setup, In, or Out.
; Find out which it is and jump to handle it.
iord ep0_mode
asl  A
jc    ep0_setup_received
asl  A
jc   ep0_in_received
asl  A
jc   ep0_out_received

ep0_done:
popA
popX
```

```
        reti
```

If it's a Setup transaction, the firmware determines which request it is and jumps to a routine to handle it:

```
ep0_setup_received:

; Clear the Setup bit to enable
; writing to Endpoint 0's buffer.
mov  A, NAK_IN_OUT
iowr ep0_mode

; Extract the 5-bit bmRequestType in
; Endpoint 0's byte 0.
mov  A, [bmRequestType]
; Bits 2, 3, and 4 are unused here, so set to 0.
and  A, E3h
push A
; Shift right 3 places to move bits 5, 6, 7
; into bits 2, 3, and 4's places.
asr  A
asr  A
asr  A
; Save the result.
mov  [int_temp], A
; OR the result  with the original value
; to restore bits 0, 1.
pop  A
or   A, [int_temp]
; Clear bits 5, 6, & 7 (unused).
and  A, 1Fh
; Shift left to multiply by two because the
; the index table's jumps are two bytes each.
asl  A
; Use a jump table to get the address to jump to
; to handle the request indicated in bmRequestType.
jacc bmRequestType_jumptable
```

Sending Data to the Host

When a request requires Endpoint 0 to send data to the host in the Data stage, the firmware stores two values and calls an initialize_control_read routine to get ready for the expected IN transaction(s). The value `maximum_data_count` is the amount of data available to send.

```
initialize_control_read:
; ep0_transtype indicates the transaction type.
; The firmware uses this value to decide how to
; respond to token packets.
;
; If the firmware has jumped here,
; it's a control Read transaction:
mov  A, TRANS_CONTROL_READ
mov  [ep0_transtype], A

; Set the data toggle to 1
mov  A, DATA_TOGGLE
mov  [ep0_data_toggle], A

; Find the lesser of the requested data (in wLengthhi
; and wLengthlo) and the maximum data available
; (in maximum_data_count).
; Store this value in maximum_data_count.

; If wLengthhi > 0,
; maximum_data_count is the smaller value.
mov  A, [wLengthhi]
cmp  A, 00h
jnz  initialize_control_read_done

; If wLengthhi = 0 and wLengthlo > maximum_data_count
; maximum_data_count is the smaller value.
mov  A, [wLengthlo]
cmp  A, [maximum_data_count]
jnc  initialize_control_read_done

; Otherwise, wLengthlo is the smaller value.
mov  A, [wLengthlo]
mov  [maximum_data_count], A

initialize_control_read_done:
jmp  control_read_data_stage
```

The firmware then loads data into Endpoint 0's buffer and configures the endpoint to return the data when the host sends an IN token packet.

```
control_read_data_stage:
; Load Endpoint 0's buffer with data to send.
; Initialize the index register.
mov  X, 00h
; If all of the data has been sent, we're done.
mov  A, [maximum_data_count]
cmp  A, 00h
jz   dmabuffer_load_done

dmabuffer_load:
; Load a byte number into the buffer.
mov  A, X
; If the buffer is full, we're done.
cmp  A, 08h
jz  dmabuffer_load_done
; The data to send begins at
; (data_start + control_read_table).
mov  A, [data_start]
index control_read_table

; Use the X register to step through
; Endpoint 0's buffer.
mov  [X + ep0_dmabuff0], A
inc  X
; data_start points to the byte to send.
inc  [data_start]
; maximum_data_count is the number of bytes
; remaining to send.
dec  [maximum_data_count]
; If no bytes remain, we're done.
jz   dmabuffer_load_done
; Otherwise, loop to load more data.
jmp  dmabuffer_load

dmabuffer_load_done:
; Unlock the counter register.
iord ep0_count
; Place the number of bytes loaded and
; the data toggle value in the counter register.
mov  A, X
or   A, [ep0_data_toggle]
iowr ep0_count
```

```
; Configure Endpoint 0 to return data on the next IN
; token packet or to check for a 0-byte data packet
; in an OUT transaction.
mov  A, ACK_IN_STATUS_OUT
iowr ep0_mode

; Toggle the data toggle.
mov  A, DATA_TOGGLE
xor  [ep0_data_toggle], A

pop  A
pop  X
reti
```

If there are more data packets, the device loads these into the endpoint buffer in the same way. When the host is finished requesting data, it sends a 0-byte data packet in the Status stage. The device's endpoint responds with ACK and the firmware jumps to routine that sets the endpoint's mode and the transaction type:

```
control_read_status_stage:
; Configure Endpoint 0 to return a 0-byte data packet
; in case there is another IN packet.
mov  A, STATUS_IN_ONLY
iowr ep0_mode

; No transaction is in progress.
mov  A, TRANS_NONE
mov  [ep0_transtype], A

pop  A
pop  X
reti
```

Receiving Data from the Host

When a request requires the host to send data to Endpoint 0 in the Data stage, the firmware calls an initialize_control_write routine to prepare to receive data in the expected OUT transaction(s). The variables wLengthlo and wLengthhi hold the amount of data the host says it will send.

```
initialize_control_write:
```

```
; ep0_transtype indicates the transaction type.
; The firmware uses this value to decide how to
; respond to token packets.

; If the firmware has jumped here,
; the transaction type is control Write:
mov  A, TRANS_CONTROL_WRITE
mov  [ep0_transtype], A

; Initialize the data toggle to 1.
mov  A, DATA_TOGGLE
mov  [ep0_data_toggle], A

;Send ACK in response to OUT packets,
;which will contain the Control Write data.
;Send NAK in response to IN packets (not expected).
mov  A, ACK_OUT_NAK_IN
iowr ep0_mode

; Return from Endpoint 0's ISR.
pop  A
pop  X
ret  i
```

When the host sends data in an OUT transaction, the device stores the data in the endpoint's buffer and triggers an interrupt to handle it. The firmware uses the token packet and ep0_transtype value to jump to the appropriate routine:

```
control_write_data_stage:
; If the data-valid bit isn't set,
; we're done with the data stage.
iord ep0_count
and  A, DATA_VALID
jz   control_write_data_stage_done

; Compare the received data toggle
; with the expected value.
iord ep0_count
and  A, DATA_TOGGLE
xor  A, [ep0_data_toggle]
; If it's incorrect,
; we're done with the data stage.
```

```
    jnz   control_write_data_stage_done

    ; Copy the received bytes to data memory.
    ; This example copies two bytes.
    mov   A, [ep0_dmabuff0]
    mov   [data_byte_0], A
    mov   A, [ep0_dmabuff1]
    mov   [data_byte_1], A

    ;Toggle the data-toggle bit.
    mov   A, DATA_TOGGLE
    xor   [ep0_data_toggle], A

    ; If all of the data has been received,
    ; configure Endpoint 0 to send a 0-byte data packet
    ; in response to an IN packet (the transfer's status
    ; stage) or to Stall an Out packet (not expected).

    mov   A, STATUS_IN_ONLY
    iowr  ep0_mode

control_write_data_stage_done:
    ; Return from Endpoint 0's ISR.
    popA
    popX
    reti
```

After the endpoint has responded to the 0-byte IN transaction in the Status stage, an interrupt triggers and the firmware re-configures the endpoint and sets ep0_transtype:

```
control_write_status_stage:
    ; Jump here if the device has received an IN token
    ; packet with ep0_transtype = TRANS_CONTROL_WRITE.
    ; The device has sent a 0-byte IN data packet to
    ; complete the transfer because ep0_mode was set to
    ; Status_In_Only at the end of the data stage.

    ; Configure Endpoint 0 to return ACK on receiving
    ; a 0-byte data packet and to return Stall on INs.
    mov   A, STATUS_OUT_ONLY
    iowr  ep0_mode
```

```
; No transfer is in progress.
mov  A, TRANS_NONE
mov  [ep0_transtype], A

; Return from Endpoint 0's ISR.
pop  A
pop  X
reti
```

Handling Interrupt Transfers

The code for handling interrupt transfers at Endpoints 1 and 2 isn't as complicated, because these transfers don't have multiple stages to manage. On an IN endpoint, the interrupt triggers after the endpoint has sent data or a NAK in a transaction. Here is code that enables Endpoint 1 to respond to IN interrupts:

```
endpoint1:
push A
; Get ready for the next transaction.
; Toggle the data toggle.
mov  A, 80h
xor  [ep1_data_toggle], A

; Set the event_machine variable to indicate that
; no transaction is in progress.
mov  A, NO_EVENT_PENDING
mov  [event_machine], A

; If the endpoint has been set to Stall,
; set the mode to Stall INs and OUTs.
mov  A, [ep1_stall]
cmp  A, FFh
jnz  endpoint1_done
mov  A, STALL_IN_OUT
iowr ep1_mode

endpoint1_done:
pop  A
reti
```

In a similar way, the interrupt-service routine for an OUT endpoint retrieves the received data (as in a Control Write transaction) and gets ready for the next transaction.

Other Responsibilities

The examples above show the essence of USB communications with the CY7C63743. There are other details, of course. For example, during control transfers the firmware must check periodically to find out if another Setup token has arrived, and if so, abandon the current transfer and start the new one. The firmware must also remember to clear the watch-dog timer in any loop that might otherwise allow the timer to run without a reset for 10 milliseconds. I also haven't covered the specifics of how to respond to each control request. Again, Cypress provides example code for the essential functions and my website (*www.Lvr.com*) has firmware examples that build on Cypress' examples.

Hardware Development Tools

For project developing for the enCoRe, Cypress offers a Development Kit for debugging code and third-party PROM programmers for storing code in the chips' PROMs.

The Development Kit

The CY3654 Development Kit enables you to test your code and circuits and find problems quickly.

The system includes a set of circuit boards (Figure 9-1) and a debugging program that together enable you to load your assembled or compiled code from a PC to the board's RAM. The RAM emulates the controller's PROM. You can run and debug code while using your PC to monitor and control program execution. Downloading to RAM makes it easy to modify the code. Manufacturers of other USB chips have similar development systems for their chips.

To use the Development Kit, you need a PC running Windows 98 or later with available USB and RS-232 ports.

The Platform Board

The Development Kit's main Platform board doesn't contain an enCoRe chip. Instead it has circuits that emulate the functions of the chip while allowing you to monitor and control program execution.

Figure 9-1 shows a typical setup. The Platform board contains the circuits that emulate the microcontroller. It has connectors for a Personality Board and an RS-232 connection to a PC. The Platform board also has a USB connector for possible future use as an alternative to the RS-232 connection.

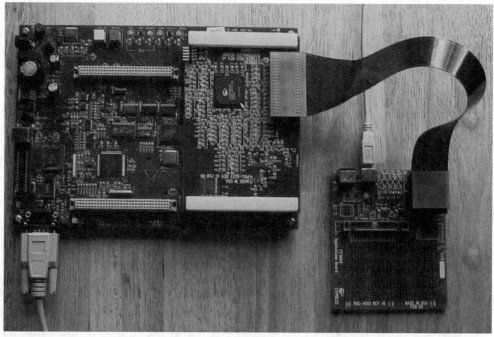

Figure 9-1: In the CY3654 Development System, a Personality Board attaches on top of the main Development Board. An RS-232 port enables communicating with the monitor program. A cable and Target Adapter connect the Personality Board to an Application Board (right), which has a USB port.

The Personality Board configures the emulator for a specific chip. A series of similar chips may share the same Personality Board. For example, all of the enCoRes use the P05 board, while the CY7C634/5/6xx chips use the P02 board.

A cable assembly connects the Personality Board to a Target Probe Adapter that in turn connects to the Application Board.

The Application Board contains the USB connector and a prototyping area. The board supports several example applications, with components for some installed. You can use your own application board in place of the one provided.

The development kit connects to a PC via both USB and RS-232 interfaces. These may, but don't have to, connect to the same PC. The USB interface of course carries the USB communications between a PC and the device's USB port. The debugger uses the RS-232 interface to send object code and to send and receive debugging information such as breakpoints and register contents. The board uses an external power supply, which is included.

The Application Board has several features for experimenting:

- Solder pads for the GPIO pins.
- A header for a cable to a logic analyzer or other circuits that connect to the GPIO pins.
- A temperature converter that uses an SPI interface (Dallas Semiconductor DS1722).
- An EEPROM that uses an SPI interface (Xicor X25020).
- Solder pads for four surface-mount LEDs, with two installed.
- Solder pads for three surface-mount push-button switches, with one installed.
- Solder pads for adding Linx Technologies' TXM and RXM RF interface modules.
- Prototyping area.

Setting Up the Development Board

Setting up the Development Board for use requires attaching five components in series. There are a few places where you can plug something in wrong, so I'll go over the steps:

1. Plug the Personality Board into the Development Board. The Personality Board rests on top of the Development Board. The bottom of the Personality Board has two headers that plug into connectors on the Development Board. The connectors are keyed so you can't plug them in backwards.

2. Plug one end of the cable assembly into the Personality Board. One end of the cable assembly has a circuit board with two 40-pin sockets (J1 and J2). These mate with the two 40-pin headers on the Personality Board. These connectors are *not* keyed, so be sure to plug the cable in correctly. The sockets and pins are labeled (J1 and J2). The cable should point away from the Development Board, not across it.

3. The Personality Board has one jumper. Leave J8 open to use bus power to power the Application Board's circuits. Jumper J8 to power the Application Board from the Development Board's supply, with a limit of 100 milliamperes.

4. Plug the other end of the cable assembly into a Target Adapter. J3 and J4 on the cable assembly are two 40-pin sockets that mate with pins on one of the provided Target Adapters. The Application Board uses the 24P DIP Adapter. These connectors are keyed.

5. Plug the Target Adapter's pins into the DIP socket on the Application Board. This connection is not keyed. The cable should point away from the Application Board, not lie across it.

6. Connect an RS-232 cable from the Development Board to your PC's serial port.

7. Connect a USB cable from the *Application Board's* USB connector to a USB port on your PC. *Don't* use the USB connector on the larger Development Board.

8. Plug the power supply into an AC outlet and the Development Board's connector.

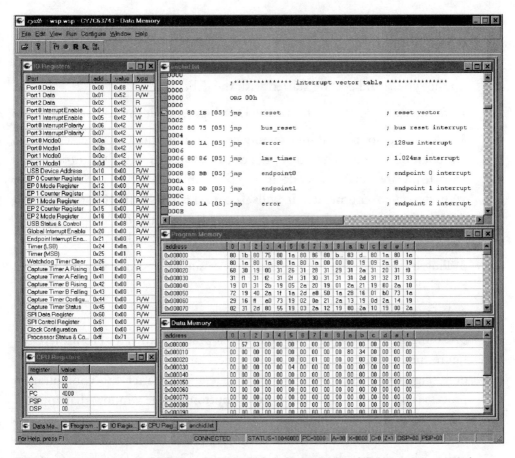

Figure 9-2: Cypress' CYDB monitor and debugger enables you to control program execution and view the status of memory and registers.

The Debugger

The companion to the development board is the CYDB debugger, or monitor program. In addition to enabling you to load and run your firmware, the debugger has features that can help enormously in tracking down program bugs.

Figure 9-2 shows the user screen, which you can customize to show the information you want. The View menu allows you to select which windows display, including program and data memory, CPU and I/O registers, and breakpoints.

The Development Kit comes with a manual that guides you through setting up the system and getting started with the debugger.

Here's an example of how to use the Development Kit to run your firmware:

1. Write your source file in assembly code and use the Cyasm assembler to create an object file. The object file can be a *.rom* or *.hex* file, and contains your firmware's machine-code instructions in an ASCII Hex format. For your device to enumerate, it will also need an INF file on the host, as described in Chapter 11. If your firmware identifies the device as HID class, you can use the HID INF file that's provided with Windows.

3. Plug in the Development Board's power supply and connect the RS-232 and USB cables to the host PC.

4. Run the debugger.

5. Configure the debugger for your development hardware. From the Configure menu, select Target to display the Configure Target/Emulator window. Figure 9-3 shows the window as it appears after the configuration process is complete. Click the Connect button. In the window that appears, select a COM port and click OK. When the debugger has finished the configuration communications, the text under the Current Emulator Configuration label changes from Not Connected to Connected, and the Connect button's caption changes to Update. Click OK to close the window.

6. Download and run your code. To download code to the emulator, click the *DL* button or select Run, Download from the menu. In the window that appears, select a *.hex* or *.rom* file and a listing file and click OK. The debugger loads the selected file into the emulator's memory and displays the selected listing file.

To run the firmware, click the *R* button or select Run, Run from the menu. If all is well, the firmware will run and Windows will enumerate the device. The *R* button will be grayed out and the *Stop* button will appear as a solid red circle.

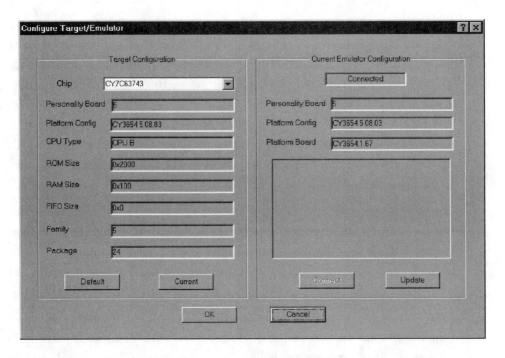

Figure 9-3: In the CYDB debugger, use the Configure Target/Emulator window to establish communications with the development board.

To stop the code, click the *Stop* button or click Run, Stop in the menu. To restart at the instruction where the firmware stopped, click *Run*. To restart from the beginning of program memory, click *Reset*.

Debugging Tips

The debugger enables you to precisely monitor and what the device's firmware is doing.

You can execute a portion of your application, then examine the states of all of the device's registers and RAM, or even change their contents on the fly. You can set a breakpoint to find out when and if a section of code executes. You can single-step through the code to find out exactly what the code does and where it branches. The Platform board's hardware and firmware disable the Watch Dog timer during single-stepping.

For example, if you suspect that a routine in your firmware never executes, you can use the monitor program to set a breakpoint in the routine. If the monitor stops program execution at the breakpoint, you know that the routine is executing. If you suspect the routine isn't doing what you intended, you can single-step through it and watch the contents of any registers and memory locations of interest in each step. The CPU Registers window shows the current value of the program counter (PC) and the listing file's display shows your code. To update the display of the emulated chip's registers and memory, click View > Refresh.

You can use your own application along with the development tools to test the firmware in its intended use. For example, you can run an application that enables users to click buttons to send and receive HID reports. You can keep the debugger open at the same time as you run your own application. This way, you can watch what's going on inside the emulated chip as your application runs.

One thing that's missing in the debugger is the ability to search a listing file for specific text. This makes it hard to find a specific line of code to set a breakpoint. So I keep a copy of the listing file loaded into a word processor and use that for searching. When I find the line of code I'm looking for, I note the line number and switch back to the debugger to set the breakpoint.

PROM Programming

When your code looks OK on the emulator and you're ready to try it out in a chip's PROM, you'll need a PROM programmer. Several vendors have programmers that are capable of this. An inexpensive one is the CY3649 Hi-Lo PROM Programmer, available from Cypress.

Programming chips in the enCoRe series requires two additional components, the CY3083-DP48 Adapter Base, which adapts the programmer for a specific package type, and the CY3083-08 Matrix Card, which routes the signals for a specific pinout. Both are available from Cypress.

Figure 9-4 shows the programmer, and Figure 9-5 shows the programmer application's display. The programmer is the same one provided with some

Figure 9-4: Cypress offers an inexpensive programmer and adapters for the enCoRe series and other chips. The photo shows an Adapter Base inserted into the programmer's ZIF socket. The Adapter Base holds a matrix card and a chip to be programmed.

of the now discontinued Starter Kits for the CY7C63000 series. If the programmer is labeled "Programmer for Starter," it's usable with the enCoRes if you update the software and get the Adapter Base and Matrix Card. If the programmer is labeled "Programmer for CY630...," it won't work with the enCoRes.

The programmer connects to the PC via an RS-232 serial port. (The unit was probably adapted from an existing design that predates USB.) As with other EPROM programmers, you place the chip to be programmed in a zero-insertion-force (ZIF) socket and flip the lever to lock in the chip.

These are the steps to program a chip:

1. Insert the Matrix Card into the Adapter Base and place the Adapter Base into the programmer's ZIF socket and lock it into place

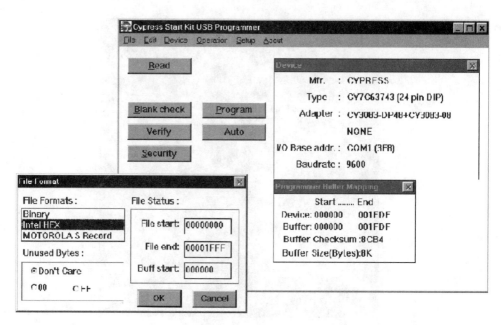

Figure 9-5: The software for Cypress Semiconductor's EPROM programmer enables you to program a file in any of several formats into Cypress chips, verify, and protect the code from copying by blowing the security fuse.

2. Place a chip to be programmed into the Adapter Base's ZIF socket and lock it into place.

3. In the Setup window, select a COM port and bit rate. A message will inform you when the software has located the programmer.

4. From the Device menu, select the device to be programmed.

5. From the File menu, select Load File to Buffer. Select a *.hex* file created by the Cyasm assembler. The programmer software is 16-bit, so long file and folder names will be truncated. In the window that appears, select file format = Intel Hex, File Start = 0000, File End = 1FFF, Buffer Start = 0000, and Unused Bytes = Don't Care.

6. Click Auto, then OK. This will cause the programmer to do four things in sequence. The programmer will verify that the chip is erased (contains all

FFs). It will program the buffer's file into the PROM, beginning at 0000h. It will verify that the chip's contents match the buffer.

The Security button blows the chip's security fuse to prevent anyone from reading the code stored in the chip. Anyone who tries to read the code in the device will see only FFs. Once the security fuse is blown, the device can no longer be programmed.

You can also do an individual blank check, program, verify, and security protection of the code. An edit menu enables you to edit individual bytes in buffer, search, move blocks of bytes, and fill areas with a value.

I found the programming software to be a little quirky. At higher bit rates, the programmer sometimes failed to read or program the device. After switching to 9600 bps, a device that failed at a higher bit rate passed the blank test but refused to be programmed until I re-erased. At slower rates, I had no problems. Because the amount to be programmed is small, the programming completes quickly enough even at a slower bit rate.

Chapter 9

10

How the Host Communicates

A USB peripheral is of no use if its host PC doesn't know how to communicate with it. Under Windows, any communication with a USB peripheral must pass through a device driver that knows how to communicate both with the system's USB drivers and with the applications that access the device.

This chapter explains how Windows applications communicate with USB devices and explores the options for device drivers.

Device Driver Basics

A device driver is a software component that enables applications to access a hardware device. The hardware device may be a printer, modem, keyboard, video display, data-acquisition unit, or just about anything controlled by circuits that the CPU can access. The device may be inside the computer's enclosure (an internal disk drive, for example) or it may use a cable to connect to the computer (as with a keyboard or mouse). The device may be a standard peripheral type or a unique design for a special purpose. It may be a one-of-a-kind, custom device. Some device drivers are class drivers that handle communications with a variety of devices that have similar functions.

Insulating Applications from the Details

A device driver insulates applications from having to know details about the physical connections, signals, and protocols required to communicate with a device. Applications are the programs that users run, including everything from popular word processors and databases to special-purpose applications that support custom hardware.

A device driver can enable application code to access a peripheral when the application knows only the peripheral's name (such as HP LaserJet) or the device's function (joystick). The application doesn't have to know the physical address of the port the peripheral attaches to (such as 378h), and it doesn't have to explicitly monitor and control the handshaking signals that the peripheral requires (Busy, Strobe, and so on). Applications don't even have to know whether a device uses USB or another interface. The application code can be the same for all interfaces, with the hardware-specific details handled at a lower level.

A device driver accomplishes its mission by translating between application-level and hardware-specific code. The application-level code uses functions supported by the operating system to communicate with device drivers. The hardware-specific code handles the protocols necessary to access the peripheral's circuits, including detecting the states of status signals and toggling control signals at appropriate times.

Windows includes application programmer's interface (API) functions that enable applications to communicate with device drivers. Applications written in Visual Basic, C/C++, and Delphi can call API functions. Three functions that device drivers may support for reading and writing to USB devices are ReadFile, WriteFile, and DeviceIoControl.

Although API functions simplify the process of communicating with hardware, they tend to have specific and rigid requirements for the values they pass and return. It's not unusual for a mistake in an API call to result in an application or even a system crash.

To make programming simpler and safer, Visual Basic has its own controls for common tasks. For example, applications can use the Printer Object to send data to printers and the MSComm control to communicate with devices that connect to RS-232 serial ports. The controls provide an easier and more failsafe programming interface for setting parameters and exchanging data. The underlying code within the control may use API functions to communicate with device drivers, but the control insulates application programmers from dealing with the sometimes arcane details of the API calls.

Visual Basic doesn't have a generic control for USB communications, however. How an application communicates with a USB device varies with the driver assigned to the device. For example, a Visual-Basic application can use the Printer object to communicate with a USB printer.

Some device drivers are monolithic drivers that handle everything from communicating with applications to reading and writing to the ports or memory addresses that connect to the device's hardware.

Other drivers, including Windows drivers for USB devices, use a layered driver model where each driver in a series performs a portion of the communication. The top layer contains a function driver that manages communications between applications and the lower-level bus drivers. The bottom layer contains a bus driver that manages communications between the function driver and the hardware. One or more filter drivers may supplement the function and bus drivers.

The layered driver model is more complicated as a whole, but it actually simplifies the job of writing drivers. Devices can share code for tasks they have in common. Plus, the drivers that handle communications with the system's USB hardware are built into Windows, so driver writers don't have to provide them. Writing a device driver for a USB device is typically much easier than writing a driver that has to handle the details of accessing the hardware.

Options for USB Devices

There are several approaches to obtaining a driver for a device. Sometimes you can use a driver that's included with Windows or provided by a chip vendor or other source. For other devices, you may need to write a custom driver. A variety of toolkits are available to simplify and speed up the task of driver writing. Sometimes more than one way will work, and the choice depends on a combination of what's easier, cheaper, and offers better performance.

Standard Device Types

Many peripherals fit into standard classes such as disk drives, printers, modems, keyboards, and mice. All of these are available with a choice of interfaces, including USB. For example, a keyboard may use the original legacy keyboard interface or USB. A disk drive may use any of a number of interfaces, including ATAPI, SCSI, printer-port, IEEE-1394, and USB.

Windows includes class drivers for many standard device types. When devices in a class may have different interfaces, supplemental drivers can support the various interface options. And if a device has features or capabilities beyond what the class driver supports, a device-specific filter driver can support these as needed.

Custom Devices

Some peripherals are custom devices intended for use only with specific applications. Examples include data-acquisition units, motor controllers, and test instruments. Windows has no knowledge of these devices, so it has no built-in drivers for them. Devices like these may use custom drivers, or they may be designed so they comply with the requirements for a supported class. For example, a data-acquisition device may be able to use the HID drivers.

How Applications Communicate with Devices

To understand what the device driver has to do, you need to understand where the driver fits in the communications path of a data transfer. Even if you don't need to write a driver for your device, understanding the driver's role will help in understanding the application-level code that you do write.

What Is a Device Driver?

In the most general sense, a device driver is any code that handles communication details for a hardware device that interfaces to a CPU. Even a short subroutine in an application can be considered a device driver. Under Windows, the code for most drivers, including USB drivers, differs from application code because the operating system allows the driver code a greater level of privilege than it allows to applications.

User and Kernel Modes

Under Windows, code runs in one of two modes: user or kernel. Each allows a different level of privilege in accessing memory and other system resources. Applications must run in user mode. Most drivers, including all USB drivers, run in kernel mode, though a USB device may also have a supplementary user-mode driver.

In user mode, Windows limits access to memory and other system resources. Windows won't allow an application to access an area of memory that the operating system has designated as protected. This enables a PC to run multiple applications at the same time, with none of the applications interfering with each other. In theory, even if an application crashes, other applications are unaffected. Of course in reality it doesn't always work that way, but that's the theory. On Pentiums and other x86 processors, user mode corresponds to the CPU's Ring 3 mode.

In kernel mode, the code has unrestricted access to system resources, including the ability to execute memory-management instructions and control access to I/O ports. On Pentiums and other x86 processors, kernel mode corresponds to the CPU's Ring 0 mode.

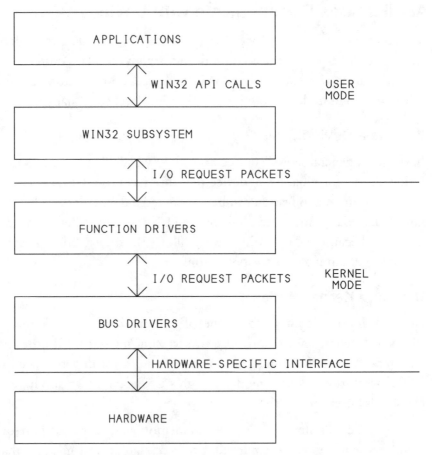

Figure 10-1: USB uses a layered driver model under Windows, with separate drivers for devices and the buses they connect to.

Under Windows 98 and Me, applications can access I/O ports directly, unless a low-level driver has reserved the port, preventing access. Under Windows NT and 2000, only kernel-mode drivers can access I/O ports.

Figure 10-1 shows the major components of user and kernel modes in a USB communication.

Applications and drivers each use their own language to communicate with the operating system. Applications use Win32 API functions. Drivers communicate with each other using structures called I/O request packets (IRPs).

Windows defines a set of IRPs that drivers can use. Each IRP requests a single input or output action. A function driver for a USB device uses IRPs to pass communications to and from the bus drivers that handle USB communications. The bus drivers are included with Windows and require no programming by applications programmers or device-driver writers.

The Win32 Driver Model

USB device drivers for Windows must conform to the Win32 Driver Model defined by Microsoft for use under Windows 98 and later, including Windows 2000 and Me. These drivers are known as WDM drivers and have the extension *.sys*. (Other file types may also use the *.sys* extension.)

Like other low-level drivers, a WDM driver has abilities not available to applications because the driver communicates with the operating system at a lower, more privileged level. A WDM driver can permit or deny an application access to a device. For example, a joystick driver can allow any application to use a joystick, or it can allow one application to reserve the joystick for its exclusive use. Other abilities that Windows reserves for WDM and other low-level drivers include DMA transfers and responding to hardware interrupts.

Driver Models for Different Windows Flavors

The Win32 Driver Model provides a common driver model for use by any device under Windows 98 and later. Earlier versions of Windows used different models for device drivers. Windows 95 used VxDs (virtual device drivers). Windows NT 4 used a type of driver called kernel-mode drivers. Developers who wanted to support both Windows 95 and Windows NT had to provide a driver for each. But a single WDM driver can work under both Windows 98 and Windows 2000.

The USB bus drivers included with Windows are WDM drivers. Although Windows 98 continues to support VxDs, USB devices must have WDM function drivers because their function drivers must communicate with the WDM bus drivers.

The Win32 Driver Model isn't completely new, but was built on existing components. A WDM driver is basically an NT kernel-mode driver with the addition of Windows 95's Plug-and-Play and power-management features. The final editions of Windows 95 (versions OSR 2.1 and higher) had some support for WDM drivers. These editions weren't available to retail customers, but were available only to vendors who installed the software on the computers they sold. Beginning with Windows 98, the WDM support was much expanded and improved.

How can two different operating systems, which previously required very different drivers, now use the same drivers? Windows 98 includes the driver *ntkern.vxd*, which tricks WDM drivers into thinking they're communicating with an NT-like operating system. All WDM drivers running on Windows 98 require this driver, which is included with Windows 98.

Programming Languages

Application programmers have a choice in programming languages, including Visual Basic, Delphi, and Visual C++. But to write a driver for a USB device, you need a tool that is capable of compiling a WDM driver, and this means using Visual C++. The exception is driver toolkits that provide a generic driver and either require no programming at all or permit you to use other C compilers or Delphi to customize a generic driver with a user-mode component.

Layered Drivers

In the layered driver model used in USB communications, each layer handles a piece of the communication process. Dividing communications into layers is efficient because it enables different devices that have tasks in common to use the same driver for those tasks. For example, all kinds of devices may use USB, so it makes sense to have one set of drivers to handle the USB-specific communications that are common to all. Including these drivers with Windows means that device vendors don't have to provide them. The alternative would be to have each device driver communicate directly with the USB hardware, with much duplication of effort.

USB Driver Layers

The portion of Windows that manages communications with devices is the I/O subsystem. The subsystem has several layers, with each layer containing one or more drivers that handle a set of related tasks. Requests pass in sequence from one layer to the next. Within the I/O subsystem, the I/O manager is in charge of communications. One element within the I/O subsystem is the USB subsystem, which includes the drivers that handle USB-specific communications for all devices.

The set of protocols used by the drivers is called a stack. (This is different from the CPU stack introduced in Chapter 8.) You can think of the layers as being stacked one above the next, with communications passing in sequence up and down the stack. Applications are at the top of the stack, and the USB hardware is at the bottom of the stack.

The Function Driver

A function driver enables applications to talk to a USB device using API functions. The API functions are part of Windows' Win32 subsystem, which is also in charge of user functions such as running applications, managing user input via the keyboard and mouse, and displaying output on the screen. To communicate with a USB device, an application doesn't have to know anything about the USB protocol, or even if the device uses USB at all.

The function driver also knows how to communicate with the lower-level bus drivers that control the hardware. Figure 10-2 shows how these work together in USB communications. The function driver is often referred to as the device driver, though a complete device driver actually encompasses both the function driver and bus drivers. The function driver may be a class driver or a device-specific driver.

When a device or subclass has requirements beyond what a class driver handles, a supplemental driver called a filter driver can add the needed capabilities. An upper filter driver resides above the class driver. Requests from

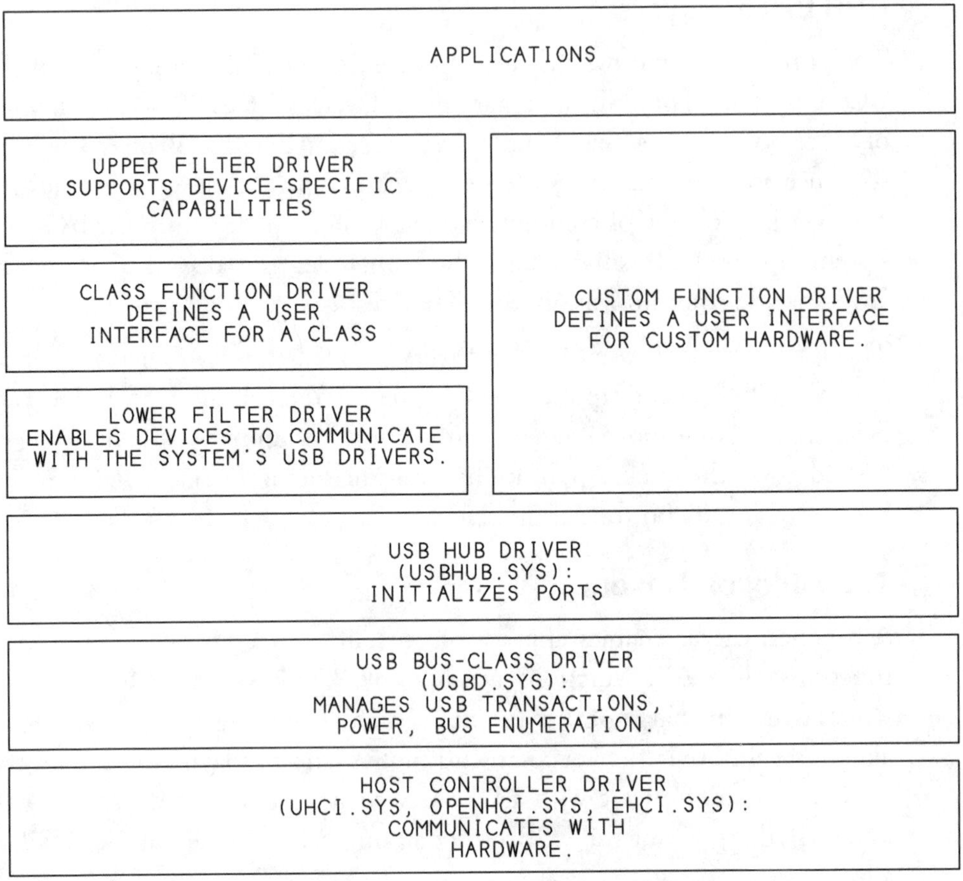

```
┌─────────────────────────────────────────────────────────────────┐
│                         APPLICATIONS                              │
└─────────────────────────────────────────────────────────────────┘

┌──────────────────────────────┐  ┌─────────────────────────────────┐
│     UPPER FILTER DRIVER       │  │                                 │
│   SUPPORTS DEVICE-SPECIFIC    │  │                                 │
│        CAPABILITIES           │  │                                 │
└──────────────────────────────┘  │                                 │
┌──────────────────────────────┐  │    CUSTOM FUNCTION DRIVER       │
│    CLASS FUNCTION DRIVER      │  │   DEFINES A USER INTERFACE      │
│       DEFINES A USER          │  │    FOR CUSTOM HARDWARE.         │
│    INTERFACE FOR A CLASS      │  │                                 │
└──────────────────────────────┘  │                                 │
┌──────────────────────────────┐  │                                 │
│     LOWER FILTER DRIVER       │  │                                 │
│ ENABLES DEVICES TO COMMUNICATE│  │                                 │
│ WITH THE SYSTEM'S USB DRIVERS.│  │                                 │
└──────────────────────────────┘  └─────────────────────────────────┘

┌─────────────────────────────────────────────────────────────────┐
│                      USB HUB DRIVER                               │
│                       (USBHUB.SYS):                               │
│                     INITIALIZES PORTS                             │
└─────────────────────────────────────────────────────────────────┘

┌─────────────────────────────────────────────────────────────────┐
│                    USB BUS-CLASS DRIVER                           │
│                        (USBD.SYS):                                │
│                  MANAGES USB TRANSACTIONS,                        │
│                   POWER, BUS ENUMERATION.                         │
└─────────────────────────────────────────────────────────────────┘

┌─────────────────────────────────────────────────────────────────┐
│                   HOST CONTROLLER DRIVER                          │
│        (UHCI.SYS, OPENHCI.SYS, EHCI.SYS):                         │
│                    COMMUNICATES WITH                              │
│                       HARDWARE.                                   │
└─────────────────────────────────────────────────────────────────┘
```

Figure 10-2: USB communications use a host controller driver, class driver, hub driver, and a function driver that may consist of one or more files.

applications pass through the upper filter driver before being passed to the class driver. A lower filter driver resides between the class driver and bus drivers. A class driver may pass requests to a lower filter driver, which in turn passes them to a bus driver. Lower filter drivers can enable a single class driver to support multiple interfaces, with each driver supporting the class-specific operations required for an interface. For example, Windows provides a driver that enables the HID-class driver to communicate with the USB bus drivers.

Some USB devices may use yet another type of driver, called a legacy virtualization driver. To communicate with the keyboard, mouse, and joystick, Windows 98 uses the virtual device drivers (VxDs) inherited from Windows 95. When one of these peripherals has a USB interface, a legacy virtualization driver translates between the device's HID interface and the VxD's interface. The legacy virtualization driver is a VxD that knows how to talk to the HID driver.

The Bus Drivers

The USB's bus drivers consist of the root-hub driver, the bus-class driver, and the host-controller driver. The root-hub driver manages the initializing of ports and in general manages communications between device drivers and the bus-class driver. The bus-class driver manages bus power, enumeration, USB transactions, and communications between the root-hub driver and the host-controller driver. The host-controller driver enables the host controller hardware to communicate with the USB system software. The host controller connects to the bus. The host-controller driver is separate from the bus-class driver because Windows supports multiple types of host controllers, each with its own driver.

The bus drivers are part of Windows, and application and device-driver writers don't have to know the details about how they work. Perhaps because of this, Microsoft provides very little in the way of documentation for them. If you want to know more about how the low-level communications work, one source of information is the source code and other documentation from the Linux USB Project.

Communication Flow

One way to better understand what happens during a USB transfer is to look at an example. The following are the steps in a USB transfer with a data-acquisition device that uses a custom function driver.

Preliminary Requirements

Before an application can communicate with a device, several things must happen. The device must be attached to the bus. Windows must enumerate the device and identify the driver for the device. And the application that will access the device must obtain a handle that identifies the device and enables communications with it.

When a device is attached, Windows' Device Manager handles enumeration automatically, as described in Chapter 5. To identify which driver to use, Windows compares the retrieved descriptors with the information in its INF files, as described in Chapter 11.

The handle is a unique identifier that Windows assigns to an instance of the device. An application gets the handle by calling the CreateFile API function with a symbolic link that identifies the device.

Some drivers explicitly define a symbolic link for each device they control. For example, Cypress' *ezusb.sys* driver identifies the first EZ-USB chip as ezusb-0. If there are additional EZ-USBs, the driver identifies them as ezusb-1, ezusb-2, and so on up.

Other drivers use a newer method supported by Windows, where the symbolic link contains a globally unique identifier (GUID). The GUID is a 128-bit number that uniquely identifies an object. The object may be any class, interface, or other entity that the software treats as an object.

Windows defines GUIDs for standard objects such as the HID class. For unique devices, developers can obtain a GUID using the *guidgen.exe* program included with Visual C++. The GUID is then included in the driver code.

The *guidgen* program uses a complex algorithm that takes into account a machine identifier, the date and time, and other factors that make it extremely unlikely that another device will end up with an identical GUID. The algorithm was originally defined by the Open Software Foundation.

The standard format for expressing GUIDs divides the GUID into five sets of hex characters, separated by hyphens. This is the GUID for the HID class: 745a17a0-74d3-11d0-b6fe-00a0c90f57da

Applications can use API calls to retrieve class and device GUIDs from the operating system.

The User's Role

When a device is attached and ready to transfer data, the host may request a transfer. To read data from a data-acquisition unit, the user might click a button in a data-acquisition application. Or a user might select an option that causes the application to request a reading once per minute. Or periodic data acquisitions might start automatically when the device's driver is loaded or when the user runs the application.

The Application's Role

The Windows API includes three functions for exchanging data with devices: ReadFile, WriteFile, and DeviceIoControl. A driver may support any combination of these. Each call includes the request, other required information such as the data to write or amount of data to read, and the device's handle. The Platform SDK section in the MSDN library documents these functions.

Although the names suggest that they're used only with files, WriteFile and ReadFile are general-purpose functions that can transfer data to and from any driver that supports them. The data read or data to be written is stored in a buffer specified by the call. A call to ReadFile doesn't necessarily cause the driver to retrieve data from the device. The call may instead return data that was requested previously and stored in a buffer. The details vary with the driver. Chapter 15 has more on how to use ReadFile and WriteFile.

DeviceIoControl is another way to transfer data to and from buffers. Included in each DeviceIoControl request is a code that identifies a specific request. Unlike ReadFile and WriteFile, a single DeviceIoControl call can transfer data in both directions. The driver specifies what data, if any, to pass in each direction for each code. Some codes are commands that don't need to pass additional data.

Windows defines control codes used by disk drives and other common devices. These are examples:

> IOCTL_STORAGE_CHECK_VERIFY determines if media is present and readable on removable media.
> IOCTL_STORAGE_LOAD_MEDIA loads media on a device.

IOCTL_STORAGE_GET_MEDIA_TYPES returns the types of media supported by a drive.

A driver may also define its own control codes. Because the codes are sent only to a specific driver, it doesn't matter if other drivers use the same codes. The driver for Cypress' thermometer application for the CY7C63001 defines codes to get the temperature and button state, set LED brightness, and read and write to the controller's RAM and ports. This is a Visual-Basic declaration for DeviceIoControl:

```
Declare Function DeviceIoControl Lib "kernel32" _
    (ByVal hDevice As Long, _
    ByVal dwIoControlCode As Long, _
    lpInBuffer As Any, _
    ByVal nInBufferSize As Long, _
    lpOutBuffer As Any, _
    ByVal nOutBufferSize As Long, _
    lpBytesReturned As Long, _
    lpOverlapped As OVERLAPPED) _
    As Long
```

This is a call that uses the control code 04h:

```
ltemp = DeviceIoControl _
    (hgDrvrHnd, _
    4&, _
    lIn, _
    lInSize, _
    lOut, _
    lOutSize,_
    lSize, _
    gOverlapped)
```

Windows may support additional API functions for transferring data with devices in a particular class. For example, the functions Hid_GetFeature and HidD_SetFeature read and send Feature reports to HID-class devices.

The Device Driver's Role

When an application calls an API function that reads or writes to a USB device, Windows passes the call to the appropriate function driver. The driver converts the request to a format the USB bus-class driver can understand.

As mentioned earlier, drivers communicate with each other using structures called I/O Request Packets (IRPs). For USB communications, the IRPs contain structures called USB Request Blocks (URBs) that specify protocols for configuring devices and transferring data. The URBs are documented in the Windows DDK.

A function driver requests a transfer by creating an URB and submitting it in an IRP to a lower-level driver. The bus and host-controller drivers handle the details of scheduling transactions on the bus. For interrupt and isochronous transfers, if there is no outstanding IRP for an endpoint when its scheduled time comes up, the transaction is skipped.

For transfers that require multiple transactions, the function driver submits a single IRP for the entire transfer. All of the transfer's transactions are then scheduled without requiring further communications with the function driver.

If you're using an existing function driver (rather than writing your own), you need to understand how to access the driver's application-level interface, but you don't have to concern yourself with IRPs and URBs. If you're writing a function driver, you need to provide the IRPs that communicate with the system's USB drivers.

The Hub Driver's Role

The host's hub driver resides between a device-specific or USB-class driver and the USB bus-class driver. The hub driver handles the initializing of the root hub's ports and any devices downstream of the ports. This driver requires no programming by device developers. Windows includes the hub driver *usbhub.sys*.

The Bus-class Driver's Role

The USB bus-class driver translates communication requests between the hub driver and the host-controller driver. It handles bus enumeration, power management, and some aspects of USB transactions. These communications require no programming by device developers. Windows includes the bus-class driver *usbd.sys*.

The Host-controller Driver's Role

The host-controller driver communicates with the host-controller hardware, which in turn connects to the bus. The host-controller driver requires no programming by device developers.

There are three types of host controllers. Two are for low- and full-speed communications only and one is for high-speed communications only. The low- and full-speed controller types are the Open Host Controller Interface (OHCI) and Universal Host Controller Interface (UHCI). High-speed controllers must use the Enhanced Host Controller Interface (EHCI). The USB Implementers Forum's website has links to the specifications.

Controllers that conform to the OHCI standard use the driver *openhci.sys*, and controllers that conform to the UHCI standard use the driver *uhci.sys*. Both drivers provide a way for the USB hardware to communicate with the bus-class driver. Although they differ in how they do so, in most cases the differences are transparent to driver developers and application programmers.

The two drivers take different approaches to implementing the host-controller's functions. UHCI places more of the communications burden on software and allows the use of simpler, cheaper hardware. OHCI places more of the burden on the hardware and allows simpler software control. UHCI was developed by Intel and OHCI was developed by Compaq, Microsoft, and National Semiconductor.

The two host controller types do have some differences in performance. An OHCI controller is capable of scheduling more than one stage of a control transfer in a single frame, while a UHCI controller always schedules each stage in a different frame. For bulk endpoints with a maximum packet size less than 64 bytes, the Windows UHCI driver attempts no more than one transaction per frame, while an OHCI driver may schedule additional transactions in a frame. And an OHCI controller will poll an interrupt endpoint at least once every 32 milliseconds, even if the endpoint descriptor requests a maximum latency of 255 milliseconds, while UHCI controllers can, but don't have to, support less-frequent polling.

An EHCI controller handles high-speed communications only. To support all three speeds, a PC must have an EHCI controller and either a companion OHCI or UHCI controller in the PC or a 2.0-compliant hub, which performs the function of a host controller for low- and full-speed devices. An EHCI host controller and a companion 1.x host controller can share a single bus. Users and application programmers don't have to know or care which host controller is communicating with a device.

The Device's Role

After a transmission leaves the host's port, data may pass through additional hubs. Eventually the data reaches the hub that connects to the device, and this hub passes the data on to the device. The device recognizes its address, reads the incoming data, and takes appropriate action.

The Response

Most communications require a response, which may include data sent in response to the request or a packet with a status code. This information travels back to the host in reverse order: through the device's hub, onto the bus, and to the PC's hardware and software. A device driver may pass a response on to an application, which may display the result or take other action.

Ending Communications

When an application closes or otherwise decides that it no longer needs to access the device, it uses the API function CloseHandle to free system resources.

More Examples

Communications with other USB devices follow a similar pattern, though there can be differences in how the transfer initiates and in how the device driver handles communications.

Other examples of a user initiating a transfer are clicking on a USB drive's icon to view a disk's folders or clicking Print in an application to send a file to a USB printer. In each of these examples, nothing happens until the application requests a communication and the device driver fills a buffer with data to send or makes a buffer available for received data.

In some cases, the driver causes the host to continuously request data from a device whether or not an application has requested it. For example, a keyboard driver causes the host to make periodic requests for keypress data because there is no way for an application to predict when a key will be pressed.

The host also sends requests to enumerate devices on system power-up or device attachment. The device's hub causes the host to initiate these requests when the hub notifies the host of the presence of a device. A device can use the USB's remote-wakeup feature to initiate a transfer by signaling its hub, and in turn the host, to request resuming communications.

Choosing a Driver Type

How do you decide whether to use an existing driver, a custom driver, or a combination? Sometimes the choice is limited by what's available for the device. From there it depends on a combination of the performance you need, cost, and speed of development.

Drivers Included with Windows

When it's feasible, the easiest approach to accessing a USB device is to use a driver included with Windows. This way, there are no drivers to write or install and any Windows computer can access the device. Chapter 12 has details about the class drivers available in Windows. For custom designs, the most useful of these are the HID drivers and possibly the mass-storage driver.

Vendor-supplied Drivers

Another way to communicate with a device is to use a driver supplied by the chip's vendor. The ideal is a ready-to-install, general-purpose driver, along with complete, commented source code in case you want to adapt it for use with a particular device. The driver should also include documentation that shows how to open a handle to the device and read and write to it in application code. The usefulness of vendor-supplied drivers varies. A driver is much less useful if it's buggy, doesn't include the features you need, or has sketchy documentation that makes it hard to understand and use.

Chapter 12 describes drivers from FTDI for use with its USB UART chip and from SigmaTel for use with its IrDA-to-USB bridge chip

Custom Drivers

Sometimes there is no generic or vendor driver that includes the transfer types you want to use or has the performance you need. Or you may want to define custom DeviceIoControl codes. In these cases, the solution is to create a custom device driver. The next section discusses this option.

Writing a Custom Driver

If you don't have experience writing device drivers, creating a WDM driver is not a trivial task. It requires an investment in tools, expertise in C programming, and a fair amount of knowledge about how Windows communicates with hardware and applications. On the positive side, writing a USB driver is easier than writing a driver for a device that connects to the ISA bus. Plus, a variety of products can help to simplify and speed up the process.

Requirements

The minimum requirement for writing a device driver from scratch is Microsoft's Visual C++, which is capable of compiling WDM drivers. The compiler also includes a programming environment and a debugger to help during development.

Beyond this basic requirement, other tools can help to varying degrees, including the Windows Device Developer's Kit (DDK), a subscription to Microsoft's Developer's Network (MSDN), driver toolkits, and advanced debuggers.

The Windows DDK includes example code and developer-level documentation. The USB-related documentation includes tutorials on WDM drivers and HIDs and source code for USB drivers.

For bulk transfers, the DDK includes source and compiled code, documentation, and an example application for the *bulkusb.sys* driver. The driver is designed to work with just about any USB chip that supports bulk transfers. Applications use ReadFile and WriteFile for data transfers. In a similar way, the DDK includes the *isousb.sys* driver for handling isochronous transfers. If you decide to use either of these, check the USB Implementers Forum's webboard for tips and fixes before you begin!

The DDK also has a filter-driver example and the *usbview* utility. The examples can be a useful starting point in developing your own drivers. You can download the Windows DDK from Microsoft's website.

MSDN is Microsoft's subscription service to massive quantities of documentation, examples, and developer's tools for Microsoft products. The topics covered include WDM driver development and USB, with quarterly updates. There are several levels of subscription that enable you to get the documentation alone or with varying amounts of Microsoft applications and development tools. Much of the information and other tools are also downloadable from Microsoft's website.

How to write a USB driver from scratch is a much bigger topic than this book has room for. Some excellent books cover the topic in detail, including WDM device-driver writing in general as well as sections specifically about USB. Three good books are *Programming the Microsoft Windows Driver Model* by Walter Oney, *Writing Windows WDM Device Drivers* by Chris Cant, and *Developing Windows NT Device Drivers* by Edward N. Dekker and Joseph M. Newcomer. (NT drivers are similar to WDM drivers, and the book includes material on WDM and USB.) Chapter 17 describes Microsoft's programs for driver testing and digital signing.

Using a Driver Toolkit

A driver toolkit provides a way to jump start driver development by doing as much of the work for you as possible. Toolkits that support creating USB drivers are available from BSQUARE, Jungo Ltd., and Compuware NuMega.

There are two general categories of toolkits. One provides a generic driver that handles USB communications, generates an INF file, and provides other assistance in enabling applications to use the driver. This approach is very fast and requires no programming at all to create the driver, but it can't handle every situation. Other toolkits provide libraries and other tools that assist in writing a custom driver for a device. This approach is more flexible but requires programming expertise.

Toolkits that Use a Generic Driver

All USB communications follow the protocols defined in the specification, so it makes sense that a single generic driver should be able to communicate with just about any device. A generic driver would have to support all four transfer types, including vendor-defined control requests, plus it should support the power management and Plug-and-Play capabilities required of all WDM drivers. Additional functions such as the ability to retrieve descriptors or select a configuration or interface are useful as well.

Two toolkits enable a device to use a generic driver: BSQUARE's WinRT for USB and Jungo's WinDriver USB. These toolkits require no driver programming at all.

WinRT for USB. WinRT for USB includes a kernel-mode driver and several supporting files. The driver supports synchronous and asynchronous transfers of all four types, retrieving descriptors and the device GUID, selecting an interface, and registering for device notification to detect when a device is removed from the bus. For example, to request an interrupt transfer, an application calls the function WinRTInterruptTransfer, passing the device handle, endpoint number, buffer length, and a buffer. The function returns a status code and the number of bytes transferred.

To create the files needed to support a device, you develop your device firmware, store the firmware in the device, and attach the device to the bus. To make the required setup files for the driver, run the WinRT for USB Con-

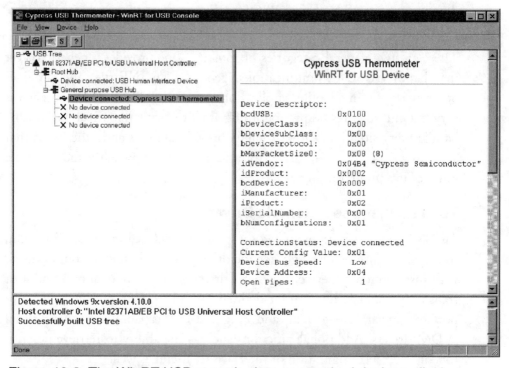

Figure 10-3: The WinRT USB console detects attached devices, displays descriptors, and creates a driver and the setup files for a device.

sole application (Figure 10-3) and select your device from the tree of detected USB devices. The Console prompts you for a symbolic name for your device, which can be anything you specify, and other optional information. The Console then makes the setup files and offers to install the driver on the current system. For testing, the WinRT for USB Wizard creates a sample Visual C++ application.

In addition to the driver file, there are two C header files containing the function prototypes and data types for calling the functions in the driver and error codes and *.dll* and *.lib* files that enable applications to access the functions in the driver. Chapter 15 has more about using *.dll* and *.lib* files.

When you distribute the device, you also distribute the INF file created by the Console application, *WinRTUsb.dll*, *WinRTUsb.sys*, and any application software you provide.

Applications can also access WinRT USB's functions from the provided ActiveX control. To enable using the control with Visual Basic, you add it to a project by clicking Project > Components > Controls and selecting the WinRT-USB control. The Object Browser then shows the supported classes and their properties, functions, and subroutines. This line of Visual-Basic code performs a bulk transfer:

```
returnlength = WinRTUsb1.BulkTransfer(0, size, buffer)
```

There are two editions of WinRT for USB. One is for use with Windows 98, Windows 2000, and Window Me. The other enables you to provide a driver for use on Windows NT 4.

WinDriver USB. Jungo's WinDriver USB takes a somewhat different approach but also can provide a driver without requiring you to write any code. The WinDriver Wizard generates files that you compile to create a custom user-mode driver in an *.exe* file. The user-mode driver communicates with the provided kernel-mode driver *windrvr.sys*. You can compile the files generated by the Wizard using Visual C++, C++ Builder, or Delphi. WinDriver will also create an INF file for the device.

The WinDriver Wizard enables you to select your device from those detected, then test it immediately by reading and writing data (Figure 10-4). You can then request the Wizard to create the driver files. When the driver is installed, applications communicate with the device using device-specific functions such as MyDevice_Open and MyDevice_GetDeviceInfo.

For faster performance, you can move portions of your code from the user-mode driver to a kernel-mode driver called a Kernel PlugIn, which you compile with Visual C++. For debugging, the included DebugMonitor application enables you to monitor activities handled by *windrvr.sys*. WinDriver USB's drivers run under Windows 98 and Windows 2000.

Toolkits that Provide Libraries for Creating a Custom Driver

The completely automated toolkits aren't suitable for every device. They can't create filter drivers, and you may want a completely custom driver to achieve the best possible performance. Three products for creating custom

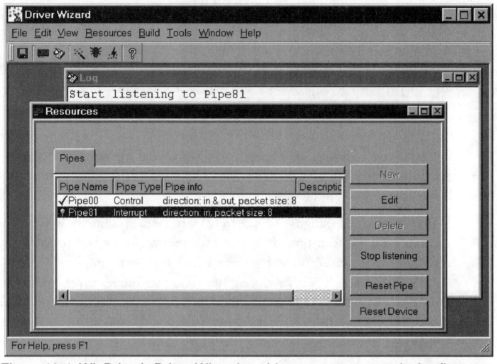

Figure 10-4: WinDriver's Driver WIzard enables you to test your device firmware by reading and writing to it, then creates the files you compile to create a custom driver for the device.

drivers are BSQUARE's WinDK, CompuWare Numega's DriverWorks, and Jungo's KernelDriver.

Each of these has Wizards and code libraries that do much of the work for you. You need to fill in the provided skeleton code and compile the driver. The driver's performance is the same as if you had written the driver from scratch.

Each of these toolkits is capable of generating driver code for any device type, not just USB devices. WinDK has an optional USB extension that enables you to use the same source code to create a driver that will run on Windows NT 4.

11

How Windows Selects a Driver

When Windows detects a new USB peripheral, one of the things it has to do is decide which device driver applications should use to communicate with the device and if necessary, load the selected driver. This is the job of Windows' Device Manager, which uses class and device installers and INF files to find a match.

This chapter explains how these components work together to select drivers for newly attached devices. I also show how to create an INF file that will cause the Device Manager to select the correct drivers.

The Process

The Device Manager is a Control-Panel applet that's responsible for installing, configuring, and removing devices. The Device Manager also adds information about each device to the system registry, which is the database that Windows maintains for storing critical information about the hardware and software installed on a system.

In Windows 98, display the Device Manager by right-clicking the My Computer icon on the desktop and selecting Properties, then the Device Manager tab. Or select Start Menu > Settings > Control Panel > System > Device Manager. In Windows 2000, it's the same except for one more click after System: System > Hardware > Device Manager.

The device and class installers are DLLs. Windows has default installers that the Device Manager uses to locate and load drivers for devices in the classes supported by the operating system (such as HIDs). The Device Manager and the installers together are also responsible for displaying dialog boxes as needed to prompt users for information.

The INF file is a text file containing information that helps Windows identify a device. The file tells Windows what driver or drivers to use and what information to store in the registry.

Searching for INF Files

When Windows enumerates a new USB device, the Device Manager compares the data in all of the system's INF files with the information in the descriptors retrieved from the device on enumerating. A typical PC can accumulate hundreds of INF files, so Windows 98 and Windows 2000 have ways to speed up the search.

To prevent having to read through all of the INF files each time a new device is detected, Windows 98 maintains a driver information database with information culled from its INF files. The database files are *drvdata.bin* and *drvidx.bin*, stored in the *windows\inf* folder.

You can view the contents of these files in a text editor or word processor. (Ignore the extra characters in the files.) Don't change the contents of the files, however; when you're finished viewing, just close the files without saving.

Drvidx.bin lists every Vendor and Product ID in the INF files, along with the manufacturer name, provider name, and description. *Drvdata.bin* matches manufacturers with INF files that contain information about their products. After retrieving the Vendor and Product IDs from a device, the Device Manager uses the information in these two files to find the manufacturer and the INF file with information about the specific product.

Windows 2000 doesn't have these database files, but instead uses PNF (precompiled INF) files to speed searching. During device installation, Windows 2000 creates a PNF file and stores it in the same folder as the device's INF file. The PNF contains much of the same information as the INF but in a format that enables quicker searching. Windows 98 systems may have PNFs also.

The Registry's Role

The system registry stores information about all installed devices, whether or not they're attached and enumerated. When a new device is enumerated, the Device Manager stores information about the device in the registry.

To learn what kinds of information the Device Manager finds and stores, you can view (and edit) the registry's contents using the *regedit.exe* utility that comes with Windows.

A word of caution: the system registry is a vital and essential component of Windows. It's so important that Windows maintains multiple backup copies in case the current copy becomes unusable. Be extremely careful about making changes to the registry. If you goof and want to restore the registry to its previous state, boot to the DOS prompt and type *scanreg /restore*. Just viewing the registry is safe, however.

The registry arranges its contents in a tree structure. Information about USB devices is in a couple of places:

> HKEY_LOCAL_MACHINE\Enum\USB

lists all USB devices.

HKEY indicates a registry key, which is an item in the registry structure. HKEY_LOCAL_MACHINE is a pointer to a data structure containing information about the system's hardware and installed software.

USB devices are also listed in this branch:

HKEY_LOCAL_MACHINE\System\CurrentControlSet\
Services\Class

The Class branch has sub-branches for various categories. The USB branch lists the USB host controller and root hub, as Figure 11-1 shows. A USB peripheral doesn't necessary show up in the USB branch; it may be in a branch that pertains to the peripheral's function. Standard peripheral types like keyboards, mice, and printers have their own branches, and will show up there. HID-class devices also have an entry in the HID branch. Other peripherals, such as digital cameras, may be in the USB branch. If the Device Manager can't figure out what to do with a device, it may call it an Unknown Device and place it in the USB branch. A custom peripheral can also create its own branch.

The Control Panel

The Device Manager is also responsible for adding attached devices to the Device Manager's window, as Figure 11-2 shows.

The Device Manager's display shows only the USB devices that are currently detected. You can unplug a device while viewing the display and watch the device's listing disappear. Plug the device back in, and its listing pops back. An exclamation point over the device's icon means that there was a problem communicating with the device or finding a driver. An X over the icon means that the device is present but disabled, possibly by the user. To view additional information about a device, select the device and click Properties.

What the User Sees

What you see on the screen when you attach a new USB peripheral depends on what drivers and INF file the device uses and whether or not the device has been attached and enumerated previously.

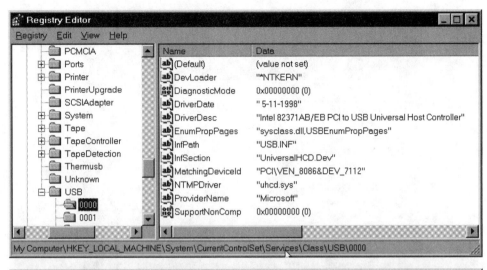

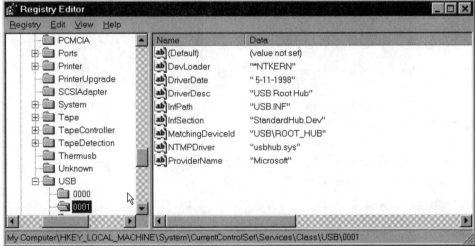

Figure 11-1: The registry's Class\USB branch has information about the system's host controller and root hub.

Specific Device Listings

When you attach a device, Windows displays a window with the message *New Hardware Found.* If the device descriptors include a Product String, under Windows 98 SE and later, the window displays the string. Otherwise,

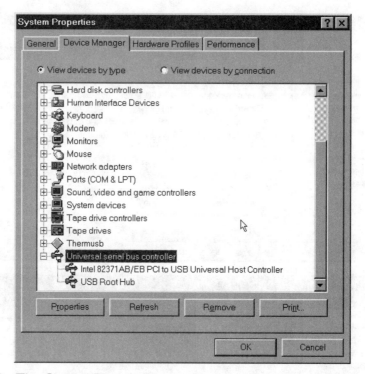

Figure 11-2: The Control Panel's Device Manager lists all attached and enumerated devices.

it displays *Unknown Device*. If the device has never been enumerated on the system, Windows will need to locate a driver.

If Windows doesn't find a matching INF file, it runs the Add New Hardware Wizard (Figure 11-3). You see a window recommending letting the Wizard search for the best driver for the device. When you accept the recommendation and select Next, the Wizard requests a location to search.

If the device comes with a driver on disk, specify the drive containing the disk. When the Wizard finds the file, it displays the filename and announces that it's ready to install the driver. (To make things as easy as possible for users, vendors should store the INF file in the root directory of the product's disk.) Click Next, and the Wizard displays *Please wait while Windows builds a driver information database.*

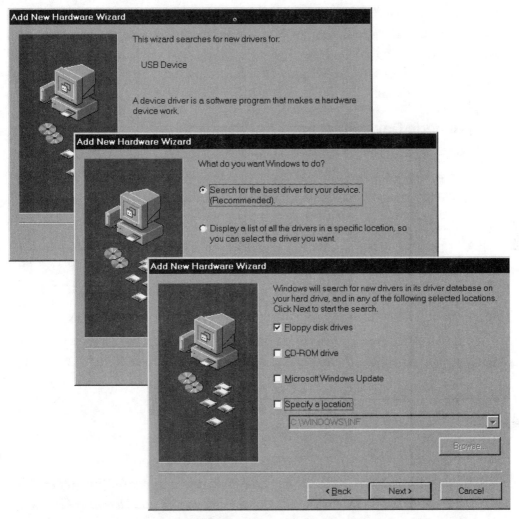

Figure 11-3: Windows' Add New Hardware Wizard searches for and installs drivers for newly attached devices.

The Wizard copies the INF file to the system's INF folder, loads the driver(s) specified in the file, lists the device in the Device Manager, and displays a window letting you know that it has finished installing the required software. The Device Manager's listing shows the device description, manufacturer, and provider name from the INF file.

If the device has been enumerated previously, the system already has the information it needs, so no windows need to be displayed. The enumeration should be invisible except for a short delay that prevents the cursor from selecting items while Windows finds the correct INF file and loads any needed drivers.

Generic Device Listings

If a newly attached device uses only the standard HID drivers, it doesn't need its own INF file to identify it. On the first attachment, the Device Manager will determine that the device belongs to the HID class, and when it can't find a Vendor and Product ID match, will decide that the generic HID drivers are the best fit.

But because there was no exact match, the Device Manager will play it safe and run the Add New Hardware Wizard to give you a chance to select a better driver (by specifying a drive to search, for example). If you accept the default selections, Windows looks for a driver in the system's INF folder, selects the INF file for the HID class *(hiddev.inf* for Windows 98 or *input.inf* for Windows 2000), and loads the HID drivers. The Device Manager lists the device as a *Standard HID Device,* with no indication of its specific function or manufacturer.

Inside an INF File

The Device Manager looks for INF files in the system's INF folder. The default locations are *\windows\inf* for Windows 98 and *\winnt\inf* for Windows 2000. By default, this is a hidden folder. If you don't see the folder in My Computer, select View > Folder Options > View, then under Hidden Files, select *Show all files.* Do *not* click *Hide file extensions for known file types.*

Examining the existing files is a good way to learn about the kinds of things contained in the files and how the information is structured. Your PC is sure to have plenty of INF files to examine. The INF file for the HID class is *hiddev.inf.* in Windows 98 and *input.inf* in Windows 2000. INF files can be long and complicated, but the basics are fairly straightforward. In most cases, you can create an INF file by adapting one that's similar to what you need. Vendors of USB controller chips often provide examples. The Windows DDK also has documentation on the contents and structure of INF files.

INF files for Windows 2000 have a few changes compared to Windows 98, including the need for a Services section that specifies how and when a driver's services are loaded. The DDK documentation has more details under *INF File Sections and Directives*.

Listing 11-1 is an INF file for a custom HID under Windows 98. I used *hiddev.inf* and Cypress' example INF files as models for the file. Figure 11-4 and Figure 11-5 show the information that the Device Manager displays after enumerating a device with this INF file.

Syntax

The information in an INF file must follow a few syntax rules, which will look familiar if you have experience with the *.ini* files commonly used in Windows 3.x.

- The information is arranged in sections, with each section containing one or more items. The section name is in square brackets [ ]. A carriage return/line feed begins a new item. Some of the section names (Version, ClassInstall) are standard names that Windows will look for. Other sections match values specified in other sections. For example, if the Manufacturer section designates the manufacturer as Lakeview, the INF file will also have a Lakeview section. The sections can be in any order, though most follow the same convention, and the order of the items within a section can be critical. So if you're adapting an example, keep the order of items in the sections the same.

- A semicolon (;) indicates a comment.

- A backslash (\) at the end of a line acts as a line continuator, unless it's enclosed in quotes ("\").

- Text enclosed in percent symbols (%sampletext%) refers to a string. For example, you might have the following item:

  ```
  provider=%Provider%
  ```

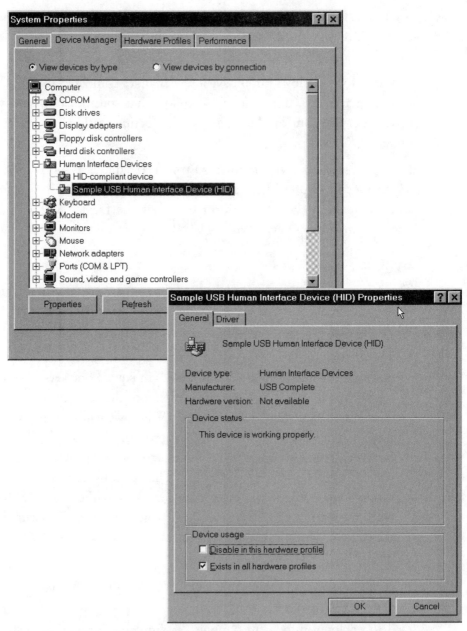

Figure 11-4: The Device Manager displays information obtained from the device's INF file. The device is listed both as an HID compliant device and as a device matching the description and Manufacturer in the INF file.

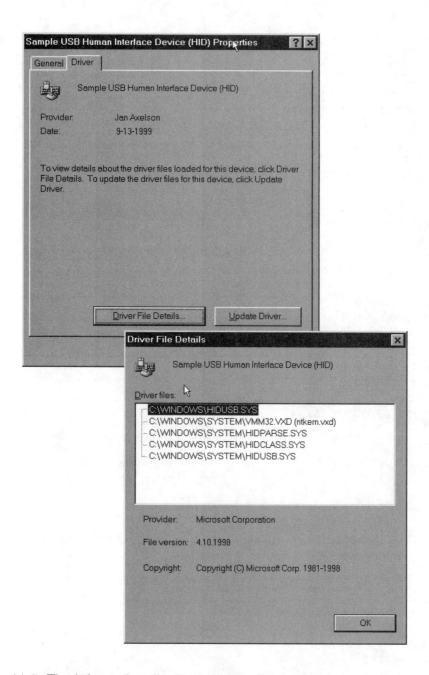

Figure 11-5: The information displayed by the Device Manager includes the Provider name and drivers specified in the device's INF file.

```
[Version]
Signature="$CHICAGO$"
Class=HID

;The GUID for HIDs
ClassGUID={745a17a0-74d3-11d0-b6fe-00a0c90f57da}

provider=%Provider%
LayoutFile=layout.inf, layout1.inf

[ClassInstall]
Addreg=Class.AddReg

[Class.AddReg]
HKR,,Installer,,mmci.dll

[Manufacturer]
%MfgName%=Lakeview

[Lakeview]
;Uses Lakeview Research's Vendor ID (0925)
;Uses the Product ID 1234
%USB\VID_0925&PID_1234.DeviceDesc%=SampleHID,
  USB\VID_0925&PID_1234

[DestinationDirs]
USBHID.CopyList = 11                 ; LDID_SYS
;------------------------------------------------------------;
```

Listing 11-1: (Sheet 1 of 2) A device's INF file helps Windows locate the driver to use for the device.

```
[SampleHID]
CopyFiles=SampleHID.CopyList
AddReg=SampleHID.AddReg

[SampleHID.AddReg]
HKR,,DevLoader,,*ntkern
HKR,,NTMPDriver,,"hidusb.sys"

[SampleHID.CopyList]
hidusb.sys
hidclass.sys
hidparse.sys
;-------------------------------------------------------------
 -;
[Strings]
Provider="Microsoft"
MfgName="USB Complete"
USB\VID_0925&PID_1234.DeviceDesc="Sample USB human interface
  device (HID)"
```

Listing 11-1: (Sheet 2 of 2) A device's INF file helps Windows locate the driver to use for the device.

with an item in the Strings section that defines the provider string:

```
Provider="USB Complete"
```

- Some items set the value of an entry. For example, this item defines the device's class entry as HID:

```
Class=HID
```

- Some items specify information to store in the system registry:

```
HKR,,Installer,,mmci.dll
```

Sections

An INF file includes sections that help Windows identify the device, find the appropriate drivers, and store information about the device in the system registry. Here is the purpose of each section in the example INF file:

Version

The Version section is the file's header. Every INF file must have one.

The Version section in the example file has these items:

```
[Version]
Signature="$CHICAGO$"
Class=HID
;The GUID for HIDs
ClassGUID={745a17a0-74d3-11d0-b6fe-00a0c90f57da}
provider=%Provider%
LayoutFile=layout.inf, layout1.inf
```

The Signature key specifies which operating system the INF file is intended for. For devices that use WDM drivers, the value can be $Windows 98$, $Windows NT$, or $Chicago$, no matter which operating system the PC is using. Chicago was a beta name used when Windows 95 was under development and its use is still valid under later editions of Windows.

The Class key specifies the class for devices installed with this file. The example specifies the HID class.

The ClassGUID key specifies the GUID in the registry for devices installed with this file. A GUID is a 128-bit identifier. The example is the GUID for the HID class. It uses the standard GUID format. There's more on GUIDs later in this chapter.

The Provider key names the creator of the INF file. In the example, %Provider% refers to a string defined later in the file.

The LayoutFile key names the source disks and files needed to install the driver for the device. Because the HID drivers are included with Windows, the example specifies files that contain installation information for the Windows setup. These files are also INF files. The information is in the Source-DisksFiles and SourceDisksNames sections of the files.

ClassInstall

The ClassInstall section installs a new class in the Class section of the registry. The Device Manager processes this section only if a device's class isn't yet installed in the operating system.

The example ClassInstall section has one item:

```
[ClassInstall]
Addreg=Class.AddReg
```

The Addreg key adds a class description to the system registry. In the example, the key's value refers to the Class.Addreg section, which specifies an installer file:

```
[Class.AddReg]
HKR,,Installer,,mmci.dll
```

HKR stands for HKEY_ROOT, which is the base registry key for the section that the AddReg appears in. This is typically under System\Current-ControlSet\Enum\Root, then a specific key for the device.

The installer file *mmci.dll* in the example is included with Windows 98 and is stored in the *windows\\system* folder.

Manufacturer

The Manufacturer section identifies the device (or devices) and names the Install section for each. Every INF file must have this section.

In the example, the MfgName string (defined later in the file) is set to the value *Lakeview*:

```
[Manufacturer]
%MfgName%=Lakeview
```

The Lakeview section has additional information:

```
[Lakeview]
;Uses Lakeview Research's Vendor ID (0925)
;Uses the Product ID 1234
%USB\VID_0925&PID_1234.DeviceDesc%=SampleHID,
USB\VID_0925&PID_1234
```

This section names the device's Vendor and Product IDs. When the Device Manager finds a match between these and the IDs retrieved from the device on enumerating, it knows that it has found the right INF file.

DestinationDirs

The DestinationDirs section names the folder or folders that any CopyFiles, RenFiles, and DelFiles items will use. In the example, SampleHID.CopyList is the name of a section that has a CopyFiles item. The value is a logical disk identifier (LDID) of 11, which is the system directory. The *Device Information (INF) File Reference* in the Windows DDK documentation lists other LDID values.

```
[DestinationDirs]
SampleHID.CopyList = 11
```

The SampleHID section has the CopyFiles item and an AddReg item:

```
[SampleHID]
CopyFiles=SampleHID.CopyList
AddReg=SampleHID.AddReg
```

These items name other sections in the file.

The SampleHID.CopyList section lists the drivers for the device:

```
[SampleHID.CopyList]
hidusb.sys
hidclass.sys
hidparse.sys
```

These are the drivers for generic HID-class devices. They're stored in *\windows\system32\drivers* or *\winnt\system32\drivers*.

The SampleHID.AddReg section adds registry information for the device:

```
[SampleHID.AddReg]
HKR,,DevLoader,,*ntkern
HKR,,NTMPDriver,,"hidusb.sys"
```

DevLoader names *ntkern.vxd* as the VxD (virtual driver) that loads the drivers. *Ntkern.vxd* in turn loads the driver named in NTMPDriver. In the example, this is *hidusb.sys*. Both files are included with Windows 98. You won't find the file *ntkern.vxd* on your system because it's archived in, or bound into, the file *vmm32.vxd* for quicker loading.

Strings

The Strings section defines the strings referred to by items in other sections. Each item matches an item surrounded by percent signs in another section.

So, for example, the provider in the Version section is equal to %Provider%, which equals *Microsoft* (since they are the source of the drivers).

```
[Strings]
Provider="Microsoft"
MfgName="USB Complete"
USB\VID_0925&PID_1234.DeviceDesc="Sample USB human
interface device (HID)"
```

The Generic INF File for HIDs

The generic INF file for HIDs is *hiddev.inf* in Windows 98 and *input.inf* in Windows 2000. Every Windows system should have one of these files. It's similar to the sample file in Listing 11-1. The Device Manager uses this file to install any HID that doesn't have its own INF file. The file also has Vendor and Product IDs and descriptions for several manufacturers' devices, so these don't need their own INF files.

Creating INF Files

If you need to create an INF file for a device, Microsoft provides several tools to help in creating the file and ensuring that it has all of the required sections in the correct format. This section describes the tools and also gives some tips that can come in handy when you're experimenting with INFs.

Tools

For creating INF files, Microsoft provides *infedit* for Windows 98 and *Geninf, ChkINF,* and *InfCatReady* for Windows 2000.

The Windows 98 DDK includes the *infedit* application (Figure 11-6), which enables you to examine and edit INF files. To protect the installed INF files, *infedit* hides the *windows\inf* folder, so to view an installed file, you'll need to copy it to a different folder. You can also use any text editor to view and edit INF files.

The Windows DDK includes two tools for Windows 2000 INF files: *Geninf* for creating files and *ChkINF* for checking a file's structure and syntax.

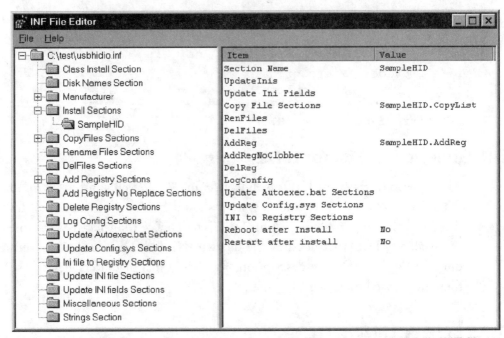

Figure 11-6: Windows 98's *infedit* tool enables you to view and edit INF files.

The *Geninf* application has an INF wizard that asks you questions about your device and creates an INF file for it. The documentation warns that the created file is a skeleton that may not be fully valid and is likely to need additions or revisions. The application includes specific support for some device classes.

ChkINF is a Perl script that requires a Perl interpreter, which you can download free from *www.activeware.com* and other sources. The script runs from an MS-DOS prompt and creates an HTML page that annotates an INF file with errors and warnings as needed.

For drivers that will use digital signing as described in Chapter 17, Microsoft provides the *InfCatReady* application, which looks for errors that could interfere with the digital signature and thus prevent driver installation. *InfCatReady* is available from the WHQL website at *www.microsoft.com/hwtest*.

Tips

Here are some tips for using and experimenting with INF files:

A commercial product's Vendor ID must be an official ID assigned by the USB Implementers Forum. My examples use the Vendor ID of 0925h, which is assigned to my company, Lakeview Research. The owner of the Vendor ID is responsible for ensuring that each product and version has a unique set of IDs. Borrowing someone else's Vendor ID can lead to conflicts if the owner of the ID uses the same values for a different product.

As described above, for experimenting with HIDs, you can use Windows' generic INF file, instead of an INF file containing your Vendor ID. The Device Manager will show the device as a generic HID, rather than using the name you provide in an INF file.

When experimenting with different settings in an INF file, you may find that at times the Device Manager remembers information from previous INF files, even if you deleted the previous file and the information about the device in the registry, powered down, and rebooted.

Under Windows 98, unless you follow a specific procedure when changing the contents of an INF file, Windows may fail to rebuild the driver information database.

To ensure that Windows 98 is aware of any changes you've made to an INF file, follow this procedure:

1. Save a copy of the new INF file that you want to use. Save it under another name (such as *mydriver.new*) or in a location other than the system's INF folder.

2. Attach the device and allow the Device Manager to enumerate it.

3. In the Device Manager's window, select the device's entry and select Remove.

4. Deleting the entry in the Device Manager causes the device's INF file to be saved in the *windows\inf\other* folder, with the vendor's name added to the beginning of the filename. For example, Lakeview's file *mydriver.inf* would become *lakeviewmydriver.inf.* Delete this file as well. In some cases,

such as the system's INF files, the *inf\other* folder won't have anything to delete.

5. Copy the INF file you want to use to the *windows\inf* folder. Be sure the file has an extension of *.inf* (such as *mydriver.inf*).

6. Unplug and re-attach the device. Windows will rebuild the driver information database using your new INF file.

Another way to accomplish the same thing under Windows 98 is described in Microsoft's article Q139206, *Hardware List Not Updated After Installing New .inf File.* The article suggests renaming the driver information database to force Windows to rebuild it. In the *windows\inf* folder, rename *drvdata.bin* to *drvdata.xxx* and rename *drvidx.bin* to *drvidx.xxx*. (By renaming the files rather than deleting them, you can restore them if necessary.) Another workaround is to use a different Product ID each time, in both the INF file and the device firmware.

Under Windows 2000, to remove all information about a device, delete or change the extension of its INF and PNF files. When Windows stores the files in *\winnt\inf*, it may rename them *oem*.inf* and *oem*pnf*, where * is a number. To find the correct files, use the *Find > Files or Folders* utility available from Windows' *Start* menu. Browse to the *\winnt\inf* folder and in the *Containing Text* text box, enter *VID_xxxx&PID_yyyy*, where *xxxx* is the vendor ID and *yyyy* is the product ID, both in hexadecimal.

If you do a lot of experimenting and don't delete each device when you're done with it, the registry will fill with entries from your various configurations. When you no longer need a registry key, you can delete it from within *regedit.exe* (but see my cautions above about the registry).

The INF files that ship with Windows all have file names with no more than eight characters plus the 3-character extension. Microsoft says that this is due to "technical issues with the product install," but that INF files added after Windows is installed may use longer file names.

12

Device Classes

Most devices aren't totally unique, but instead share many qualities with other devices. For example, all printers receive and print data and send status information back to the host. All mice send information about mouse movements and button clicks to the host. All disk drives transfer files between a disk and the host.

When a group of devices or interfaces share many attributes or when they provide or request similar services, it makes sense to define the attributes and services in a class specification. The specification then serves as a guide for device developers and device-driver writers.

This chapter describes USB's defined classes and takes a closer look at both common and more unusual peripheral types and how you can use classes to simplify developing on both the host and device sides.

Uses of Classes

Classes offer several advantages. They make it easier to develop device drivers and firmware because the work of defining the attributes and services the device will use has been done, leaving only the implementation details. If both the driver writer and firmware developer follow the same specification, the driver should have no problem communicating with the device. Windows and other operating systems include drivers for common classes. If your device's class is supported by the operating system, you don't have to provide a driver with the device.

When a device in a supported class has unique features or abilities, the device vendor can provide a filter driver that adds capabilities to the class driver included with the operating system. Adding a filter driver is easier than writing the complete driver.

Even if the device's class isn't supported by the operating system, it may be in the future. If you design the firmware and driver to comply with the class specification, it will be compatible with any driver added in future editions of the operating system.

The USB Implementers Forum releases class specifications developed by Device Working Groups whose members have expertise and interest in a particular area. A special case is the hub class, which is defined in the main USB specification rather than in its own document. The operating system must support the hub class because the host requires a root hub to do any communications at all.

Elements of a Class Specification

All class specifications are based on the Common Class specification, which describes what information a class specification should contain and how the specification document should be organized. A class specification defines the number and type of endpoints supported by the class. A specification may also define formats for data to be transferred, including both general data and status and control information. Many class specifications also define functions or capabilities that describe how the data being transferred will be used. For example, the HID class has Usage Tables that define how to interpret data sent by keyboards, mice, joysticks, and other devices.

A class specification may define class-specific items for the standard descriptors as well as class-specific descriptors, interfaces, endpoint usages, and control requests. For example, the device descriptor for a hub includes a bDeviceClass value of 09h to indicate that the device belongs to the hub class. The hub must also have a hub-class descriptor, with a descriptor type of 29h. Hubs also support class-specific requests. When the host sends a Get_Port_Status request to a hub with a port number in the Index field, the hub responds with status information for the port. (Chapter 18 has more on hubs.) A class may also require a device to support specific endpoints or comply with tighter timing for standard requests.

Defined Classes

In addition to the hub class, specifications for several other classes have been released. However, just because a specification exists doesn't mean that Windows includes drivers for the class. Table 12-1 shows the class drivers added in each edition of Windows.

The following are classes with released specifications:

Audio Device. Devices that transfer audio, voice, or sound and related controls. Windows 98 Gold (original) and later include an audio driver. Windows 2000 and Me also have a **MIDI** driver that supports the MIDI protocol for music control.

Chip/Smart Card Interface Devices. For devices that conform to the ISO/IEC 7816 specification.

Communications Device. Telephones, modems, and other telecommunications devices. Windows 98 SE and later include a modem driver.

Content Security. Supports protected and controlled distribution of digital content.

Device Firmware Upgrade. For updating program code in a device.

Table 12-1: Microsoft adds new USB driver support with each release of Windows. The releases are listed top to bottom from earliest to latest. Each release also includes the drivers provided with earlier releases.

Windows Edition	USB Version Compliance	USB Drivers Added
Windows 98 Gold (original)	1.0	Audio
		HID 1.0 (includes keyboard, pointing devices)
Windows 98 SE	1.1	Communications (modem)
		HID 1.1 (adds the ability to do interrupt OUT transfers)
		Still image capture (scanner, camera) (first phase/preliminary)
Windows 2000, Windows Me	1.1 (2.0 support expected in an update)	Mass storage
		MIDI (in the audio driver)
		Printer. This driver can also be distributed for use with Windows 98.
		Still image capture (scanner, camera) (enhanced)

Human Interface Device (HID). Keyboards, mice, joysticks, or any device that transfers blocks of information to or from the host at moderate rates, using control or interrupt transfers. Windows 98 Gold and later include HID 1.0 drivers. Windows 98 SE and later include HID 1.1 drivers, which support interrupt OUT transfers. The **Monitor** class describes HIDs that provide user controls on display monitors (not the display interface itself). The **Physical Interface** class supports HIDs that use real-time physical feedback, such as force-feedback joysticks. The **Power** class describes HIDs that provide power-supply control, including control for power conservation and uninterruptible power supplies.

IrDA Bridge Device. To replace or supplement a motherboard-mounted IrDA transceiver.

Mass Storage. For CD-ROM, tape, floppy drives, etc. Windows 2000 and Windows Me include a mass-storage driver (*usbstor.sys*).

Printer. The printer interface (not the page-description protocols). Windows 2000 and Windows Me include a printer driver (*usbprint.sys*), and the driver can be distributed for use with Windows 98.

Imaging. For scanners and still-image (not video) cameras. Windows 98 SE included a preliminary version that was enhanced in Windows 2000 and Windows Me (*usbscan.sys*).

Other class specifications under development are Device Bay Controllers and PC Legacy Compatibility. All of the specifications are available from the USB Implementers Forum website.

For more details about a class, see the class specification and for most classes supported under Windows, the DDK has further documentation.

The provided class drivers aren't installed until a device requires them. So for example, a Windows 2000 system won't show the mass-storage driver *usb-stor.sys* until a device that requires it is attached and the device's INF file causes the driver to be installed. A driver may be archived in a file on the system's hard drive, or the user may have to insert the Windows install disk to retrieve the file.

Matching a Device to a Class

Many peripherals are standard types such as the keyboards, mice, printers, and disk drives found on most desktop systems (though not always with USB interfaces). Other peripherals perform non-standard functions such as data acquisition or motor control for specific applications. The following sections contain advice on how to select a class for various applications.

Standard Peripheral Types

Standard peripheral types are likely to have built-in drivers. For the most part, users and application programmers don't have to know or care whether a device uses USB or another interface type. The hardware-specific communications are handled at a lower level and present a common interface to applications. For example, users can access files on a hard drive in exactly the same ways whether the drive uses USB, ATAPI, SCSI, IEEE-1394, or a parallel-port interface.

Keyboard, Mouse and Joystick

The keyboard, mouse, and joystick are the big three of the HID class. "Mouse" includes trackballs and other pointing devices. HIDs also encompass various other game controls. All Windows editions support USB versions of these peripherals.

Many applications don't need to access these devices directly. For example, a Visual-Basic application doesn't have to read mouse clicks to find out if a user has clicked on an option button because the button's click event executes automatically when this occurs.

Windows provides two ways for applications to communicate directly with HIDs: Windows API functions and the APIs supported by DirectX, which enables faster, more direct access to the hardware. However, Windows 2000 doesn't allow applications to use API calls or DirectX to access the system keyboard or mouse.

Besides supporting standard peripherals, the HID class is a good, general-purpose class for other uses. For this reason, the following chapters have much more detail about how to use HIDs.

Mass Storage Devices

The mass-storage class encompasses disk drives, including floppies, hard drives, CDs, and so on. Other devices that transfer files in one or both directions can use this class as well.

On a PC, all devices that use a mass-storage driver appear as drives in My Computer. Users can use the same interface to copy, move, and delete files. For example, for a digital camera that uses a mass-storage driver, the camera's memory appears to the operating system like any other drive. There's no need for proprietary software to access the images in the camera.

The many types of media supported by the mass-storage class have different internal structures. Several industry-standard sets of command blocks, or command descriptor blocks, enable controlling and reading status information from different device types. Floppies, CDs, tape drives, and Flash memory each typically use a different command-block set.

The mass-storage class supports two transport protocols that determine which transfer types the device and host use to send command, data, and status information.

Bulk-only transport uses bulk transfers for most communications. It uses control transfers only to clear a Stall condition on a bulk endpoint and to send class-specific requests. The two class-specific requests supported are Bulk Only Mass Storage Reset (reset the device) and Get Max Lun (get the number of logical units the device supports).

Control/bulk/interrupt (CBI) transport uses bulk transfers for transferring data and control transfers to clear a Stall condition on a bulk endpoint and to send class-specific requests. The single class-specific request is Accept Device-Specific Command, which enables the host to send a command block. A CBI device may use either interrupt or control transfers to signal the completion of commands.

In the device's interface descriptor, the value 08h in the bInterfaceClass field indicates that the device is mass-storage class. The bInterfaceSubClass field specifies the supported command-block set. The bInterfaceProtocol field contains a code indicating the supported transport protocol.

There are separate specifications for each transport protocol, plus a UFI Command Specification for removable media.

There are several approaches to writing or obtaining a mass-storage driver for a device. Windows 2000 and Windows Me include a driver that supports bulk-only and CBI devices. Microsoft hasn't provided much documentation for the driver, but the class specification can serve as a guide to firmware design, and applications can access devices in the same way they access other system drives.

Windows 98 doesn't have a mass-storage driver, so device vendors will have to provide one. Microsoft provides source code for a mass-storage driver for use under Windows 98 (described in knowledge base Article ID Q257751). Cypress Semiconductor has a mass-storage reference design for its EZ-USB chip. The design works with Windows 2000's driver and with a free driver provided by Cypress for use with Windows 98.

For OEMs (original equipment manufacturers) whose existing devices have standard SCSI, ATA, or ATAPI interfaces, SCM Microsystems has USB Intelligent Cables and drivers that quickly add USB capability to the devices. Many hard drives, CD drives, tape drives, and some scanners use either SCSI, ATA (AT attachment), originally known as IDE, or ATAPI (AT attachment packet interface), an extension to EIDE. The EUSB-S1 product contains a microcontroller and an ASIC that convert between the device's existing SCSI interface and USB. In a similar way, the EUSB-C product converts between ATA and ATAPI devices and USB. The cables are available only to OEMs, not to end users.

Printers

Windows 2000 and Windows Me include a USB printer driver and Microsoft also permits distributing the driver for use with Windows 98. The printer vendor must supply a high-level, user-mode driver that is layered above the print spooler. The interface to the USB printer driver is similar to the interface for parallel printers, so a single driver often works without modification with both USB and the parallel port.

Cameras and Scanners

The still-image capture, or imaging, specification was created to support still-image (not video) digital cameras. Other devices that have similar requirements, such as scanners, fit into the class as well. Version 1.0 was released in July 2000.

The Photographic and Imaging Manufacturers Association (PIMA) developed the PIMA 15740 Standard, which describes requirements for transferring files and for controlling digital still cameras. USB's specification is based on this standard.

The class supports bulk IN and bulk OUT endpoints for sending both image and non-image data, plus an interrupt IN endpoint for event data. Three class-specific requests are required and one is optional. The required requests are Cancel Request (cancel a bulk transfer), Device Reset Request (the device returns to the Idle state if the bulk pipe has stalled), and Get Device Status (the host receives information about a transfer cancelled by the device). Optional is Get Extended Event Data (the device returns information about an event or condition.)

The interface descriptor in the device identifies a still-image device, with the bInterfaceClass field set to 06h to indicate an image interface and bInterfaceSubClass set to 01h to indicate a still-image capture device.

Windows 98 SE included a preliminary version of a still-image driver that was enhanced in Windows 2000 and Windows Me. The driver supports USB, SCSI, and IEEE-1394.

Windows 2000 and Windows Me support the Microsoft Windows Image Acquisition (WIA) architecture, which is built on the Microsoft Still Image Architecture (STI) used in previous Windows editions. The device vendor needs to supply only a user-mode WIA minidriver that provides a device-specific interface to the generic still-image driver. The Windows DDK has more details about how to use the driver.

For Windows 98 Gold and probably Windows SE, you'll need to provide a device driver.

If all that is needed is a way to transfer image files from a camera, another option is to use a mass-storage driver, as described earlier.

Audio Applications

Audio has been supported beginning with Windows 98 Gold, so there should be no need to write an audio driver. Windows 2000 and Windows Me added a MIDI driver. Audio functions are often part of a device that also supports video, storage, or other functions.

An audio function consists of an Audio Interface Collection containing one or more device interfaces. The AudioControl interface accesses controls such as volume, mute, bass, and treble. One or more AudioStreaming interfaces transport data representing audio to or from the device. One or more MIDIStreaming interfaces transport MIDI data to or from the device.

The default control endpoint responds to class-specific requests. Isochronous endpoints transfer data for the streaming interfaces. Some isochronous endpoints may require an additional isochronous synch endpoint. An optional interrupt IN endpoint transfers status information.

MIDI (musical instrument digital interface) is a standard for controlling synthesizers, sound cards, and other electronic devices that generate music. A MIDI representation of a sound includes values for pitch, length, volume, and other characteristics. A pure MIDI hardware interface carries asynchronous data at 31.25 kilobits per second. USB MIDI carries MIDI data but doesn't use MIDI's hardware interface.

The audio and MIDI specifications have the details needed to implementing an audio interface.

Modems

The modem driver included with Windows 98 SE and later (*usbser.sys*) is compatible with modems that use the Abstract Control Model defined in the communications class specification. A modem used by programs that call the Windows Telephony Application Programming Interface (TAPI) to make data, fax, or voice calls must have its own INF file; descriptors that place the device in the communications class aren't sufficient. The Windows DDK includes a Modem Development Kit with tools, sample INF files, and information for creating and testing INF files for AT (data) and AT+V (data + voice) command modems.

Non-standard Functions

One of the great things about USB is that you're not limited to a few standard peripheral types. Applications can communicate with any peripheral if the operating system has a driver for the it. Some peripherals require custom drivers. But even when a device's purpose is very different from typical peripherals, it's often possible to design the device to fit into a defined class.

Devices that Transfer Data at Moderate Speeds

Motor controllers and data-acquisition units are two examples of specialized peripherals that aren't found on most PCs. For a motor controller, the host may send configuration and control requests to the device, which then provides the signals required to carry out the requested tasks. A controller may also send status information to the host. For data acquisition, a device may collect data from sensors and sends the results periodically to the host, and the host may send configuration or control requests to the device.

For devices in both of these categories, or any device that transfers data at low to moderate speeds, you may be able to design the device to fit the HID class, eliminating the need to provide a custom driver.

A HID doesn't have to be a standard peripheral type, and it doesn't even need a human interface. The only requirement is that the descriptors stored in the device must conform to the requirements for HID-class descriptors, and the device must send and receive data using interrupt or control transfers as defined in the HID specification.

The main limitation to HID communications is the available transfer types. For device-to-host data transfers, HIDs can use interrupt or control transfers. For host-to-device transfers, Windows 98 SE or later, including Windows 2000 and Me, will use interrupt transfers if an OUT interrupt pipe is available. Otherwise the host will use control transfers to send data to the device. The original release of Windows 98 complies only with the HID 1.0 specification and uses control transfers for all host-to-device data.

As Chapter 3 explained, interrupt transfers aren't the fastest transfer type, and they don't have the guaranteed transfer rate of isochronous transfers (though they do have guaranteed maximum latency). Control transfers have no guaranteed rate or latency. But even with these limitations, the simplicity of using the HID functions makes the class attractive when the limits are acceptable.

Upgrading RS-232 Devices

The RS-232 serial port is a good, general-purpose interface that has been with the PC since its beginning. There are probably thousands of different RS-232 peripherals in use. Microsoft and Intel's *PC 2001 System Design Guide* doesn't forbid RS-232 ports, but it discourages them in favor of newer, more powerful and flexible interfaces like USB. Just about any device that uses RS-232 can be implemented with USB. There are several approaches to making the switch.

RS-232 modems of course can be designed for USB's modem class.

For many other devices, FTDI's FT8U232AM USB UART provides a quick way to upgrade a design to USB. The chip converts an existing RS-232 serial device to USB while requiring minimal design changes and no changes to host software. (Figure 12-1).

A typical device with an RS-232 interface contains a UART that converts between the serial data used in RS-232 communications and the parallel data used by the CPU's internal buses. The signals on the line side of the UART connect to converters that translate between RS-232 voltages and the 5V logic used by the CPU. The line side of the converter connects to a cable that connects to the remote device.

The USB UART converts between USB and RS-232, including not just the data lines but also RTS, CTS, and the other status and control signals used in RS-232 communications. One set of pins on the USB UART looks like the line side of a conventional UART, with pins for data and handshaking signals. Two other pins connect to a USB transceiver.

The chip requires no programming except the optional storing of Vendor, Product, and Device IDs and strings in a serial EEPROM.

To adapt an RS-232 design for USB, you replace the original UART's connections to the RS-232 converters with connections to the complimentary signals on the USB UART. Store the IDs and other optional information in a serial EEPROM that connects to the USB UART and add a USB connection to the USB transceiver. The device firmware requires no changes because the original UART will think it's talking to an RS-232 device as usual.

But providing the device hardware is only half of the job. The other half is the device driver. For the least disruption to existing applications, the driver should cause application software to treat the device as if it were still attached to a COM port. FTDI provides drivers that do just that under

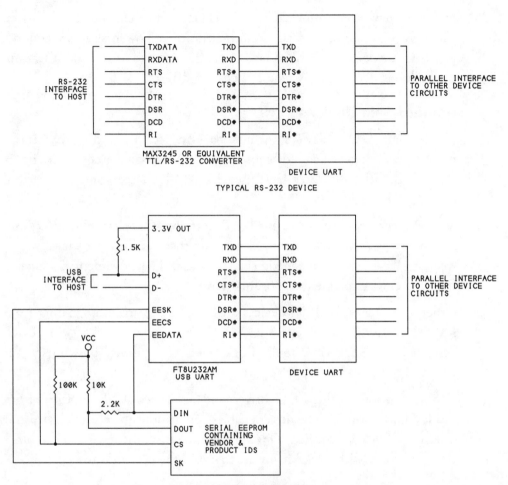

Figure 12-1: FTDI's USB UART can convert devices with RS-232 interfaces to USB. A free device driver provided by FTDI causes the device to appear like a conventional COM-port device to host applications.

Windows and other operating systems. An RS-232 design converted for USB with an FTDI UART can use exactly the same application software as the RS-232 version.

Another approach to upgrading RS-232 devices is to redesign the device to eliminate the COM-port interface entirely. The device will probably be cheaper to manufacture because there's no need for a UART, but the device will need new application software and possibly a custom device driver. Many RS-232 devices, such as uninterruptible power supplies and the point-of-sale devices described below, can be designed as HIDs. Others will use bulk transfers and may require a custom driver.

Point-of-Sale Devices

Point-of-sale (POS) devices include bar-code scanners, displays, receipt printers, cash drawers, coin dispensers, and other devices used in sales transactions. Traditionally these have used RS-232 interfaces, and they're ideal candidates to upgrade to USB.

Most POS devices can be designed to fit into the HID class. The *HID Point of Sale Usage Tables* document defines data formats for bar-code scanners, weighing devices, and magnetic stripe readers. The document is available from the USB Implementers Forum's website.

Other approaches for POS devices are designed to make upgrading from RS-232 as easy as possible. RS-232 POS devices can use the USB UART described above to enable applications to access the device the same as if it were still connected to a COM port.

Another option is the EPiC driver and associated USB protocol from Inside/Out Networks. The driver enables applications to access a device as if it were a COM-port device. This approach requires the device to contain a USB controller with device firmware that uses the licensed protocol.

Replacing Non-standard Parallel Port Devices

Besides the RS-232 serial port, another port that all PCs had from the beginning was the parallel port, originally intended for connecting a printer. Like the serial port, the parallel port has found many other uses over the years. The parallel port is faster than the serial port, so it became a favored connection for scanners and disk drives. This became even more true when the ports began supporting the new, faster PS/2, enhanced parallel port (EPP) and extended capabilities port (ECP) modes. In each of its modes, the parallel port uses a defined protocol for exchanging bytes of data along with status and control information.

Another category of parallel-port devices uses custom protocols. The original port had 8 outputs, 5 inputs, and 4 open-collector, bidirectional lines. Under Windows 3.x and 9x, applications can read and write directly to the port addresses, and under Windows NT and 2000 all that's needed to access the ports is a kernel-mode driver available at low cost or free from several sources. What resulted was an assortment of devices following no standard use of the port's input and outputs. For example, one popular use involved connecting combinations of decoders, flip-flops, and data selectors to expand the number of inputs and outputs applications could access.

But as with RS-232, Microsoft and Intel are discouraging the parallel port's use in favor of USB and IEEE-1394. And this brings up the question of what to do with all of the existing designs.

For drives, scanners, and other standard device types, the logical solution is to design the device to comply with the appropriate USB class specification.

A quick solution for parallel printers is to use a USB printer adapter. The adapter's driver causes the operating system to see the printer as a network printer. Adapters are available from several vendors. A printer adapter isn't a solution for parallel-port scanners, drives, and so on, because the firmware and driver are designed for use only with the PC's printer drivers.

For devices that use non-standard parallel-port communications, the solution is to redesign the interface for USB. This requires adding a USB microcontroller to the device, possibly providing a device driver, and revising the application software to match the driver's requirements. The parallel port has 17 signal pins, so to emulate them all requires at least that many I/O pins on the microcontroller. But many designs can get by with the 16 I/O pins available on smaller, cheaper controller chips. If you must have 17 bits on a chip with a small footprint, Cypress' CY7C63743 has 16 I/O pins plus two additional inputs that are available if the chip uses the internal oscillator or an external source for D-'s pull-up.

Applications that access the port at low and moderate speeds can probably use the HID drivers included with Windows. This means there are no drivers to write, but you'll need to rewrite the application software to use the API calls for accessing HIDs.

If you want to make minimal changes to the application software, provide a driver that supports custom DeviceIoControl functions that emulate the functions used by the original application. For example, you could define an IoControlCode for a status-port read function that reads five inputs with bit values of bit 3 through bit 7 and even inverts bit 7 to match what the parallel-port hardware does. Instead of reading the status-port address with an Inp function, applications would call DeviceIoControl with your IoControlCode for the status-port read emulation.

PC-to-PC Connections

USB doesn't allow peripherals to exchange data directly. All communications must go through a host. There's no way for two hosts to send data to each other without going through a peripheral. There is, however, a way to enable two PCs to communicate using their USB ports. Each PC can connect to a USB peripheral, and the two peripherals can communicate with each other via a shared buffer.

Cypress Semiconductor's AN2720SC is designed for this purpose. It's a single chip containing two USB cores. Each core connects to a USB transceiver and a shared 2-Kilobyte buffer. Cypress provides a driver that causes each PC to see the other as a network-connected PC. You add only a single crystal, an EEPROM for storing a VID and PID, and few other components.

But you don't have to build your own PC-to-PC cable. It's a popular enough application that ready-made products are available, including Cypress' EZ-Link.

Wireless Links

Replacing a USB cable with a wireless connection isn't a simple task. The main reason is that USB transactions involve communicating in both directions with tight timing requirements. For example, when a host sends a token and data packet in the data stage of an interrupt transaction, the device must respond quickly with ACK or another code in the handshake packet. Designing a wireless link to do this while also meeting all of USB's timing and other requirements would be a challenge.

An easier solution when you need a wireless connection is to use a conventional wired connection to a USB device that also supports a wireless interface. The device at the other end of the wireless link doesn't have to support USB at all.

SigmaTel's STIr4200s takes this approach with its IrDA-to-USB bridge chip for wireless applications. IrDA is a standard for communications that use infrared energy instead of cables. The bridge's USB interface connects to a USB hub, and the IrDA interface communicates with IrDA-capable devices. The bridge translates between the two interfaces. SigmaTel provides a driver for use with the chip.

A similar approach would work for devices that use radio-frequency wireless communications.

Chapter 12

13

Human Interface Devices: Firmware Basics

The human interface device (HID) class was one of the first USB classes to be supported under Windows. On PCs running Windows 98 or later, applications can communicate with HIDs using the drivers built into the operating system. For this reason, USB devices that fit into the HID class are some of the easiest to get up and running.

This chapter shows how to determine whether a peripheral will fit into the human-interface class, explains the firmware requirements that define a device as a HID and enable it to exchange data with its host, and introduces the six HID-specific control requests. The next three chapters describe the reports that HIDs use to exchange information and how to access HIDs from applications.

What is a HID?

Before you can know whether or not you can use Windows' HID drivers to communicate with a device, you need to know whether your device fits in the HID class.

The designation *human interface* suggests that the device interacts directly with people. A device may detect when someone presses a key or moves a mouse or joystick, or the host may send a message that translates to a joystick effect that the user experiences. The classic examples of HIDs are keyboards, mice, and joysticks. Other HIDs include front panels with knobs, switches, buttons, and sliders; remote controls; telephone keypads; and game controls such as data gloves and steering wheels.

But a HID doesn't have to have a human interface at all. It just needs to be able to function within the limits of the class's specification. These are the major abilities and limitations of HID-class devices:

- The data exchanged resides in structures called reports. The device's firmware must support the HID report format. The host sends and receives data by sending and requesting reports in control or interrupt transfers. The report format is flexible, and can handle just about any type of data.

- Each transaction can carry a small to moderate amount of data. For a low-speed device, the maximum is 8 bytes per transaction. For a full-speed device, the maximum is 64 bytes per transaction. For a high-speed device, the maximum is 1024 bytes per transaction. A long report can use multiple transactions.

- A device may send information to the computer at unpredictable times. For example, there's no way for the computer to know when the user will press a key on the keyboard, so the host's driver polls the device periodically to obtain new data.

- The maximum speed of transfers is limited, especially at low and full speeds. As Chapter 4 explained, a host can guarantee a low-speed interrupt endpoint no more than 1 transaction per 10 milliseconds, for a maximum of 800 bytes per second. A host can guarantee a full-speed endpoint up to 1 transaction per millisecond, for a maximum of 64,000 bytes per second, or a high-speed endpoint up to 3 transactions per 125 microseconds, for a maximum of 24.576 Megabytes per second.

- There is no guaranteed *rate* of transfer. If the device is configured for 10-millisecond intervals, the time between transactions may be any period equal to or less than this. The exception is devices configured to transfer data every frame at full speed or every microframe at high speed. Since these are the fastest possible polling rates, the endpoint is guaranteed to have this exact bandwidth available.

- Under Windows 98 Gold (original), interrupt OUT transfers aren't supported, so all host-to-device data must use control transfers.

Although many HIDs mostly send data from the device to the host, a HID can also receive data from the host. The classic example of host-to-device HID communications is the force-feedback joystick, where users experience effects that match their actions, such as greater resistance when pulling the stick to cause a simulated airplane to climb or when getting a bite on a simulated fishing rod.

Any device that can live within the class's limits is a candidate to be a HID. The specification mentions bar-code readers, thermometers, and voltmeters as examples of HIDs that may not have a conventional human interface. Each of these sends data to the computer and may also receive requests that configure the device. Examples of devices that mostly receive data are remote displays, control panels for remote devices, robots, and devices of any kind that receive occasional or periodic commands from the host.

The HID interface may be just one of multiple USB interfaces supported by a device. A video display may have a HID interface for software control of brightness, contrast, and refresh rates, while using the conventional video interface to send the data to be displayed. A USB speaker that uses isochronous transfers for audio may also have a HID interface for controlling volume, balance, treble, and bass. A HID interface is often cheaper than traditional physical controls.

Two essential documents for working with HIDs are *Device Class Definition for Human Interface Devices*, which defines the HID class, and *HID Usage Tables*, which defines values that help the host understand and use the HID data. Both documents are products of a USB Device Working Group. The members are affiliated with the member companies of the USB Implementers Forum. The documents are published by the Implementers Forum and available on the Forum's website.

Hardware Requirements

A HID interface must conform to the requirements of the HID class as defined in the specification. The document describes the required descriptors, the frequency of transfers, and the transfer types available.

To comply with the specification, the interface's endpoints and descriptors must meet several requirements.

Endpoints

All HID transfers use either the Default Control Pipe or an interrupt pipe. A HID must have an interrupt IN endpoint for sending data to the host. An interrupt OUT endpoint is optional.

The specification defines uses for each pipe. Table 13-1 shows the transfer types and their uses in HIDs.

You can think of the data that the host and device exchange as being of two types: low-latency data that must get to its destination as soon as possible, and configuration data or other data that doesn't have critical timing requirements. (By configuration data, I'm referring to data sent in HID reports, not the host's requesting and selecting of device configurations on enumerating.)

The Control Pipe

The control pipe for a HID carries the standard USB requests as well as six class-specific requests defined in the HID specification. Two of the HID-specific requests, Set_Report and Get_Report, provide a way for the host and device to transfer a block of any kind of data to or from the device. The host uses Set_Report to send reports and Get_Report to receive reports.

The other four requests relate to configuring the device. Set_Idle and Get_Idle set and read the Idle rate, which determines whether or not a

Table 13-1: The transfer type used in a HID transfer depends on the chip's abilities and the requirements of the data being sent.

Transfer Type	Source of Data	Type of Data	Required Pipe?	Windows Support
Control	Device (IN transfer)	Data that doesn't have critical timing requirements.	yes	Windows 98 and later
	Host (OUT transfer)	Data that doesn't have critical timing requirements, or any data if there is no OUT interrupt pipe.		
Interrupt	Device (IN transfer)	Periodic or low-latency data.	yes	
	Host (OUT transfer)	Periodic or low-latency data.	no	Windows 98 SE and later

device resends data that hasn't changed since the last poll. Set_Protocol and Get_Protocol set and read a protocol value, which can enable a device to function with a simplified protocol when the HID drivers aren't loaded on the host.

Interrupt Transfers

The interrupt pipe or pipes provide an alternate way of exchanging device data, especially when the receiver must get the data quickly or periodically. An interrupt IN pipe carries data to the host, and an interrupt OUT pipe carries data to the device. Control transfers can be delayed if the bus is very busy, but once the device is configured, the bandwidth for interrupt transfers is guaranteed to be available. HIDs aren't required to have interrupt OUT pipes. If there is no interrupt OUT pipe, the host sends all reports on the control pipe, using Set_Report requests.

The ability to do Interrupt OUT transfers was added in version 1.1 of the USB specification, and the option to use an interrupt OUT pipe was added to version 1.1 of the HID specification. A HID driver that complies only with version 1.0 (including the drivers in Windows 98 Gold) won't support interrupt OUT transfers.

Firmware Requirements

For the host's drivers to communicate with a HID, the device's firmware must meet certain requirements. The device's descriptors must identify the device as having a HID interface, and the firmware must support an interrupt IN endpoint in addition to the Default Control Pipe. The firmware must also contain a report descriptor that defines the format for transmitted and received device data.

To send data, the specification requires the firmware to support Get_Report control transfers and interrupt IN transfers, and to receive data, the firmware must support Set_Report control transfers and may also support interrupt OUT transfers.

All HID data must use a defined report format that defines the size and contents of the data in the report. Devices may support one or more reports. A report descriptor in the device's firmware describes the reports, and may also include information about how the receiver of the data should use it.

A value in each report defines the report as an Input, Output, or Feature report. The host receives data in Input reports and sends data in Output reports. Feature reports may travel in either direction.

For Input reports, the HID drivers in all releases of Windows 98 and later use interrupt transfers. For Output reports, the transfer type depends on what endpoints the device supports and which edition of Windows is installed. The original release of Windows 98 (Windows 98 Gold) complies only with version 1.0 of the HID specification, and the HID driver uses control transfers for Output reports. Windows 98 SE, Windows 2000, and Windows Me comply with version 1.1 of the specification, so the HID driver uses interrupt transfers for Output reports if the interface has an interrupt OUT endpoint. Otherwise it uses control transfers. If the HID interface doesn't have an interrupt OUT endpoint or if the firmware supports both transfer types for Output reports, the HID will be compatible with any Windows edition. Feature reports always use control transfers.

A report format can be simple or complex. The rest of this chapter and Chapter 14 have much more about report formats.

Identifying a Device as a HID

As with any USB device, a HID's descriptors tell the host what it needs to know to communicate with the device. Listing 13-1 shows example device, configuration, interface, class, and endpoint descriptors for a HID-class joystick. The host learns about the HID interface when it sends a Get_Descriptor request for the configuration containing the HID interface. The configuration's interface descriptor identifies the interface as HID-class. The HID class descriptor specifies the number of report descriptors supported by the interface. During enumeration, the HID driver retrieves the HID class and report descriptors.

Descriptor Contents

The device and configuration descriptors have no HID-specific information. The device descriptor contains a field for a class code, but this isn't where the device is defined as a HID. Instead, the interface descriptor is where the host learns that a device, or more properly, a device interface, belongs to the HID class. If the class-code byte in the device's interface descriptor is 3, the interface is a HID.

Other fields that contain HID-specific information in the interface descriptor are the subclass and protocol fields, which can specify a boot interface.

Boot Interfaces

The subclass field has just one active setting. A subclass of 1 indicates that the device supports a boot interface. When a device has a boot interface, the device will be usable when the host's HID drivers aren't loaded. This might occur when the computer boots directly to DOS, or when viewing the system setup screens that you can access on bootup, or when using Windows' Safe mode for system troubleshooting. A keyboard or mouse with a boot interface can use a predefined, simplified protocol supported by the BIOS of many hosts. The BIOS loads from ROM or other non-volatile memory on bootup and is available in any operating-system mode. The HID specification defines boot-interface protocols for keyboards and mice.

```
device_desc_table:
    db 12h              ; Descriptor length (18 bytes)
    db 01h              ; Descriptor type (Device)
    db 00h,01h          ; Complies to USB Spec. Release (1.00)
    db 00h              ; Class code (0)
    db 00h              ; Subclass code (0)
    db 00h              ; Protocol (No specific protocol)
    db 08h              ; Max. packet size for EP0 (8 bytes)
    db B4h,04h          ; Vendor ID (Cypress)
    db 1Fh,0Fh          ; Product ID (joystick = 0x0F1F)
    db 88h,02h          ; Device release number (2.88)
    db 00h              ; Mfr string descriptor index (None)
    db 00h              ; Product string descriptor index (None)
    db 00h              ; Serial No. string descriptor index (None)
    db 01h              ; Number of possible configurations (1)
end_device_desc_table:

config_desc_table:
    db 09h              ; Descriptor length (9 bytes)
    db 02h              ; Descriptor type (Configuration)
    db 22h,00h          ; Total data length (34 bytes)
    db 01h              ; Interface supported (1)
    db 01h              ; Configuration value (1)
    db 00h              ; Index of string descriptor (None)
    db 80h              ; Configuration (Bus powered)
    db 32h              ; Maximum power consumption (100mA)

Interface_Descriptor:
    db 09h              ; Descriptor length (9 bytes)
    db 04h              ; Descriptor type (Interface)
    db 00h              ; Number of interface (0)
    db 00h              ; Alternate setting (0)
    db 01h              ; Number of endpoints supported
    db 03h              ; Class code (HID)
    db 00h              ; Subclass code (None)
    db 00h              ; Protocol code (None)
    db 00h              ; Index of string(None)
```

Listing 13-1: Descriptors for a HID-class joystick (Sheet 1 of 2)

```
Class_Descriptor:
    db 09h              ; Descriptor length (9 bytes)
    db 21h              ; Descriptor type (HID)
    db 00h,01h          ; HID class release number (1.00)
    db 00h              ; Localized country code (None)
    db 01h              ; # of HID class descriptors to follow (1)
    db 22h              ; Report descriptor type (HID)
                        ; Total length of report descriptor
    db (end_hid_report_desc_table - hid_report_desc_table),00h

Endpoint_Descriptor:
    db 07h              ; Descriptor length (7 bytes)
    db 05h              ; Descriptor type (Endpoint)
    db 81h              ; Encoded address (Respond to IN, 1 endpnt)
    db 03h              ; Endpoint attribute (Interrupt transfer)
    db 06h,00h          ; Maximum packet size (6 bytes)
    db 0Ah              ; Polling interval (10 ms)

end_config_desc_table:
```

Listing 13-1: Descriptors for a HID-class joystick (Sheet 2 of 2)

If a device does have a boot interface, the protocol field indicates if the device supports the keyboard (1) or mouse (2) interface. A value of zero indicates no device, and values 3–255 are reserved. A subclass of zero means that the device doesn't support a boot protocol. Values 2 through 255 are reserved.

The HID Usage Tables document defines the keyboard and mouse boot descriptors. The BIOS doesn't need to read a descriptor from the device because it knows what the boot protocol is and assumes that the device will support it. So a boot device doesn't have to include a boot-interface descriptor in firmware; it just has to support the boot protocol if the host hasn't requested the protocol defined in the report descriptor. When the operating system loads, the HID drivers use the HID-specific request Set_Protocol to cause the device to switch from the boot protocol to the report protocol.

Draft 4 Compliance

During the development of the HID 1.0 specification, a change was made to the ordering of descriptors in HID firmware. In the early versions, the descriptors were stored and retrieved in this order:

Configuration
Interface
Endpoint
HID

By Draft 4 of the specification, the order had changed to:

Configuration
Interface
HID
Endpoint

The change means that the HID descriptor is associated with an interface, rather than an endpoint. If a HID has two endpoints, the device doesn't need a HID descriptor for each.

A device that complies with HID 1.0 or later uses the Draft 4 ordering. A USB test utility (such as HIDView, described in Chapter 17) that checks for Draft 4 compliance is examining the order of the descriptors.

HID Class Descriptor

The main purpose of the HID class descriptor is to identify additional descriptors for use in HID communications. The class descriptor has seven or more fields, depending on the number of additional descriptors. Table 13-2 shows the fields.

The Descriptor

bLength. The length in bytes of the descriptor.

bDescriptorType. The value 21h indicates the HID class.

Table 13-2: The HID class descriptor has 7 or more fields in 9 or more bytes.

Offset (decimal)	Field	Size (bytes)	Description
0	bLength	1	Descriptor size in bytes
1	bDescriptorType	1	21h indicates the HID class
2	bcdHID	2	HID specification release number (BCD)
4	bCountryCode	1	Numeric expression identifying the country for localized hardware (BCD)
5	bNumDescriptors	1	Number of subordinate class descriptors supported
6	bDescriptorType	1	The type of class descriptor
7	wDescriptorLength	2	Total length of report descriptor
9	bDescriptorType	1	Constant identifying the type of descriptor. Optional, for devices with more than one descriptor.
10	wDescriptorLength	2	Total length of descriptor. Optional, for devices with more than one descriptor. May be followed by additional wDescriptorType and wDescriptorLength fields.

The Class

bcdHID. The HID specification number that the device and its descriptors comply with. In BCD (binary-coded decimal) format. The value is a 4-character hexadecimal value with a decimal point assumed in the middle. For example, Version 1.0 is 0100h; Version 1.1 is 0110h.

bCountryCode. If the hardware is localized for a specific country, this field is a code identifying the country. The HID specification lists the codes. If the hardware isn't localized, this field is 00h.

bNumDescriptors. The number of class descriptors that are subordinate to this descriptor.

bDescriptorType. The type (report or physical) of a descriptor that is subordinate to the HID class descriptor. Every HID must support at least one report descriptor. An interface may support multiple report descriptors and one or more physical descriptors.

wDescriptorLength. The length of the descriptor described in the previous field.

Additional bDescriptorType, wDescriptorLength (optional). If there are additional subordinate descriptors, the descriptor type and length for each follow in sequence.

Report Descriptors

A report descriptor defines the format and uses of the data that carries out the purpose of the device. If the device is a mouse, the data reports mouse movements and button clicks. If the device is a relay controller, the data contains codes that specify which relays to open and close.

The report descriptor needs to be flexible enough to handle devices with very different purposes. The data should be stored in a concise form so it doesn't waste storage space in the device or bus time when the data transmits. The HID report descriptor achieves both of these at a price of a format that's more complex and less readable than a more verbose format might be. The format doesn't limit the type of data in a report, but the report descriptor must describe the size and contents of the report in advance. A report descriptor's contents and length vary with the device, and can be short and simple, long and complex, or anywhere in between.

A report descriptor is a type of class descriptor. The host retrieves the descriptor by sending a Get_Descriptor request with the Value field containing 22h in the high byte and the report ID in the low byte. The default report ID is 00h.

One way to get a feel for what a report descriptor contains and how it's structured is to look at one. Listing 13-2 is a bare-bones report descriptor that describes an Input report that sends two bytes of data to the host and an Output report that sends two bytes of data to the device. Other report descriptors build on this basic format, so a short descriptor like this is a good place to start understanding report descriptors in general.

The items in the example descriptor are required in all descriptors. Some items apply to the entire descriptor, while others are specified separately for the input and output data. More complicated report descriptors may use additional instances of these same items along with other optional items.

```
hid_report_desc_table:

    db 06h, A0h, FFh ;        Usage Page (vendor defined)
    db 09h, A5h      ;        Usage (vendor defined)

    db A1h, 01h      ;        Collection (Application)
    db 09h, A6h      ;        Usage (vendor defined)

;The input report
    db 09h, A7h      ;        Usage (vendor defined)
    db 15h, 80h      ;        Logical Minimum (-127)
    db 25h, 7Fh      ;        Logical Maximum (128)
    db 75h, 08h      ;        Report Size (8)  (bits)
    db 95h, 02h      ;        Report Count (2)  (fields)
    db 81h, 02h      ;        Input (Data, Variable, Absolute)

;The output report
    db 09h, A9h      ;        Usage (vendor defined)
    db 15h, 80h      ;        Logical Minimum (-128)
    db 25h, 7Fh      ;        Logical Maximum (127)
    db 75h, 08h      ;        Report Size (8)  (bits)
    db 95h, 02h      ;        Report Count (2)  (fields)
    db 91h, 02h      ;        Output (Data, Variable, Absolute)

    db C0h           ;        End Collection

end_hid_report_desc_table:
```

Listing 13-2: This report descriptor enables sending and receiving of two bytes.

Each item in the example report consists of a byte that identifies the item and one or more bytes containing the item's data. Here is what each item in the example descriptor specifies:

The **Usage Page** item is identified by the value 06h and specifies the general function of the device, such as generic desktop control, game control, or alphanumeric display (to name just a few). You can think of the Usage Page as a subset of the HID class. In the example descriptor, the Usage Page is the vendor-defined value FFA0hh. The HID specification lists values for different Usage Pages and values reserved for vendor-defined Usage Pages.

The **Usage** item is identified by the value 09h and specifies the function of the individual report. Just as the Usage Page is a subset of the class, the Usage is a subset of the Usage Page. For example, Usages available for generic desktop controls include mouse, joystick, and keyboard. Because the example's Usage Page is vendor-defined, all of the Usages in the Usage Page are vendor-defined also. In the example, the Usage is A5h.

The **Collection (Application)** item begins a group of items that together perform a single function, such as keyboard or mouse. Each report descriptor must have an Application Collection to enable Windows to enumerate it. The Usage item that follows the Collection item names the function of the collection. In the example, it's the vendor-defined value A6.

The Logical Minimum and Maximum have values of 15h and 25h and specify the range of values that the report can contain. Negative values may be expressed as two's complements. In the example, the values 80h and 7Fh indicates a range of -128 to +127.

The Report Size item has a value of 75h and indicates how many bits are in each reported data item. In the example, each data item is eight bits.

The Report Count item has a value of 95h and indicates how many data items the report contains. In the example, each report contains two data items.

The final item specifies whether the report carries data from the host to the device (91h) or from the device to the host (81h), along with other information about the data.

The End Collection item closes the Application Collection.

HID-specific Requests

The HID specification defines six HID-specific control requests. Table 13-3 lists the requests, and the following pages describe each request in more detail.

All HIDs must support Get_Report, and boot devices must support Get_Protocal and Set_Protocol. The other requests (Set_Report, Get_Idle,

Table 13-3: In addition to the eleven standard control requests, HIDs may support up to six HID-specific requests.

Request #	Request	Data source	Value	Index	Data Length (bytes)	Data stage contents	Required ?
01h	Get_ Report	device	report type, report ID	interface	report length	report	yes
02h	Get_ Idle	device	report ID	interface	1	idle duration	no
03h	Get_ Protocol	device	0	interface	1	protocol	required for boot devices
09h	Set_ Report	host	report type, report ID	interface	report length	report	no
0Ah	Set_ Idle	host	idle duration, report ID	interface	0	none	no
0Bh	Set_ Protocol	host	protocol	interface	0	none	required for boot devices

and Set_Idle) are optional. If a device doesn't have an Interrupt OUT endpoint or if it is communicating with a 1.0 host such as Windows 98 Gold, it will need to support Set_Report to receive data from the host. Devices that don't support Feature reports will send data using interrupt transfers only and thus have no use for Get_Report, but to comply with the specification, they should support the request in case a host should decide to use it. A device will enumerate and transfer data under Windows without supporting this request, however.

Get_Report

Purpose: Enables the host to receive data from a device in control transfers.

Request Number: 01h

Source of Data: device

Data Length: length of the report

Contents of Value field: The high byte contains the report type (1=Input, 2=Output, 3=Feature), and the low byte contains the report ID. The default report ID is 0.

Contents of Index field: the number of the interface that supports this request.

Contents of data packet in the Data stage: the report

Comments: The HID specification advises that the host should not use this request to obtain periodic data. (It should use interrupt transfers instead.) The request is intended only for obtaining the state of feature items or other information that the host needs to know when it initializes the device. However, a host using a boot protocol might use Get_Report to receive keypress or mouse data.

All HIDs must support this request.

Set_Report

Purpose: Enables a device to receive data from the host in control transfers.

Request Number: 09h

Source of Data: host

Data Length: length of the report

Contents of Value field: The high byte contains the report type (1=Input, 2=Output, 3=Feature), and the low byte contains the report ID. The default report ID is 0.

Contents of Index field: the number of the interface that supports this request.

Contents of data packet in the Data stage: the report

Comments: If a device doesn't have an Interrupt OUT endpoint or if the host complies only with version 1.0 of the HID specification, this request is the only way the host can send data to the device. For other devices, the host may use this request to send Feature reports or other information that that isn't time-sensitive. HIDs aren't required to support this request.

Get_Idle

Purpose: The host reads the current Idle rate from a device.

Request Number: 02h

Source of Data: device

Data Length: 1

Contents of Value field: The high byte is 0. The low byte indicates the report ID that the request applies to. If the low byte is 0, the request applies to all of the device's Input reports.

Contents of Index field: the number of the interface that supports this request.

Contents of data packet in the Data stage: the Idle rate, expressed in units of 4 milliseconds.

Comments: See Set_Idle for more details. HIDs aren't required to support this request.

Set_Idle

Purpose: Saves bandwidth by limiting the reporting frequency of an interrupt IN endpoint when the data hasn't changed since the last report.

Request Number: 0Ah

Source of Data: none

Data Length: 0

Contents of Value field: The high byte sets the duration, or the maximum amount of time between reports. A value of 0 means that there is no maximum and the device will report only when the report data has changed. Otherwise, the device returns a NAK. The low byte indicates the report ID that the request applies to. If the low byte is 0, the request applies to all of the device's Input reports.

Contents of Index field: the number of the interface that supports this request.

Contents of data packet in the Data stage: none

Comments: The duration is in units of 4 milliseconds, which gives a range of 4 to 1,020 milliseconds. No matter what the duration value is, if the report data has changed since the last report sent, on receiving a request, the device sends a report. If the data hasn't changed and the amount of time specified in the duration value hasn't elapsed since the last report, the device returns a NAK. If the data hasn't changed and the amount of time specified in the duration value has elapsed since the last report, the device sends a report. A duration value of 0 indicates an infinite duration; the device sends a report only if the report data has changed, and responds to all other interrupt IN requests with NAK.

HIDs aren't required to support this request. On enumerating a HID, the Windows HID driver attempts to set the idle rate to 0. If the HID supports the request, it will send a report only if the report data has changed. If the HID returns a Stall in response to this request, the request isn't supported and the device can send reports whether or not the data has changed.

Get_Protocol

Purpose: The host learns whether the boot or report protocol is currently active on the device.

Request Number: 03h

Source of Data: device

Data Length: 1

Contents of Value field: 0

Contents of Index field: the number of the interface that supports this request.

Contents of data packet in the Data stage: The protocol. 0=boot protocol, 1=report protocol.

Comments: Boot devices must support this request.

Set_Protocol

Purpose: The host specifies whether to use the boot or report protocol.

Request Number: 0Bh

Source of Data: host

Data Length: 1

Contents of Value field: 0

Contents of Index field: the number of the interface that supports this request.

Contents of data packet in the Data stage: 0=Boot Protocol; 1=Report Protocol

Comments: Boot devices must support this request.

Transferring Data

When enumeration is complete, the host has done all of the following: it has identified the device interface as a HID, it has established pipes with the supported endpoints, and it has learned what report formats to use in sending and receiving data.

The host uses control transfers to send and receive Feature reports containing additional configuration data or other data that doesn't have critical timing requirements. For example, a control-panel application for a video monitor may use control transfers to send settings to the monitor. The host uses interrupt transfers to send and receive periodic, low-latency data in Input and Output reports. The device's firmware must have the complementary code to respond to the host's requests.

Sending Data to the Host

The host receives data after requesting it in an interrupt or control transfer. To respond to an interrupt transfer, the device's firmware needs only to have the requested data in its transmit buffer and to be configured to send the data in response to an interrupt IN request. For Cypress' enCoRe series, doing this requires writing a value to Endpoint 1's transmit configuration register to enable transmitting and to specify the number of bytes to send and the data-toggle bit's value.

Below is example code for the enCoRe that prepares two bytes to transmit on the next interrupt IN transfer:

On receiving a Set_Configuration request, enable the Endpoint 1 interrupt:

```
; Set the endpoint mode to NAK Ins and Outs
mov  A, NAK_IN_OUT
iowr ep1_mode
; Enable Endpoint 0 and 1 interrupts.
mov  A, EP0_INT | EP1_INT
iowr endpoint_int
mov  A, 00h
; Reset the data toggle.
mov  [ep1_data_toggle], A
```

To prepare to send data to the host, copy the data to Endpoint 1's buffer and configure the endpoint to return data in an IN transaction:

```
mov  A, [data_byte_0]
mov  [ep1_dmabuff0], A
mov  A, [data_byte_1]
mov  [ep1_dmabuff1], A
; Configure Endpoint 1 to send 2 bytes.
mov  A, 02h
; Keep the data toggle the same.
or   A, [ep1_data_toggle]
iowr ep1_count
; Configure the endpoint to send data in IN
; transactions.
mov  A, ACK_IN
iowr ep1_mode
```

After sending the data, in Endpoint 1's interrupt service routine, toggle the data toggle so it will be correct for the next transaction:

```
; Toggle the data toggle.
mov  A, 80h
xor  [ep1_data_toggle], A
```

The details will vary for other chips. When the device has no data to send, the endpoint should be configured to return NAK.

Responding to a Get_Report request for a Feature report is much like responding to any control Read request. Control transfers are more complicated than interrupt transfers because of their multiple stages, but you can use the code for other control Read requests as a model. The device must be able to detect the request in the Setup stage, write the requested report data to the USB output buffer for transmitting in the Data stage, and acknowledge the host's 0-length data packet in the Status stage.

Receiving Data from the Host

The host receives data after requesting it in an interrupt or control transfer. As explained earlier, a host may use control or interrupt transfers for Output reports. The chip's architecture and descriptors determine whether or not the HID interface has an interrupt OUT pipe available. The host always uses Set_Report control requests to send Feature reports.

If the interface has an interrupt OUT endpoint and needs to receive low-latency data, the endpoint should be configured to receive report data. Typically, when new data arrives, an interrupt informs the device of the event. An interrupt-service routine in the firmware then does whatever is necessary with the data, either using the data right away or storing it for later use. The interrupt-service routine should also do whatever is needed to prepare the endpoint to receive a new report.

If the interface doesn't have an interrupt OUT endpoint, the firmware must detect Set_Report control requests and handle the report data in the requests. The chip must do the same to receive Feature reports. A device that has an interrupt OUT endpoint should also be able to receive reports in Set_Report control transfers so it can receive Feature reports, or Output reports if it happens to communicate with a 1.0 host.

A Set_Report request consists of at least three transactions. The host initiates a Setup transaction that specifies the request and the number of bytes in the report, followed by one or more data transactions with the report data. The device returns a response in the Status stage.

For a Set_Report request, the device must be able to detect the request in the Setup stage, receive the report data in the Data stage, and send a handshake in the Status stage. These are the steps a device typically follows to handle a Set_Report request:

1. The device detects a Setup packet, stores the data in the transaction's data packet, returns ACK, and triggers an interrupt that causes the firmware to jump to an interrupt-service routine.

2. The interrupt-service routine does the following:

- Detects the code that indicates the arrival of a Set_Report request.
- Reads the report-length, report-type, and report-ID parameters in the Setup transaction.
- Ensure that Endpoint 0 is configured to accept the data following an OUT token packet.

3. When the interrupt-service routine ends, the device returns to normal operation until it receives an OUT token packet indicating that the host is

sending data to the control endpoint in the Data stage. After receiving the data, the endpoint returns a status code in the handshake packet. An interrupt causes the firmware to jump to an interrupt-service routine for the endpoint.

4. The interrupt-service routine does whatever is needed with the received data.

5. If additional data packets are expected in the Data stage, repeat steps 3 and 4 for any additional OUT transactions, up to the Length value in the Setup transaction.

6. In response to an IN token packet in the Status stage, the endpoint sends a 0-length data packet and the host returns ACK.

Below is enCoRe code that executes on detecting a Set_Report request. The code finds out how many bytes to read and configures Endpoint 0 to receive data in an OUT transaction. This involves setting two configuration bits.

```
set_report:
; Find out how many bytes to read in the OUT
; transaction(s) that will follow.
; This value is in WLengthlo.
; (WLengthhi is unused for this device).
; Save the length in data_count.
mov   A, [wLengthlo]
mov   [data_count], A
mov   A, 0
mov   [wLengthhi], A

; Unlock the counter register so it can be updated
; with the number of bytes in the data stage.
   iord ep0_count

; Enable receiving data in an OUT transaction.
jmp   initialize_control_write

initialize_control_write:
; The firmware uses the value in ep0_transtype to
; decide how to respond to a token packet.
mov   A, TRANS_CONTROL_WRITE
mov   [ep0_transtype], A
```

```
    ; Set the data toggle.
    mov  A, DATA_TOGGLE
    mov  [ep0_data_toggle], A

    ; Send ACK in response to OUT packets,
    ; which will contain the Control Write data.
    ; Send NAK in response to IN packets (not expected).
    mov  A, ACK_OUT_NAK_IN
    iowr ep0_mode

    ;Return from the Endpoint 0 ISR.
    pop  A
    pop  X
    reti
```

The chip then waits for the arrival of the OUT token packet to begin the Data stage. When an Endpoint 0 interrupt occurs, the code checks for an OUT packet, and if one has arrived, it stores the received data and returns a 0-byte data packet in the Status stage:

```
    control_write_data_stage:
    ; Jump here on receiving an Out packet in the
    ; Data stage of a Control Write transfer.

    ; If the data-valid bit isn't set,
    ; we're done with the data stage.
    iord ep0_count
    and  A, DATA_VALID
    jz   control_write_data_stage_done

    ; Check the data-toggle bit. If it's incorrect,
    ; we're done with the Data stage.
    iord ep0_count
    and  A, DATA_TOGGLE
    xor  A, [ep0_data_toggle]
    jnz  control_write_data_stage_done

    ; Copy the report's bytes to data memory.
    mov  A, [ep0_dmabuff0]
    mov  [data_byte_0], A
    mov  A, [ep0_dmabuff1]
    mov  [data_byte_1], A
```

```
;Toggle the data-toggle bit.
mov  A, DATA_TOGGLE
xor  [ep0_data_toggle], A

; Configure Endpoint 0 to send a 0-byte data packet
; in response to an IN packet (the transfer's Status
; stage) and to Stall an Out packet.

mov  A, STATUS_IN_ONLY
iowr  ep0_mode

control_write_data_stage_done:

; Return from Endpoint 0's ISR.
  pop  A
  pop  X
  reti
```

After sending the 0-byte data packet, the endpoint is ready for another transfer.

14

Human Interface Devices: Reports

Chapter 13 introduced the reports that HIDs use to exchange data. A report can be a buffer of undefined bytes, or it can be a complex assortment of items, each with assigned functions and units. This chapter shows how to design a report to fit a specific application.

Report Structure

A report descriptor may contain any of dozens of items arranged in various combinations. It can be long and complex, short and simple, or anywhere in between. The advantage of a more complex descriptor is that the device can provide detailed information about the data it sends and expects to receive. The descriptor can specify the values' uses and what units to apply to the raw data, and it can tell applications whether or not a device supports a particular feature, such as force feedback on a joystick.

But just because the specification supports an item that applies to a device doesn't mean that the report has to include it. For custom devices that are intended for use with a single application, the application often knows the report format in advance, so there's no need to request the information from the device. For example, when the vendor of a data-acquisition unit creates an application for use with the unit, the vendor already knows what data format the device will use in its reports. At most, the application might check the product ID and version number from the device descriptor to learn whether it can request a particular setting or action.

Some of the details about report structures can get tedious, and it's not necessary to understand every nuance about them in most cases. So feel free to skim through the details. You can always come back to them later if you need to.

The report descriptor consists of a series of items that describe the values to be transferred. Each item has a defined scope, and some items may apply to multiple values, eliminating the need to repeat.

Using the HID Descriptor Tool

The HID Descriptor Tool (Figure 14-1) is a free utility available from the USB Implementers Forum. It helps in creating report descriptors, and will also check your descriptor's structure, reporting any errors it finds. Instead of having to look up the values that correspond to each item in your report, you can select the item from a list and enter the value you want to assign to it, and the software will add the item to the descriptor. You can also add items manually. The Parse Descriptor function displays the raw and interpreted values in your descriptor and comments on any errors found. When you have a descriptor with no errors, you can convert it to the syntax required by your firmware. The tool has limited support for vendor-specific items, and may flag these as errors.

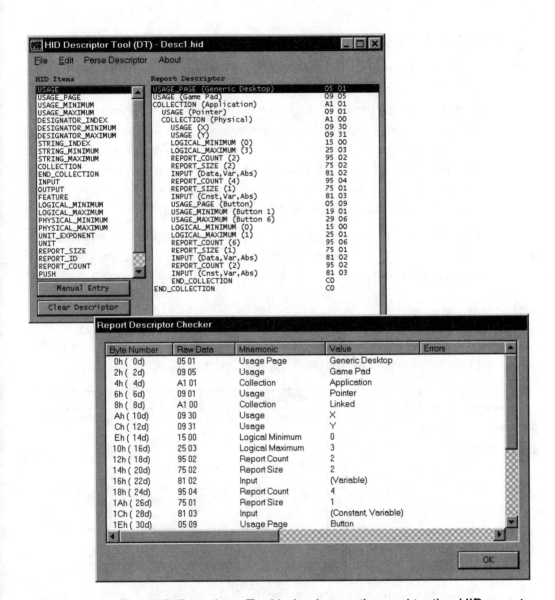

Figure 14-1: The HID Descriptor Tool helps in creating and testing HID report descriptors.

Predefined Values

A report descriptor can contain values that describe specific uses. There are several documents that define the Usage and other values that reports may contain. The first place to look is the *HID Usage Tables* document. This has tables of values for generic desktop controls, simulation controls, game controls, LEDs, buttons, telephony devices, and more. The document also tells you where to find values that are defined elsewhere. Some are in the HID specification, while others are in the class specifications for specific device types such as monitor, power, and image-class devices.

The HID specification defines two report item types: short items and long items. As of HID 1.1, there are no defined Long items, and the type is just reserved for future use.

Short Items

A Short item's 1-byte prefix specifies the item type, item tag, and item size. These are the elements that make up the prefix byte:

Bit Number	Contents	Description
7	Item Tag	Numeric value that indicates the item's function
6		
5		
4		
3	Item Type	Item scope: Main, Global, or Local
2		
1	Item Size	Number of bytes in the item
0		

The item tag (bits 4-7) indicates the item's function.

The item type (bits 3 and 2) describes the scope of the item: Main (00), Global (01), or Local (10). Main items define or group the data fields in the descriptor. Global items describe the reported data. Local items define characteristics of individual controls in the data. (This chapter has more information about these.)

The item size (bits 1 and 0) indicates how many data bytes the item contains. Note that an item size of 3 (11 in binary) corresponds to 4 data bytes:

Item Size (binary)	Number of Data Bytes
00	0
01	1
10	2
11	4

Long Items

A Long item uses multiple bytes to store the same information as the Short item's 1-byte prefix. A Long item's 1-byte prefix (FEh) identifies the item as a Long item. In addition, the item has a byte that specifies the number of data bytes, a byte containing the item tag, and up to 255 bytes of data.

The Main Item Type

A Main item defines or groups data items within a report descriptor. There are five subtypes with the Main item type. The Input, Output, and Feature items each define fields in the report. Collection and End Collection items don't define fields, but instead group related items within a report. The default value for all Main items is 0.

Input, Output, and Feature Items

Table 14-1 shows the supported values for the Input, Output, and Feature items, including the item tag and the meanings of the bits in the value that follows the tag.

An Input item can apply to any control, sensor reading, or other information that the device sends to the host. An Input report contains one or more Input items. The host uses interrupt IN transfers to request Input reports.

An Output item applies to information that the host sends to the device. An Output report contains one or more Output items. Output reports contain data that reports the states of controls, such as whether to open or close a

Table 14-1: The data included with Input, Output, and Feature Item Tags describes the report data.

Main Item Tag	Bit Number	Meaning if bit = 0	Meaning if bit = 1
Input (100000nn, where nn=the number of data bytes)	0	Data	Constant
	1	Array	Variable
	2	Absolute	Relative
	3	No wrap	Wrap
	4	Linear	Non-linear
	5	Preferred state	No preferred state
	6	No null position	Null state
	7	Reserved	
	8	Bit field	Buffered bytes
	9-31	Reserved	
Output (100100nn, where nn=the number of data bytes)	0	Data	Constant
	1	Array	Variable
	2	Absolute	Relative
	3	No wrap	Wrap
	4	Linear	Non-linear
	5	Preferred state	No preferred state
	6	No null position	Null state
	7	Non-volatile	Volatile
	8	Bit field	Buffered bytes
	9-31	Reserved	
Feature (101100nn, where nn=the number of data bytes)	0	Data	Constant
	1	Array	Variable
	2	Absolute	Relative
	3	No wrap	Wrap
	4	Linear	Non-linear
	5	Preferred state	No preferred state
	6	No null position	Null state
	7	Non-volatile	Volatile
	8	Bit field	Buffered bytes
	9-31	Reserved	

switch or the intensity to apply to an effect. As explained earlier, if an interrupt OUT pipe is available, a HID 1.1-compliant host uses interrupt OUT transfers to send Output reports. Otherwise, the host uses Set_Report control requests.

A Feature item normally applies to information that the host sends to the device. However, it's also possible for the host to read Feature items from a device. A Feature report contains one or more Feature items. Feature reports typically contain configuration settings that affect the overall behavior of the device or one of its components. Feature reports normally control settings that you might otherwise adjust in a physical control panel. For example, the host may have a virtual (on-screen) control panel to enable users to select and control features. The host uses control transfers with Set_Report and Get_Report requests to send and receive Feature reports.

Following each item tag are 32 bits that describe the data. At most, only 9 of the bits are used, with the rest reserved. The device firmware and host software may use or ignore this information.

The bit functions are the same for Input, Output, and Feature items, except that Input items don't support the volatile/non-volatile bit. These are the uses for each bit:

Data | Constant. Data means that the contents of the item are modifiable (read/write). Constant means the contents are not modifiable (read-only).

Array | Variable. This bit specifies whether the data reports the state of every control or just reports the controls that are active. Reporting only the active controls results in a more compact report for devices such as keyboards, where there are many controls (keys) but only one or a few are active at the same time.

For example, if a keypad has eight keys, setting this bit to Variable would mean that the keypad's report would contain a bit for each key. In the report descriptor, the report size would be one bit, the report count would be eight, and the total amount of data sent would be eight bits. Setting the bit to Array would mean that each key has an assigned index, and the keypad's report would contain only the index of the keys that are active. With eight keys, the report size would be three bits, which can report a key number from 0 through 7. The report count would equal the maximum number of simultaneous keypresses that could be reported. If the user can press only one key at a time, the report count would be 1 and the total amount of data sent would be just 3 bits. If the user can press all of the keys at once, the report count would be 8 and the total amount of data sent would be 24 bits.

The specification recommends returning 0 when no controls are active, and specifying a Logical Minimum of 1 and a Logical Maximum equal to the number of controls.

Absolute | Relative. Absolute means that the value is based on a fixed origin; Relative means that the data indicates the change from the last reading. A joystick normally reports absolute data (the joystick's current position), while a mouse reports relative data (how far the mouse has moved since the last report).

No Wrap | Wrap. Wrap indicates that the value rolls over if it continues to increment after reaching its maximum or continues to decrement after reaching its minimum. A value specified as No Wrap that exceeds the limits may report a value outside the specified limits. This bit doesn't apply to Array data.

Linear | Non-linear. Linear indicates that the measured data and the reported value have a linear relationship. A graph of the reported data and the property being measured forms a straight line. In non-linear data, a graph of the reported data and the property being measured forms a curve. This bit doesn't apply to Array data.

Preferred State | No Preferred State. Preferred state indicates that the control will return to a particular state when the user isn't interacting with it. A momentary pushbutton has a preferred state (out) when no one is pressing it. A toggle switch has no preferred state; it remains in the state selected by the last user. This bit doesn't apply to Array data.

No Null Position | Null State. Null state indicates that the control supports a state where it isn't sending meaningful data. A control indicates that it's in its null state by sending a value outside the range defined by its Logical Minimum and Maximum. No Null Position indicates that the control can always be assumed to be sending meaningful data. A hat switch on a joystick is in a null position when it isn't being pressed. This bit doesn't apply to Array data.

Non-volatile | Volatile. The Volatile bit applies only to Output and Feature reports. Volatile means that the device can change the value on its own, without host interaction, as well as when the host sends a report requesting the device to change the value. For example, a control panel may have a control that users can set in two ways. They may use a mouse to click a setting in a window on the host to cause the host to send a report to the device, or they may press a physical button on the device. Non-volatile means that the device changes the value only when the host requests it in a report.

When the host is sending a report and doesn't want to change a volatile item, the value to assign depends on whether the data is defined as relative or absolute. If a volatile item is defined as relative, a report that assigns a value of 0 should result in no change. If a volatile item is defined as absolute, a report that assigns an out-of-range value should result in no change.

This bit doesn't apply to Array data.

Bit Field | Buffered Bytes. Bit Field means that each bit or a group of bits in a byte can represent a separate piece of data and the field doesn't represent a single quantity. The application interprets the contents of the field. Buffered Bytes means that the data consists of one or more bytes. The report size for Buffered Bytes must be eight. This bit doesn't apply to Array data.

Collection and End Collection Tags

All of the report types can use Collection and End Collection items to group related items.

There are three defined types of collections: application, physical, and logical. Vendors can also define their own collection types. Collections can be nested. Table 14-2 shows the values of the Collection and End Collection tags and the defined values for the different collection types.

An application collection contains items that have a common purpose or together carry out a single function. For example, the boot descriptor for a

Table 14-2: Data values for the Collection and End Collection Main Item Tags.

Main Item Type	Value	Description
Collection (A1h)	00h	Physical
	01h	Application
	02h	Logical
	03h-7Fh	Reserved
	80h-FFh	Vendor-defined
End Collection (C0h)	None	Closes a collection

keyboard groups the keypress and LED data in an application collection. All reports must be in an application collection

A physical collection contains items that represent data at a single geometric point. A device that collects a variety of sensor readings from multiple locations might group the data for each location in a collection. The boot descriptor for a mouse groups the button and position indicators in a physical collection.

A logical collection forms a data structure consisting of items of different types that are linked by the collection. An example is the contents of a data buffer and a count of the number of bytes in the buffer.

Each collection begins with a Collection item and ends with an End Collection item. All Main items between the Collection and End Collection items are part of the collection. Each collection must have a Usage tag (described below).

If a report contains an unknown vendor-defined collection type, the host should ignore all Main items in the collection. If a known collection type has an unknown Usage, the host should ignore all items in the collection.

The Global Item Type

Global items identify reports and describe the data in them, including characteristics such as the data's function, maximum and minimum allowed values, and the size and number of report items. A Global item tag applies to every item that follows until the next Global tag. This saves storage space because there's no need to repeat values that don't change from one item to the next. There are 12 defined Global items, shown in Table 14-3.

Identifying the Report

Report ID is a prefix that may precede the report data in a data packet. A device can support multiple reports of the same type, with each containing different data and having its own ID. This way, a transfer doesn't have to include every piece of data every time. However, in many cases the simplicity of having a single report is more important than the need to reduce the bandwidth used by reports to the absolute minimum.

In a descriptor, a Report ID item applies to all items that follow until a new Report ID. If there is no Report ID item, the default ID of zero is assumed. A descriptor should not declare a Report ID of zero. Input, Output, and Feature reports can share a Report ID.

If one or more report types has multiple Report IDs, every report must have a declared ID. For example, if an interface supports Report IDs 1 and 2 for Feature reports, any Input or Output reports must also have a Report ID greater than 0.

In a transfer that uses a Set_Report or Get_Report request, the host specifies a report ID in the Setup transaction, in the low byte of the Value field. In an interrupt transfer, if the interface supports more than one report ID, the report ID should be the first byte sent with a report. If the interface supports only the default report ID of zero, the report ID should not be sent with the report in an interrupt transfer.

Under Windows, applications should always precede a report to be sent with a report ID. If the ID is 0, the HID driver doesn't send it on the bus with the report data. In a similar way, reports read into an application always begin with a report ID. The HID driver inserts an ID of zero before the report data if necessary.

When a HID supports multiple report IDs for Input reports of different sizes, Windows' HID driver always uses buffers large enough to hold the longest report. Shorter reports that are a multiple of the maximum packet

Table 14-3: There are twelve defined Global items.

Global Item Type	Value (nn indicates the number of bytes that follow)	Description
Usage Page	000001nn	Defines the data's usage or function.
Logical Minimum	000101nn	Smallest value that an item will report.
Logical Maximum	001001nn	Largest value that an item will report.
Physical Minimum	001101nn	The logical minimum expressed in physical units.
Physical Maximum	010001nn	The logical maximum expressed in physical units.
Unit exponent	010101nn	Base 10 exponent of units.
Unit	011001nn	Unit values
Report Size	011101nn	Size of an item's fields in bits.
Report ID	100001nn	Prefix that identifies a report.
Report Count	100101nn	The number of data fields for an item
Push	101001nn	Places a copy of the global item state table on the stack.
Pop	101101nn	Replaces the item state table with the last structure pushed onto the stack.
Reserved	110001nn to 111101nn	For future use.

size must terminate with a 0-length data packet to let the host know that all of the data has been sent.

Windows' HID driver uses interrupt transfers to retrieve Input reports. When there are multiple Input Report IDs, the driver has no way to request a specific report. On receiving the IN token packet, the device returns whatever report is in its buffer, so the device firmware must decide which report to make available. The HID driver stores the received report and its ID in its buffer.

Describing the Data's Use

The items that describe how the data will be used are Usage Page, Logical and Physical Maximums and Minimums, Unit, and Unit Exponent. All of these help the receiver of the report to interpret the report's data. All but the Usage Page are involved with converting raw report data to values with units attached. These items make it possible for a report to contain data in a compact form, with the receiver of the data having the responsibility of converting the data to meaningful values. However, the sender of the report data may instead choose to do some or all of the converting.

Usage Page. An item's Usage is a 32-bit value that describes its function. The Usage is made up of two 16-bit parts: the Usage Page, which is a Global item, and the Usage Index, which is a Local item. Multiple items may share a Usage Page while having different Usage Indexes. After a Usage Page appears in a report, all Usage Indexes that follow will use that Usage Page until a new one is declared. Re-using the Usage Page reduces the amount of data that the descriptor has to store and send.

The HID Usage Tables document lists the defined Usage Pages and their values and also names the document section or other document that describes each page and its indexes. There are Usage Pages for many common device types, including generic desktop controls (mouse, keyboard, joystick), digitizer, bar-code scanner, camera control, and various game controls. Specialized devices may not have a defined Usage Page. In this case, a vendor can define the Usage Page. Values from FF00h to FFFFh are reserved for vendor-defined Usage Pages.

Logical Minimum and Logical Maximum. The Logical Minimum and Maximum define the limits for reported values. The limits are expressed in "logical units," which means that they use the same units as the values they describe. For example, if a device reports readings of up to 500 milliamperes in units of 2 milliamperes, the Logical Maximum is 250.

Negative values may be expressed as two's complements. Bit 7 is a sign bit that indicates whether the value is positive (0) or negative (1). The values 0 to 7Fh are the positive decimal values 0 through 127, and FFh to 80h are the negative decimal values -1 through -128. To find the negative value represented by a two's complement, complement each bit and add 1 to the result. Here are some examples:

Negative Value Expressed as a Two's Complement:	FFh	FDh	80h
Complement each bit:	00h	02h	7Fh
Add 1:	01h	03h	80h
Value Expressed as a Negative Number (decimal):	-1	-3	-128

The HID specification says that if both the Logical Minimum and Maximum are considered positive, there's no need for a sign bit. For example, a range from 0 to 255 can have a Logical Minimum of 00h and a Logical Maximum of FFh. A device will enumerate and transfer data without problems whether the Logical Minimum and Maximum are expressed as signed or unsigned values. The receiver of the data has to know whether or not the data can be negative.

The HIDView utility (described in Chapter 17) assumes the use of signed values. With a Logical Minimum of 00h and a Logical Maximum of FFh, it reports the error, "Logical Minimum must be less than the Logical Maximum." It doesn't report this error with a minimum of 80h (-128) and maximum of 7F (+127). On the other hand, the HID Descriptor Tool reports an error if you use a minimum of 80h and maximum of 7Fh, while it accepts 00h and FFh.

The Physical Minimum, Physical Maximum, Unit Exponent, and Unit items define how to convert the reported values into more meaningful units.

Physical Minimum and Physical Maximum. The Physical Minimum and Maximum define the limits for the value when expressed in the units defined by the Units tag. In the earlier example of values of 0 through 250 in units of 2 milliamperes, the Physical Minimum is 0 and the Physical Maximum is 500. The receiving device uses the logical and physical limit values to obtain the value in the desired units. In the example, reporting the data in units of 2 milliamperes means that the value can transfer in a single byte, with the receiver of the data using the Physical Minimum and Maximum values to translate to milliamperes. The price is a loss in resolution, compared to reporting 1 bit per milliampere. If the report doesn't specify the values, they default to the same as the Logical Minimum and Maximum.

Unit Exponent. The Unit Exponent specifies what power of 10 to apply to the value obtained after using the logical and physical limits to translate the value into the desired units. The exponent can range from -8 to +7. A value of 0 causes the value to be multiplied by 10^0, or 1, which is the same as applying no exponent. These are the codes:

Exponent	0	1	2	3	4	5	6	7	-8	-7	-6	-5	-4	-3	-2	-1
Code	00h	01h	02h	03h	04h	05h	06h	07h	08h	09h	0Ah	0Bh	0Ch	0Dh	0Eh	0Fh

For example, if the value obtained is 1234 and the Unit Exponent is 0Eh, the final value is 12.34.

Unit. The Unit tag specifies what units to apply to the report data after it's converted using the Physical and Unit Exponent items. The HID specification defines codes for the basic units of length, mass, time, temperature, current, and luminous intensity. Most other units can be derived from these.

Specifying a Unit value can be more complicated than you might expect. Table 14-4 shows values you can work from. The value can be as long as four bytes, with each nibble having a defined function. Nibble 0 (the least significant nibble) specifies the measurement system, either English or SI (International System of Units), and whether the measurement is in linear or angular units. Each of the nibble positions that follow represents a quality to be measured, with the value of the nibble representing the exponent to apply to the value. For example, a nibble with a value of 2 means that its corresponding value is in units squared. A nibble with a value of 0Dh, which represents -3, means that the units are expressed as $1/units^3$. These exponents are separate from the Unit Exponent value, which is a power of ten applied to the data, rather than an exponent applied to the units.

Converting Raw Data

To convert raw data to values with units attached, three things must occur. The firmware's report descriptor must contain the information needed for

Table 14-4: The units to apply to a reported value are a function of the measuring system and exponent values specified in the Unit item

Nibble Number	Quality Measured	Measuring System (Nibble 0 value)				
		None (0)	SI Linear (1)	SI Rotation (2)	English Linear (3)	English Rotation (4)
1	Length	None	Centimeters	Radians	Inches	Degrees
2	Mass	None	Grams		Slugs	
3	Time	None	Seconds			
4	Temperature	None	Kelvin		Fahrenheit	
5	Current	None	Amperes			
6	Luminous Intensity	None	Candelas			
7	Reserved	None				

the conversion. The sender of the data must send data that matches the specification in the descriptor. And the receiver of the data must apply the conversions specified in the descriptor.

Below are examples of descriptors and raw and converted data. Remember that just because a tag exists in the HID specification doesn't mean you have to use it. If the application knows what format and units to use for the values it's going to send or receive, the firmware doesn't have to specify it.

To measure time in seconds, up to a minute, the report descriptor might include this information:

Logical Minimum: 0

Logical Maximum: 60

Physical Minimum: 0

Physical Maximum: 60

Unit: 1003h. Nibble 0 = 3 to select the English Linear measuring system (though in this case, any value from 1 to 4 would work). Nibble 3 = 1 to select time in seconds.

Unit Exponent: 0

With this information, the receiver knows that the value sent equals a number of seconds.

Now, what if instead you want to measure time in tenths of seconds, again up to a minute? You would need to increase the Logical and Physical Maximums and change the Unit Exponent:

> Logical Minimum: 0
>
> Logical Maximum: 600
>
> Physical Minimum: 0
>
> Physical Maximum: 600
>
> Unit: 1003h. Nibble 0 = 3 to select the English Linear measuring system. Nibble 3 = 1 to select time in seconds.
>
> Unit Exponent: 0Fh. This represents an exponent of -1, to indicate that the value is expressed in tenths of seconds rather than seconds.

Sending values as large as 600 will require 3 bytes, which the firmware specifies in the Report Size tag.

To send a temperature value using one byte to represent temperatures from -20 to 110 degrees Fahrenheit, the report descriptor might contain the following:

> Logical Minimum: -128 (80h expressed as a two's complement)
>
> Logical Maximum: 127 (7Fh)
>
> Physical Minimum: -20 (ECh expressed as a two's complement)
>
> Physical Maximum: 110 (6Eh)
>
> Unit: 10003h. Nibble 0 is 3 to select the English Linear measuring system, though in this case, any value from 1 to 4 is OK. Nibble 4 is 1 to select degrees Fahrenheit.
>
> Unit Exponent: 0

These values ensure the highest possible resolution, because the transmitted values can span the full range from 0 to 255.

In this case the logical and physical limits differ, so converting is required. To find the resolution, or number of bits per unit, use this equation:

```
Resolution = _
    (Logical_Maximum - Logical_Minimum) / _
    ((Physical_Maximum - Physical_Minimum) * _
    (10 ^ Unit_Exponent ))
```

With the example values, this works out to 1.96 bits per degree, or 0.51 degree per bit.

To convert a value to the specified units, use this equation:

```
Value = _
   Value_In_Logical_Units *
   ((Physical_Maximum - Physical_Minimum) * _
   (10 ^ Unit_Exponent )) /
   (Logical_Maximum - Logical_Minimum)
```

If the value in logical units (the raw data) is 63, the converted value in the specified units is 32 degrees Fahrenheit.

Specifying velocity in centimeters per second requires a Unit value that contains units of both centimeters and seconds. From Table 14-4, the Unit value to use is 1011h. Nibble 0 = 1 to select the SI measuring system, nibble 1 = 1 to select length in centimeters, and nibble 3 = 1 to select time in seconds.

To illustrate how complicated it can get, the Unit value for volts is F0D121h, which indicates the SI Linear measuring system in units of $(cm^2)*(gm)*(sec^{-3})*(amp^{-1})$. However, remember that the Unit value only specifies the units. All the receiver has to do is identify the Units value and assign the units to received data; there's no need to do the calculations implied in the Units value.

Describing the Data's Size and Format

Two Global items describe the size and format of the report data.

Report Size specifies the size in bits of an Input, Output, or Feature item's fields. Each field contains one piece of data.

Report Count specifies how many fields an Input, Output, or Feature item contains. For example, for two 8-bit fields, Report Size is 8 and Report Count is 2. For ten 4-bit fields, Report Size is 4 and Report Count is 10. For one 16-bit field, Report Size is 16 and Report Count is 1.

A single Input, Output, or Feature report can have multiple items, each with its own Report Size and Report Count.

Saving and Restoring Global Items

The final two Global items enable saving and restoring sets of Global items. These allow flexibility in the report formats while using minimum storage space in the device.

Push places a copy of the Global-item state table on the CPU's stack. The Global-item state table contains the current settings for all previously defined Global items.

Pop is the complement to Push. It restores the saved states of the previously pushed Global item states.

The Local Item Type

Local items define qualities of the knobs, switches, buttons, and other controls that a report returns data for. A Local item applies to all controls that follow within the Main item, until a new value is assigned. Local items don't carry over to the next Main item. Each Main item begins fresh, with no Local items defined.

Local items relate to general usages, body-part designators, and strings. A Delimiter item enables grouping sets of Local items. Table 14-5 shows the values and meaning of each of the items.

Usage. The Local Usage item is the Usage Index that works together with the Global Usage Page to describe the function of an item or collection. As with the Usage Page, the HID Usage Tables document lists many Usage Indexes. For example, the Buttons Usage Page uses Local Usage Indexes from 1 to FFFFh to specify individual buttons, with a value of 0 meaning no button pressed.

A report may assign one Usage to multiple controls, or it may assign a different Usage to each control. If a report item is preceded by a single Usage, that Usage applies to all of the item's controls. If a report item is preceded by more than one Usage, and the number of controls equals the number of Usages, each Usage applies to one control, with the Usages and controls

Table 14-5: There are ten defined Local items.

Local Item Type	Value (nn indicates the number of bytes that follow)	Description
Usage	000010nn	An index that describes the use for an item or collection.
Usage Minimum	000110nn	The starting Usage associated with an array or bitmap.
Usage Maximum	001010nn	The ending Usage associated with an array or bitmap.
Designator Index	001110nn	Designates the body part used for a control.
Designator Minimum	010010nn	The starting Designator associated with an array or bitmap.
Designator Maximum	010110nn	The ending Designator associated with an array or bitmap.
String Index	011110nn	Associates a string with an item or control.
String Minimum	100010nn	The first string index when assigning a group of sequential strings to controls in an array or bitmap.
String Maximum	100110nn	The last string index when assigning a group of sequential strings to controls in an array or bitmap.
Delimiter	101010nn	The beginning (1) or end (0) of a set of Local items.
Reserved	101011nn to 111110nn	For future use.

pairing up in sequence. In the following example, the report contains two bytes. The first byte's Usage is X, and the second byte's Usage is Y.

```
Report Size (8),
Report Count (2),
Usage (X),
Usage (Y),
Input (Data, Variable, Absolute),
```

If a report item is preceded by more than one Usage and the number of controls is greater than the number of Usages, each Usage pairs up with one control, and the final Usage applies to all of the remaining controls. In the following example, the report is 16 bytes. Usage X applies to the first byte,

Usage Y applies to the second byte, and a vendor-defined Usage applies to the third through 16th bytes.

```
Usage (X)
Usage (Y)
Usage (vendor defined)
Report Count (16),
Report Size (8),
Input (Data, Variable, Absolute)
```

Usage Minimum and Maximum. The Usage Minimum and Maximum can assign a single Usage to multiple controls. The following example reports the state (0 or 1) of each of three buttons. The Usage Minimum and Maximum assign the Button Usage Page to all three items. The item uses one bit per button.

```
Logical Minimum (0)
Logical Maximum (1)
Report Count (3)
Report Size (1)
Usage Page (Button Page)
Usage Minimum (1)
Usage Maximum (3)
Input (Data, Variable, Absolute)
```

The Usage Minimum and Maximum can also assign a single Usage to a series of array items.

Designator Index. For items with a Physical descriptor, the Designator Index specifies the body part the control uses.

Designator Minimum and Maximum. When a report contains multiple controls with the same Designator, the Designator Minimum and Maximum can specify which controls the Usage applies to.

String Index. An item or control can include a string index to associate a string with that item or control. The strings are stored in the same format described in Chapter 5 for product, manufacturer, and serial-number strings.

String Minimum and Maximum. When a report contains multiple controls with the same String Index, the String Minimum and Maximum can specify which controls the Usage applies to.

Delimiter. The Delimiter defines the beginning (1) or end (0) of a local item. A delimited local item may contain alternate usages for a control. This enables different applications to define a device's controls in different ways. For example, a button may have a generic use (Button1) and a specific use (Send, Quit, etc.).

Physical Descriptors

A physical descriptor describes the part or parts of the body intended to activate a control. For example, each finger might have its own assigned control.

A physical descriptor is a type of class descriptor. The host can retrieve a physical descriptor by sending a Get_Descriptor request with 23h in the high byte of the Value field and 00h in the low byte of the Value field.

Physical descriptors are optional. For most devices, they either don't apply at all or the information they could provide has no practical use. The HID specification has more information on how to use physical descriptors, for those devices that need them.

Padding

To pad a descriptor so it contains a multiple of eight bits, the descriptor may include a Main item with no assigned Usage. The following example describes an Input report that transfers three bits with data and five bits of padding:

```
Report Count (3)
Report Size (1)
Usage Page (Button Page)
Usage Minimum (1)
Usage Maximum (3)
Input (Data, Variable, Absolute)
Report Size (5),
Input (Constant)
```

15

Human Interface Devices: Host Application Primer

Chapter 13 and Chapter 14 described human-interface-device communications from the device's perspective and the report format that HIDs use to exchange data with the host. This chapter introduces the Windows functions that applications can use to communicate with HIDs. Applications may use any programming language that can call API functions. Chapter 16 has example code in Visual Basic and Visual C++. Much of the information in this chapter applies to communicating with any USB device, not just HIDs.

Host Communications Overview

Windows 98 and Windows 2000 include everything applications need to communicate with HID-class devices. There's no need to install drivers because Windows has them built in.

How the Host Finds a Device

Communicating with a HID isn't as simple as opening a port, setting a few parameters, and then reading and writing data, as you can do with RS-232 and parallel ports. Before an application can exchange data with a HID, it has to identify the device and get information about its reports. To do this, the application has to jump through a few hoops by calling a series of API functions. The application first finds out what HIDs are attached to the system. It then examines information about each until it finds one with the desired attributes. For a custom device, the application can search for specific Vendor and Product IDs. Or the application can search for a device of a particular type, such as a mouse or joystick.

After finding a device, the application can exchange information with it by sending and receiving reports.

Table 15-1 lists API functions used in establishing communications and exchanging data with a HID. The functions are listed in a typical order that an application might call them.

Table 15-1: Communicating with HIDs uses a variety of API functions. These are the major functions used in identifying a HID and sending and receiving reports.

API Function	DLL	Purpose
HidD_GetHidGuid	hid.dll	Obtain the GUID for the HID class
SetupDiGetClassDevs	setupapi.dll	Return a device information set containing all of the devices in a specified class.
SetupDiEnumDeviceInterfaces	setupapi.dll	Return information about a device in the device information set.
SetupDiGetDeviceInterfaceDetail	setupapi.dll	Return a device pathname.
SetupDiDestroyDeviceInfoList	setupapi.dll	Free resources used by SetupDiGetClassDevs.
CreateFile	kernel32.dll	Open communications with a device.
HidD_GetAttributes	hid.dll	Return a Vendor ID, Product ID, and Version Number.
HidD_GetPreparsedData	hid.dll	Return a handle to a buffer with information about the device's capabilities
HidP_GetCaps	hid.dll	Return a structure describing the device's capabilities.
HidD_FreePreparsedData	hid.dll	Free resources used by HidD_GetPreparsedData.
WriteFile	kernel32.dll	Send an Output report to the device.
ReadFile	kernel32.dll	Read an Input report from the device.
HidD_SetFeature	hid.dll	Send a Feature report to the device.
HidD_GetFeature	hid.dll	Read a Feature report from the device.
CloseHandle	kernel32.dll	Free resources used by CreateFile.

Documentation

The functions are in three DLLs whose documentation is spread among several areas in the Windows DDK documentation and the MSDN library. These are DLLs that contain functions used in HID communications:

Filename	Type of Functions Included
hid.dll	HID communications.
setupapi.dll	Finding and identifying devices
kernel32.dll	Exchanging data, other general functions

The functions that relate only to HID communications are in *hid.dll* and are documented in the DDK, under *Kernel-Mode Drivers > Drivers for Input Devices*. Functions related to detecting devices are in *setupapi.dll* and are documented in the DDK under *Setup, Plug & Play, and Power Management > Device Installation Functions* and also in the Platform SDK under *Device Management Functions*. These functions apply to all Plug-and-Play devices, including USB devices. Functions relating to opening communications, reading Input reports, and writing Output reports are in *kernel32.dll* and are documented in the MSDN library, in the Platform SDK under *File I/O*. Many other devices also use these functions.

Windows 98 SE added seven HID functions to those supported by Windows 98 Gold. Windows 2000 and Windows Me support the new functions as well. The Windows 2000 DDK documentation includes the added functions; the Windows 98 DDK doesn't.

The HID Functions

Hid.dll supports many more functions than the essentials listed in Table 15-1. The following three tables together comprise a complete list of the HID functions grouped by purpose. Functions whose names begin with HidP are available to both applications and device drivers. Functions whose names begin with HidD are available only to applications.

Table 15-2 lists functions that applications use to learn about a HID. Table 15-3 lists functions that applications use in reading and writing reports. Table 15-4 lists functions that applications use in configuring the input buffer to receive reports. The documentation also names three functions for future use: HidD_GetConfiguration, HidD_SetConfiguration, and HidP_TranslateUsagesToI8042ScanCodes.

You can use these functions with just about any HID-class device, including custom designs. Windows 2000 doesn't allow applications to use the functions to access the system keyboard or mouse, but applications don't normally need to do so because the operating system provides other ways to communicate with the keyboard and mouse.

Table 15-2: Applications can use these functions in *hid.dll* to learn about a device.

Function	Purpose
HidD_GetAttributes	Retrieves the HID's Vendor ID, Product ID, and Version Number.
HidD_FreePreparsedData	Frees resources used by HidD_GetPreparsedData.
HidD_GetHidGuid	Obtains the GUID for the HID class.
HidD_GetIndexedString*	Retrieves a string identified by an index.
HidD_GetManufacturerString*	Retrieves the string that identifies the device manufacturer.
HidD_GetPhysicalDescriptor*	Retrieves the string that identifies the physical device.
HidD_GetPreparsedData	Retrieves a handle to a buffer with information about the device's capabilities.
HidD_GetProductString*	Retrieves the string that identifies the product.
HidD_GetSerialNumberString*	Retrieves the string containing the device's serial number.
HidP_GetButtonCaps	Retrieves the capabilities of all buttons in a report.
HidP_GetCaps	Retrieves a pointer to a structure describing the device's capabilities.
HidP_GetLinkCollectionNodes	Retrieves an array of structures that describes the relationship of link collections within a top-level collection.
HidP_GetSpecificButtonCaps	Retrieves the capabilities of buttons in a report. The request can specify a Usage Page, Usage, or Link Collection.
HidP_GetSpecificValueCaps	Retrieves the capabilities of values in a report. The request can specify a Usage Page, Usage, or Link Collection.
HidP_GetValueCaps	Retrieves the capabilities of all values in a report.
HidP_MaxUsageListLength	Retrieves the maximum number of buttons that a report can return. Can specify a Usage Page.
HidP_UsageListDifference	Compares two button lists and find the buttons that are set in one list and not in the other.
*not supported under Windows 98 Gold.	

DirectX

An alternative to using API functions for accessing HIDs is to use Microsoft's DirectX components. DirectX enables control of system hardware, including HIDs. DirectX originated as a tool for game programmers with a goal of providing fast access to hardware. Instead of having to poll an

Table 15-3: Applications can use these functions in *hid.dll* to read and write reports.

Function	Purpose
HidD_GetFeature	Retrieves a Feature report.
HidD_SetFeature	Sends a Feature report.
HidP_GetButtons	Returns a pointer to a buffer containing the Usage of each button that is pressed. Can specify a Usage Page.
HidP_GetButtonsEx	Returns a pointer to a buffer containing the Usage and Usage Page of each button that is pressed.
HidP_GetScaledUsageValue	Returns the signed result of a value that has been adjusted for its scaling factor.
HidP_GetUsageValue	Returns a pointer to a value.
HidP_GetUsageValueArray	Returns data for a Usage that contains multiple data items.
HidP_SetButtons	Sets button data.
HidP_SetScaledUsageValue	Takes a signed, physical (scaled) number, converts it to the logical representation used by the device, and inserts it in a report.
HidP_SetUsageValue	Sets a value.
HidP_SetUsageValueArray	Sets data for a Usage that contains multiple data items.

input buffer with ReadFile, you can configure the DirectX software components to notify an application when data is available to read.

The DirectInput components of DirectX enable communications with HIDs under C++, Delphi, or Visual Basic. The DirectX SDK has examples in Visual C++ and Visual Basic. The samples are oriented towards communicating with standard device types. The documentation suggests that you can use DirectX to communicate with any HID, but provides few details on how to do so.

Using API Functions

The examples in this chapter use Microsoft's Visual Basic and Visual C++. As explained in Chapter 10, an API function is a part of Windows' Application Programmer's Interface, which contains thousands of functions that applications can use to communicate with the operating system. The execut-

Table 15-4: Applications can use these functions in *hid.dll* to control the driver's input buffer for reading reports.

Function	Purpose
HidD_FlushQueue*	Empty the input buffer.
HidD_GetNumInputBuffers*	Retrieves the size of the ring buffer the driver uses to store input reports. The default is 8.
HidD_SetNumInputBuffers*	Sets the size of the ring buffer the driver uses to store input reports.
*Not supported under Windows 98 Gold.	

able code for the functions resides in dynamic linked library (DLL) files provided with Windows.

Before getting into the details of the functions themselves, I'll present some background on how to call API functions from Visual Basic and Visual C++ applications. If you're already familiar with using API calls, or if you want to get right to the HID-specific functions, you can skip over the these introductory sections. I'll begin with Visual C++.

Using Visual C++

To use an API function, a Visual C++ application needs three things: the ability to locate the file containing the function's compiled code, a function declaration, and a call that causes the function to execute.

Applications that access HIDs will call functions contained in *hid.dll* and *setupapi.dll*. Each of the DLLs has two companion files, a library file (*hid.lib* and *setupapi.lib*) and one or more header files (*hidpi.h, hidsdi.h, hidusage.h,* and *setupapi.h*). The header file contains the prototypes, structures, and symbols for the functions that applications may call, and the library file eliminates the need for the application to get a pointer to the function in the DLL.

A DLL contains compiled code for the functions that it exports, or makes available to applications. For each exported function, the DLL's library file contains a stub function whose name and arguments match the name and arguments of one of the DLL's functions. The stub function calls its corresponding function in the DLL. During the compile process, the linker incorporates the code in the library file into the application's executable file. When the application calls a function in the library file, the function of the same name in the DLL executes.

The *hid.dll* and *setupapi.dll* files are included with Windows. They're typically stored in the *windows\system* or *windows\system32\drivers* folder. (In Windows 2000, substitute *winnt* for *windows*.) Both are standard locations that Windows searches when DLL functions are called. The library and header files are included in the DDK.

The header files for other common Windows functions are included automatically when you create a project. For example, *afxwin.h* adds headers for common Windows and MFC functions.

To include a API function in an application, you need to do the following:

1. Add the library files to the project. In Visual C++, click Project > Settings > Link > Category: Input. In the *Object/library* modules box enter *hid.lib* and *setupapi.lib*. In the same window, if necessary, you can enter a path for the library files under *Additional library path*.

2. Include the header files in one of the application's files. Here's an example:

```
extern "C" {
#include "hidsdi.h"
#include <setupapi.h>
}
```

The `#include` directive causes the contents of the named file to be included in the file, the same as if they were copied and pasted into it.

The `extern "C"` modifier enables a C++ module to include header files that use C naming conventions. The difference is that C++ uses name decoration, or name mangling, on external symbols. The punctuation around the file name determines where the compiler will search for the file, and in what order. This is relevant if you have different versions of a file in multiple locations!

Enclosing the file name in brackets (`<setupapi.h>`) causes the compiler to search for the file first in the path specified by the compiler's */I* option, then in the paths specified by the Include environment variable. Enclosing the file name in quotes (`"hidsdi.h"`) causes the compiler to search for the file first in the same directory as the file containing the `#include` directive, then in the directories of any files that contain `#include` directives for that file, then in the path specified by the compiler's */I* option, and finally in the paths specified by the Include environment variable.

3. Call the function. Here is code that declares the variable `HidGuid` and passes a pointer to it in the function `HidD_GetHidGuid` in *hid.dll*:

```
GUID    HidGuid;
HidD_GetHidGuid(&HidGuid);
```

Using Visual Basic

In Visual Basic, the process of calling API functions is different than in Visual C++. In place of an include file, the application needs a module containing Visual-Basic declarations for the DLL's functions and structures. Some of these, but not all, are provided with Visual Basic. You don't need library files, as Visual Basic requires only the DLL's name and the DLL itself in a standard or specified location.

You can write a lot of Visual-Basic applications without ever coding an API call. Visual Basic provides its own syntax and controls for performing common functions. For example, to print a file, you can use Visual Basic's Printer Object instead of API functions. The Printer Object provides an easier and more fail-safe way to access printers. When you run the application, the code that executes may call API functions, but Visual-Basic programmers are insulated from having to make the calls directly.

But sometimes you may want to do something that Visual Basic doesn't support explicitly. In these cases, which can include communicating with HIDs, Visual-Basic applications can call API functions.

In a Visual-Basic application, the code to call an API function follows the same syntax rules as the code to call any function. But instead of placing the function's executable code in a routine within the application, the API function requires only a declaration that enables Windows to find the DLL containing the function's code.

Calling API functions in Visual Basic requires some extra knowledge. The documentation included with Visual Basic doesn't offer much guidance. Microsoft's documentation for the API functions uses C syntax to show how to declare and call the functions. The DDK includes the declarations in header files that Visual C++ programmers can include in applications. To use an API function in Visual Basic, you need to translate the declaration and function call from C to Visual Basic.

The process is more complicated than a simple word-for-word translation, mainly because Visual Basic doesn't support all of C's structures, and it stores string variables in a different format. Before you can translate, you need to understand exactly what the function is passing and returning. Even if you have an example to work from, understanding what the function is doing helps in using it correctly.

For greater detail on API calls in Visual Basic, I recommend Dan Appleman's books, especially *Dan Appleman's Win32 API Puzzle Book and Tutorial for Visual Basic Programmers*. This is the book I used as a reference in figuring out how to call the API functions in this chapter.

To use an API function in a Visual Basic program, you need three things: the DLL containing the function, a declaration that enables the application to find and use the function, and a call that causes the function to execute.

The Declaration

This is a Visual-Basic declaration for the API function WriteFile, which you can use to write data to a HID (as well as to files and other devices):

```
Public Declare Function WriteFile _
    Lib "kernel32" _
    (ByVal hFile As Long, _
    ByRef lpBuffer As Byte, _
    ByVal nNumberOfBytesToWrite As Long, _
    ByRef lpNumberOfBytesWritten As Long, _
    ByVal lpOverlapped As Long) _
    As Long
```

The declaration includes several pieces of information:

• The function's name (WriteFile).

- The values the function will pass to the operating system (hFile, lpBuffer, nNumberOfBytesToWrite, lpNumberOfBytesWritten, and lpOverlapped). The names use the convention of adding a prefix to indicate the type of data the variable contains: h=handle, lp=long pointer, and so on.

- The data types of the values passed (Long, Byte).

- Whether the values will be passed by value (ByVal) or by reference (ByRef).

- The name of the file that contains the executable code for the function (*kernel32.dll*).

- The data type of the value returned for the function (Long). A few API calls have no return value and may be declared as subroutines rather than functions.

The declaration must be in the Declarations section of a module. You might want to place the declarations for API functions and the user-defined types they pass in a separate module (a *.bas* file) in your project. This will make them easy to add to multiple projects.

Visual Basic's documentation includes the file *win32api.txt*, which contains declarations for many API calls. You can add this file as a module in your project, or you can cut and paste the declarations you need into another module in the project. However, the file doesn't include every API call, especially newer ones like those that relate to HID communications.

To declare a function not included in *win32api.txt*, the starting point is Microsoft's documentation, which includes a declaration in C, comments, and sometimes an example. You can also find C declarations in the header files included in the DDKs. Sometimes these header files have useful comments as well. The header files are text files that you can view in any word processor.

These are header files that have HID-related declarations:

File Name	Contents
hid.h	HID user-mode declarations and functions
hidpi.h	Public interface to the HID parsing library
hidsdi.h	Public definitions for the code that implements the HID DLL
hidusage.h	HID usages
setupapi.h	Setup services

Sometimes the function's documentation names the header file. If not, a quick way to find it is to use the *Find > Files or Folders* utility available from Windows' *Start* menu. In the *Named* text box, enter **.h*, and in the *Containing Text* text box, enter the name of the function whose declaration you want to find. Be sure that *Include Subfolders* is checked, and let Windows go to work finding the file for you.

In some cases, the translation from C to Visual-Basic syntax is fairly straightforward. In others, the C parameters don't correspond in a simple way to the alternatives in Visual Basic.

These are some general guidelines for creating Visual-Basic declarations:

Variable Types

C and Visual Basic each use different terms to specify variable types, and C supports more variable types than Visual Basic. However, to specify a variable type for an API call, all you really have to do is determine the variable's length, then use a Visual-Basic type that matches. These are some of the C types and their Visual-Basic equivalents:

C Type	Visual-Basic Type
CHAR	Byte
USHORT USAGE	Integer
ULONG HWND BOOLEAN DWORD LP_ (long pointer prefix) P_ (long pointer prefix)	Long
PCTSTR	String

To avoid problems that can result from passing the wrong variable type, an API declaration should declare variables as specific types if possible. In some cases, an application may use a variable in multiple ways, each requiring a different type. There are two ways to handle this. You can create multiple declarations, using the Alias keyword to give each a different name, or you can declare the variable As Any and specify the variable type in the function call.

ByRef and ByVal

For each variable, you have a choice of passing it by reference (ByRef) or by value (ByVal). These parameters have the same meanings as when you use them in the functions and subroutines you write in Visual-Basic applications. Often either will work. But the concept is important to understand when calling API functions, because many of the functions have variables that must be passed a specific way.

ByRef and ByVal determine what information the call passes to enable the function to access the variable. Every variable has an address in memory where its value is stored. When an application passes a variable to a function, it can pass the variable's address or the value itself. The information is passed by placing it on the stack, which is a temporary storage location used (among other things) to pass values to functions.

Passing a variable ByRef means that the function call places the address of the variable on the stack. If the function changes the value by writing a new value to the address, the new value will be available to the calling application because the new value will be stored at the address where the application expects to find it. The address passed is called a pointer, because it points to, or indicates, the address where the value is stored.

Passing a variable ByVal means that the function call places the value of the variable on the stack. The value at the variable's original address in memory is unchanged. If the function changes the value, the calling application won't know about it because the function has no way to pass the new value back to the application.

Passing ByRef is the default, but you can include the ByRef parameter in declarations if you wish. This way, you can quickly see if you've forgotten to assign the parameter to a value. If the declaration doesn't include ByVal or ByRef, you can specify either when you call the function.

For all variable types except strings, there are two situations where you must pass a variable ByRef:

- The called function changes the value and the calling application needs to use the new value. Passing ByRef enables the calling application to access the new value.

- The variable is a user-defined type. You can't pass user-defined types ByVal in Visual Basic.

String variables are a special case. Visual Basic uses a format called BSTR for storing strings in memory. The BSTR format differs from the format expected by API calls. In memory, a BSTR string consists of four bytes containing the string's length in bytes followed by the string's characters in Unicode (2 bytes per character). In contrast, most Windows 98 API functions expect a string to consist of a series of ANSI character codes (1 byte per character), followed by a null (0) termination. Windows 2000 supports two versions of most functions, one that uses Windows 98's ANSI format and one that uses Unicode characters followed by a null termination.

Fortunately, there is a solution that doesn't require the application code to translate between formats. If the string is declared ByVal, Visual Basic creates a copy of the string in ANSI format and passes a pointer to the string. In other words, declaring a Visual-Basic string ByVal actually causes the string to be passed ByRef in the expected format. If the function will change the contents of the string, the application should initialize the string to be at least as long as the longest expected returned string.

For various reasons, some structures can't be passed either ByRef or ByVal. In these cases, there is an alternate way. It requires creating a byte array equal to the structure's size, then using Visual Basic's undocumented VarPtr operator to pass the byte array's address ByVal. When the function returns, the application can copy the data from the byte array into a structure, which is a user-defined variable type.

Passing Nulls

When an optional parameter is a pointer, a function may accept a null value (zero) to indicate that the function call isn't using the pointer.

For example, CreateFile includes a parameter that points to a security-attributes structure. The parameter is declared ByRef:

```
ByRef lpSecurityAttributes As SECURITY_ATTRIBUTES
```

If the call isn't using security attributes, the application should pass zero. But if you pass a value of zero ByRef, the function actually passes the address of a memory location that contains zero. Windows 98 handles the call without error, but Windows 2000 returns *Invalid access to memory location.*

In Visual C++, the solution is to pass a NULL constant. In Visual Basic, declare the parameter ByVal as a Long:

```
ByVal lpSecurityAttributes As Long
```

Then pass a value of 0 in the function call.

If a parameter is declared As Any and you want to pass a Long, use a trailing & (for example, 0&) to ensure that the value is passed as a Long.

Functions and Subroutines

Most API routines are functions, which have a return value that the declaration must also specify. A few are subroutines, with no return value. You can declare these as subroutines, or as functions with the returned value ignored.

Providing the DLL's Name

Each declaration must also name the file that contains the function's executable code. The file is a DLL. When the application runs, Windows loads the named DLLs into memory (unless they're already loaded).

In most cases, the declaration only has to include the file name and not the location. The DLLs used for HID communications are included with Windows. When the first HID enumerates on the system, the DLLs are stored in standard locations (such as *\windows\system*) that the operating system searches automatically. The operating system also searches the application's working directory for a DLL. In the Visual-Basic environment, the working directory is Visual Basic's directory, not your application's directory. If you use a DLL that isn't stored in a standard Windows directory or the application's working directory, the declaration must specify the location.

For some system files, such as *kernel32*, the *.dll* extension is optional in the declaration.

Strings

As mentioned earlier, Windows 98 and Windows 2000 differ in how they store strings. Windows 98 stores each character as an 8-bit ANSI code, while Windows 2000 stores each character as a 16-bit Unicode. To handle the difference, there are two versions of API calls that pass string variables. The 8-bit version ends in *A* (ANSI), and the 16-bit version ends in *W* (wide). For example, there is a SetupDiGetClassDevsA function and a SetupDiGet-ClassDevsW function.

Both Windows 98 and Windows 2000 support the ANSI versions. Windows 98 supports very few Unicode functions. Windows 2000 uses Unicode internally, but can convert to and from ANSI as needed.

Structures

Some of the API functions used in HID applications pass and return structures, which contain multiple items that may be of different types. The documentation for the API functions includes documentation for the structures used by the calls. The header files contain declarations for the structures in C syntax.

Here again, Visual Basic uses different syntax and translating is required. In Visual Basic, you can declare structures as user-defined types. Some of the structures translate in a straightforward way. For example, the Visual-Basic declaration for the HIDD_ATTRIBUTES structure consists of Long and Integer variables that translate directly from the USHORT and ULONG types in the C declaration:

```
Public Type HIDD_ATTRIBUTES
    Size As Long
    VendorID As Integer
    ProductID As Integer
    VersionNumber As Integer
End Type
```

You can then declare a variable of the user-defined type:

```
Dim DeviceAttributes As HIDD_ATTRIBUTES
```

Before passing the structure in an API call, the Size property must be set to the size of the structure in bytes. The LenB operator will do this:

```
DeviceAttributes.Size = LenB(DeviceAttributes)
```

The HidD_GetAttributes API function can then pass the structure ByRef:

```
Public Declare Function HidD_GetAttributes _
    Lib "hid.dll" _
    (ByVal HidDeviceObject As Long, _
    ByRef Attributes As HIDD_ATTRIBUTES) _
As Long
```

When an application calls the function, the function can change the values in the structure, and the application will see the new values.

Calling a Function

After the code has declared a function and any user-defined types it passes, the application may call the function.

Here is a call to the HidD_GetAttributes function declared above:

```
Dim Result as Long
Result = HidD_GetAttributes _
    (HidDevice, _
     DeviceAttributes)
```

HidDevice is a Long value returned by a previous API call. Result is non-zero on success. DeviceAttributes is a structure containing the Vendor ID, Product ID, and product version number retrieved from the device during enumeration.

Two Useful Routines

In addition to the basic API functions for USB communications, there are a couple of other API functions that I've found useful in HID and other applications. One copies data in memory, and the other returns text describing the last error detected by the operating system.

Moving Data in Memory

The API function RtlMoveMemory transfers a series of bytes from one location in memory to another. This function is useful for copying raw data between byte arrays and structures. This is the declaration:

```
Public Declare Function RtlMoveMemory _
    Lib "kernel32" _
    (dest As Any, _
     src As Any, _
     ByVal Count As Long) _
As Long
```

Rather than declaring the data address's (src) and destination (dest) as specific types, the values are declared As Any to allow flexibility in using the function. Count is the number of bytes to copy.

Here RtlMoveMemory copies four bytes from a structure into a byte array whose address will be passed in a call to the SetupDiGetDeviceInterfaceDetail function.

```
Call RtlMoveMemory _
    (DetailDataBuffer(0), _
    MyDeviceInterfaceDetailData, _
    4)
```

Viewing Errors

The second useful function is FormatMessage, which returns text describing the last error that Windows detected.

This is the function's declaration:

```
Public Declare Function FormatMessage _
    Lib "kernel32" _
    Alias "FormatMessageA" _
    (ByVal dwFlags As Long, _
    ByRef lpSource As Any, _
    ByVal dwMessageId As Long, _
    ByVal dwLanguageId As Long, _
    ByVal lpBuffer As String, _
    ByVal nSize As Long, _
    ByVal Arguments As Long) _
As Long
```

The function also uses the following system constant:

```
Public Const FORMAT_MESSAGE_FROM_SYSTEM = &H1000
```

I use FormatMessage in a Visual-Basic function that returns the string containing the error message. During debugging, I call the function after making an API call and display the error, either in a list box or using a debug.print statement in the immediate window. This code is adapted from an example in Dan Appleman's *Win32 API Puzzle Book*:

```
Private Function GetErrorString _
    (ByVal LastError As Long) _
As String

'Returns the error message for the last error.

Dim Bytes As Long
```

```
Dim ErrorString As String
ErrorString = String$(129, 0)
Bytes = FormatMessage _
    (FORMAT_MESSAGE_FROM_SYSTEM, _
    0&, _
    LastError, _
    0, _
    ErrorString$, _
    128, _
    0)

'Subtract two characters from the message to
'strip the CR and LF.
If Bytes > 2 Then
    GetErrorString = Left$(ErrorString, Bytes - 2)
End If

End Function
```

Device Attachment and Removal

Other capabilities an application might want are detecting when a device is attached or removed from the bus and controlling whether or not an attached device is enabled. Windows provides ways to do this.

USBView

One way to search for a device is to search a list of every attached device. The Windows DDK includes C source code for the USBView application (Figure 15-1), which displays in tree form all hosts, hubs, and devices attached to the hubs. You can also view each device's descriptors. The code uses DeviceIoControl functions to retrieve the information. For a Visual-Basic application that does the same thing, I recommend the DisplayUSB example in John Hyde's book, *USB Design by Example*, which, by the way, is an excellent companion to this book.

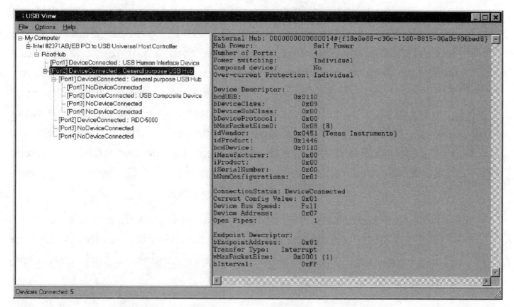

Figure 15-1: The USBView utility in the Windows DDK displays all hosts, hubs, and device attached to hubs.

Searching for a Device

To find out if a specific device is attached, an application can search using the Plug and Play/Device Management functions listed in Table 15-1 and described in greater detail in the next chapter. Searching can also reveal if a previously attached device has been removed. An application will also learn that a device is removed when it attempts to communicate and receives the error *invalid handle*.

Device Notification

Another way to learn of newly attached or removed devices uses Windows' RegisterDeviceNotification function. In calling the function, an application can pass a pointer to a structure containing the GUID of a device interface to monitor and a handle to a window to receive the event notifications.

When a device with a matching interface is attached or removed, the window receives a message such as DBT_DEVICE_ARRIVAL or DBT_DEVICE_REMOVE_COMPLETE with a pointer to a structure that identifies the device. Attachment or removal of a device also results in a DBT_DEVNODES_CHANGED message that indicates that an event of some type has occurred. Another way to detect a specific device's arrival or removal is to investigate further on receiving a DBT_DEVNODES_CHANGED message. To find out whether a device has been removed, attempt to open a handle to it. To search for newly attached devices, use the Plug-and-Play functions.

A call to UnRegisterDeviceNotification causes the notifications to cease. A Windows 2000 application should call this function before closing. Because of buggy behavior, Windows 98 applications shouldn't use UnRegisterDeviceNotification.

Enabling and Disabling Devices

The Windows 2000 DDK documents Setup functions that can enable or disable a device in software.

The CM_Request_Device_Eject function prepares a device for safe removal and physically ejects media that are ejectable. The SetupDiChangeState function can disable a device or load drivers for and start a device.

16

Human Interface Devices: Host Application Example

With the previous chapters' information about reports and how to call API functions, we're now ready to communicate with a HID. In this chapter, I present code that applications can use to communicate with HID-class devices. The examples are in both Visual-Basic and Visual C++. Headings identify text that is specific to a language. Much of the information applies to communications with any USB device.

Finding a Device

The first task is to find the device you want to communicate with. This involves examining properties of the HIDs available on a system and looking for a match, either in Vendor and Product IDs or in device capabilities. A series of API calls will accomplish this. The process uses many of the same Setup functions you would use to locate other USB devices.

Obtain the GUID for the HID Class

Before an application can communicate with a HID, it must obtain the globally unique identifier (GUID) for the HID class. Chapter 10 introduced the GUID, which is a 128-bit value that uniquely identifies an object. In this case, the object is the HID class. The GUID value is included in the file *hidclass.h*, so in theory you could hard-code it into the application. But you can also obtain the GUID by using an API function that reads the value from the system. Doing it this way, you'll be sure to have the correct value in the expected format.

The API call to retrieve the GUID for the HID class is HidD_GetHidGuid. The application doesn't have to do anything with the GUID itself. It just passes the GUID's address to other API functions.

Visual C++

This is the function's declaration:

```
VOID
   HidD_GetHidGuid(
     OUT LPGUID HidGuid
     );
```

This is the code to call the function:

```
HidD_GetHidGuid(&HidGuid);
```

Visual Basic

This is the function's declaration:

```
Public Declare Sub HidD_GetHidGuid _
     Lib "hid.dll" _
```

```
(ByRef HidGuid As GUID)
```

This routine has no return value, so it can be declared as a subroutine, as above. Or you can declare it as a function, with a return value of type Long, and ignore the returned value:

```
Public Declare Function HidD_GetHidGuid _
    Lib "hid.dll" _
    (ByRef HidGuid As GUID)
as Long
```

The GUID is returned in the variable HidGuid, which has the following user-defined type:

```
Public Type GUID
    Data1 As Long
    Data2 As Integer
    Data3 As Integer
    Data4(7) As Byte
End Type
```

HidGuid is declared byRef because Visual Basic requires user-defined types to be passed byRef.

The call to get the GUID is:

```
Call HidD_GetHidGuid(HidGuid)
```

or

```
Dim Result as Long
Result = HidD_GetHidGuid(HidGuid)
```

Get an Array of Structures with Information about the HIDs

The GUID enables the application to get information about a system's HIDs. The functions to do this are Windows Device Management Functions. There are two sets of essentially identical documentation for these in the Windows DDK documentation and in the Platform SDK in the MSDN documentation.

The SetupDiGetClassDevs function returns the address of an array of structures containing information about all attached and enumerated HIDs.

Visual C++

This is the function's declaration:

```
HDEVINFO
  SetupDiGetClassDevs(
    IN LPGUID  ClassGuid,  OPTIONAL
    IN PCTSTR  Enumerator,  OPTIONAL
    IN HWND  hwndParent,  OPTIONAL
    IN DWORD  Flags
    );
```

This is the code to call the function:

```
hDevInfo=SetupDiGetClassDevs
  (&HidGuid,
  NULL,
  NULL,
  DIGCF_PRESENT|DIGCF_INTERFACEDEVICE);
```

Visual Basic

This is the function's declaration:

```
Public Declare Function SetupDiGetClassDevs _
    Lib "setupapi.dll" _
    Alias "SetupDiGetClassDevsA" _
    (ByRef ClassGuid As GUID, _
    ByVal Enumerator As String, _
    ByVal hwndParent As Long, _
    ByVal Flags As Long) _
As Long
```

This is the code to call the function:

```
Public Const DIGCF_PRESENT = &H2
Public Const DIGCF_DEVICEINTERFACE = &H10

DeviceInfoSet = SetupDiGetClassDevs _
    (HidGuid, _
    vbNullString, _
    0, _
    (DIGCF_PRESENT Or DIGCF_DEVICEINTERFACE))
```

Details

ClassGuid is HidGuid, the value returned in the last call. Enumerator and hwndParent are unused. The flags are two system constants defined in the file *setupapi.h*.

The flags tell the function to look only for device interfaces that are currently present (attached and enumerated) and that are members of the HID class, as specified in the ClassGuid parameter.

The value returned, hDevInfo or DeviceInfoSet, is the address of an array of structures containing information about all attached and enumerated HIDs. Again, there's no need to access the individual elements in the collection. You need the value only so you can pass it on in the next API call.

When the application is finished using the array pointed to by hDevInfo or DeviceInfoSet, it should free the resources used by calling the API function SetupDiDestroyDeviceInfoList, as described later in this chapter.

Identify Each HID Interface

The next call is to SetupDiEnumDeviceInterfaces, which retrieves a pointer to a structure that identifies an interface in the previously retrieved hDevInfo or DeviceInfoSet array. Each call must specify one interface by passing an array index. To retrieve information about all of the interfaces, an application can use a loop to step through the array, incrementing the array index until the function returns zero, indicating that there are no more interfaces. The GetLastError API call will then return *No more data is available*.

How do you know if an interface is the one you're looking for? You don't, yet. The application needs more information before it can decide if it wants to use an interface. If the function returns multiple interfaces, the application will need to investigate each in turn, until it either finds what it's looking for or determines that the desired interface isn't present.

Again, the use for any returned pointers is to pass them on to the next function so we can learn more about the interfaces.

Visual C++

This is the function's declaration:

```
BOOLEAN
  SetupDiEnumDeviceInterfaces(
    IN HDEVINFO  DeviceInfoSet,
    IN PSP_DEVINFO_DATA  DeviceInfoData,  OPTIONAL
    IN LPGUID  InterfaceClassGuid,
    IN DWORD  MemberIndex,
    OUT PSP_DEVICE_INTERFACE_DATA  DeviceInterfaceData
    );
```

This is the declaration for DeviceInterfaceData's type:

```
typedef struct _SP_DEVICE_INTERFACE_DATA {
    DWORD cbSize;
    GUID InterfaceClassGuid;
    DWORD Flags;
    ULONG_PTR Reserved;
} SP_DEVICE_INTERFACE_DATA,
*PSP_DEVICE_INTERFACE_DATA;
```

And this is the code to call the function:

```
devInfoData.cbSize = sizeof(devInfoData);
Result=SetupDiEnumDeviceInterfaces
  (hDevInfo,
  0,
  &HidGuid,
  MemberIndex,
  &devInfoData);
```

Visual Basic

This is the function's declaration:

```
Public Declare Function SetupDiEnumDeviceInterfaces _
    Lib "setupapi.dll" _
    (ByVal DeviceInfoSet As Long, _
    ByVal DeviceInfoData As Long, _
    ByRef InterfaceClassGuid As GUID, _
    ByVal MemberIndex As Long, _
    ByRef DeviceInterfaceData _
        As SP_DEVICE_INTERFACE_DATA) _
    As Long
```

DeviceInterfaceData is a user-defined type:

```
Public Type SP_DEVICE_INTERFACE_DATA
    cbSize As Long
    InterfaceClassGuid As GUID
    Flags As Long
    Reserved As Long
End Type
```

This is the code to call the function:

```
Dim Result as Long
Dim MemberIndex as Long
Dim MyDeviceInterfaceData As SP_DEVICE_INTERFACE_DATA
'Store the size of the structure
MyDeviceInterfaceData.cbSize = _
  LenB(MyDeviceInterfaceData)
Result = SetupDiEnumDeviceInterfaces _
    (DeviceInfoSet, _
    0, _
    HidGuid, _
    MemberIndex, _
    MyDeviceInterfaceData)
```

Details

The parameter cbSize is the size of the SP_DEVICE_INTERFACE_DATA structure in bytes. Before calling SetupDiEnumDeviceInterfaces, the size must be stored in the structure that the function will pass. Use the `sizeof` operator in Visual C++ or the `LenB` operator in Visual Basic to retrieve the size, which is 28 bytes: 4 for each Long and 16 for the GUID, which contains one Long (4 bytes), two Integers (4 bytes), and eight Bytes. The other values in the structure should be zero.

Two of the values passed to this function are values returned previously: HidGuid and hDevInfo or DeviceInfoSet. DeviceInfoData is an optional pointer to an SP_DEVINFO_DATA structure that limits the search to interfaces of a particular device. MemberIndex is the index of the hDevInfo or DeviceInfoSet array. MyDeviceInterfaceData is the returned structure that identifies an interface of the requested type, which in this case is a HID.

Get the Device Pathname

The next API call, SetupDiGetDeviceInterfaceDetail, returns yet another structure. This time the structure relates to a device interface identified in the previous call. The structure's DevicePath member is a device pathname that the application can use to open communications with the device.

Before calling this function for the first time, there's no way to know the value of DeviceInterfaceDetailDataSize, which must contain the size in bytes of the DeviceInterfaceDetailData structure. Yet the call won't return the structure unless it has this information. The solution is to call the function twice. The first time, GetLastError will return the error *The data area passed to a system call is too small,* but the RequiredSize parameter will contain the correct value for DeviceInterfaceDetailDataSize. The second time, you pass the returned value and the function succeeds.

Visual C++

This is the function's declaration:

```
BOOLEAN
  SetupDiGetDeviceInterfaceDetail(
    IN HDEVINFO  DeviceInfoSet,
    IN PSP_DEVICE_INTERFACE_DATA  DeviceInterfaceData,
    OUT PSP_DEVICE_INTERFACE_DETAIL_DATA
      DeviceInterfaceDetailData,  OPTIONAL
    IN DWORD  DeviceInterfaceDetailDataSize,
    OUT PDWORD  RequiredSize,  OPTIONAL
    OUT PSP_DEVINFO_DATA  DeviceInfoData  OPTIONAL
    );
```

This is the declaration for DeviceInterfaceDetailData's structure:

```
typedef struct _SP_DEVICE_INTERFACE_DETAIL_DATA {
    DWORD cbSize;
    TCHAR DevicePath[ANYSIZE_ARRAY];
} SP_DEVICE_INTERFACE_DETAIL_DATA,
 *PSP_DEVICE_INTERFACE_DETAIL_DATA;
```

This is the code to call the function twice, first to get the structure's size, and second to get a pointer to the structure:

```
// Get the Length value.
```

```
// The call will return with a "buffer too small"
// error which can be ignored.
Result = SetupDiGetDeviceInterfaceDetail
  (hDevInfo,
  &devInfoData,
  NULL,
  0,
  &Length,
  NULL);

// Allocate memory for the detailData structure,
// using the returned Length.
detailData =
  (PSP_DEVICE_INTERFACE_DETAIL_DATA)malloc(Length);

// Set cbSize in the detailData structure.
detailData -> cbSize =
  sizeof(SP_DEVICE_INTERFACE_DETAIL_DATA);

// Call the function again, this time passing it the
// returned buffer size.
Result = SetupDiGetDeviceInterfaceDetail
  (hDevInfo,
  &devInfoData,
  detailData,
  Length,
  &Required,
  NULL);
```

Visual Basic

The function's declaration is:

```
Public Declare Function _
   SetupDiGetDeviceInterfaceDetail _
   Lib "setupapi.dll" _
   Alias "SetupDiGetDeviceInterfaceDetailA" _
   (ByVal DeviceInfoSet As Long, _
   ByRef DeviceInterfaceData _
       As SP_DEVICE_INTERFACE_DATA, _
   ByVal DeviceInterfaceDetailData As Long, _
   ByVal DeviceInterfaceDetailDataSize As Long, _
   ByRef RequiredSize As Long, _
   ByVal DeviceInfoData As Long) _
```

```
    As Long
```

The structure returned in DeviceInterfaceDetailData is a user-defined type:

```
Public Type SP_DEVICE_INTERFACE_DETAIL_DATA
    cbSize As Long
    DevicePath As Byte
End Type
```

Because of the different string formats used by Visual Basic and C, you can't pass this structure in the usual way, using ByRef to pass the structure's address. But there is a way around the problem. The first step is to allocate a buffer in memory to hold the structure. Then you can use the VarPtr operator to get the starting address of the buffer, and pass the address ByVal. When the function returns, you can copy the data in the buffer into a DeviceInterfaceDetailData structure, or just extract the data of interest, which is the device pathname.

This is the code for the first call:

```
Dim Needed as Long
Result = SetupDiGetDeviceInterfaceDetail _
    (DeviceInfoSet, _
    MyDeviceInterfaceData, _
    0, _
    0, _
    Needed, _
    0)
```

DeviceInfoSet and MyDeviceInterfaceData are structures returned by previous calls. After calling this function, Needed contains the buffer size to pass in the next call.

Before calling the function again, we need to take care of a few things.

The DetailData variable to be passed in the next call is set to equal the value returned in Needed:

```
Dim DetailData as Long
DetailData = Needed
Dim DetailDataBuffer() as Byte
```

The size of the structure to be returned is stored in its cbSize parameter:

```
'Store the structure's size.
```

```
MyDeviceInterfaceDetailData.cbSize = _
Len(MyDeviceInterfaceDetailData)
```

Because we're going to pass only the address of a byte array for the returned structure, we need to allocate enough memory in the array to hold the structure:

```
ReDim DetailDataBuffer(Needed)
```

The first four bytes of the byte array hold the array's size, which can be copied from the cbSize property in the MyDeviceInterfaceDetailData structure:

```
Call RtlMoveMemory _
    (DetailDataBuffer(0), _
    MyDeviceInterfaceDetailData, _
    4)
```

Now we're ready to call SetupDiGetDeviceInterfaceDetail again:

```
'Call SetupDiGetDeviceInterfaceDetail again.
'This time, pass the address
'of the first element of DetailDataBuffer
'and the returned required buffer size in DetailData.
Result = SetupDiGetDeviceInterfaceDetail _
        (DeviceInfoSet, _
        MyDeviceInterfaceData, _
        VarPtr(DetailDataBuffer(0)), _
        DetailData, _
        Needed, _
        0)
```

VarPtr(DetailDataBuffer(0)) is the starting address of the byte array that will contain the MyDeviceInterfaceDetailData structure. DetailData holds the size returned by the previous call.

The item of interest in the returned structure is the device pathname to be used in additional API calls. To extract the pathname from the byte array, convert the byte array to a string, convert the result to Unicode for compatibility with Visual Basic, and strip the cbSize characters from the beginning of the string.

```
'Convert the byte array to a string.
DevicePathName = CStr(DetailDataBuffer())
'Convert to Unicode.
DevicePathName = StrConv(DevicePathName, vbUnicode)
```

```
'Strip cbSize (4 characters) from the beginning.
DevicePathName = _
    Right$(DevicePathName, Len(DevicePathName) - 4)
```

Get a Handle for the Device

Now that we have a device pathname, we're ready to open communications with the device itself. The first step is the all-purpose function CreateFile, which can open a handle to a file or any device whose driver supports CreateFile. Devices with HID interfaces are among these.

On success, the value returned by CreateFile is a handle that other API functions can use to exchange data with the device.

Visual C++

This is the function's declaration:

```
HANDLE CreateFile(
  LPCTSTR lpFileName,
  DWORD dwDesiredAccess,
  DWORD dwShareMode,
  LPSECURITY_ATTRIBUTES lpSecurityAttributes,
  DWORD dwCreationDisposition,
  DWORD dwFlagsAndAttributes,
  HANDLE hTemplateFile
);
```

This is the code to call the function:

```
DeviceHandle=CreateFile
  (detailData->DevicePath,
  GENERIC_READ|GENERIC_WRITE,
  FILE_SHARE_READ|FILE_SHARE_WRITE,
  (LPSECURITY_ATTRIBUTES)NULL,
  OPEN_EXISTING,
  0,
  NULL);
```

Visual Basic

This is the function's declaration:

```
Public Declare Function CreateFile _
    Lib "kernel32" _
```

```
    Alias "CreateFileA" _
    (ByVal lpFileName As String, _
    ByVal dwDesiredAccess As Long, _
    ByVal dwShareMode As Long, _
    ByVal lpSecurityAttributes _
        As SECURITY_ATTRIBUTES, _
    ByVal dwCreationDisposition As Long, _
    ByVal dwFlagsAndAttributes As Long, _
    ByVal hTemplateFile As Long) _
As Long
```

And this is the code to call the function:

```
Dim HidDevice As Long
HidDevice = CreateFile _
    (DevicePathName, _
    GENERIC_READ Or GENERIC_WRITE, _
    (FILE_SHARE_READ Or FILE_SHARE_WRITE), _
    Security, _
    OPEN_EXISTING, _
    0, _
    0)
```

The function passes a pointer to the DevicePathName string returned in the previous call. The parameter is declared as a String to be passed ByVal, because of Visual Basic's different string format, as explained earlier. Security is a structure of type SECURITY_ATTRIBUTES with lpSecurityDescriptor=0, bInheritHandle=True, and nLength=Len(Security), The constants passed by the call are defined in several locations, including *winnt.h* and *wdm.h*, and must be declared in a declarations section of a module in the Visual-Basic application:

```
Public Const GENERIC_READ = &H80000000
Public Const GENERIC_WRITE = &H40000000
Public Const FILE_SHARE_READ = &H1
Public Const FILE_SHARE_WRITE = &H2
Public Const OPEN_EXISTING = 3
```

Details

When the application no longer needs to access the device, it should free system resources by calling the CloseHandle API function, as described later in this chapter.

Read the Vendor and Product IDs

One way to identify whether or not a device is the one you want is to get its Vendor and Product IDs and compare them with the IDs for the product you're looking for. This is the way to find custom devices that don't fit standard usages. For other devices, this information may not be important, and if not, you can skip this step.

The API function HidD_GetAttributes retrieves a pointer to a structure containing the Vendor and Product IDs and the product's version number.

Visual C++

This is the function's declaration:

```
BOOLEAN
  HidD_GetAttributes(
    IN HANDLE HidDeviceObject,
    OUT PHIDD_ATTRIBUTES Attributes
    );
```

The HIDD_ATTRIBUTES structure contains the information about the device:

```
typedef struct _HIDD_ATTRIBUTES {
  ULONG   Size;
  USHORT  VendorID;
  USHORT  ProductID;
  USHORT  VersionNumber;
} HIDD_ATTRIBUTES, *PHIDD_ATTRIBUTES;
```

This is the code to retrieve the structure:

```
// Set the Size member to the number of bytes
// in the structure.
Attributes.Size = sizeof(Attributes);
Result = HidD_GetAttributes
  (DeviceHandle,
  &Attributes);
```

Visual Basic

This is the declaration for the function:

```
Public Declare Function HidD_GetAttributes _
```

```
        Lib "hid.dll" _
        (ByVal HidDeviceObject As Long, _
        ByRef Attributes As HIDD_ATTRIBUTES) _
    As Long
```

The HIDD_ATTRIBUTES structure contains the information about the device:

```
    Public Type HIDD_ATTRIBUTES
        Size As Long
        VendorID As Integer
        ProductID As Integer
        VersionNumber As Integer
    End Type
```

This is the code to retrieve the structure:

```
    Dim DeviceAttributes As HIDD_ATTRIBUTES
    'Set the Size property to the number of bytes
    'in the structure.
    DeviceAttributes.Size = LenB(DeviceAttributes)
    Result = HidD_GetAttributes _
        (HidDevice, _
        DeviceAttributes)
```

Details

The HidDeviceObject parameter is the handle returned by CreateFile. If the function returns a non-zero value, the DeviceAttributes structure filled without error.

The application can then compare the retrieved values with the desired Vendor and Product IDs and version number.

If it isn't a match, the application should use the CloseHandle API call to close the handle to the interface. The application can then move on to test the next HID detected by SetupDiEnumDeviceInterfaces. When the application is finished examining the HIDs, it should free the resources reserved by SetupDiGetClassDevs by calling SetupDiDestroyDeviceInfoList.

Get a Pointer to a Buffer with Device Capabilities

Another way to find out more about a device is to examine its capabilities. You can do this for a device whose Vendor and Product IDs matched the values you were looking for, or you can examine the capabilities for an unknown device.

The first task is to get a pointer to a buffer with information about the device's capabilities. The API call to do this is HidD_GetPreparsedData.

Visual C++

This is the function's declaration:

```
BOOLEAN
  HidD_GetPreparsedData(
    IN HANDLE HidDeviceObject,
    OUT PHIDP_PREPARSED_DATA *PreparsedData
    );
```

This is the code to call the function:

```
PHIDP_PREPARSED_DATA PreparsedData;
HidD_GetPreparsedData
  (DeviceHandle,
  &PreparsedData);
```

Visual Basic

This is the function's declaration:

```
Public Declare Function HidD_GetPreparsedData _
    Lib "hid.dll" _
    (ByVal HidDeviceObject As Long, _
    ByRef PreparsedData As Long) _
  As Long
```

This is the code to call the function:

```
Result = HidD_GetPreparsedData _
    (HidDevice, _
    PreparsedData)
```

HidDeviceObject is the handle returned by CreateFile. PreparsedData is a pointer to the buffer containing the data. The application doesn't need to access the data in the buffer; it just needs to pass its starting address to another API function.

When the application no longer needs to access the PreparsedData, it should free system resources by calling HidD_FreePreparsedData, as described later in this chapter.

Get the Device's Capabilities

The HidP_GetCaps function returns a structure that contains information about the device's capabilities. The structure contains the device's Usage, Usage Page, report lengths, and the number of button capabilities, value capabilities, and data indices for Input, Output, and Feature reports, as stored in the device's firmware. If you didn't use the Vendor and Product IDs to identify the device, the capabilities information can help you decide if you want to continue communicating with the device. Even if you know that you have the device you're looking for, the report lengths and other information are useful in determining what kinds of data you can transfer. Not every item in the structure applies to all devices.

Visual C++

This is the function's declaration:

```
NTSTATUS
  HidP_GetCaps(
    IN PHIDP_PREPARSED_DATA PreparsedData,
    OUT PHIDP_CAPS Capabilities
    );
```

This is the declaration for the HIDP_CAPS structure:

```
typedef struct _HIDP_CAPS {
  USAGE Usage;
  USAGE UsagePage ;
  USHORT InputReportByteLength ;
  USHORT OutputReportByteLength ;
  USHORT FeatureReportByteLength ;
  .
  .
  USHORT NumberLinkCollectionNodes ;
  USHORT NumberInputButtonCaps ;
```

```
    USHORT NumberInputValueCaps ;
    USHORT NumberOutputButtonCaps ;
    USHORT NumberOutputValueCaps ;
    USHORT NumberFeatureButtonCaps ;
    USHORT NumberFeatureValueCaps ;
} HIDP_CAPS, *PHIDP_CAPS ;
```

This is the code to call the function:

```
HidP_GetCaps
  (PreparsedData,
  &Capabilities);
```

Visual Basic

This is the declaration for the function:

```
Public Declare Function HidP_GetCaps _
    Lib "hid.dll" _
    (ByVal PreparsedData As Long, _
    ByRef Capabilities As HIDP_CAPS) _
As Long
```

The information is returned in a HIDP_CAPS structure:

```
Public Type HIDP_CAPS
    Usage As Integer
    UsagePage As Integer
    InputReportByteLength As Integer
    OutputReportByteLength As Integer
    FeatureReportByteLength As Integer
    Reserved(16) As Integer
    NumberLinkCollectionNodes As Integer
    NumberInputButtonCaps As Integer
    NumberInputValueCaps As Integer
    NumberInputDataIndices As Integer
    NumberOutputButtonCaps As Integer
    NumberOutputValueCaps As Integer
    NumberOutputDataIndices As Integer
    NumberFeatureButtonCaps As Integer
    NumberFeatureValueCaps As Integer
    NumberFeatureDataIndices As Integer
End Type
```

This is the code to call the function:

```
Result = HidP_GetCaps _
```

```
(PreparsedData, _
Capabilities)
```

Details

PreparsedData is the pointer returned by HidD_GetPreparsedData. When the function returns, you can examine and use whatever values are of interest in the Capabilities structure. For example, if you're looking for a mouse, you can look for a Usage Page of 01h and a Usage of 02h.

The report lengths are useful for setting buffer sizes for sending and receiving reports.

An application designed for use with a custom device may already know what it needs to know about the device's capabilities. In this case, if the application identifies the device by its Vendor and Product IDs, it can skip examining the capabilities because it has no need for the information.

Get the Capabilities of the Values

The device capabilities aren't all that an application can retrieve from the device. It can also get the capabilities of each value and button in a report.

HidP_GetValueCaps returns a pointer to an array of structures containing information about each value in a report. The NumberInputValueCaps property of the HIDP_CAPS structure is the number of values in the interface.

The items in the structure include many familiar values from the device's report descriptor, as described in Chapter 14. The items include the Report ID, whether a value is absolute or relative, whether it has a null state, and logical and physical minimums and maximums A LinkCollection identifier distinguishes between controls with the same Usage and Usage Page in the same collection.

In a similar way, the HidP_GetButtonCaps function can retrieve information about a report's buttons. The information is stored in a HidP_ButtonCaps structure.

If the application has no use for this information, it doesn't have to retrieve it.

Reading and Writing Data

All of the previous API calls are concerned with finding a device that matches what the application is looking for. When this is accomplished, the application and a device are finally ready to exchange data in reports.

There are four API calls for exchanging report data, depending on the report type. The USB request type that the host uses also varies with the report type and in one case on the operating system and the supported endpoints:

Report Type	API Function	USB Transfer Type	When Used
Input	ReadFile	Interrupt IN	Always
Output	WriteFile	Control Transfer with Set_Report	Under Windows 98 Gold or when the HID interface has no interrupt OUT endpoint
		Interrupt OUT	Under Windows 98 SE and later if the HID interface has an interrupt OUT endpoint
Feature IN	HidD_GetFeature	Control Transfer with Get_Report	Always
Feature OUT	HidD_SetFeature	Control Transfer with Set_Report	Always

Sending an Output Report to the Device

An application can send an Output report when it has a handle to the HID interface and knows the number of bytes in the report. To write data, the application copies the data to send to a buffer and calls WriteFile. The buffer size should equal the size reported in the OutputReportByteLength property of the HIDP_CAPS structure returned by HidP_GetCaps. This size equals the report size in bytes plus one byte for the Report ID, which is the first byte in the buffer.

Like CreateFile, WriteFile is a generic API call that can be used with a file or any device whose driver supports the function.

As Chapter 13 explained, the type of transfer the HID driver uses to send the Output report depends on the edition of Windows and whether the HID interface has an interrupt OUT endpoint. The application doesn't have to know or care which transfer type the driver uses, because it's handled at a lower level.

Visual C++

This is the function's declaration:

```
BOOL WriteFile(
  HANDLE hFile,
  LPCVOID lpBuffer,
  DWORD nNumberOfBytesToWrite,
  LPDWORD lpNumberOfBytesWritten,
  LPOVERLAPPED lpOverlapped
);
```

This the code to call the function:

```
// The report's data can reside in a byte array.
// The array's size = report length in bytes + 1.
CHAR OutputReport[3];
// The first byte in the buffer containing the report
// is the Report ID.
OutputReport[0]=0;
// (The application should fill the following bytes
// with the report's data.)
Result = WriteFile
  (DeviceHandle,
  OutputReport,
  Capabilities.OutputReportByteLength,
  &BytesWritten,
  NULL);
```

Visual Basic

This is the function's declaration:

```
Public Declare Function WriteFile _
    Lib "kernel32" _
    (ByVal hFile As Long, _
    ByRef lpBuffer As Byte, _
    ByVal nNumberOfBytesToWrite As Long, _
    ByRef lpNumberOfBytesWritten As Long, _
    ByVal lpOverlapped As Long) _
    As Long
```

The data to send is in a Byte array that contains the Report ID in the first byte, followed by the report data. This code creates and fills a SendBuffer Byte array:

```
Dim SendBuffer() As Byte
'The SendBuffer array begins at 0,
'so subtract 1 from OutputReportByteLength.
ReDim SendBuffer _
    (Capabilities.OutputReportByteLength - 1)
'The first byte is the Report ID
SendBuffer(0) = 0
'The next bytes are data.
'This example copies the data from an OutputReportData
'Byte array filled earlier by the application.
For Count = _
        1 To Capabilities.OutputReportByteLength - 1
        SendBuffer(Count) = OutputReportData(Count - 1)
Next Count
```

This is the code to call WriteFile to send a report to the device:

```
Dim NumberOfBytesWritten As Long
NumberOfBytesWritten = 0
Result = WriteFile _
    (HidDevice, _
    SendBuffer(0), _
    CLng(Capabilities.OutputReportByteLength), _
    NumberOfBytesWritten, _
    0)
```

SendBuffer(0) is the first element in a Byte array containing the Report ID and report data. The parameter is passed ByRef to cause the function to pass the byte's address. CLng(Capabilities.OutputReportByteLength) is the size of the output report returned by HidP_GetCaps, converted to a Long to match the declaration.

Details

The hFile parameter is the handle returned by CreateFile. The lpNumberOfBytesWritten parameter returns the number of bytes the function successfully wrote to the device. If the Result value returned by the function is non-zero, the function succeeded.

If the interface supports only the default Report ID of 0, the Report ID doesn't transmit on the bus, but it must be present in the buffer the application passes to WriteFile.

Probably the most common error returned by WriteFile in HID communications is *CRC Error*. This error indicates that the host controller attempted to send the report, but didn't receive an expected response from the device. In spite of the error message, the problem isn't likely to be due to an error detected in a CRC calculation. The error is more likely to be due to a firmware problem that is keeping the device from responding in the expected way.

Reading an Input Report from the Device

The complement to WriteFile is ReadFile. When the application has a handle to the HID interface and knows the number of bytes in the device's Input report, the application can use ReadFile to read an Input report from a device.

Like CreateFile and WriteFile, ReadFile is a generic API call that can be used with a file or any device whose driver supports the function.

To read a report, the application declares a buffer to hold the data and calls ReadFile. The buffer size should equal the size reported in the InputReportByteLength property of the HIDP_CAPS structure returned by HidP_GetCaps.

Visual C++

This is the function's declaration:

```
BOOL ReadFile(
    HANDLE hFile,
    LPVOID lpBuffer,
    DWORD nNumberOfBytesToRead,
    LPDWORD lpNumberOfBytesRead,
    LPOVERLAPPED lpOverlapped
);
```

This is the code to call the function:

```
Result = ReadFile
```

```
(ReadHandle,
InputReport,
Capabilities.InputReportByteLength,
&BytesRead,
NULL);
```

Visual Basic

This is the function's declaration:

```
Public Declare Function ReadFile _
    Lib "kernel32" _
    (ByVal hFile As Long, _
    ByRef lpBuffer As Byte, _
    ByVal nNumberOfBytesToRead As Long, _
    ByRef lpNumberOfBytesRead As Long, _
    ByVal lpOverlapped As Long) _
As Long
```

The data read is in a Byte array that contains the report ID in the first byte and the report data in the following bytes. This code creates and fills a Read-Buffer Byte array:

```
Dim NumberOfBytesRead As Long
'Allocate a buffer for the report.
Dim ReadBuffer() As Byte
Dim NumberOfBytesRead As Long

'The ReadBuffer array begins at 0,
'so subtract 1 from the number of bytes to read.
ReDim ReadBuffer _
    (Capabilities.InputReportByteLength - 1)
```

This is the code to call the function:

```
Result = ReadFile _
    (HidDevice, _
    ReadBuffer(0), _
    CLng(Capabilities.InputReportByteLength), _
    NumberOfBytesRead, _
    0)
```

ReadBuffer(0) is the first element in the Byte array that will contain the report. The parameter is passed ByRef, so the function passes the address of the byte. CLng(Capabilities.InputReportByteLength) is the size of the input report returned by HidP_GetCaps, converted to a Long to match the declaration. NumberOfBytesRead will return the number of bytes the function successfully read from the device.

Details

The hFile parameter is the handle returned by CreateFile. If the Result value returned is non-zero, the function was successful. Byte 0 of the read buffer contains the report ID, and the following bytes contain the report data read from the device. If the interface supports only one Report ID, the ID doesn't transmit on the bus, but it is always present in the buffer returned by Read-File.

A call to ReadFile doesn't initiate traffic on the bus. It just retrieves a report that the host previously requested in one of its periodic interrupt IN transfers, or if there are no unread reports, waits for the next scheduled transfer to complete. The host begins requesting reports after enumeration, when the HID driver is loaded. The driver stores the reports in a ring buffer. When the buffer is full and a new report arrives, the oldest report is overwritten. A call to ReadFile reads the oldest report in the buffer. Under Windows 98 SE and later, the default buffer size is eight reports, and an application can set the buffer size with the HidD_SetNumInputBuffers function.

If the application doesn't request reports as frequently as they're sent, some will be lost. If you need to be absolutely sure not to lose a report, use Feature reports instead. Also see the tips in Chapter 4 about performing time-critical transfers

The Idle rate determines whether or not the device sends a report if its data hasn't changed since the last transfer. During enumeration, Windows' HID driver attempts to set the Idle rate to 0, which means that the HID won't send a report unless the report data has changed. There is no API call that enables applications to change the Idle rate. To prevent setting an Idle rate of 0, the HID can return a Stall to the Set_Idle request. This informs the host that the request isn't supported. Not all chips have hardware support for the Idle rate, though support can be implemented with a timer in firmware. Chapter 13 has more on the Idle rate.

If Set_Idle isn't supported and the application wants to retrieve a report once and only once, the firmware can be programmed to send a report only once. After sending a report, the firmware can configure the endpoint to return NAK in response to IN token packets. When the device has a new report to send, the firmware can configure the endpoint to send the data. Otherwise, the device will continue to send the same report every time the host polls the endpoint, and the application is likely to read the same report multiple times.

Reading Reports without Blocking the Thread

There is one caution about using ReadFile to retrieve HID reports. ReadFile is blocking call. If an application calls ReadFile when the read buffer is empty, the application's thread will hang until a report is available, or the user closes the application with Control-Alt-Delete or removes the device from the bus. There are three ways to prevent this from happening: be sure the device always has data to send, use overlapped ReadFiles with timeouts, or call the ReadFiles in their own program thread.

To ensure that the device always has data to send, you can write the firmware so that the IN endpoint is always enabled and ready to respond to a request for data. If there is no new data to send, the device can send the same data as last time, or it can return a vendor-defined code that indicates that there is nothing new to report. Another approach requires cooperation from the application that accesses the device. Before each ReadFile, the application can call WriteFile to send a report. The report can contain a vendor-defined item that tells the firmware to get ready to send data. Then when the application calls ReadFile, the device's endpoint is enabled, with data ready to transmit. These solutions aren't ideal, but they're workable.

A more elegant solution is to use ReadFile's overlapped option. In an overlapped read, the ReadFile returns immediately, even if the data isn't ready, and the application can then use the WaitForSingleObject API function to retrieve the data. The advantage of WaitForSingleObject is the ability to set a timeout. If the data hasn't arrived when the timeout period has elapsed, the function returns a code to indicate this and the application can use the CancelIo function to cancel the read operation. This approach works well if reports are normally available without delay, but the application needs to regain control if for some reason there is no report.

To use overlapped I/O, CreateFile must pass an overlapped structure in the dwFlagsAndAttributes parameter. The application also calls the CreateEvent function to create an event object that will be set to the signaled state when the ReadFile operation completes. When the application calls ReadFile, it passes a pointer to an overlapped structure whose hEvent parameter is a handle to the event object. The application then calls WaitForSingleObject, again passing the event handle along with a timeout value in milliseconds. The function returns when the read operation is complete or a timeout has occurred.

Visual C++

This is the code for doing an overlapped ReadFile:

```
// Declare an overlapped structure.
OVERLAPPED  HIDOverlapped;

// Create an event object to signal completion
// of a ReadFile.
hEventObject = CreateEvent
  (NULL,
  TRUE,
  TRUE,
  "");

// Assign values to the members of the overlapped
// structure.
HIDOverlapped.hEvent = hEventObject;
HIDOverlapped.Offset = 0;
HIDOverlapped.OffsetHigh = 0;

// Obtain a handle with FILE_FLAG_OVERLAPPED.
ReadHandle=CreateFile
  (detailData->DevicePath,
  GENERIC_READ|GENERIC_WRITE,
  FILE_SHARE_READ|FILE_SHARE_WRITE,
  NULL,
  OPEN_EXISTING,
```

```
      FILE_FLAG_OVERLAPPED,
      NULL);

   // Read a report, passing a pointer to the
   // overlapped structure.
   Result = ReadFile
      (ReadHandle,
      InputReport,
      Capabilities.InputReportByteLength,
      &BytesRead,
      (LPOVERLAPPED) &HIDOverlapped);

   // Wait for the ReadFile to complete or a timeout.
   Result = WaitForSingleObject
      (hEventObject,
      5000);
```

Visual Basic

These are the declarations required to do an overlapped ReadFile:

```
   Public Type OVERLAPPED
       Internal As Long
       InternalHigh As Long
       Offset As Long
       OffsetHigh As Long
       hEvent As Long
   End Type

   Public Const FILE_FLAG_OVERLAPPED = &H40000000

   Public Declare Function CreateEvent _
       Lib "kernel32" _
       Alias "CreateEventA" _
       (ByVal SecurityAttributes As Long, _
       ByVal bManualReset As Long, _
       ByVal bInitialState As Long, _
       ByVal lpName As String) _
   As Long

   Public Declare Function ReadFile _
       Lib "kernel32" _
       (ByVal hFile As Long, _
       ByRef lpBuffer As Byte, _
```

```
        ByVal nNumberOfBytesToRead As Long, _
        ByRef lpNumberOfBytesRead As Long, _
        ByRef lpOverlapped As OVERLAPPED) _
As Long

Public Declare Function WaitForSingleObject _
    Lib "kernel32" _
    (ByVal hHandle As Long, _
    ByVal dwMilliseconds As Long) _
As Long
```

This the code to do an overlapped ReadFile:

```
Dim EventObject As Long
Dim HIDOverlapped As OVERLAPPED

'Create an event object to signal completion
'of a ReadFile.
EventObject = CreateEvent _
    (0&, _
    True, _
    True, _
    "")

'Assign values to the members of the overlapped
'structure.
HIDOverlapped.Offset = 0
HIDOverlapped.OffsetHigh = 0
HIDOverlapped.hEvent = EventObject

'Obtain a handle using FILE_FLAG_OVERLAPPED.
ReadHandle = CreateFile _
    (DevicePathName, _
    GENERIC_READ Or GENERIC_WRITE, _
    (FILE_SHARE_READ Or FILE_SHARE_WRITE), _
    0, _
    OPEN_EXISTING, _
    FILE_FLAG_OVERLAPPED, _
    0)

'Read a report, passing a pointer to the
'overlapped structure.
Result = ReadFile _
    (ReadHandle, _
```

```
    ReadBuffer(0), _
    CLng(Capabilities.InputReportByteLength), _
    NumberOfBytesRead, _
    HIDOverlapped)

'Wait for the ReadFile to complete or a timeout.
Result = WaitForSingleObject _
    (EventObject, _
    5000)
```

ReadFileEx and WaitForSingleObjectEx offer another way to do overlapped I/O. Instead of requiring the program thread to wait for a read operation to complete or a timeout, ReadFileEx enables the calling thread to perform other operations while it waits. A call to ReadFileEx passes a pointer to a completion routine that executes when the read operation completes.

Another option is to put the ReadFile calls in a separate thread using Visual C++, Delphi, or another compiler that supports multithreading.

Visual C++

This example shows one way to do ReadFiles in a separate thread. When the HID interface has been identified, open a separate handle to use for reading:

```
ReadHandle=CreateFile
    (detailData->DevicePath,
    GENERIC_READ|GENERIC_WRITE,
    FILE_SHARE_READ|FILE_SHARE_WRITE,
    NULL,
    OPEN_EXISTING,
    0,
    NULL);
```

Then create a thread for reading reports from the device:

```
ThreadHandle = CreateThread
    (NULL,
    0,
    (LPTHREAD_START_ROUTINE)StaticIO_Thread,
    this,
    0,
    &ThreadID);
```

StaticIO_Thread is a static member that accepts the "this" pointer and casts it to a pointer to the ReadReport routine, which does the ReadFile. Here is an example:

```
DWORD CUsbhidiocDlg::StaticIO_Thread(LPVOID Param)
{
  if (Param != NULL)
    return ((CUsbhidiocDlg*)Param)->ReadReport();
  else
    return -1;
}
```

A ReadReport routine can then read reports continuously while the main application thread can go on to other things.

```
DWORD WINAPI CUsbhidiocDlg::ReadReport()
{
  CStringByteToDisplay = "";
  ULONGInputReportLength = 0;
  CStringMessageToDisplay = "";
  ULONGResult;

  //Read a report from the buffer.
  InputReportLength=
    Capabilities.InputReportByteLength;

  do
  {
    Result = ReadFile
      (ReadHandle,
      InputReport,
      Capabilities.InputReportByteLength,
      &BytesRead,
      NULL);

    if (Result == 0)
    {
      // The ReadFile failed, so close the handle,
      // display a message, and
      // set DeviceDetected to FALSE.
      CloseHandle(ReadHandle);
      DisplayData("Can't read from device");
      DeviceDetected = FALSE;
    }
```

```
    }
// Exit the loop if the device is no longer detected
// or the user has clicked the close button.
while ((DeviceDetected == TRUE) &&
   (ApplicationActive == TRUE));
return 0;
}
```

The application can read a retrieved report in the InputReport buffer.

Visual Basic

What about Visual Basic's support for multi-threading? As of version 6, applications can't use the CreateThread API function. Visual Basic does support multi-threading in ActiveX EXE servers. The server can continuously attempt to read from the device, notifying an application when data has been received, without blocking the application while it waits. For more about ActiveX EXE servers, I recommend Dan Appleman's book *Developing ActiveX Components in Visual Basic*.

Or you can write a multi-threaded DLL that performs the ReadFiles. Power-Basic's PB/DLL compiler enables you to write a multi-threaded DLL in Basic. PowerBasic's website (www.powerbasic.com) has a good tutorial on multi-threaded programming.

Writing a Feature Report to the Device

To send a Feature report to a device, use the HidD_SetFeature function. The call will send a Set_Feature request and report in a control transfer.

Visual C++

This is the function's declaration:

```
BOOLEAN
   HidD_SetFeature(
      IN HANDLE HidDeviceObject,
      IN PVOID ReportBuffer,
      IN ULONG ReportBufferLength
      );
```

This is the code to call the function:

```
Result = HidD_SetFeature
   (HidDevice,
   SendBuffer,
   Capabilities.FeatureReportByteLength);
```

Visual Basic

This is the function's declaration:

```
Public Declare Function HidD_SetFeature _
   Lib "hid.dll" _
   (ByVal HidDeviceObject As Long, _
   ByRef ReportBuffer As Byte, _
   ByVal ReportBufferLength As Long) _
As Long
```

This is the code to call the function:

```
Result = HidD_SetFeature _
   (HidDevice, _
   SendBuffer(0), _
   CLng(Capabilities.FeatureReportByteLength))
```

Reading a Feature Report from a Device

To read a Feature report from a device, use the HidD_GetFeature API function. The call will send a Get_Feature request in a control transfer, with the device returning the report in the data stage.

Visual C++

This is the function's declaration:

```
BOOLEAN
   HidD_GetFeature(
      IN HANDLE HidDeviceObject,
      OUT PVOID ReportBuffer,
      IN ULONG ReportBufferLength
      );
```

This is the code to call the function:

```
Result = HidD_GetFeature
   (HidDevice,
   ReadBuffer,
   Capabilities.FeatureReportByteLength);
```

Visual Basic

This is the function's declaration:

```
Public Declare Function HidD_GetFeature _
    Lib "hid.dll" _
    (ByVal HidDeviceObject As Long, _
    ByRef ReportBuffer As Byte, _
    ByVal ReportBufferLength As Long) _
As Long
```

This is the code to call the function:

```
Result = HidD_GetFeature _
    (HidDevice, _
    ReadBuffer(0), _
    CLng(Capabilities.FeatureReportByteLength))
```

Closing Communications

When an application is finished communicating with a HID, it should free the resources previously reserved for it. Three of the API functions used earlier have complementary functions for freeing resources.

The declarations and calls are short. Each passes a single parameter obtained from its complementary function. For each, a non-zero Result indicates success. Be sure to include each of these in code that executes before the application closes.

When an application is finished communicating with a device, it should call CloseHandle, the complement to CreateFile. When an application is finished using the DeviceInfoSet array returned by SetupDiGetClassDevs, it should call SetupDiDestroyDeviceInfoList. And when an application is finished using the PreparsedData buffer returned by HidD_GetPreparsedData, it should call HidD_FreePreparsedData.

Visual C++

These are the functions' declarations:

```
BOOL CloseHandle(
  HANDLE hObject);

BOOL SetupDiDestroyDeviceInfoList(
```

```
      HDEVINFO DeviceInfoSet
);

BOOLEAN
  HidD_FreePreparsedData(
    IN PHIDP_PREPARSED_DATA PreparsedData
    );
```

This is the code to call the functions:

```
CloseHandle(DeviceHandle);

SetupDiDestroyDeviceInfoList(hDevInfo);

HidD_FreePreparsedData(PreparsedData);
```

Visual Basic

These are the functions' declarations:

```
Public Declare Function CloseHandle _
    Lib "kernel32" _
    (ByVal hObject As Long) _
As Long

Public Declare Function SetupDiDestroyDeviceInfoList _
    Lib "setupapi.dll" _
    (ByVal DeviceInfoSet As Long) _
As Long

Public Declare Function HidD_FreePreparsedData _
    Lib "hid.dll" _
    (ByRef PreparsedData As Long) _
As Long
```

This is the code to call the functions:

```
Result = CloseHandle _
    (HidDevice)

Result = SetupDiDestroyDeviceInfoList _
    (DeviceInfoSet)

Result = HidD_FreePreparsedData _
    (PreparsedData)
```

17

Device Testing

Users expect installing and using USB peripherals to be easy, and the burden is on the developer to make it so. The USB interface is complex, and misbehaving software or firmware can make a peripheral irritating or impossible to use. So don't skimp on testing.

The peripheral's firmware and the host's applications must of course know what data to send and what to do with the data they receive. But that's not all. In addition, device installation should be as invisible as possible for users. Users must be able to attach and remove a device at any time. And the device should transfer data as efficiently as possible while co-existing peacefully with whatever other peripherals happen to be sharing the bus. Anything short of this and users will look elsewhere for their products.

Fortunately, there are many tools that help in testing new peripheral designs. This chapter introduces a variety of these, including the free software and other resources available from the USB Implementers Forum and the protocol analyzers and other test equipment available from other sources. These are in addition to the development boards and monitor programs available from chip vendors and described in Chapter 9. For electrical tests, Chapter 20 describes the test modes that all high-speed host controllers and devices must support.

USB Check's Test Suite

USB Check is a suite of test applications for USB devices. You can view descriptors, send control requests, view the results, and run further tests on hubs, communication-class devices, and HID-class devices. USB Check is available free from the USB Implementers Forum's website.

The software runs only under Windows 2000. This is because problems with remote wake-up under Windows 98 made remote wake-up impossible to test with a standard Windows 98 system. Passing the tests under Windows 2000 indicates that the device will also function properly under Windows 98.

Detecting a Device

When you run USB Check, the software identifies the device to test by displaying a window asking you to attach the device (or remove and re-attach if it's already attached). When you do this, USB Check replaces the driver normally used by the device with its own driver, *usbdiag.sys*. Your device's normal listing in the Device Manager disappears and is replaced with a listing under *Other Detected Devices,* described as a *USB Diagnostic Device.* To get this far in the test, the device has to be functional enough to respond to the standard requests.

When you want to use the device in its intended way, you *must* close the USB Check application and again remove and re-attach your device so Windows can restore the device's normal drivers. The device listing will also return to its proper location in the Device Manager's window.

The Tests

The first tests are the Device Framework tests, which cover material in Chapter 9 of the USB specification. The tests read the descriptors and send standard requests. These tests are extremely useful as an initial check that Windows is retrieving the expected information from your device.

To start, it's interesting to view the descriptors for whatever USB peripherals you may have on your system. Figure 17-1 shows a hub's descriptors, which tell you several things. The device descriptor identifies the device as a hub. The configuration descriptor says that the hub may be self- or bus-powered and that is draws no more than 100 milliamperes from the bus. The interface descriptor says that the hub has one endpoint in addition to Endpoint 0. And the endpoint descriptor describes the hub's required interrupt endpoint, which has an interval of 255 milliseconds and a maximum packet size of 1 byte.

In a similar way, you can use the tests to retrieve descriptors from devices you develop, to verify that Windows is reading the expected information from the device. Once you have that much working, you can move on to the other tests.

Listing 17-1 is a report for the complete set of Device Framework tests on a custom HID. You can run individual tests, such as sending a Get_Descriptor or Set_Interface request, or run all of the tests at once and view the results. If your device supports remote wakeup, the test will ask you to send a Remote Wakeup signal to the host. You can skip this test if you're not set up to trigger a remote wakeup.

The other tests are for devices in specific classes, including hubs and HIDs.

HIDView

After running USB Check's Device Framework tests on a HID-class device, a window will appear advising you to run the HIDView tests. Figure 17-2 shows the options for testing.

If you run all of the tests, you'll see a display like Figure 17-3's. From the Full Test window you can also run individual tests and view the results. Figure 17-4 shows the result of retrieving a device's report descriptor.

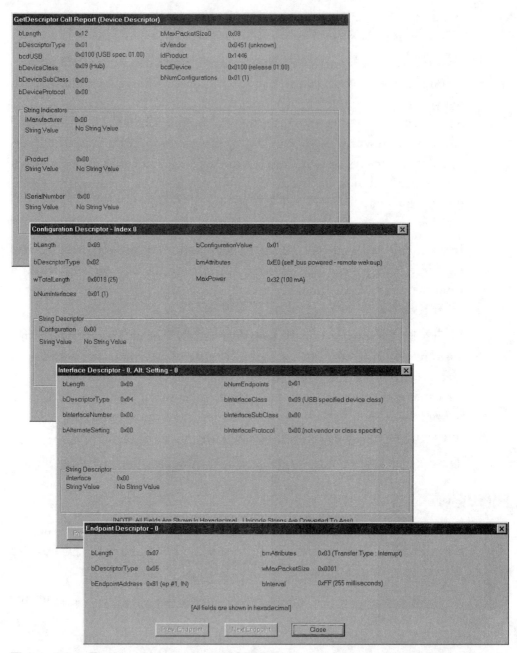

GetDescriptor Call Report (Device Descriptor)

bLength	0x12	bMaxPacketSize0	0x08
bDescriptorType	0x01	idVendor	0x0451 (unknown)
bcdUSB	0x0100 (USB spec. 01.00)	idProduct	0x1446
bDeviceClass	0x09 (Hub)	bcdDevice	0x0100 (release 01.00)
bDeviceSubClass	0x00	bNumConfigurations	0x01 (1)
bDeviceProtocol	0x00		

String Indicators
iManufacturer 0x00
String Value No String Value

iProduct 0x00
String Value No String Value

iSerialNumber 0x00
String Value No String Value

Configuration Descriptor - Index 0

bLength	0x09	bConfigurationValue	0x01
bDescriptorType	0x02	bmAttributes	0xE0 (self _bus powered - remote wakeup)
wTotalLength	0x0019 (25)	MaxPower	0x32 (100 mA)
bNumInterfaces	0x01 (1)		

String Descriptor
iConfiguration 0x00
String Value No String Value

Interface Descriptor - 0, Alt. Setting - 0

bLength	0x09	bNumEndpoints	0x01
bDescriptorType	0x04	bInterfaceClass	0x09 (USB specified device class)
bInterfaceNumber	0x00	bInterfaceSubClass	0x00
bAlternateSetting	0x00	bInterfaceProtocol	0x00 (not vendor or class specific)

String Descriptor
iInterface 0x00
String Value No String Value

[NOTE: All Fields Are Shown In Hexadecimal. Unicode Strings Are Converted To Ansi]

Endpoint Descriptor - 0

bLength	0x07	bmAttributes	0x03 (Transfer Type : Interrupt)
bDescriptorType	0x05	wMaxPacketSize	0x0001
bEndpointAddress	0x81 (ep #1, IN)	bInterval	0xFF (255 milliseconds)

[All fields are shown in hexadecimal]

Prev. Endpoint   Next Endpoint   Close

Figure 17-1: These windows from USB Check show the contents of a hub's descriptors.

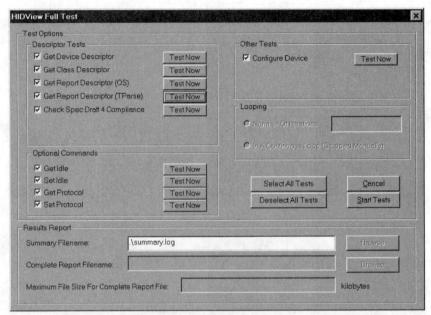

Figure 17-2: The HIDView utility enables you to test HID-class devices.

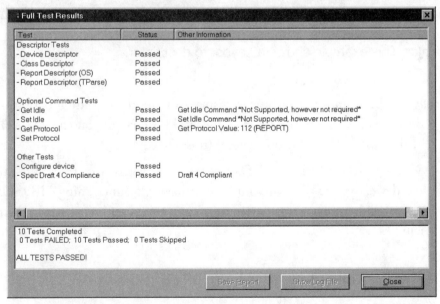

Figure 17-3: HIDView examines the device's report descriptors and sends other requests related to HID functions.

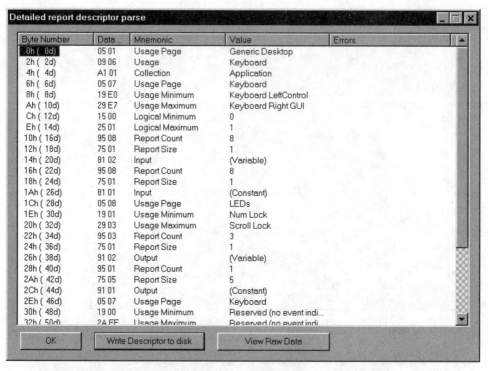

Figure 17-4: HIDView also enables you to examine your device's report descriptor. This example shows a keyboard descriptor.

A *Get Data from Device* button displays the result of reading data from the device, either one time or continuously. This enables you to test the ability of the host to receive Input reports from the device.

When a HID passes the HIDView tests and you're able to read data from the device, you're well on your way to having a functioning HID. On the other hand, failing one or more tests gives an indication of where the problem lies.

DEVICE 00 Vid (0x0925) Pid (0x1234) Tests:

- Get Device Descriptor Passed.
Returned Device Descriptor:
0x12 0x01 0x10 0x01 0x00 0x00 0x00 0x08
0x25 0x09 0x34 0x12 0x01 0x00 0x01 0x02
0x00 0x01
Descriptor Fields:
bLength   : 0x12
bDescriptorType   : 0x01 (Dev. Descriptor)
bcdUSB   : 0x0110 (USB spec. 01.10)
bDeviceClass   : 0x00 (ifc's specify own)
bDeviceSubClass : 0x00
bDeviceProtocol : 0x00
bMaxPacketSize0 : 0x08
idVendor   : 0x0925 (unknown)
idProduct   : 0x1234
bcdDevice   : 0x0001 (release 00.01)
iManufacturer   : 0x01
- Get String Descriptor 0 (Language ID's) Passed.
- Checking Language ID's Passed.
Language ID   : 0x0409
- Get String Descriptor Index 1, Language ID 0x0409 Passed.
USB C
iProduct   : 0x02
Language ID   : 0x0409
- Get String Descriptor Index 2, Language ID 0x0409 Passed.
HID
iSerialNumber   : 0x00
bNumConfigurations : 0x01 (1)
CONFIGURATION Index 0 Tests:

- Get Configuration Descriptor Passed. Configuration Value = 0x01

Configuration Descriptor:
0x09 0x02 0x22 0x00 0x01 0x01 0x00 0x80
0x32 0x09 0x04 0x00 0x00 0x01 0x03 0x00
0x00 0x00 0x09 0x21 0x00 0x01 0x00 0x01
0x22 0x34 0x00 0x07 0x05 0x81 0x03 0x06
0x00 0x0a

Listing 17-1: (Sheet 1 of 3) USB Check's Device Framework test report shows the result of the tests, which retrieve descriptors and send other control requests. This report is for a custom HID.

Get Configuration Descriptor with Transfer size 0x22 for Config# 0x0

Descriptor Fields:
bLength   : 0x09
bDescriptorType   : 0x02
wTotalLength   : 0x0022 (34)
bNumInterfaces   : 0x01 (1)
bConfigurationValue : 0x01
iConfiguration   : 0x00
bmAttributes   : 0x80 (bus powered)
MaxPower   : 0x32 (100 mA)
- Get Configuration Passed. Device Is Unconfigured

- Set Configuration Passed. Set To 0x01

- Get Configuration Passed. Returned 0x01.

- Unconfigure Device Passed. Set To 0x00

- Get Configuration Passed. Device Is Unconfigured

- Set Configuration Passed. Set To 0x01

- Get Configuration Passed. Returned 0x01.

- Check If Alt. Setting For Ifc 0 is 0 Passed. Single interface responded with STALL

INTERFACE 0x0 Tests:

INTERFACE Number 0x00, Alt. Setting 0x00 Tests:

bLength   : 0x09
bDescriptorType   : 0x04
bInterfaceNumber : 0x00
bAlternateSetting : 0x00
bNumEndpoints   : 0x01
bInterfaceClass   : 0x03 (USB specified device class)
bInterfaceSubClass : 0x00
bInterfaceProtocol : 0x00 (not vendor or class specific)
iInterface   : 0x00
- Set Interface Passed. Single interface responded with STALL

- Get Interface Passed. Single interface responded with STALL

Listing 17-1: (Sheet 2 of 3) USB Check's Device Framework test report shows the result of the tests, which retrieve descriptors and send other control requests. This report is for a custom HID.

Descriptor (Endpoint 0x00) Fields:
bLength   : 0x07
bDescriptorType : 0x05
bEndpointAddress : 0x81 (ep #1, IN)
bmAttributes   : 0x03 (Transfer Type : Interrupt)
wMaxPacketSize   : 0x0006
bInterval   : 0x0A (10 milliseconds)
ENDPOINT With Address 0x81 Tests:

- GetStatus Passed. Endpoint NOT Stalled

- Set Feature (STALL) Passed.

- GetStatus Passed. Set Stall Confirmed

- Clear Feature (STALL) Passed.

- GetStatus Passed. Clear Stall Confirmed

NonStandard Descriptor
Size : 0x09 Bytes
Type : 0x21
Data : 0x00 0x01 0x00 0x01 0x22 0x34 0x00

More DEVICE Tests For Current Configuration:
- Get Status Passed. Remote Wakeup Not Supported - Remote Wakeup Disabled,
Bus-Powered

00 Vid (0x0925) Pid (0x1234): All Selected Test(s) PASSED!
DEVICE IS CHAPTER 9 COMPLIANT
bcdDevice: 0x0001 (release 00.01)

Listing 17-1: (Sheet 3 of 3) USB Check's Device Framework test report shows
the result of the tests, which retrieve descriptors and send other control
requests. This report is for a custom HID.

Test Equipment

Test equipment for USB includes protocol analyzers to monitor bus traffic
and other devices for generating traffic and performing other tests.

Protocol Analyzers

The ultimate tool for USB development is a protocol analyzer. The analyzer is a combination of hardware and software that enables you to view every detail of the traffic on the bus. The analyzer does the work for you, collecting the data you request, then decoding and displaying it in a variety of formats. You can watch what happens during enumeration, detect and examine protocol and signaling errors, view the data being transferred during control, interrupt, bulk, and isochronous transfers, or focus on any aspect of a communication that you want.

For developing a commercial product, a protocol analyzer is essential. For experimenting and learning, you can do a lot with the tools provided by chip vendors and the USB Implementers Forum's free utilities, but a protocol analyzer will make things much easier and will open your eyes to many new things.

Protocol analyzers are complex instruments, and even though there are many developers working on USB products, the market for analyzers is limited in comparison to, for example, the market for generic PCs. This means that analyzers aren't cheap. But as with many other electronic devices, prices have come down as USB has become more popular and more vendors have entered the market.

Sources for USB protocol analyzers include Catalyst Enterprises, Computer Access Technology Corporation (CATC), Crescent Heart Software, Data Transit, FuturePlus, Hitex Development Tools, and QualityLogic.

Any analyzer should perform the basic tasks of decoding USB traffic and displaying the results in useful formats. Not all analyzers support USB 2.0. The user interface may be via a PC or a logic analyzer. An analyzer that connects to a PC may use a USB, parallel-port, Ethernet, or ISA-board connection. If you own a generic logic analyzer, a USB analyzer that connects to it will probably be less expensive than other options. Crescent Heart Software's analyzers connect to Tektronix analyzers, and FuturePlus's analyzers connect to Agilent analyzers.

As an example of what you can do with a protocol analyzer, I'll describe QualityLogic's USB Expert. Other analyzers have similar abilities, and new and improved products are constantly being developed, so be sure to check for the latest information when you're ready to buy.

Hardware

The USB Expert's hardware consists of two pieces: the main unit and the probe (Figure 17-5). The main unit contains the buffer that stores the USB traffic and an embedded PC to manage the storage and transferring of the analyzer's data to a PC. The probe connects in series with the USB segment to be monitored, with an additional parallel connection that carries the segment's data to the Expert's main unit for analyzing. The parallel connection

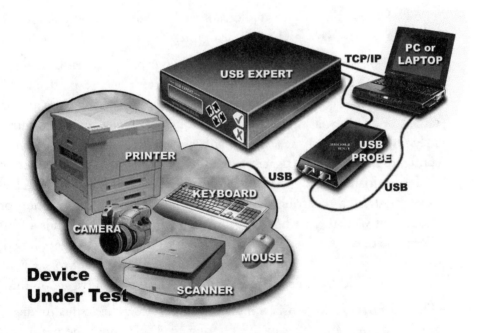

Figure 17-5: QualityLogic's USB Expert protocol analyzer collects USB data and sends it to a PC over a TCP/IP connection. An application on the PC displays the data in a variety of formats.

enables the Expert to monitor the USB traffic without affecting it. The probe also has a connector for hardware triggering and a manual trigger button.

The Expert communicates with a PC via a TCP/IP Network connection. To use the Expert, you need a PC with an Ethernet interface configured for TCP/IP. An Ethernet interface is fast, and is inexpensive to add if your PC doesn't already have one. If the PC connects to a network, both the PC and USB Expert can connect to the same 10 BaseT Ethernet hub. If the PC doesn't have a network connection, the Expert can use the provided Direct-Connect 10-BaseT cable to connect to the PC. The same PC that connects to the Expert can serve as the host of the bus being tested. The TCP/IP interface also enables remote testing.

Software

The USB Expert's software application enables you to begin and stop data logging and view, save, and print the results.

Figure 17-6 shows the screen you use to begin capturing data. Data logging can begin on detecting any of a number of event types: a particular USB event (such as a Setup packet or STALL), a programmed trigger in an application, or an external signal. Or you can just start collecting data immediately. If you want to see what happens during enumeration, you can configure the Expert to trigger on the first Setup packet sent to the device's address, initiate data logging, then attach the device. The Expert will begin storing traffic on detecting the first Setup packet in the enumeration process. If you want to see what happens when your application sends a Write-File to the device's driver, you can add a call to the Expert's trigger function just before calling WriteFile in your application. If you want to see if your device is responding to any requests with STALL, you can trigger on this.

When the data collection is complete, you can view the results in any of a number of formats. You can use filtering to display only the items you're interested in. I'll mention only some of the available screens and reports.

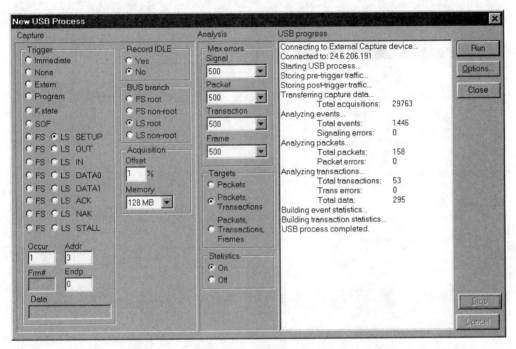

Figure 17-6: The USB Expert gives you many options for triggering and recording data.

The Transactions tab (Figure 17-7) displays each occurrence of the transaction types you specify. Right-clicking on a transaction displays additional information about it. In a similar way, the Events and Data tabs display the information formatted by event (including Idle, Reset, and Resume states, End-of-Packet signals, and errors) or focusing on the data transferred, rather than on the events. You can search for invalid packets or other errors, then see exactly where they occurred and view details about each error.

You can also view all of the information that transferred in any control request. Figure 17-8 shows a Set_Address request. The Expert decodes class-specific requests, including those for hubs, HIDs, and printers. A Signal-Layer display shows data as you would see it on a logic analyzer, and a Transfer-Layer display shows all transactions associated with a transfer.

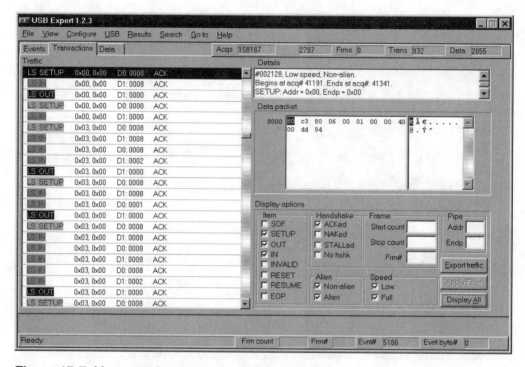

Figure 17-7: You can view each transaction by type, and right-click for more information.

Other Test Equipment

Protocol analyzers are great for watching what happens on the bus. Also useful is the ability to control bus traffic and signaling beyond what you can do by accessing devices from applications. And there are instruments that can do this as well.

One example is Catalyst Enterprises' SBAE-10 protocol analyzer, which can also function as a host that generates traffic on the bus. Other instruments from CATC and RPM Systems offer various combinations of capabilities and may be used alone or in combination with a protocol analyzer.

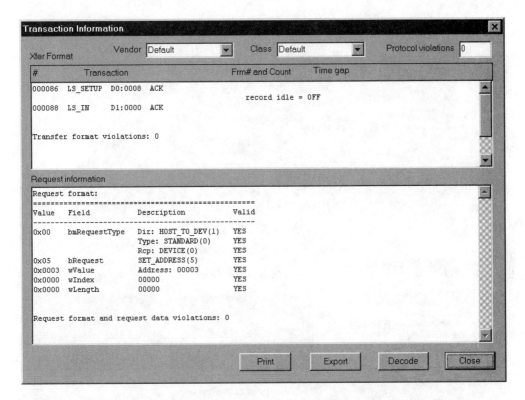

Figure 17-8: This display of a Set_Address request shows that the host assigned an address of 03h to the device.

CATC Traffic Generator

CATC's Traffic Generator is an example of an instrument that offers precise control over bus traffic and events. You control the Traffic Generator via a parallel-port connection to a PC running the Traffic Generator software.

The Traffic Generator enables you to generate both legal and illegal messages and bus conditions. You can control the state of individual bits and the bit width. Some of the illegal bus conditions you can generate are bad PID, bad CRC, bad bit stuffing, short Idle, short Single-Ended-Zero time, narrow bits, and clock jitter.

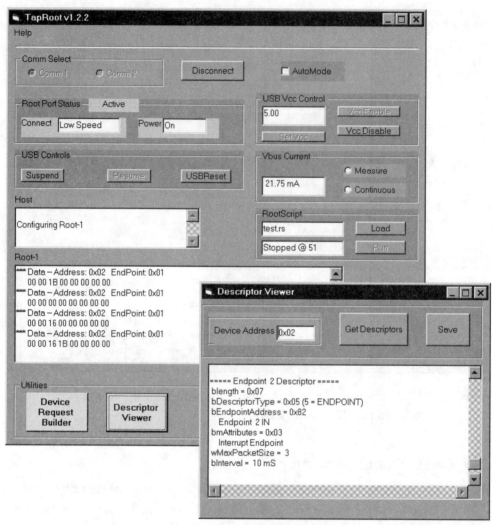

Figure 17-9: RPM Systems' Root 1 Test Adapter and TapRoot software enable you to generate bus traffic and perform other tests.

Root 1 Test Adapter

RPM Systems' Root 1 USB Functional Verification Adapter performs many of the functions of a host and root hub. When you connect a device to the Root 1, the Root 1 enumerates the device and can initiate other traffic and perform various tests. Figure 17-9 shows the TapRoot application, which enables you to monitor and control the Root 1's bus using an RS-232 connection.

TapRoot enables you to view the descriptors retrieved during enumeration, specify requests to send, and view the results. You can suspend, resume, and reset the bus. You can control the bus voltage and measure bus current.

Rootscript is a Visual C++ application that enables you to write scripts to generate traffic on the Root 1's bus. A script can initiate control, bulk, interrupt, or isochronous transfers. A script can loop to repeat a test or series of tests.

Testing and Logos

The USB Implementers Forum and Microsoft offer testing opportunities for developers of USB devices and their host software. Passing the tests can earn a product the right to display the USB Logo or the Microsoft Windows Logo. This in turn gives users confidence that the device is thoroughly tested and reliable.

The USB Implementers Forum Compliance Program

One advantage USB has that other interfaces don't have is that the developers of the specification didn't stop with the release of the specification document. The USB Implementers Forum remains involved in helping developers design and test USB products. I've already mentioned that the Forum's website has documents and tools, including USB Check, available to everyone. In addition, joining the Implementers Forum gives you access to resources that will help ensure that your product complies with the specification and causes no problems for users.

For a thorough testing of a product under a variety of conditions, Forum members can enroll a device in the Implementers Forum's Compliance Program. When a device meets the program's criteria, the Forum deems it to have "reasonable measures of acceptability" and adds it to its Integrators List of compliant devices. On receiving a signed license agreement and payment, the Forum authorizes the device to display the USB Logo.

The program's two criteria are checklists and compliance testing.

Checklists

The checklists contain questions relating to your product and its behavior. Filling out the appropriate checklists is the first step in achieving compliance. You do this step on your own.

There are checklists for vendors of peripherals, hubs, systems with USB hosts, and cables. Some products require multiple checklists. I'll focus on peripheral testing.

The Peripheral checklist is several pages of questions about your device. They cover mechanical design, device states and signals, and operating voltages and power consumption. You should be able to answer yes to everything. Accompanying each question is a reference to a page in the specification where you can find more information.

The checklists are available from the Forum's website.

Compliance Testing

When you can answer yes to everything on the checklists that apply to your product, you're ready for compliance testing. The USB Implementers Forum sponsors compliance workshops that enable you to test your device with a variety of hardware. Every workshop has many vendors and products available. You can schedule private tests with vendors of host hardware. And you can participate in one of the Implementers Forum's Plugfests, where as many vendors as possible connect their devices to a single host to find out if all can co-exist peacefully. The Forum also authorizes some private labs to perform compliance tests.

Before attending a workshop, the Forum recommends performing the tests as fully as possible on your own. The Compliance Test Procedure document has detailed descriptions of the tests, which cover responding to standard requests, power consumption and distribution, signal quality, and interoperability.

The interoperability tests are where you emulate the user's experience using your product on a system with a variety of other USB peripherals attached and in use with a variety of software. The goal is "an enjoyable end-user experience." These tests are important!

The Compliance Test Procedure document spells out what should be self-evident: your device should function without ever causing a device-not-detected error or a system crash, hang, or reboot.

The following are the minimal situations that you must test for a low- or full-speed device. In each case, the specified actions shouldn't interfere with the operation of the device being tested or any other attached devices.

The device must pass the tests not only on a bus with just your device, but also on a bus that connects a variety of hubs and other common peripherals. The Forum's website lists devices that are verified to have no interopability problems of their own. The Guidelines document calls this topology the Gold Tree. The minimum configuration includes your device plus four hubs, a disk drive, a camera, a keyboard, and a mouse. A low- or full-speed device is tested with both UHCI and OHCI host controllers.

Using an OHCI host controller:

- With the system powered, attach the device to the fifth hub in series, using a 5-meter or captive cable. The operating system must identify the device and load the appropriate drivers. Rebooting should not be required.

- Install any application software the device uses. Rebooting should not be required. The device should demonstrate its intended operation. For example, a printer would print documents sent to it, a keyboard would send keystrokes in a format the operating system understands, and a camera would transfer images to the host.

- Suspend and resume. The device, device driver, and application software must operate normally after resuming from the Suspend state.

- If remote wakeup is supported, suspend and initiate a remote wakeup event. The device, device driver, and application software must operate normally after the remote wakeup.

Using a UHCI host controller:

- With the system powered, attach the device to the fifth hub in series, using a 5-meter or captive cable. The operating system must identify the device and load the appropriate drivers. Rebooting should not be required.

- Each device in the Gold Tree must operate while other devices are operating.

- With the system powered, detach and re-attach the device. The device, device driver, and application software must operate normally after re-attaching.

- With the system powered, detach the device and attach it to a different port. The device, device driver, and application software must operate normally after re-attaching.

- Warm boot: click Start > Shutdown > Restart. The device, device driver, and application software must operate after the reboot.

- Cold boot: click Start > Shutdown > Shutdown and turn the PC back on. The device, device driver, and application software must operate after powering up.

The Compliance Test Procedure document has more specifics about these tests.

If your device has one or more isochronous endpoints, you must also test what happens when the host can't configure a device because there isn't enough bandwidth for the requested pipe. When the device can't be configured, it must inform the user of what has happened and advise the user to stop using other devices that use isochronous transfers in order to enable the device to be configured.

For this test, you can use the Bandwidth Load Application available from the Implementers Forum. The application requires a dummy device that will receive isochronous OUT data. The device doesn't have to have any isochronous endpoints. The application uses a replacement driver that configures the device with isochronous endpoints and causes the data to be sent. Because there are no handshake packets for the device to return, it doesn't matter if the device never sees the data.

Figure 17-10: Devices that pass compliance testing can display the USB Logo. The logo indicates if the device supports high speed.

If your device supports a boot interface, you must test this as well, to ensure, for example, that a keyboard with a boot interface will work with BIOSes that have keyboard support.

The USB Logo

If your device passes Compliance testing, it's eligible to display the official USB Logo. There are two logos, one for low-and full-speed devices and one for high-speed-capable devices (Figure 17-10). To qualify for the logo, a high-speed device must also be fully functional at full speed. To use the logo, you must sign the USB-IF Trademark License Agreement. If you're not a member of the Implementers Forum, you also must pay a logo administration fee of $1500 every two years. The logo is different than the USB icon described in Chapter 21.

Windows Hardware Quality Labs Testing

For devices that will attach to Windows PCs, Microsoft provides Windows Hardware Quality Labs (WHQL) testing. These tests qualify devices to display a Microsoft Windows logo and to be included in Microsoft's Hardware Compatibility List (HCL) of devices that have been shown to be compatible with Windows. The device's driver may also be included in the Microsoft Windows Driver Library.

Microsoft provides test kits for hardware and device drivers. You can download the kits that apply to your device and run the tests. When you believe your device can pass all tests, you submit a test package to an authorized testing site. The test package contains the device, any driver and related files, signed agreements, test logs, and fees. If your device passes, your device and marketing materials can display the Microsoft Windows Logo.

You can find more information and downloads relating to WHQL at *www.microsoft.com/hwtest.*

Driver Signing

Beginning with Windows 98, Microsoft began supporting and promoting digital signing to improve the quality of device drivers and to provide a way of controlling whether untested drivers can be installed.

To qualify for signing, a driver must pass WHQL testing. A signed driver has a catalog (CAT) file containing a digital signature provided by Microsoft and INF file that references the catalog file. The signature enables Windows to detect if a driver file has been modified since it passed WHQL testing.

For specified device classes, Windows looks for a signature when using an INF file to install hardware. When an INF file specifies an unsigned driver, operating-system settings control whether Windows blocks installation, or installs the driver with a warning, or installs with no warning.

Each INF file has its own CAT file. A single INF file can support multiple devices. A change in an INF file, to support a new Product ID or version number for example, invalidates the CAT file and requires new testing, even if the driver is unchanged.

The support for driver signing has been enhanced with each edition of Windows. For many common device classes, Windows 2000's default setting warns the user when it detects the installation of a device with an unsigned driver. You can change the default policy in the Control Panel, under System > Hardware.

18

Hubs: the Link between Devices and the Host

Every USB device must connect to a hub. As Chapter 2 explained, a hub is an intelligent device that provides attachment points for devices and manages each device's connection to the bus. Devices that plug directly into a PC connect to the root hub. Other devices connect to external hubs downstream from the root hub.

A hub's two main jobs are managing its devices' connections and passing traffic to and from the host. Managing the connections includes helping to get newly attached devices up and communicating and blocking communications from misbehaving devices so they don't interfere with other devices' use of the bus. The hub's role in passing traffic to and from the host depends on the speed of the host, device, and the hubs between them. A hub may

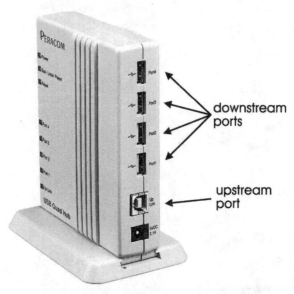

downstream
ports

upstream
port

Figure 18-1: A hub has one upstream port and one or more downstream ports. (Photo of Peracom hub courtesy of B & B Electronics.)

just repeat what it receives or it may convert the traffic to a different speed and manage the transaction with the device.

This chapter presents essentials about hub communications. You don't need to know every detail about hubs in order to design a USB peripheral, but some understanding of what the hub must do will help understanding how your device communicates with the host.

Hub Basics

Each external hub has one port, or attachment point, that connects in the upstream direction (toward the host) (Figure 18-1). This upstream port may connect directly to the host's root hub, or it may connect to a downstream port on another external hub. Each hub also has one or more ports downstream from the host. Most downstream ports have a connector for attaching a cable. An exception is a hub that is part of a compound device whose ports connect to functions embedded in the device. Hubs with one, two, four, and seven downstream ports are common. A hub may be self-powered or bus-powered. As Chapter 19 explains, bus-powered hubs are limited because you can't attach high-power devices to them.

Every external hub has a hub repeater and a hub controller. (Figure 18-2). The hub repeater is responsible for passing USB traffic between the host's root hub or another upstream hub and whatever downstream devices are attached and enabled. The hub controller manages the communications between the host and the hub repeater. State machines contain the logic to respond to events at the hub repeater and upstream and downstream ports. A 2.0 hub also has one or more transaction translators and routing logic that enable low- and full-speed devices to communicate on a high-speed bus.

The host's root hub is a special case. The host controller performs many of the functions performed by the hub repeater and hub controller in an external hub, so a root hub may contain little more than routing logic and downstream ports.

The Hub Repeater

The hub repeater re-transmits, or repeats, the packets it receives, sending them on their way either upstream or downstream with minimal changes. The hub repeater also detects when a device is attached and removed, establishes the connection of a device to the bus, detects bus faults such as over-current conditions, and manages power to the device.

The hub repeater in a 2.0 hub has two modes of operation, depending on the upstream bus speed. When the hub connects upstream to a full-speed bus segment, the repeater functions as a low- and full-speed repeater. When the hub connects upstream to a high-speed bus segment, the repeater functions as a high-speed repeater. The repeaters in 1.x hubs always function as low- and full-speed repeaters.

The Low- and Full-speed Repeater

The hub repeater in a 1.x hub handles low- and full-speed traffic. A 2.0 hub also uses this type of repeater when its upstream port connects to a

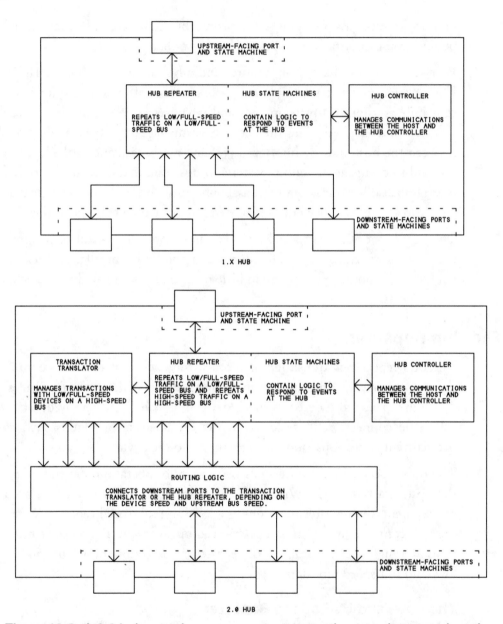

Figure 18-2: A 2.0 hub contains one or more transaction translators and routing logic that enable a hub on a high-speed bus to communicate with low- and full-speed devices. In a 1.x hub, the hub repeater is routed directly to the downstream ports.

full-speed bus. In this case, the 2.0 hub doesn't send or receive high-speed traffic but instead functions identically to a 1.x hub.

A 1.x hub repeats all low- and full-speed packets received from the host (including data that has passed through one or more additional hubs) to all enabled, full-speed, downstream ports. Enabled ports include all ports with attached devices that are ready to receive communications from the hub. Exceptions would include a device that the host controller has stopped communicating with due to errors or other problems, a device in the Suspend state, or a device that isn't yet ready to communicate because it has just been attached or is in the process of exiting the Suspend state.

The hub repeater doesn't translate or process traffic to or from full-speed ports in any way. It just regenerates the edges of the signal transitions and passes them on.

Low-speed devices never see full-speed traffic. A 1.x hub repeats only low-speed packets to low-speed devices. The hub identifies a low-speed packet by the PRE packet identifier that precedes it. The hub repeats the low-speed packets, and only these packets, to any enabled low-speed devices. The hub also repeats low-speed packets to its full-speed downstream ports, because a full-speed port may connect to a hub that in turn connects to a low-speed device. To give the hubs time to make their low-speed ports ready to receive data, the host adds a delay of at least four full-speed bit widths between the PRE packet and the low-speed packet.

Compared to full speed, low-speed traffic varies not only in speed, but also in edge rate and polarity. In transmitting to a low-speed device, the repeater converts received full-speed transitions to the slower edge rate required by the low-speed device. In receiving data from a low-speed device, the repeater converts received low-speed transitions to the faster edge rate used by full-speed devices. Low-speed traffic also uses an inverted polarity compared to full speed, so the repeater inverts all data sent to and received from a low-speed device. Chapter 20 has more on the signal polarities, and Chapter 21 has more about edge rates.

The High-speed Repeater

A 2.0 hub uses a high-speed repeater when the hub's upstream port connects to a high-speed bus segment. When this is the case, the hub sends and receives all upstream traffic at high speed, even if the traffic is from or to a low- or full-speed device. The path that traffic takes through a hub with a high-speed repeater depends on the speeds of the attached devices. Routing logic in the hub determines whether or not traffic to or from a downstream port passes through a transaction translator.

Unlike the low- and full-speed repeater, a high-speed repeater re-clocks received data to minimize accumulated jitter. In other words, instead of just repeating received transitions, a high-speed repeater extracts the data and uses its own local clock to time the transitions when retransmitting. The edge rate and polarity are unchanged. An elasticity buffer allows for small differences between the two clock frequencies. When the buffer is half full, the received data begins to be clocked out.

High-speed devices don't use the transaction translator. Traffic is routed from the receiving port on the hub, through the high-speed repeater, to the hub's transmitting port.

For traffic to and from low- and full-speed devices, the high-speed repeater communicates with the transaction translator that manages the transactions with the devices. Traffic received from upstream is routed to the high-speed repeater, then passes through the transaction translator, which communicates at the appropriate speed with the downstream ports. In the other direction, traffic from low- and full-speed devices is routed to the transaction translator, which processes the received data and takes appropriate action. The following section has more about the transaction translator.

The Transaction Translator

Every 2.0 hub must have a transaction translator to manage communications with low- and full-speed devices. The transaction translator communicates upstream at high speed but enables 1.x devices to communicate at low and full speeds in exactly the same way as they do with 1.x hosts.

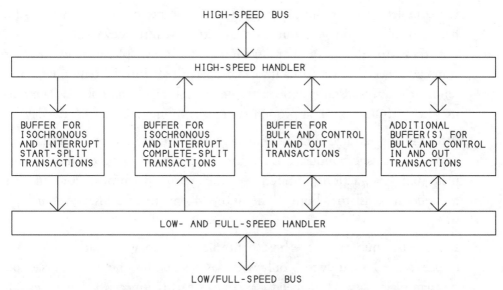

Figure 18-3: A transaction translator contains a high-speed handler for upstream traffic, buffers for storing information in split transactions, and a low- and full-speed handler for downstream traffic to low- and full-speed devices.

The transaction translator frees bus time by enabling other bus communications to occur while a device is completing a low- or full-speed transaction. It can also enable low- and full-speed devices to use more bandwidth than they would have on a shared 1.x bus.

The transaction translator contains three sections (Figure 18-3). The high-speed handler communicates with the host at high speed. The low/full-speed handler communicates with devices at low and full speeds. Buffers store information in split transactions with low- and full-speed devices.

As Chapter 3 explained, when a 2.0 host on a high-speed bus wants to communicate with a low- or full-speed device, the host initiates a start-split transaction with the 2.0 hub that is nearest the device and communicating upstream at high speed. One or more start-split transactions contain the information the hub needs to complete the transaction with the device. The transaction translator stores the information received from the host and completes the start-split transaction with the host.

On completing a start-split transaction, the hub performs the function of a host controller in carrying out the transaction with the device. The transaction translator initiates the transaction in the token phase, sends data or stores returned data or status information as needed in the data phase, and sends or receives a status code as needed in the handshake phase. The hub uses low or full speed, as appropriate, in its communications with the device.

After the hub has had time to exchange data with the device, in all transactions except isochronous OUTs, the host initiates one or more complete-split transactions to retrieve the returned information in the transaction translator's buffer. The hub performs these transactions at high speed.

Because the hub acts as a host controller in managing transactions, 1.x devices share 1.x bandwidth only with devices that use the same transaction translator. So if two full-speed 1.x devices each connect to their own 2.0 hubs on a high-speed bus, each can use all of the full-speed bandwidth it wants. When the hub converts to high speed, the 1.x communications will use little of the high-speed bandwidth.

A hub can have one transaction translator for all ports, or it can have a translator for each port that connects to a low- or full-speed device. Each transaction translator has to have at least four buffers: one for interrupt and isochronous start-split transactions, one for interrupt and isochronous complete-split transactions, and two for control and bulk transfers.

The Hub Controller

The hub controller manages communications between the host and the hub. This includes enumeration along with other communications and actions due to events at downstream ports.

As it does for all devices, the host enumerates a newly detected hub to find out its abilities. The hub descriptor retrieved during enumeration tells the host how many ports the hub has. After enumerating the hub, the host requests the hub to tell it whether there are any devices attached and if so, the host enumerates these as well.

The host finds out if a device is attached to a port by sending the hub-class request Get_Port_Status. This is similar to a Get_Status request, but sent to a hub with a port number in the Index field. The hub returns two 16-bit values that indicate whether a device is attached as well as other information, such as whether the device is low power or in the Suspend state.

The hub controller is also responsible for disabling any port that was responsible for loss of bus activity or babble. Loss of bus activity occurs when a packet doesn't end with the expected End-of-Packet signal. Babble occurs when a device continues to transmit beyond the End-of-Packet signal.

In addition to Endpoint 0, which all devices must have for control transfers, hubs must have a Status Change endpoint configured for interrupt IN transfers. The host polls this endpoint to find out if there have been any changes at the hub. On each poll, the hub controller returns either a NAK if there have been no changes, or data that indicates a specific port or the hub itself as the source of the change. If there is a change, the host sends requests to find out more about the change and to take whatever action is needed. For example, if the hub reports the attachment of a new device, the host attempts to enumerate it.

Speed

An external 2.0 hub's downstream ports must support all three speeds. The EHCI host-controller specification says that a host must also support all speeds except for the unusual situation where every port has a permanently attached high-speed device. Because an EHCI controller supports high speed only, to support low and full speeds, a 2.0 host must have a companion 1.x host controller in addition to its high-speed host controller.

In the upstream direction, if a 2.0 hub's upstream segment is high speed, the hub communicates at high speed. Otherwise, it communicates at low and full speeds.

A 1.x hub's upstream port must support low- and full-speed communications. All downstream ports with connectors must support both low- and full-speed communications. 1.x hubs never support high speed.

Filtering Traffic according to Speed

Low-speed devices aren't capable of receiving full-speed data, so hubs don't repeat full-speed traffic to low-speed devices. This is necessary because a low-speed device would try to interpret the full-speed traffic as low-speed data and might even mistakenly see what it thinks is valid data. Full- or high-speed data on a low-speed cable would also cause radiated electromagnetic interference (EMI). In the other direction, hubs receive and repeat any low-speed data upstream.

Low- and full-speed devices aren't capable of receiving high-speed data, so 2.0 hubs don't repeat high-speed traffic to these devices, including 1.x hubs.

Keeping Devices from Entering the Suspend State

Start-of-Frame packets keep full- and high-speed devices from entering the Suspend state on an otherwise idle bus. When there is no data on a full-speed bus, the host continues to send a Start-of-Frame packet once per frame, and all hubs pass these packets on to their full-speed devices. When there is no data on a high-speed bus, the host continues to send a Start-of-Frame packet once per microframe, and all hubs pass these packets on to their high-speed devices.

A full-speed device that connects to a 2.0 hub that communicates upstream at high speed will also receive a Start-of-Frame once per frame.

Low-speed devices don't see the Start-of-Frame packets. Instead, at least once per frame, hubs must send their low-speed devices a low-speed End-of-Packet (EOP) signal (defined in Chapter 20). This functions as a keep-alive signal that keeps a device from entering the Suspend state on a bus with no low-speed activity. Chapter 19 has more on how hubs manage the Suspend state.

Detecting Device Speed

On attachment, every device must support either low or full speed. A hub detects whether an attached device is low or full speed by detecting which

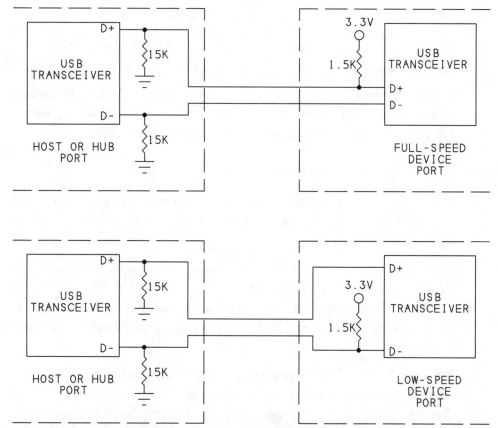

Figure 18-4: The device's port has a stronger pull-up than the hub's. The location of the pull-up tells the hub whether the device is low- or full-speed. High-speed devices are full speed at attachment.

signal line is more positive on an idle line. Figure 18-4 illustrates. As Chapter 5 explained, the hub has a 15-kilohm pull-down resistor on each of the port's two signal lines, D+ and D-. A newly attached device has a 1.5-kilohm pull-up resistor on D+ for a full-speed device or D- for a low-speed device. When a device is attached to a port, the device's pull-up is stronger than the hub's pull-down, so the line with the pull-up is pulled high. When the voltage on one of the lines is more positive than the hub's logic-high input threshold, the hub assumes a device is attached, and detects the speed by which line it is.

After detecting a full-speed device, a 2.0 hub determines whether the device supports high speed by using the high-speed detection handshake. The handshake occurs during the Reset state that the hub initiates during enumeration. When the handshake succeeds, the device removes its pull-up and communications are at high speed. A 1.x hub ignores the attempt to handshake, and the failure of the handshake informs the device that it must use full speed. Chapter 20 has more details about the handshake.

How Many Hubs in Series?

USB was designed as a desktop bus. It's not intended for long-distance links. But that hasn't stopped people from wondering just how far a USB peripheral can be from its host.

The specification doesn't give a maximum length for cable segments, but the maximum allowed propagation delay limits the length to about 5 meters for full and high speed and 3 meters for low speed. You can increase the distance between a device and its host by using a series of hubs, each with a 5-meter cable.

But how many hubs in series can you use? The number of hubs you can connect in series is limited by the electrical properties of the hubs and cables and the resulting delays in propagating signals along the cable and through a hub. The limit is five hubs in series, with each hub and the final device each using a 5-meter cable. This means that a device can be 30 meters (96 feet) from its host. If the device is low speed, the limit is 28 meters because the device's cable can be no more than 3 meters. Chapter 21 has more about extending the distance between a USB device and its host.

The Hub Class

Hubs are members of the Hub class, which is the only class defined in the main USB specification. Each hub supports the standard descriptors as well as descriptors that are specific to hubs.

Hub Descriptors

A 1.x hub has a series of five descriptors: device, hub class, configuration, interface, and endpoint. A 2.0 hub has more descriptors because it must support all speeds, and because it may offer a choice of using one or multiple transaction translators.

A 2.0 hub's descriptors include the device_qualifier descriptor and the other_speed_configuration_descriptor required for all high-speed-capable devices. The device_qualifier descriptor contains an alternate value for bDeviceProtocol in the device descriptor. The hub uses the alternate value when it switches between high and full speeds.

The other_speed_configuration_descriptor tells the number of interfaces supported by the configuration not currently in use, and is followed by the descriptors for that configuration. A configuration that supports multiple transaction translators has two interface descriptors: one for use with a single transaction translator and an alternate setting for use with multiple transaction translators. The bInterfaceProtocal field specifies whether an interface setting supports one or multiple transaction translators.

Hub Values for the Standard Descriptors

The specification assigns class-specific values for some parameters in a hub's device, and interface descriptors. It also specifies the contents of the endpoint descriptor for the hub's status-change endpoint:

Device Descriptor

bDeviceClass = HUB_CLASSCODE (09H)

bDeviceSubClass =0

bDeviceProtocol = 0 for low/full speed, 1 for high speed when the hub supports a single transaction translator, 2 for high speed when the hub supports multiple transaction translators

These fields also apply to the Device_Qualifier_Descriptor in 2.0 hubs.

Interface Descriptor

bNumEndpoints =1

bInterfaceClass = HUB_CLASSCODE (09H)

bInterfaceSubClass = 0

bInterfaceProtocol = 0 for a low/full speed hub or a high-speed hub that supports only a single transaction translator. For a hub that supports single and multiple transaction translators, 1 indicates a single transaction translator, and 2 indicates multiple transaction translators.

Endpoint Descriptor (for Status Change Endpoint)

bEndpointAddress = Implementation-dependent; Bit 7: Direction = In(1)

wMaxPacketSize = Implementation-dependent

bmAttributes = Transfer Type = Interrupt

bInterval = FFh for full speed, 0Ch for high speed (Maximum allowable interval)

The Hub Descriptor

Each hub must also have a hub-class descriptor. The hub descriptor contains the following fields:

Identifying the Descriptor

bDescLength. The number of bytes in the descriptor.

bDescriptorType. Hub Descriptor, 29h.

Hub Description

bNbrPorts. The number of downstream ports the hub supports.

wHubCharacteristics:

Bits 1 and 0 specify the power-switching mode. 00=Ganged; all ports are powered together. 01=Ports are powered individually. 1X: used only on 1.0 hubs with no power switching.

Bit 2 indicates whether the hub is part of a compound device (1) or not (0).

Bits 4 and 3 are the Overcurrent Protection mode. 00 = Global protection and reporting. 01=Protection and reporting for each port. 1X = No protection and reporting (for bus-powered hubs only).

Bits 6 and 5 are the Transaction Translator Think Time. These bits indicate the maximum number of full-speed bit times required between transactions on a low- or full-speed downstream bus. 00 = 8; 01 = 16; 10 = 24; 11 = 32. Applies to 2.0 hubs only.

Bit 7 indicates whether the hub supports Port Indicators (1) or not (0). Applies to 2.0 hubs only.

Bits 8 through 15 are reserved.

bPwrOn2PwrGood. The maximum delay between beginning the power-on sequence on a port and when power is good on the port. The value is in units of 2 milliseconds. (Set to 100 for a 200-millisecond delay.)

bHubContrCurrent. The maximum current required by the Hub Controller's electronics only, in milliamperes.

DeviceRemovable. Indicates whether the device(s) attached to the hub are removable (0) or not (1). The number of bits in this value equals the number of the highest port with an attached device + 1. Bit 0 is reserved. Bit 1 is for Port 1, bit 2 is for Port 2, and so on up.

PortPowerCtrlMask. All bits should be 1s. This field is only for compatibility with 1.0 software. Each port has one bit, and the field should be padded with additional 1s so that the field's size in bits is a multiple of 8.

Hub-class Requests

All hubs accept or return data for seven of the USB's eleven standard requests. Some 2.0 hubs support an additional request. Of the other requests, one is optional and the other two are undefined for hubs. Like all devices, hubs must return STALL for unsupported requests.

Hubs respond in the standard way to Clear_Feature, Get_Configuration, Get_Descriptor, Get_Status, Set_Address, Set_Configuration, and Set_Feature requests. Set_Descriptor is optional and should return STALL if

Table 18-1: The 2.0 hub class has 12 class-specific requests, while the 1.x hub class has 9. Many are hub-specific variants of USB's standard requests.

Specific Request	USB Versions	bRequest	Data source	Value	Index	Data Length (bytes) (Data stage)	Data (in the Data stage)
Clear Hub Feature	all	Clear_ Feature	none	feature	0	0	none
Clear Port Feature	all	Clear_ Feature	none	feature	port	0	none
Clear TT Buffer	2.0 only	Clear_TT _Buffer	none	device address, endpoint #	TT_port	0	none
Get Bus State	1.x only	Get_State	Hub	0	port	1	per-port bus state
Get Hub Descriptor	all	Get_ Descriptor	Hub	descriptor type & index	0 or language ID	descriptor length	descriptor
Get Hub Status	all	Get_ Status	Hub	0	0	4	hub status and change indicators
Get Port Status	all	Get_ Status	Hub	0	port	4	port status and change indicators
Get TT State	2.0 only	Get_TT State	hub	TT flags	port	TT state, length	TT state
Reset TT	2.0 only	Reset_TT	none	0	port	0	none
Set Hub Descriptor (optional)	all	Set_ Descriptor	host	descriptor type & index	0 or language ID	descriptor length	descriptor length
Set Hub Feature	all	Set_ Feature	none	feature	0	0	none
Set Port Feature	all	Set_ Feature	none	feature	port	0	none
Stop TT	2.0 only	Stop_TT	none	0	port	0	none

Table 18-2: The host can monitor and control Status bits in a hub using Get_Hub_Status, Set_Hub_Feature, and Clear_Hub_Feature.

Field	Bit	Status Indicator	Meaning, with 0 state first, followed by 1 state.
Hub Status	0	HUB_LOCAL_POWER	Local power supply is good/not active.
	1	HUB_OVER_CURRENT	An over-current condition exists/does not exist.
	2-15	reserved	Returns 0 when read.
Hub Change	0	C_HUB_LOCAL_POWER	Local power status has not changed/changed.
	1	C_HUB_OVER_CURRENT	Over-current status has not changed/changed.
	2-15	reserved	Returns 0 when read.

not supported. Only 2.0 hubs that support multiple transaction translators support Get_Interface and Set_Interface. A hub can't have an isochronous endpoint, so Synch_Frame is undefined.

The hub class defines eight hub-specific requests that build on the standard requests with hub-specific values. For example, a Get_Status request directed to a hub with an Index value of 0 causes the hub to return a value in a Data packet indicating whether the hub is using an external power supply and whether an over-current condition exists.

Table 18-1 shows the hub-specific requests. One request from the 1.x specification, Get_Bus_State, isn't included in the 2.0 spec. This request enables the host to read the states of D+ and D- at a specified port on the hub.

The host uses many of the hub-specific requests to monitor and control the status of the hub and its ports. Get_Hub_Status reads status bits in a hub. Set_Hub_Feature and Clear_Hub_Feature set and clear status bits in a hub. Table 18-2 shows the bits and their meanings. In a similar way, Get_Port_Status, Set_Port_Feature, and Clear_Port_Feature enable the host to read and control status bits for a selected port in a hub. Table 18-3 shows the bits and their meanings.

In 2.0 hubs, Set_Port_Feature can place a port in one of five Test Modes. Chapter 20 has more about these modes.

Table 18-3: The host can monitor and control Status bits at a port using Get_Port_Status, Set_Port_Feature, and Clear_Port_Feature.

Field	Bit	Status Indicator	Meaning, with 0 state first, followed by 1 state.
Port Status	0	PORT_CONNECTION	A device is not present/present.
	1	PORT_ENABLE	The port is disabled/enabled.
	2	PORT_SUSPEND	The port is not/is in the Suspend state.
	3	PORT_OVERCURRENT	An over-current condition exists/does not exist.
	4	PORT_RESET	The hub is not/is asserting Reset at the port.
	5-7	reserved	Returns 0 when read.
	8	PORT_POWER	The port is/is not in the Powered Off state.
	9	PORT_LOW_SPEED	The attached device is full or high speed/low speed.
	10	PORT_HIGH_SPEED	The attached device is full speed/high speed. (2.0 hubs only)
	11	PORT_TEST	The port is not/is in the Port Test mode. (2.0 hubs only)
	12	PORT_INDICATOR	Port indicator displays default/software controlled colors. (2.0 hubs only)
	13-15	reserved	Returns 0 when read.
Port Status Change	0	C_PORT_CONNECTION	Connect status has not changed/changed.
	1	C_PORT_ENABLE	A Port Error condition does not/does exist.
	2	C_PORT_SUSPEND	Resume signaling is not/is complete.
	3	C_PORT_OVERCURRENT	The over-current condition has not/has changed.
	4	C_PORT_RESET	Reset processing is not/is complete.
	5-15	reserved	Returns 0 when read.

The four new requests in the 2.0 spec all relate to controlling and trouble-shooting the transaction translator (TT). The requests enable the host to clear a buffer in the TT, stop the TT, retrieve the state of a stopped TT using a vendor-specific format, and restart the TT by resetting it.

Port Indicators

The 2.0 specification defines optional indicators to indicate port status to the user. Many hubs have status LEDs. The 2.0 specification assigns standard meanings to the LEDs' colors and blinking property. Bit 7 in the wHubCharacteristics field in the hub descriptor indicates whether a hub has port indicators.

Each downstream port on a hub can have an indicator, which can be either a single bi-color green/amber LED or a separate LED for each color. The indicator tells the state of the hub's port, not the attached device. These are the meanings of the indicators to the user:

> Green: fully operational
> Amber: error condition
> Blinking off/green: software attention required
> Blinking off/amber: hardware attention required
> Off: not operational

Chapter 18

19

Managing Power

One very convenient feature of USB is the ability for peripherals to draw power from the bus. Many devices can be entirely bus powered. But drawing power from the bus also carries the responsibility to live within the limits of available power, including entering the low-power Suspend state when required.

This chapter will help you decide whether or not your design can use bus power. And whether your design is bus-powered or self-powered, you'll find out how to ensure that your design follows the specification's requirements for power management and conservation.

Powering Options

Inside a typical PC is a power supply with amperes to spare. Many USB peripherals can take advantage of this existing capability rather than having to provide their own redundant supplies.

The ability to draw power from the same cable that carries data to and from the PC has several advantages. From the user's point of view, it eliminates the need for an electrical outlet near the peripheral and makes the peripheral smaller and lighter. From the manufacturer's point of view, it makes peripherals cheaper to manufacture. A bus-powered device can also save energy, because power supplies in PCs use efficient switching regulators rather than the cheap linear regulators in the "wall bugs" that many peripherals provide in place of an internal supply. (But most self-powered hubs use wall bugs.)

Before USB, most peripherals used the PC's RS-232 serial and printer ports. Neither of these includes a power-supply line. The ability to use bus power is so compelling that the designers of some peripherals that connect to these ports use schemes that borrow the small amount of current available from unused data or control outputs in the interface. With a super-efficient regulator, you can get a few milliamperes from a serial or parallel port to power a device. Another approach used by some peripherals is to kludge onto the keyboard connector, which does have access to the PC's power supply. With USB, you don't have to resort to these tricks.

Voltages

The nominal voltage between the VBUS and GND wires in a USB cable is 5V, but the actual value can be a little more or quite a bit less. A device that's using bus power must be able to handle the variations and still comply with the specification.

These are the minimum and maximum voltages allowed at a hub's downstream ports:

Hub Type	Minimum Voltage	Maximum Voltage
High Power	4.75	5.25
Low Power	4.4	5.25

To allow for cable and other losses, devices should be able to function with supply voltages a few tenths of a volt less than the minimum available at the hub's connector. In addition, transient conditions can cause the voltage at a low-power hub's port to drop briefly to as low as 4.07V.

If components in the device need a higher voltage, the device can contain a step-up switching regulator. Most USB controller chips require a +5V or +3.3V supply. Components that use 3.3V are handy because the device can use an inexpensive, low-dropout linear regulator to obtain 3.3V.

Which Peripherals Can Use Bus Power?

Not every peripheral can take advantage of bus power. Although USB can provide generous amounts of current in comparison to other interfaces, the current available from the PC's power supply or an external hub does have limits. Figure 19-1's chart will help you decide whether a device can use bus power.

Advances in semiconductor technology have reduced the power required by electronic devices. This is good news for designers of bus-powered devices. Thanks to CMOS processes used in chip manufacturing, lower supply voltages for components, and power-conserving modes in CPUs, you can do a lot with 100 milliamperes.

A peripheral that requires up to 100 milliamperes can be bus powered and will work when attached to any host or hub. A peripheral that requires up to 500 milliamperes can use bus power with limitations: not every battery-powered computer and no bus-powered hub supports peripherals that draw more than 100 milliamperes from the bus.

Of course, some devices need to function when they're not attached to the host at all. A digital camera is an example. These will need their own supplies. Self power can use batteries or power from a wall socket. To save battery power without requiring users to plug in a supply, a device can be designed to be bus-powered when connected to the bus and self-powered otherwise.

A device in the Suspend state can draw very little current from the bus, so some devices will need their own supplies to enable operating when the host has put the device in the Suspend state.

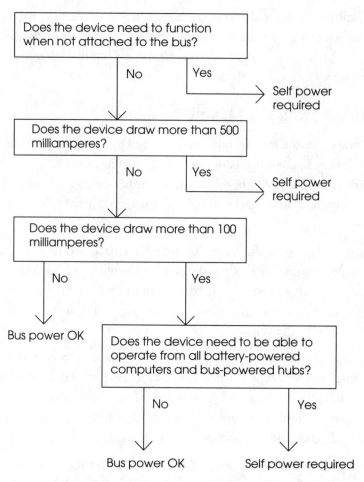

Figure 19-1: Not every device can use bus power alone. A bus-powered device must also meet the specification's limits for Suspend current.

Power Needs

The specification defines a low-power device as one that draws up to 100 milliamperes from the bus, and a high-power device as one that draws up to 500 milliamperes from the bus. A self-powered device has its own power supply and can draw as much power as its supply is capable of.

On power-up, any device can draw up to 100 milliamperes from the bus until the device is configured. This enables self-powered devices to be enumerated even if the user hasn't yet attached or switched on an external supply.

A high-power device can't draw more than 100 milliamperes until the host has said it's OK to do so. This typically happens during enumeration. After retrieving a configuration descriptor, the host examines the amount of current requested in MaxPower, and if the current is available, it sends a Set_Configuration request specifying the configuration. So a high-power device must be able to enumerate at low power.

A self-powered device may also draw up to 100 milliamperes from the bus at any time. This enables the device's USB interface to function when the device's power supply is off, so the host can detect and enumerate the device. Otherwise, if a device's pull-up is bus-powered but the rest of the interface is self-powered, the host will detect the device but won't be able to communicate with it.

These limits are absolute maximums, not averages. And remember that the bus's power-supply voltage can be as high as 5.25V, which may result in greater current consumption. A device never provides upstream power. Even the pull-up resistor must remain unpowered until VBUS is present. So a self-powered device must have a connection to VBUS to detect the presence of bus power even if the device never uses it.

Informing the Host

During enumeration, the host learns whether the device is self powered or bus powered and the maximum current the device will draw from the bus. As Chapter 5 explained, each device's configuration descriptor holds a MaxPower value that specifies the maximum bus current the device requires. All hubs have over-current protection that prevents excessive current from flowing to a device.

If you connect a high-power device to a low-power hub, Windows will display a message informing you that the hub doesn't have enough power available and offering assistance. If the bus has a low-power device connected to a

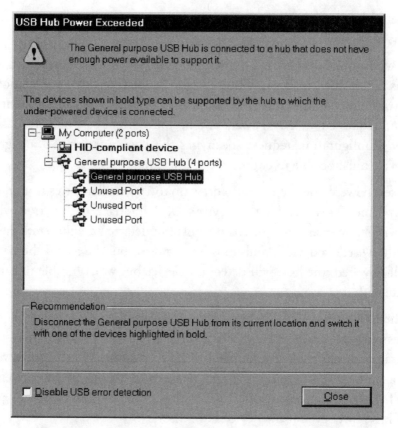

Figure 19-2: Windows warns users when they connect a high-power device to a low-power hub, and helps them find an alternate connection.

high-power port, Windows will recommend swapping the device with the high-power device (Figure 19-2).

A device can support both bus-powered and self-powered options, using self power when available and bus power (possibly with limited abilities) otherwise. When the power source changes, the host must re-enumerate the hub. To enable forcing a re-enumeration, power to the device's bus pull-up resistor may be controlled by a FET. Switching the FET off briefly, then back on, simulates a disconnect and re-connect. If the device doesn't have this feature, users will need to remove the device from the bus before attaching or removing the power supply. The device reports its use of bus or self power in response to a Get_Status (Device) request from the host.

Hub Power

Powering options for hubs are similar to those for other devices, but hubs have some special considerations. A hub must also control power to its devices and monitor power consumption, taking action when the devices are using too much current and presenting a safety hazard.

Power Sources

Like other devices, all hubs except the root hub are self-powered or bus-powered. The root hub gets its power from the host.

If the host uses AC power from a wall socket or another external source, the root hub must be high power and capable of supplying 500 milliamperes to each port on the hub. If the host is battery-powered, the hub may supply either 500 or 100 milliamperes to each port on the hub. If it supplies 100 milliamperes, the hub is defined as a low-power hub.

Bus-powered hubs are limited. All of a bus-powered hub's downstream devices must be low power. This is because the hub can draw no more than 500 milliamperes and the hub itself will use some of this, leaving less than 500 milliamperes for all attached devices combined. Many peripherals can function with 100 milliamperes or less. If you connect two bus-powered hubs in series, the upstream hub can guarantee no more that 100 milliamperes to each downstream port, and that doesn't leave enough current to power a second hub that also has one or more downstream ports, each requiring 100 milliamperes.

An exception is a bus-powered compound device, which consists of a hub and one or more downstream, non-removable devices. In this case, the hub's configuration descriptor can report the maximum power required by the hub electronics plus its non-removable device(s). The configuration descriptors for the non-removable device(s) report that they are self-powered, with MaxPower equal to zero. The hub descriptor indicates whether a hub's ports are removable.

Like other high-power, bus-powered devices, a bus-powered hub can draw up to 100 milliamperes until it's configured, and up to 500 milliamperes after being configured. During configuration, the hub must manage the available current so that its devices and the hub combined don't exceed the allowed current. A possible use for a bus-powered hub would be a hub with an embedded keyboard and pointing device. The keyboard and mouse use little power, so the hub can easily use bus power.

Like other self-powered devices, a self-powered hub may also draw up to 100 milliamperes from the bus so the hub interface can continue to function when the hub's power supply is off. If the hub's power is from an external source, such as AC power from a wall socket, the hub is full power and must be capable of supplying 500 milliamperes to each port on the hub. If the hub uses battery power, the hub may supply 500 or 100 milliamperes to each port on the hub. Because of the confusion that can result when high-power devices are attached to low-power hubs, Microsoft and Intel's *PC 2001 System Design Guide* requires most hubs to be self powered. The exceptions are hubs that are integrated into keyboards or mobile systems.

Over-current Protection

As a safety precaution, hubs must be able to detect an over-current condition, which occurs when the current used by the total of all devices attached to the hub exceeds a preset value. When the port circuits on a hub detect an over-current condition, they limit the current at the port and the hub informs the host of the problem. Windows warns the user when a device exceeds the current limits of its hub port (Figure 19-3).

The specification doesn't name a value to trigger the over-current actions, but it must be less than 5 amperes. To allow for transient currents, the over-current value should be greater than the total of the maximum allowed currents for the devices. In the worst case, seven high-power, bus-powered downstream devices can legally draw up to 3.5 amperes. So a supply for a self-powered hub with up to seven downstream ports would provide much less than 5 amperes at all times unless something goes very wrong.

The specification allows a device to draw larger inrush currents when it attaches to the bus. However, this current is typically provided by the stored

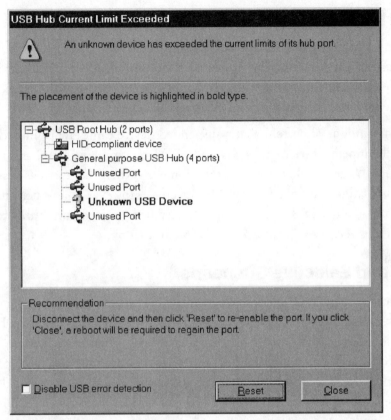

Figure 19-3: When a device exceeds the current limit of its hub's port, Windows warns the user and offers assistance.

energy in a capacitor that is downstream from the over-current protection circuits.

Power Switching

A bus-powered hub must have circuits that can provide and cut off power to its downstream ports. A single switch may control all ports, or the ports may switch individually. The *PC 2001 System Design Guide* requires the ports on bus-powered hubs to be individually power switchable. A self-powered hub must support switching to the Powered Off state, and may also support power switching to its downstream ports.

Saving Power

The USB's Suspend state ensures that a device doesn't consume power from the bus when the host has no reason to communicate with it. A device enters the Suspend state when there is no activity on the bus for a time, or when the host sends a request to suspend to the device's hub.

The amount of current that a suspended device can draw is limited to a few milliamperes if it's high power and supports remote wakeup, and much less if not. A device that needs to function even when the host has ceased communicating may need to be self-powered. However, many peripheral controllers can shut down, consuming very little power, and still detect when there is activity requiring attention on an I/O pin.

Global and Selective Suspends

Most suspends are global, where the host stops communicating with the entire bus. When a PC detects no activity for a period of time, the PC enters a low-power state and stops sending Start-of-Frame packets on the bus. When a full-or high-speed device detects that no Start-of-Frame packet has arrived for 3 milliseconds, it enters the Suspend state. Low-speed devices do the same when they haven't received a low-speed keep-alive signal for 3 milliseconds.

A host may also suspend an individual device by sending a Set_Port_Feature request to the device's hub with the Index field set to the port number and the Value field set to Port_Suspend. (See Chapter 18.) This instructs the hub to stop sending any traffic, including Start-of-Frames or low-speed keep-alives, to the named port. The specification defines this as a selective suspend.

Current Limits for Suspended Devices

A low-power device can draw no more than 500 *micro*amperes from the bus when in the Suspend state. This is very little current, and it includes the current through the device's bus pull-up resistor. As Figure 19-4 shows, the

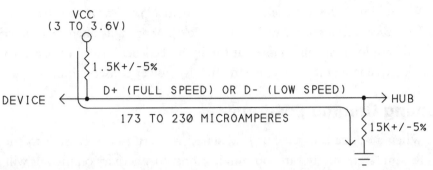

Figure 19-4: The allowed bus current in the Suspend state includes the current through the device's pull-up.

pull-up current flows from the device's pull-up supply, which must be between 3.0 and 3.6V, through the 1.5-kilohm pullup and the hub's 15-kilohm pull-down, to ground. In the worst case, with a pull-up voltage of 3.6V and resistors that are 5% less than their nominal values, the pull-up current is 230 microamperes, leaving just 270 microamperes for everything else.

High-speed devices, which don't use pull-ups in normal communications, must switch to full speed and use a pull-up when entering the Suspend state. So high-speed devices have the same restriction on available current.

A high-power device that supports remote wakeup and whose remote-wakeup feature has been enabled by the host can draw up to 2.5 milliamperes from the bus. This also includes current through the pull-up resistor. Every device connects as low power, so every device should be able to meet the 500-microampere limit if the host suspends the device before configuring it as high power with remote wakeup enabled.

The limits are averages over intervals of up to 1 second, so brief peak currents can be greater. For example, a flashing LED that draws 20 milliamperes for one tenth of each second draws an average of 2 milliamperes per second.

A device should begin to enter the Suspend state after its bus segment has been in the Idle state for 3 milliseconds. The device must be in the Suspend state after its bus segment has been in the Idle state for 10 milliseconds.

When USB 2.0 was released, the document *USB Feature Specification: Interface Power Management* was under development. This document describes a protocol for managing power at the interface level instead of just the device level, to enable more precise and effective power conservation.

Resuming Communications

When a device is in the Suspend state, two actions can cause it to enter the Resume state and restart communications. Any activity on the bus will cause the device to enter the Resume state. And if the device's remote wakeup feature is enabled by the host, the device itself may request a resume at any time.

To resume, the host places the bus in the Resume state (the K state, defined in Chapter 20) for at least 20 milliseconds. The host follows the Resume with a low-speed End-of-Packet signal. (Some hosts incorrectly send the End-of-Packet after just a few hundred microseconds.) The host then resumes sending Start-of-Frame packets and any other communications requested by the device driver.

A device causes a Resume by driving its upstream bus segment in the Resume state for between 1 and 15 milliseconds. The device then places its drivers in a high-impedance state to enable receiving traffic from its upstream hub. A device may send the Resume at any time on a suspended bus, as long as the bus has been suspended for at least 5 milliseconds. The host controller software must allow all devices at least 10 milliseconds to recover from a Resume.

Monitoring the bus to determine whether to enter the Suspend state may require firmware support. The resume signaling is normally handled by the device's SIE and requires no firmware support.

On some early Intel host controllers, a suspended root port didn't respond correctly to a remote wakeup. In addition, using remote wake-up requires work-arounds under Windows 98 Gold, Windows 98 SE, and Windows Me. With these operating systems, the device may wake up properly, but the device's driver isn't made aware of it, so communications can't resume. A white paper from Intel titled *Understanding WDM Power Management* by

Kosta Koeman details the problem and solutions. In short, a device using these operating systems shouldn't place itself in the Suspend state unless the host requests it, and the device driver requires extra code to ensure that the wake-up completes successfully. This isn't a problem under Windows 2000. The white paper is available from the USB Implementers Forum's website.

Chapter 19

20

Signals and Encoding

You can design a USB peripheral without knowing all of the details about how the data is encoded on the bus. But understanding something about these helps in understanding USB's abilities and limits.

This chapter presents the essentials of the USB's encoding and data formats. The specification has the details. Another good source for detailed information on the low-level signaling is the book *Universal Serial Bus Architecture* by Don Anderson and Dave Dzatko.

Bus States

The specification defines several bus states that correspond either to signal voltages on the bus or conditions that these voltages signify. Different segments on a bus may be in different states at the same time. For example, in response to a request from the host, a hub might place one of its downstream ports in the Reset state while its other ports are in the Idle state. Low/full speed and high speed each have different defined bus states, though with many similarities.

Low- and Full-speed Bus States

Low and full speed support the same bus states, though some are defined differently depending on the speed.

Differential 1 and Differential 0

When transferring data, the two states on the bus are Differential 1 and Differential 0. A Differential 1 exists when D+ is a logic high and D- is a logic low. A Differential 0 exists when D+ is a logic low and D- is a logic high. Chapter 21 has details about the voltages that define logic low and high.

The Differential 1s and 0s don't translate directly into 1s and 0s in the bytes being transmitted, but instead indicate either a change in logic level, no change in logic level, or a bit stuff, as explained later in this chapter.

Single-Ended Zero

The Single-Ended-Zero state occurs when both D+ and D- are logic low. The bus uses the SingleEnded-Zero state when entering the End-of-Packet, Disconnect, and Reset states.

Single-Ended One

The complement of the Single-Ended Zero is the Single-Ended One. This occurs when both D+ and D- are logic high. This is an invalid bus state and should never occur.

Data J and K States

In addition to the Differential 1 and 0 states, which are defined by voltages on the lines, USB also defines two Data bus states, J and K. These are defined by whether the bus state is Differential 1 or 0 and whether the cable segment is low or full speed:

Bus State	Data State	
	Low Speed	Full Speed
Differential 0	J	K
Differential 1	K	J

Defining the J and K states in this way makes it possible to use one terminology to describe an event or logic state even though the voltages on low- and full-speed lines differ. For example, a Start-of-Packet state exists when the bus changes from Idle to the K state. On a full-speed segment, this means that D- becomes more positive than D+, while on a low-speed segment, it means that D+ becomes more positive than D-.

Idle

In the Idle state, no drivers are active. On a full-speed line, D+ is more positive, while on a low-speed line, D- is more positive. Shortly after device attachment, the hub determines whether a device is low or full speed by checking the voltages on the Idle bus.

Resume

When a device is in the Suspend state, the Data K state signifies a resume from the state.

Start-of-Packet

The Start-of-Packet bus state exists when the lines change from the Idle state to the K data state. Every transmitted low- or full-speed packet begins with a Start of Packet.

End-of-Packet

The End-of-Packet state exists when a receiver has been in the Single-Ended-Zero state for at least one bit time, followed by a Data J state for at least one bit time. A receiver may optionally define a shorter minimum time for the Data J state. At the driver, the Single-Ended Zero is approximately two bit widths. Every transmitted low- or full-speed packet ends with an End of Packet.

Disconnect State

A downstream port is in the Disconnect state when a Single-Ended Zero has lasted for at least 2.5 microseconds.

Connect

A downstream port enters the Connect state when the bus has been in the Idle state for at least 2.5 microseconds and no more than 2.0 milliseconds.

Reset State

When a Single-Ended Zero has lasted for 10 milliseconds, the device must be in the Reset state. A device may enter the Reset state after the Single-Ended Zero has lasted for as little as 2.5 microseconds. A full-speed device that is capable of high-speed communications performs the high-speed handshake during the Reset state.

When a device exits the Reset state, it must be operating at its correct speed and must respond to communications directed to the default address (00h).

High-speed Bus States

Many of the high-speed bus states are similar to those for low and full speed. A few are unique to high speed, and some low- and full-speed bus states have no equivalent at high speed.

High-speed Differential 1 and Differential 0

The two bus states that exist when transferring high-speed data are High-speed Differential 1 and High-speed Differential 0. As with low and full speeds, a High-speed Differential 1 exists when D+ is a logic high and D- is a logic low, and a High-speed Differential 0 exists when D+ is a logic low and D- is a logic high. The voltage requirements differ at high speed, however, and high speed has additional requirements for AC differential levels.

High-speed Data J and K States

The definitions for High-speed Data J and K states are identical to those for full-speed J and K:

Bus State	Data State, High Speed
Differential 0	K
Differential 1	J

Chirp J and Chirp K

The Chirp J and Chirp K bus states are present only during the high-speed detection handshake. This occurs when a 2.0 hub has placed a downstream bus segment in the Reset state. Chirp J and K are defined as DC differential voltages. In a Chirp J, D+ is more positive, and in a Chirp K, D- is more positive.

A high-speed device must use full speed when it first attaches to the bus. The high-speed detection handshake enables a high-speed device to tell a 2.0 hub that it supports high speed and then to transition to high-speed communications.

As Chapter 5 explained, shortly after detecting device attachment, a device's hub places a device's port and bus segment in the Reset state. When a high-speed-capable device detects the Reset, it sends a Chirp K to the hub for 1 to 7 milliseconds. A 2.0 hub that is communicating upstream at high speed detects the Chirp K and in response, sends an alternating sequence of Chirp Ks and Js. The sequence continues until shortly before the Reset state ends. At the end of Reset, the hub places the port in the High-speed Enabled state.

On detecting the Chirp K and J sequence, the device disconnects its full-speed pull-up, enables its high-speed terminations, and enters the high-speed Default state.

A 1.x hub ignores the device's Chirp K. When the device doesn't see the answering sequence, it knows that it must remain at full speed.

High-speed Squelch

The High-speed Squelch state indicates an invalid signal. High-speed receivers must include circuits that detect the Squelch state, indicated by a differential bus voltage of 100 millivolts or less.

High-speed Idle

In the High-speed Idle state, no high-speed drivers are active and the low/full-speed drivers assert Single-Ended Zeroes. Both D+ and D- are between -10 and +10 millivolts.

Start of High-speed Packet

The Start-of-High-speed-Packet (HSSOP) state exists when a segment changes from the High-speed Idle state to the High-speed Data K or J state. Every high-speed packet begins with a Start of High-speed Packet.

End of High-speed Packet

The End-of-High-speed-Packet (HSEOP) bus state exists when the bus changes from the High-speed Data K or J state to the High-speed Idle state. Every high-speed packet ends with an End of High-speed Packet.

High-speed Disconnect

Removing a high-speed device from the bus also removes the high-speed line terminations at the device. This causes the differential voltage at the hub to double. A differential voltage of 625 millivolts or more indicates the High-speed Disconnect state. A 2.0 hub contains circuits that detect this voltage.

Data Encoding

All data on the bus is encoded. The encoding format, called *Non-Return to Zero Inverted (NRZI) with bit stuffing,* ensures that the receiver remains synchronized with the transmitter without the overhead of sending a separate clock signal or Start and Stop bits with each byte.

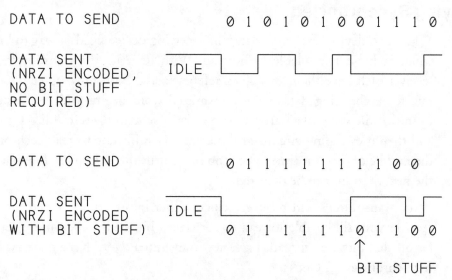

Figure 20-1: In NRZI encoding, a 0 causes a change and a 1 causes no change. Bit stuffing adds a 0 after six consecutive 1s.

If you use an oscilloscope or logic analyzer to view USB data on the bus, you'll find that unlike other interfaces, reading the bits isn't as easy as matching voltage levels to logic levels.

Instead of defining logic 0s and 1s as voltages, USB defines logic 0 as a voltage change, and logic 1 as a voltage that remains the same. Figure 20-1 shows an example. Each logic 0 results in a change from the previous state. Each logic 1 results in no change in the voltages. The bits transmit least-significant-bit (LSB) first.

Fortunately, the USB hardware does all of the encoding and decoding automatically, so device developers and programmers don't have to worry about it. The encoded data makes it difficult to interpret the data on an oscilloscope or logic analyzer, but the solution is to use a protocol analyzer that decodes the data for you.

Staying Synchronized

When two devices exchange data, the receiving device needs a way to know when each bit is available to be read. With RS-232, the transmitter and receiver each have their own clock reference, and both must agree on a bit rate for exchanging data. Each transmitted word begins with a transition from the Idle state to a Start bit. The receiver synchronizes to this transition and then uses timing circuits and the agreed-on bit rate to read each bit in the middle of each bit time. The Stop bit returns the link to the Idle state so the next Start bit can be detected.

If the transmitter's and receiver's clocks differ by up to a few percent, the receiver will still be able to read ten or eleven bits before the timing gets so far off that bits are misread. Each new transmitted word has a Start bit that resynchronizes the clocks.

But adding a Start and Stop bit to each data byte adds 25 percent overhead. A 9600-bps link with 8 data bits and one Start and Stop bit transmits only 7680 data bits (960 bytes) per second.

Another approach used by SPI, I²C, and Microwire interfaces is to send a clock signal along with the data. The protocol defines when to read the bits, either on detecting a rising or falling edge or a high or low logic level. Sending a clock requires an extra signal line, however, and a noise glitch on the clock line can cause misread data.

NRZI requires no Start and Stop bits or clock line. Instead, USB uses two other techniques to remain synchronized: bit stuffing and SYNC fields. Each adds some overhead to each transaction, but the amount is minimal with larger packets.

Bit Stuffing

Bit stuffing is required because the receiver synchronizes on transitions. If the data is all 0s, there are plenty of transitions. But if the data contains a long string of 1s, the lack of transitions could cause the receiver to get out of sync.

If data has six consecutive 1s, the transmitter stuffs, or inserts, a 0 (represented by a transition) after the sixth 1. This ensures at least one transition for every seven bit widths. The receiver detects and discards any bit that follows six consecutive 1s.

Considering just the data bytes, there are only three values with six consecutive 1s:

    00111111
    01111110
    11111100

Bit stuffing can increase the number of transmitted bits by up to 17 percent. In practice the average is much less. The bit-stuffing overhead for random data is just 0.8 percent, or one stuff bit per 125 data bits.

SYNC Field

Bit stuffing alone isn't enough to ensure that the transmitting and receiving clocks in a transfer are synchronized. Because devices and the host don't share a clock, the receiving device has no way of knowing exactly when a transmitting device will send a transition that marks the beginning of a new packet. A single transition isn't enough to ensure that the receiver will remain synchronized for the duration of a packet.

To keep things synchronized, each packet begins with a SYNC field to enable the receiving device to align, or synchronize, its clock to the transmitted data. For low and full speeds, the SYNC pattern is eight bits: KJKJKJKK. The transition from the Idle to the first K serves as a sort of Start bit that indicates the arrival of a new packet. There's one SYNC field per packet, rather than a Start bit for each byte.

For high speed, the SYNC pattern is 32 bits: fifteen KJ repetitions, followed by KK. A high-speed hub repeating a packet can drop up to four bits from the beginning of the sync field, so a SYNC field repeated by the fifth external hub series can be as short as 12 bits.

The alternating Ks and Js provide the transitions for synchronizing, and the final two Ks mark the end of the field. By the end of the SYNC pattern, the receiving device can determine precisely when each of the remaining bits in the packet will arrive. The price to pay for synchronizing is the addition of 8 to 32 bit times to each packet. This means that large packets are much more efficient than smaller ones.

End of Packet

An End-of-Packet signal returns the bus to the Idle state in preparation for the next SYNC field. The End-of-Packet signal is different for low/full and high speed.

The low- or full-speed End of Packet is a Single-Ended-Zero that lasts for two bit widths.

At high speed, it's more complicated. High-speed receivers treat any bit-stuff error as an End of Packet, so the End of High-speed Packet must cause a bit-stuff error.

For all high-speed packets except Start-of-Frame packets, the End of High-speed Packet is an encoded byte of 01111111, without bit stuffing. If the preceding bit was a J, the End of High-speed Packet is KKKKKKKK. The initial 0 causes the first bit to be a change of state from J to K, and the following 1s mean that the rest of the bits don't change. If the preceding bit was a K, the End of High-speed Packet is JJJJJJJJ. The initial 0 causes the first bit to be a change of state from K to J, and the following 1s mean that the rest of the bits don't change. In either case, a sequence of seven bits without a transition causes a bit stuff error.

In high-speed Start-of-Frame packets, the End of High-speed Packet is 40 bits. This allows a hub time to detect the doubled differential voltage that indicates that a device has been removed from the bus. The encoded byte begins with a zero, followed by 39 ones, which results in an End of High-speed Packet consisting of 40 Js or 40 Ks. As with low and full speeds, this results in a bit-stuff error that the receiver treats as an End of Packet.

Timing Accuracy

A tradeoff of speed is more stringent timing requirements. USB's high speed has the most critical timing, followed by full and low speeds.

Devices typically derive their timing from a crystal. Many factors can affect a crystal's frequency, including initial accuracy, capacitive loading, aging of the crystal, supply voltage, and temperature. Crystal accuracy is often specified as parts per million (ppm), which is the maximum number of cycles the crystal may vary in the time required for 1 million cycles at the rated frequency.

High speed's bit rate of 480 Megabits per second can vary no more than 0.05 percent, or 500 ppm. Full speed's bit rate of 12 Megabits per second can vary no more than 0.25 percent, or 2500 ppm. Low speed's bit rate can vary up to 1.5%, or 15,000 ppm. Low-speed devices can use inexpensive ceramic resonators rather than quartz crystals. Low speed's greater tolerance means that low-speed devices can use less expensive components and cables, though the need for slower edge rates actually increases the manufacturing cost of low-speed chips.

The data rate at the host or a 2.0 hub must be within 0.05%, or 500 ppm, of the specified rate at all speeds. The frame intervals must be accurate as well, at 1 millisecond ±500 nanoseconds per frame or 125.0 ±62.5 microseconds per microframe. To maintain this accuracy, hubs must be able to adjust their frame intervals to match the host's. Each hub has its own timing source and synchronizes its transmissions to the host's Start-of-(micro)Frame signals.

The specification also defines limits for data jitter, or small variations in the timing of the individual bit transitions. The limits allow small differences in the rise and fall times of the drivers as well as clock jitter and other random noise.

Packet Format

As Chapter 3 explained, all USB data travels in packets, which are blocks of information with a defined format. The packets in turn contain fields, with each field type holding a particular type of information. The field types are SYNC, PID, address, endpoint, frame number, data, and CRC. Table 20-1 lists the fields and their purposes.

Table 20-1: All USB traffic is in packets. Packets are made up of fields. The field type determines its contents.

Name	SIze (bits)	Packet Types	Purpose
SYNC	8	all	Start-of-packet and synchronization
PID	8	all	Identify the packet type
Address	7	IN, OUT, Setup	Identify the function address
Endpoint	4	IN, OUT, Setup	Identify the endpoint
Frame Number	11	SOF	Identify the frame
Data	0 to 8192 (1024 bytes) for 2.0 hardware; 0 to 8184 (1023 bytes) for 1.x hardware	Data0, Data1	Data
CRC	5 or 16	IN, OUT, Setup, Data0, Data1	Detect errors

SYNC Field

Each packet begins with an 8-bit SYNC field, as described earlier. The SYNC Field serves as the Start-of-Packet delimiter. This field may transmit only on an Idle bus.

Packet Identifier Field

The packet identifier field (PID) is 8 bits. Bits 0 through 3 identify the type of packet and bits 4 through 7 are the one's complement of these bits, for use in error checking.

There are 16 defined PID codes for token, data, handshake and special packets. Chapter 3 introduced these codes. The lower two bits identify the PID type, and the upper two bits identify the specific PID.

Address Field

The address field is seven bits that identify the function that the host is communicating with. The function is a device (which may be a hub), or a specific function in a compound device.

Endpoint Field

The endpoint field is four bits that identify an endpoint number within a function. A low-speed function can have no more than 3 endpoint numbers. A full- or high-speed function can have up to 16 numbers.

Frame Number Field

The frame-number field is eleven bits that identify the specific frame. The host sends this field in the Start-of-Frame packet that begins each frame or microframe. The number rolls over to 0 at 7FFh. A full-speed host maintains an 11-bit counter that increments once per frame. A high-speed host maintains a 14-bit counter that increments once per microframe. Only bits 3-13 of the microframe counter transmit in the frame number field, so the frame number increments once per frame, with eight microframes in sequence having the same frame number.

Data Field

The data field may range from 0 to 1024 bytes, depending on the transfer type, the amount of data in the transaction, and the USB version. 1.x devices support data fields of up to 1023 bytes.

CRC Fields

The CRC field is 5 bits for address and endpoint fields and 16 bits for data fields. The bits are used in error-checking. The transmitting hardware inserts the CRC bits and the receiving hardware does the required calculations; there's no need for program code to do it.

Inter-packet Delay

USB carries data from multiple sources, in both directions, on one pair of wires. Data can travel in just one direction at a time. To ensure that the previous transmitting device has had time to switch off its driver, the bus requires a brief delay between the end of one packet and the beginning of the next packet in a transaction. This delay time is limited, however, and devices must be able to switch directions quickly.

The specification defines the delays differently for low/full and high speed. The delays are handled by the hardware and require no support in code.

Test Modes

For use in compliance testing, the 2.0 specification adds five new test modes that all host controllers, hubs, and high-speed-capable devices must support.

Entering and Exiting Test Modes

An upstream-facing port enters a test mode in response to a Set_Feature request with TEST_MODE in the wValue field. A downstream-facing port enters a test mode in response to the hub-class request Set_Port_Feature with PORT_TEST in the wValue field. In both cases, the wIndex field contains the port number and the test number. All downstream ports on a hub with a port to be tested must be in the suspended, disabled, or disconnected state.

An upstream-facing port exits the test mode when the device powers down and back up. A downstream-facing port exits the test mode when the hub is reset.

The Modes

These are the five test modes:

Test_SEO_NAK
Value. 01h.

Action. The transceiver enters and remains in high-speed receive mode. Upstream-facing ports respond to IN token packets with NAK.

Purpose. Test output impedance, low-level output voltage, and loading characteristics. Test device squelch-level circuits. Provide a stimulus-response test for basic functional testing.

Test_J

Value. 02h.

Action. The transceiver enters and remains in the High-speed Data J state.

Purpose. Test the high output drive level on D+.

Test_K

Value. 03h.

Action. The transceiver enters and remains in the High-speed Data K state.

Purpose. Test the high output drive level on D-.

Test_Packet

Value. 04h.

Action. Repetitively transmit the test packet defined by the specification.

Purpose. Test rise and fall times, eye pattern, jitter, and other dynamic waveform specifications.

Test_Force_Enable

Value. 05h.

Action. Enable downstream-facing hub ports in high-speed mode. Packets arriving at the upstream-facing port are repeated at the port being tested. The disconnect-detect bit can be polled while varying the loading on the port.

Purpose. Measure the disconnect-detection threshold.

Chapter 20

Other Values

Test-mode values 06h through 3Fh are reserved for future standard tests. Value C0h through FFh are available for vendor-defined tests. All other values are reserved.

21

The Electrical Interface

All of the protocols and program code in the world are no use if the signals don't make it down the cable in good shape. The electrical interface plays an important part in making USB a reliable way to transfer information.

From a practical point of view, if you're using compliant cables and components, you don't need to know much about the electrical interface. You can just use the products you have and trust that the hardware designers have done their job. But if you're designing USB transceivers or cables, printed-circuit boards with USB interfaces, or a protocol analyzer that must unobtrusively monitor the bus, you do need to understand the electrical interface and how it applies to your project.

This chapter presents the essentials about the electrical interface of the USB's drivers and receivers and details about the cables that carry the signals.

Transceivers and Signals

The electrical properties of the signals carried by a USB cable vary depending on the speed of the cable segment. Low-, full-, and high-speed signaling each have a different edge rate, which is a measure of the rise and fall times or amount of time required for an output to switch. The transceivers and supporting circuits that produce and detect the bus signals also vary depending on speed.

At any speed, the components that connect to a USB cable must be able to withstand the shorting of any line to any other line or the cable shield without component damage.

Cable Segments

A cable *segment* is a single physical cable that connects a device (which may be a hub) to an upstream hub (which may be the root hub at the host). The speed, edge rate, and polarity of the data in a segment depend on whether the segment is low, full, or high speed. Figure 21-1 illustrates.

Low-speed segments exist only between low-speed devices and their hubs. A low-speed segment carries only low-speed data, using low-speed's edge rate and inverted polarity compared to full speed.

A full-speed segment exists when the downstream device is full speed. The upstream device may be a 1.x or 2.0 hub. When the downstream device is a hub, the segment may also carry data to and from low-speed devices that are downstream from that hub. When this is the case, the low-speed data on the full-speed segment uses low-speed's bit rate but full speed's polarity and edge rate. The hub that connects to the low-speed device converts between low and full speed's polarity and edge rates. Full-speed segments never carry high-speed data. If a high-speed-capable device connects to a 1.x hub, communications are at full speed. High-speed devices must at least respond to enumeration requests at full speed.

High-speed segments exist only where the upstream device is a 2.0 hub and the downstream device is high speed. When the downstream device is a hub, the segment may also carry data to and from low- and full-speed devices that

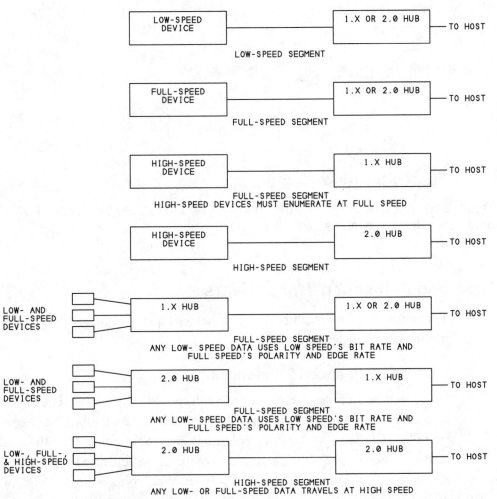

Figure 21-1: The speed of data in a segment depends on the capabilities of the device and its upstream hub.

are downstream from that hub. The data in the high-speed segment travels at high speed, and the transaction translator in a downstream hub converts between low or full speed and high speed as needed.

On attachment, all devices must communicate at low or full speed. When possible, a high-speed-capable device transitions from full to high speed during the high-speed handshake.

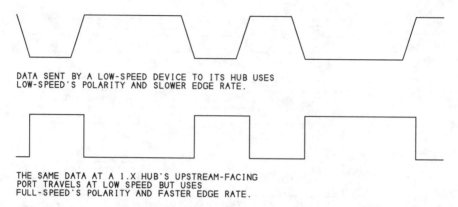

DATA SENT BY A LOW-SPEED DEVICE TO ITS HUB USES
LOW-SPEED'S POLARITY AND SLOWER EDGE RATE.

THE SAME DATA AT A 1.X HUB'S UPSTREAM-FACING
PORT TRAVELS AT LOW SPEED BUT USES
FULL-SPEED'S POLARITY AND FASTER EDGE RATE.

Figure 21-2: A 1.x hub converts between low- and full-speed's polarities and edge rates. (Not drawn to scale)

Low- and Full-speed Transceivers

The transceiver for low and full speeds has a simpler design compared to the transceiver for high speed.

Low- and Full-speed Differences

Low-speed data differs electrically from full speed in three ways. The bit rate is slower, at 1.5 Megabits per second compared to 12 Megabits per second for full speed. Low speed traffic's polarity is inverted compared to full speed. And low speed has a slower edge rate compared to full speed. Figure 21-2 illustrates. The slower edge rate reduces reflected voltages on the line and makes it possible to use cables that have less shielding and are thus cheaper to make and physically more flexible.

The transceiver's hardware doesn't care about the signal polarity. It just transmits and receives whatever logic levels are at its inputs. A transceiver that is fast enough for full speed can also support low speed, but a driver that supports both speeds must be able to switch between the two edge rates.

The Circuits

Figure 21-3 shows the circuits inside a Philips' PDIUSB11 USB transceiver for low- and full-speed communications. The chip converts between low-

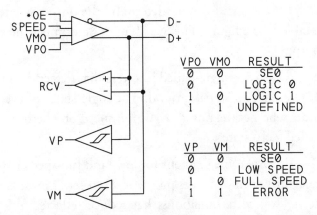

VPO	VMO	RESULT
0	0	SE0
0	1	LOGIC 0
1	0	LOGIC 1
1	1	UNDEFINED

VP	VM	RESULT
0	0	SE0
0	1	LOW SPEED
1	0	FULL SPEED
1	1	ERROR

Figure 21-3: Philips' PDIUSBP11 transceiver includes a differential driver and receiver as well as two single-ended receivers for detecting bus speed and Single-Ended Zeros.

and full-speed voltages on the bus and TTL logic levels. Any low- or full-speed USB controller chip contains similar circuits.

The transceiver contains the differential driver and receiver required to send and receive data on the bus. When transmitting data, the driver has two outputs that are 180 degrees out of phase. When one output is high, the other is low. The receiver detects the voltage difference between the lines. This type of interface called a balanced line.

Other interfaces that use balanced lines, such as RS-485, define logic levels strictly as the difference between the voltages on the two lines, with no reference to a signal ground (though the interface does require a common ground for the small amount of return current due to component mismatches). An interface whose inputs are defined as the difference between two inputs is a differential interface. USB differs because it specifies absolute voltages in addition to the required voltage difference.

The differential receiver's output can interface directly to a TTL-compatible input.

The differential driver has four TTL-compatible inputs. When *OE is a logic high, the driver is disabled and the transceiver can receive data. When *OE is a logic low, the driver is enabled. When the driver is enabled, the

VPO and VMO inputs together determine the output's state, as shown by the truth table in the figure. The Speed input determines the edge rate of the driver's output.

The chip also has two single-ended receivers that detect the D+ and D- voltages with reference to signal ground. The logic states of the receivers' outputs indicate whether the bus is low or full speed or whether the bus is in the Single-Ended-Zero state.

Figure 21-4 shows a cable segment for low- and full-speed communications. The drivers' output impedances plus a 36-ohm series resistor at each driver's output act as source terminations that reduce reflected voltages when the outputs switch. The series resistors may be on or off chip. The 1.5-kilohm pull-up resistor on D+ or D- at the downstream device enables the upstream hub to detect the device's speed. The upstream hub has 15-kilohm pull-down resistors on D+ and D-.

High-speed Transceivers

A high-speed device must support control requests at full speed, so it must contain transceivers to support both full and high speeds and the logic to switch between them. A high-speed-capable device's upstream transceivers aren't allowed to support low speed. In a 2.0 hub, the downstream transceivers at ports with user-accessible connectors must support all three speeds.

Why 480 Megabits per Second?

High speed's rate of 480 Megabits per second was chosen for several reasons. The frequency is slow enough to allow using existing cables and connectors. Components can use CMOS processes and don't require the advanced compensation used in high-speed digital signal processors. Tests of high-speed drivers showed 20 to 30 percent jitter at 480 Megabits per second. Because receivers can be designed to tolerate 40 percent jitter, this speed leaves a good margin of error. And 480 is an even multiple of 12, so the same crystals can be used for full and high speed.

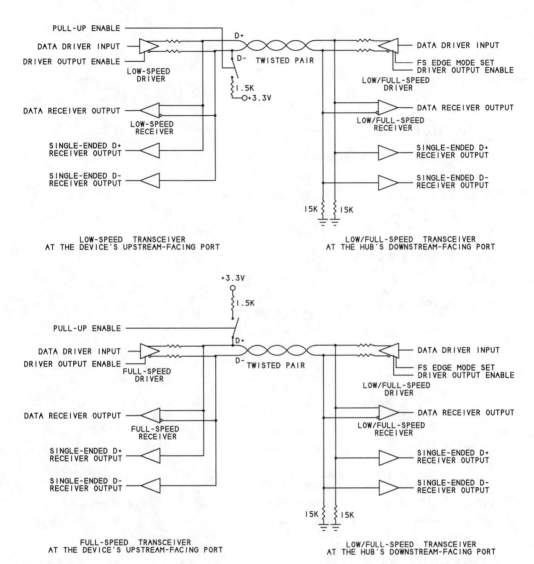

Figure 21-4: The downstream-facing ports on a 1.x hub must support both low and full speeds (except for ports with embedded or permanently attached devices). A device's upstream-facing port normally supports just one speed.

The use of separate drivers for high speed makes it easy to add high speed to the existing interface. Current-mode drivers were chosen because they're fast.

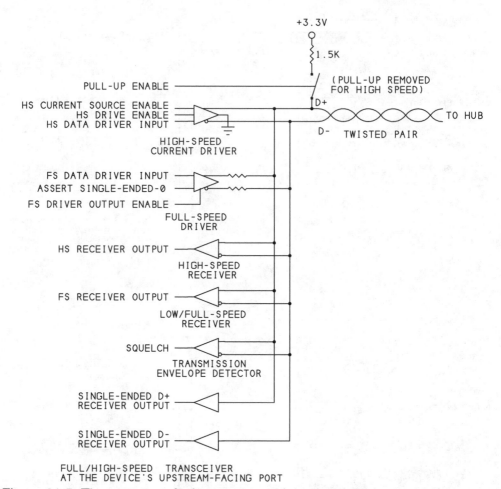

Figure 21-5: The upstream-facing port on a high-speed device must also support full speed communications.

The Circuits

Figure 21-5 shows the upstream-facing transceiver circuits in a high-speed-capable device, and   Figure 21-6 shows the same for the down-stream-facing circuits in a 2.0 hub.

High speed requires its own drivers, so a high-speed device must contain two sets of drivers. For receiving, a transceiver may use a single receiver to handle all supported speeds, or it may have separate receivers for high speed.

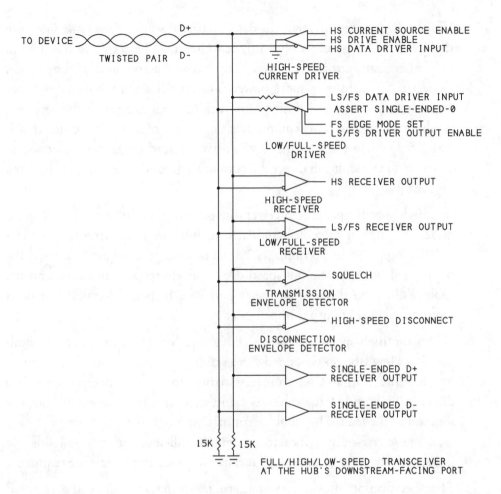

Figure 21-6: The downstream-facing ports on 2.0 hubs must support all three speeds (except for ports with embedded or permanently attached devices).

When a high-speed driver sends data, a current source drives one line with the other line at ground. The current source may be active all the time or only when transmitting. A current source that is active all the time is easier to design but consumes more power. The specification requires devices to meet the amplitude and timing requirements beginning with the very first symbol in a packet. This complicates the design of a current source that is active only when transmitting. If the driver instead keeps its current source active all the time, it can direct the current to ground when not transmitting on the bus.

In a high-speed-capable transceiver, the output impedance of the full-speed drivers has tighter tolerance compared to full-speed only drivers (45 ohms ±10%, compared to 36 ohms ±22%). The change is required because the high-speed bus uses the full-speed drivers as electrical terminations on the cable. Full-speed drivers that aren't part of a high-speed transceiver don't require a change in output impedance.

When the high-speed drivers are active, the full-speed drivers bring both data lines low (the Single-ended-Zero state). Each driver and its series resistor then function as a 45-ohm termination to ground. Because there is a driver at each end of the cable segment, there is a termination at both the source and the load. This double termination quiets the line more effectively than the source-only series terminations in full-speed segments. Using the full-speed drivers as terminations means no extra components are required.

The specification provides eye-pattern templates that show the required high-speed transmitter outputs and receiver sensitivity. High-speed receivers must also meet new specifications that require the use of a differential time-domain reflectometer (TDR) to measure impedance characteristics.

All high-speed receivers must include a differential envelope detector to detect the Squelch (invalid signal) state, indicated by a differential bus voltage of 100 millivolts or less. The downstream ports on all 2.0 hubs must also include a high-speed disconnect detector that detects when a device has been removed from the bus.

Other new responsibilities for high-speed-capable devices include managing the switch from full to high speed, and handling new protocols for entering and exiting the Suspend and Reset states.

Switching Speeds

In a low- or full-speed device, a 1.5-kilohm pull-up on one of the signal lines indicates device speed. When a low- or full-speed device is attached or removed from the bus, the voltage change due to the pull-up informs the hub of the change. High-speed devices always attach at full speed, so the hub detects attachment in the same way.

As Chapter 20 explained, the switch to high speed occurs after the device has been detected, during the Reset sent by the hub. A high-speed-capable device must support the high-speed handshake that informs the hub that the device is capable of high speed, and switches to high speed when possible. When switching to high speed, the device removes its pull-up from the bus.

Detecting Removal of a High-speed Device

A 2.0 hub must also detect the removal of a high-speed device. Because at high speed the device has no pull-up, the hub has to use a different method to detect device removal. When a device is removed from the bus, its differential terminations are removed. This causes the differential voltage at the hub's port to double. When the hub detects the doubled voltage, it knows the device has been removed.

The hub detects the voltage by measuring the differential bus voltage during the extended End of High-speed Packet (HSEOP) in each high-speed Start-of-Frame Packet (HSSOP). A differential voltage of at least 625 millivolts indicates a disconnect.

Suspending and Resuming at High Speed

As Chapter 19 explained, devices must enter the low-power Suspend state when the bus has been in the Idle state for at least 3 and no more than 10 milliseconds. When the bus has been idle for 3 milliseconds, a high-speed device switches to full speed. The device then checks the state of the full-speed bus to determine whether the host is requesting a Suspend or Reset. If the bus state is Single-Ended Zero, the host is requesting a Reset, so the device prepares for the high-speed-detect handshake. If the bus state is Idle, the device enters the Suspend state. The device must return to high speed on exiting the Suspend state.

Signal Voltages

Chapter 20 introduced USB's bus states. The voltages that define the states vary depending on the speed of the cable segment. In any case, the difference between the minimum transmitted and received voltages means that a signal can have some noise or attenuation and the receiver will still see the correct logic level.

Low and Full Speeds

Table 21-1 shows the driver output voltages for low/full and high speeds. At low and full speeds, a Differential 1 exists at the driver when the D+ output is at least 2.8V and the D- output is no greater than 0.3V, referenced to the driver's signal ground. A differential 0 exists at the driver when D- is at least 2.8V and D+ is no greater than 0.3V, referenced to the driver's signal ground.

At a low- or full-speed receiver, a differential 1 exists when D+ is at least 2V, referenced to the receiver's signal ground, and the difference between D+ and D- is greater than 200 millivolts. A differential 0 exists when D- is at least 2V, referenced to the receiver's signal ground, and the difference between D- and D+ is greater than 200 millivolts. However, a receiver may optionally have less stringent definitions that require only a differential voltage greater than 200 millivolts, ignoring the requirement for one line to be at least 2V.

High Speed

At high speed, a differential 1 exists at the driver when the D+ output is at least 0.36V and the D- output is no greater than 0.01V, referenced to the

Table 21-1: High speed requires different drivers and has different output specifications, compared to low and full speed. The receiver specifications differ as well.

Parameter	Low/Full Speed (V)	High Speed (V)
Vout low minimum	0	-0.010
Vout low maximum	0.3	0.010
Vout high minimum	2.8	0.360V
Vout high maximum	3.6	0.440V
Vin low maximum	0.8	Limits are defined by the eye-pattern templates in the specification
Vin high minimum	2.0	

driver's signal ground. A differential 0 exists at the driver when D- is at least 0.36V and D+ is no greater than 0.01V, referenced to the driver's signal ground.

At a high-speed receiver, the input must meet the requirements shown in the eye-pattern templates in the specification. The eye patterns specify maximum and minimum voltages, rise and fall times, maximum jitter in a transmitted signal, and the maximum jitter a receiver must tolerate. The specification has details about how to make the measurements.

Cables

The USB specification includes detailed requirements for cables. The requirements help to ensure that any compliant cable will be able to carry the bus's fast digital signals without resulting in errors due to noise in the cable or large amounts of noise radiating from the cable.

Conductors

USB cables have four conductors: VBUS, GND, D+ and D-.

VBUS is the +5V supply.

GND is the ground reference for VBUS as well as for D+ and D-.

D+ and D- are the differential signal pair.

Chapter 19 described the voltage and current limits for VBUS.

The USB icon embossed on the plug connector identifies a USB cable (Figure 21-7). (Don't confuse the icon with the USB Logo described in Chapter 17.) PCs and hubs may also use the icon to identify their USB connectors. A "+" added to the icon indicates USB 2.0 performance at a downstream-facing port.

Cables to be used in full- or high-speed segments have different requirements from those for low-speed segments. Table 21-2 compares the two cable types..

The 2.0 specification tightened the requirements for low-speed cables. A 1.1-compliant low-speed cable required no shielding at all. A 2.0-compliant low-speed cable must have the same inner shield and drain wire required for full speed. The specification also recommends, but doesn't require, a braided outer shield and a twisted pair for data, as on full- and high-speed cables.

Both full-and high-speed cables use the same cables. When the 2.0 specification was under development, an Engineering Change Notice (ECN) to the 1.x specification added new requirements to ensure that full-speed cables would also work at high speed. The 2.0 specification also uses these require-

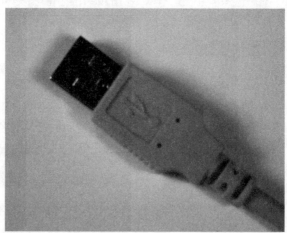

Figure 21-7: The USB icon identifies a USB cable and also indicates the top surface of the plug when attached.

Table 21-2: The requirements for cables and related components differ for full/high speed and low speed.

Specification	Low Speed	Full/High Speed
Maximum length (meters)	3	5
Inner shield and drain wire required?	yes (new in USB 2.0)	yes
Braided outer shield required?	no, but recommended	yes
Twisted pair required?	no, but recommended	yes
Common-mode impedance (ohms)	not specified	30 ±30%
Differential Characteristic impedance (ohms)	not specified	90
Cable skew (picoseconds)	< 100	
Wire gauge (AWG#)	28 or lower	
DC resistance, plug shell to plug shell (ohms)	0.6	
Cable delay	18 nanosecs. (one way)	5.2 nanoseconds/meter
Pull-up location at the device	D-	D+
Detachable cable OK?	no	yes
Captive cable OK?	yes	

ments. They describe what was typically found in compliant full-speed cables, so most providers with compliant cables had no changes to make.

In a full/high-speed cable, the signal wires must have a differential characteristic impedance of 90 ohms. This value is a measure of the input impedance of an infinite, open line and determines the initial current on the lines when the outputs switch. The characteristic impedance for a low-speed cable isn't defined because the slower edge rates mean that the initial current doesn't affect the logic states seen by the receiver.

The specification lists requirements for the cable's conductors, shielding, and insulation. These are the major requirements for full/high-speed cables:

Data wires: twisted pair, #28 AWG.
Power and ground: non-twisted, #20 to #28 AWG.
Drain wire: stranded, tinned copper wire, #28 AWG
Inner shield: aluminum metallized polyester
Outer shield: braided, tinned copper

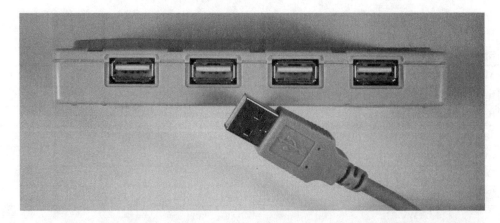

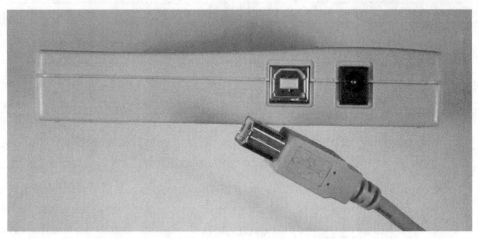

Figure 21-8: The series-A plug (top) is on the upstream end of the cable and mates with a series-A receptacle on a hub or the host. The series-B plug (bottom) is on the downstream end of the cable and mates with a series-B receptacle on the device.

The specification also lists requirements for the cable's durability and performance.

A low-speed device can use a full-speed cable if the cable meets all of the low-speed cable requirements. These include not using the standard A or B connector at the device end and a maximum length of 3 meters.

Figure 21-9: The mini-B connector was added as an option in response to comments that the original series-B connector was too bulky for some devices. (photo courtesy of Tyco Electronics)

Connectors

The 2.0 specification describes two connector types: series A for the upstream end of the cable and series B for the downstream end (Figure 21-8). The series-B connectors were bulky for some devices, so an Engineering Change Notice to the 2.0 specification added an option for new mini-B connectors (Figure 21-9). A mini-B receptacle is less than half the height of a series-B receptacle. You can use the mini-B connectors anywhere you can use the series-B connectors. Every cable must have a series-A connector, but not all cables require a series-B or mini-B connector.

A typical hub will have a series-B receptacle at its upstream port. The receptacle accepts the series-B plug on a cable that connects to the root hub or another upstream hub. A hub with external, downstream ports will also have one or more series-A receptacles. These accept the series-A plugs on cables that connect to devices or other downstream hubs.

The connectors are keyed so you can't plug them in upsidedown. The signal connections are recessed slightly to ensure that the power lines connect first when a cable is attached. The receptacle should be mounted so the icon on the plug is visible when attached.

All of the connectors have connections for the bus's two signal wires, the VBUS supply, and ground. The mini-B connector has an additional ID pin. Devices that support the USB On-The-Go specification will use the ID pin to identify a device's default mode (host or function). The specification gives the following pin and color assignments for the cable and connectors:

Series A/B pin	Mini-B pin	Conductor	Cable Wire
1	1	VBUS (+5V)	red
2	2	D-	white
3	3	D+	green
4	5	GND	black
-	4	ID	not connected
shell		shield	drain wire

Detachable and Captive Cables

The specification defines cables as being either detachable or captive. From the names, you might think that a detachable cable is one you can remove, while a captive cable is permanently attached to its downstream device. But in fact, a captive cable can be removable as long as its downstream connector is *not* the standard series-B or series-A type.

A detachable cable must be full/high speed, with a series-A plug for the upstream connection and a series-B or mini-B plug for the downstream connection. The generic USB cables offered by various vendors are of this type. A captive cable may be low- or full/high-speed. The upstream end has a series-A plug. For the downstream connection, the cable can be permanently attached, or it can be removable with a non-standard connector type. The non-standard connector doesn't have to be hot pluggable, but the series-A connector must be hot pluggable. Requiring low-speed cables to be captive eliminates the possibility of using a low-speed cable in a full- or high-speed segment.

Cable Length

Version 1.0 of the USB specification gave maximum lengths for cable segments. A full-speed segment could be up to 5 meters and a low-speed segment could be up to 3 meters. Version 1.1 dropped the length limits in favor of a discussion of characteristics that limit a cable's ability to meet the interface's timing and voltage requirements. On full- and high-speed cables, the limits are due to signal attenuation, cable propagation delay (the amount of time it takes for a signal to travel from driver to receiver), and the voltage drops on the VBUS and GND wires. On low-speed cables, the length is limited by the rise and fall times of the signals, the capacitive load presented by the segment, and the voltage drops on the VBUS and GND wires.

The original limits of 3 and 5 meters are still good general guidelines. A 2.0-compliant 5-meter full-speed cable will also work at high speed. Cables of these lengths that meet the specifications are readily available. Chapter 19 explained how the length limits translate to a maximum distance of 30 meters between a host and its peripheral, assuming the use of five hubs and six 5-meter cable segments.

The USB specification prohibits extension cables, which would extend the length of a segment by adding a second cable in series. An extension cable for the upstream side of a cable would have a series A plug on one end and a series-A receptacle on the other, while an extension cable for the downstream side would have a series-B plug and receptacle.

Prohibiting extension cables eliminates the temptation to stretch a segment beyond the interface's physical limits. Extension cables are available, but just because you can buy one doesn't mean that it's a good idea or that it will work. Instead, buy a single cable of the length you need, and add hubs as necessary.

There is an exception: an *active* extension cable contains a hub, a downstream port, and a cable. This will work fine, because it contains the required hub.

An option for longer distances is to use a standard USB cable that connects to a device that translates between USB and RS-485 or another interface designed for use over long distances. The remote device would then need to support the long-distance interface, rather than USB.

Ensuring Signal Quality

The specifications for drivers, receivers, and cable design ensure that virtually all data transfers occur without errors. Requirements that help to ensure signal quality include the use of balanced lines and shielded cables, twisted pairs required for full/high-speed cables, and slower edge rates required for low-speed drivers.

Sources of Noise

Noise can enter a wire in many ways, including by conductive, common-impedance, magnetic, capacitive, and electromagnetic coupling. If a noise voltage is large enough, and if it's present when the receiver is attempting to detect a transmitted bit, the noise can cause the receiver to misread the received logic level. Very large noise voltages can damage components.

Conductive and common-impedance coupling require ohmic contact between the signal wire and the wire that is the source of the noise. Conductive coupling occurs when a wire brings noise from another source into a circuit. For example, a noisy power-supply line carries noise into the circuit it powers. Common-impedance coupling occurs when two circuits share a wire, such as a ground return.

The other types of noise coupling result from interactions between the electric and magnetic fields of the wires themselves and signals that couple into the wires from outside sources, including other wires in the interface.

Capacitive and inductive coupling can cause crosstalk, where signals on one wire enter another wire. Capacitive coupling, also called electric coupling, occurs when two wires carry charges at different potentials, resulting in an electric field between the wires. The strength of the field, and of the resulting capacitive coupling, varies with the distance between the wires. Inductive, or magnetic, coupling occurs because current in a wire causes the wire to emanate a magnetic field. When the magnetic fields of two wires overlap, the energy in each wire's field induces a current in the other wire.

When wires are greater then 1/6 wavelength apart, the captive and inductive coupling is considered together as electromagnetic coupling. An example of electromagnetic coupling is when a wire acts as a receiving antenna for radio waves.

Balanced Lines

One way that USB eliminates noise is with the balanced lines that carry the bus's differential signals. Balanced lines are electrically quiet. Any noise that couples into the interface is likely to couple equally into both signal wires. Because the receiver detects only the difference between the two wires' voltages, any noise that is common to both cancels out.

In contrast, in the unbalanced, single-ended lines used by RS-232 and other interfaces, the receiver detects the difference between a signal wire and a ground line shared by other circuits. The ground line is likely to be carrying noise from a number of sources, and the receiver sees this noise when it detects the difference between the signal voltage and ground.

Twisted Pairs

In a full/high-speed USB cable, the two signal wires must form a twisted pair. Twisted pairs are recommended, but not required, for low-speed cables. A twisted pair is two insulated conductors that spiral around each other with a twist every few inches (Figure 21-10). The twisting reduces noise in two ways: by reducing the amount of noise in the wires and by canceling whatever noise does enter the wires. Twisting is most effective at eliminating low-frequency, magnetically coupled signals such as 60-Hz power-line noise.

Twisting reduces noise by minimizing the area between the conductors. The magnetic field that emanates from a circuit is proportional to the area between the conductors. Twisting the conductors around each other reduces the total area between them. The tighter the twists, the smaller the area.

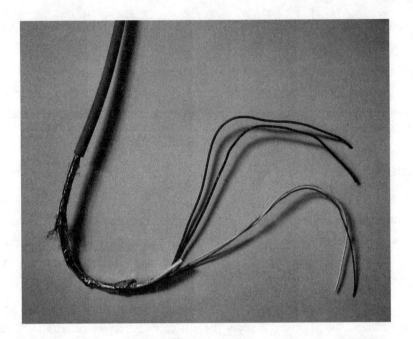

Figure 21-10: A full/high-speed USB cable contains a twisted pair for data, plus VBUS and GND lines, plus aluminum metallized polyester and braided copper shields.

Reducing the area shrinks the magnetic field emanating from the wires and thus reduces the amount of noise coupling into the field.

A twisted pair tends to cancel any noise that does enters the wires because the conductors swap physical positions with each twist. Any noise that magnetically couples into the wires reverses polarity with each twist. The result is that the noise present in one twist is cancelled by a nearly equal, opposite noise signal in the next twist. Of course, the twists aren't perfectly uniform, so the canceling isn't perfect, but noise is much reduced.

Shielding

Metal shielding prevents noise from entering or emanating from a cable. Shielding is most effective at blocking noise due to capacitive, electromagnetic, and high-frequency magnetic coupling.

The 2.0 specification requires both low-speed and full/high-speed cables to be shielded, though the requirements differ.

In a full/high-speed cable, an aluminum metallized polyester shield surrounds the four conductors. Surrounding this is an outer shield of braided, tinned copper wire. Between the shields and contacting both is a copper drain wire. The outside layer is a polyvinyl chloride jacket. The shield terminates at the connector plug.

A low-speed cable has the same requirements except that the braided outer shield is recommended but not required. The 1.x specification required no shielding for low-speed cables on the premise that the slower rise and fall times made shielding unnecessary. The shielding requirement was added in 2.0 not because the USB interface is noisy in itself, but because the cables are likely to attach to computers that are noisy internally. Shielding helps to keep the cable from radiating this noise and helps the cable pass FCC tests. The downside is that 2.0-compliant low-speed cables are more expensive to make and physically less flexible.

The specification leaves the grounding details to the user, with the advice that the grounding method must be consistent with accepted industry practices and regulations with respect to safety, electromagnetic interference (EMI), radio-frequency interference (RFI), and electrostatic discharge (ESD). In a typical design, the shield is AC-coupled to a local ground reference at each end, using a 0.01-microfarad ceramic capacitor between the shield and ground.

Edge Rates

Low speed's slower data rate enables the drivers to use slower edge rates, or rise and fall times, that reduce both the reflected voltages seen by receivers and the noise that emanates from the cable.

When a digital output switches, a mismatch between the line's characteristic impedance and the load presented by the receiver can cause reflected voltages that affect the voltage at the receiver. If the reflections are large enough and last long enough, the receiver may misread a transmitted bit.

In low-speed cables, the slower edge rate ensures that any reflections have died out by the time the output has finished switching. The slow edge rate also means that the signals contain less high-frequency energy and thus the noise emanated by the cables is less.

Isolation

Galvanic isolation can be useful in preventing electrical noise and power surges from coupling into a circuit. Circuits that are galvanically isolated from each other have no ohmic connection. Typical methods of isolation include using a transformer that transfers power by magnetic coupling and optoisolators that transfer digital signals by optical coupling.

USB is designed as a desktop bus and should require no additional protection in typical environments. USB's timing requirements and use of a single pair of wires for both directions make it difficult to completely isolate a USB device from its host. It is feasible, however, to isolate the circuits that the peripheral controller connects to, using conventional methods. For example, in a motor controller with a USB interface, the motor and control circuits may be isolated from the USB controller and bus.

Index

I

Index

saving, 452–4
surges, 494
Power class, 278
power switching, 451
predefined values descriptor, 324
Preferred State | No Preferred State bit, 328
PRE packets, 55, 56, *59*
printers
    Parallel Printer Port, *4*, 14–6
    printer driver, 282
    Printer Object, 233, 351
    selecting device classes for, 282
    transfer type used for, *48*
    USB printer adapter, 289
problems with USB. *See* disadvantages of
        USB
Processor Status and Control Register, 203,
        205
Product IDs, 104
    in Drvidx.bin file, 256–7
    obtaining, 15
    reading, 378–9
program memory, 144–6
programming
    assembly-language, 174–5
    in C, 180–1
    languages for developing device driver,
        36
    PROM programming, 226–9
    and protocol complexity, 14–5
    Visual Basic, calling API functions
        with, 351–2
    Visual C++
        calling API functions with, 349–51
        compilers for, 350–1
    Windows Telephony Application Pro-
        gramming Interface (TAPI), 284
    to write driver for USB device, 238,
        250

Program Stack Pointer (PSP), 185–7
PROM programming, 226–9
protocol analyzers, 410–4
protocol, complexity of, 14–5
protocol stalls, 63
Provider key, 268
PS/2 Pullup Enable bit, 192
PSP (Program Stack Pointer), 185–7

Q

QualityLogic, 410–413

R

RAM (random-access memory), 146
ReadFile function, 387–96
reading data
    feature report from device, 397–8
    input report from device, 387–96
read-only memory (ROM), 145
Read transfers, control
    amount of data returned by device, 76
    data travel, 72, *74*
    detecting and handling errors, 78
    reporting status of, 65–6
RegisterDeviceNotification function, 363–
        4
registers, 146–7
reliability of USB, 7
remote-wakeup feature, 32, 191, 248, 453
ReNum register bit, 162
Report Count item, 306
report descriptors, 298, 304–6, 304–6,
        321–2
    creating, 322–3
    testing, 322–3
Report ID item, 331
Report Size item, 306
requirements, computer, 22–3
Reset bus state, 458
ROM (read-only memory), 145